# Social Welfare

## A Response to Human Need

**Louise C. Johnson**
**University of South Dakota**

**Charles L. Schwartz**
**University of South Dakota**

Allyn and Bacon, Inc.
Boston  London  Sydney  Toronto

Library of Congress Cataloging-in-Publication Data

Johnson, Louise C., 1923–

   Includes bibliographies and index.
   1. Social service—United States.   2. Public
welfare—United States.   3. Social workers—United States.
I. Schwartz, Charles L., 1948–   .   II. Title.
HV91.J625  1987   361′.973  87-18826
ISBN 0-205-10614-5

*Production coordinator:* Helyn Pultz
*Copyeditor:* Jane Schulman
*Cover administrator:* Linda K. Dickinson
*Cover designer:* Lynda Fishbourne

Printed in the United States of America

10  9  8  7  6  5  4  3     92  91  90  89

# Contents

Preface   ix

**Part One   Social Welfare as a Response to Societal Concern   ■   1**

Chapter 1   An Introduction to the Social Welfare System in
the United States   3
Human Needs   3
Societal Responses   5
Development of the United States Social
Welfare System   16
Motivators of Social Welfare Decisions   24
Summary   26
Key Terms   26
Questions for Discussion   27
Notes   27
Suggested Readings   28

Chapter 2   The Emergence of Professionalism within
Social Welfare   29
Roots of Social Work   29
The Beginning of Professionalism in the
United States   30
The Search for Professionalism   31
The Emergence of Training Schools   33
Further Professionalization: The Establishment
of Professional Organizations   35
Is Social Work a Profession?   36
Who Are Professional Social Workers?   39
Summary   41
Key Terms   42
Questions for Discussion   42

Notes   42
Suggested Readings   44

**Part Two   Conditions that Give Rise to Human Need   ■   45**

Chapter 3     Social Change   47
              Society as a Social System   48
              Change as It Affects the Societal System   51
              Social Change as It Affects Individuals   58
              Summary   59
              Key Terms   60
              Questions for Discussion   60
              Notes   60
              Suggested Readings   60

Chapter 4     Poverty, Human Needs, and Social Welfare   62
              What Is Poverty?   63
              Who Are the Poor?   66
              Causes of Poverty   69
              Discovery and Rediscovery of Poverty: Societal
                 Responses   75
              Professional Responses to Poverty   79
              Summary   80
              Key Terms   80
              Questions for Discussion   80
              Notes   81
              Suggested Readings   82

Chapter 5     Social Welfare Resources   83
              Need for Resources   83
              Life Span Needs   87
              Availability of Resources   89
              Discontinuity of Needs and Services   90
              Summary   91
              Key Terms   91
              Questions for Discussion   91
              Notes   92
              Suggested Readings   92

Chapter 6     Racism and Discrimination   93
              Racism, Prejudice, and Discrimination—
                 Definitions   93
              Causes of Racism and Discrimination   95
              Discrimination toward Blacks   98

Discrimination toward Native Americans   101
Discrimination toward Hispanics   102
Discrimination toward Asian Americans   105
Discrimination toward Other Groups   107
Social Welfare Responses to Prejudice and
    Discrimination   109
Summary   112
Key Terms   112
Questions for Discussion   113
Notes   113
Suggested Readings   114

## Part Three   Fields of Practice   ■   115

Chapter 7      Income Maintenance as a Response to
               Human Need   117
               Definitions of Income Mantenance   117
               The Structure of Income Maintenance
                   Programs   118
               Historical Development of Income Maintenance
                   Programs and Services   119
               Current Income Maintenance Programs   125
               Looking Ahead: Alternatives to Income
                   Maintenance   130
               The Role of Social Work in Income Maintenance
                   Services   135
               Summary   137
               Key Terms   138
               Questions for Discussion   138
               Notes   139
               Suggested Readings   140

Chapter 8      Services for Children   141
               The Scope of Child Welfare Services   142
               The Historical Development of Services
                   to Children   142
               Current Children Welfare Services   150
               Substitute Care Services for Children   156
               Summary   163
               Key Terms   163
               Questions for Discussion   164
               Notes   165
               Suggested Readings   166

Chapter 9    Services to Families   168
The Contemporary United States Family   169
Family-Centered Problems   173
Social Services Agencies Serving Families   177
Summary   180
Key Terms   181
Questions for Discussion   181
Notes   182
Suggested Readings   183

Chapter 10    Health Care and Social Welfare   184
Health Care and the Social Welfare System   185
Social Services and Social Policy in
    Health Care   189
Social Work in Health Care   191
Issues in the Relationship of Health Care and
    Social Welfare   200
Summary   203
Key Terms   204
Questions for Discussion   204
Notes   205
Suggested Readings   206

Chapter 11    Social Welfare and Mental Health   208
Definition of Mental Health Services   209
Development of Mental Health Services   210
The Developmentally Disabled   216
Substance Abuse   217
History of Social Work in Mental Health   217
The Social Worker in the Mental Health
    Setting   218
Current Issues and Concerns in the Mental
    Health Field   224
Summary   227
Key Terms   228
Questions for Discussion   228
Notes   229
Suggested Readings   231

Chapter 12    Social Work and Corrections
Structure of the Criminal Justice System   233
The Juvenile Corrections System   235
The Role of Social Work in Juvenile
    Corrections   240
The Adult Corrections System   243

Causes of Crime and Criminal Behavior   243
Correctional Services and Human Diversity   247
Social Work in Adult Correctional Services   249
Summary   251
Key Terms   252
Questions for Discussion   252
Notes   253
Suggested Readings   254

Chapter 13   Gerontological Social Work   255
Who Are the Aged?   256
Arrangements Used to Meet Need   258
Current Problems and Issues   264
Social Work Practice with Older People   272
Summary   273
Key Terms   274
Questions for Discussion   274
Notes   275
Suggested Readings   276

Chapter 14   Old-New Fields of Practice: Industrial and Rural   277
Industrial Social Work: An Historical Perspective   278
Practice in the Industrial Setting   282
Issues in Industrial Social Work   285
Rural Social Work: An Historical Perspective   286
Practice in Rural Settings   291
Issues in Rural Social Work   293
Development of Fields of Practice   294
Summary   295
Key Terms   295
Questions for Discussion   296
Notes   296
Suggested Readings   298

Part Four   The Contemporary Response to Human Need   ■   301

Chapter 15   Social Work as a Profession   303
What Is Social Work?   303
Social Work's Knowledge Base   305
Social Work, a Value-based Profession   306
The Skills of Social Work   310
Methods and Approaches of Social Work Practice   312

Current Conceptualizations of Social
  Work Practice  313
Professional Concerns  317
The Future of Social Work  320
Key Terms  321
Questions for Discussion  321
Notes  322
Suggested Readings  323

Chapter 16  The Contemporary Social Welfare System  324
Framework for Analysis  324
Major Issues in the Contemporary Social
  Welfare System  329
Change in the System  334
A Student's Next Step  336
Summary  337
Questions for Discussion  337
Notes  338
Suggested Readings  338

Index  339

# Preface

We have written this book for students in introductory social work courses and social service courses that focus on understanding the nature of the social welfare system in the United States. As a background for these courses and the book, an introductory course in sociology or social problems and some understanding of U.S. history are helpful but not necessary.

We view the social welfare system as one way we, as a people, attempt to respond to human needs within our society. Although these needs are individual in nature, they also have a universal quality. The social welfare system, then, is defined as a system of arrangements, programs, and mechanisms that can be formal or informal, governmental or nongovernmental, that tries to meet the needs of individuals and families who cannot fulfill such needs through their own resources. The theme carried throughout our book is society's response to human need. We examine the social welfare system from an historical as well as from a contemporary perspective. History is presented in a way that emphasizes its relevance to the current functioning of the system.

We have divided the book into four major parts. In Part One, we consider how societal values and philosophies, as well as "the needs of the times," have influenced the development of the social welfare system. We also trace the emergence of professionalism with social welfare. In the second part, we deal with the conditions that make it difficult for individuals and families to meet their needs, thereby requiring them to rely on the social welfare system. We discuss the availability of resources to meet these needs, and conclude with a discussion of specific types of prejudice and discrimination. In Part Three, we provide a thorough look at the fields of practice and service areas that constitute the social welfare system. Services specifically for children and families are covered in two chapters. In the remainder of this section of the book we deal with health care services, mental health services, the structure of the criminal justice system and the role of social work in juvenile corrections, gerontological social work, and two fields of practice, industrial and rural social work, that lay fallow for many years but are now reemerging. In the fourth and final part, we look at social work as a profession. In so doing, we provide an organizing framework for integrating the various themes and cases discussed throughout the book.

Each chapter includes a listing of key terms developed for the first time within that chapter. Thoughtful questions are provided, along with a brief selection of suggested readings for those who wish to further develop their understanding of the material presented.

We have found the writing of this book an exciting challenge. The opportunity to explore the development of the U.S. social welfare system and to develop an analytic framework for understanding that system was stimulating.

We wish to thank the following people who reviewed portions of our manuscript. Their insightful comments were greatly appreciated.

Joseph D. Anderson
Shippensburg University

Richard M. Coughlin
University of New Mexico

Bettyann Dubansky
University of Missouri, Columbia

Mary Ellen Elwell
Western Maryland College

Donald F. Fausel
Arizona State University

Barbara B. Johnson
University of South Dakota

Thomas L. Kruse
Millersville University of Pennsylvania

Diana M. Langhorst
James Madison University

Elizabeth T. Ortiz
California State University, Long Beach

Betty Piccard
Florida State University

Albert R. Roberts
Indiana University

Calvin Y. Takagi
University of Washington

Our hope is that through the use of this book, students of social work will develop sufficient knowledge, values and skills needed for analyzing policy issues, for understanding the various roles and functions of professional social workers, and for working within the structure of the contemporary social welfare system. The book is dedicated to all students beginning their journey toward becoming effective social work practitioners. We hope that you become excited about joining a host of social workers who labor to meet human need, and to help those who, for whatever reason, cannot help themselves.

# Part One

## Social Welfare as a Response to Societal Concern

Part One introduces the basic concepts and gives a framework for understanding the social welfare system in the United States. In Chapter 1 six different arrangements that are used by our society to provide for the needs of those who are a part of the societal system are defined and discussed. These arrangements give one facet of the framework of the book. A second facet is the history of the development of the U.S. social welfare system. Important milestones are introduced in Chapter 1. (This history will be expanded in later sections of the book.) A third facet is a discussion of the motivations that influence the decisions that affect our social welfare programs and policies.

Chapter 2 considers the professionalization of social welfare. It discusses professional attributes particularly as they relate to social work—the core profession in the social welfare system. The historical development of social work is also discussed in Chapter 2.

These two chapters are an introduction to the material that will deal with specific fields of practice in Part Three. They provide an overview of the whole social welfare system so that the reader may better understand the specific discussion of services to various segments of the population.

# Chapter 1

## An Introduction to the Social Welfare System in the United States

This chapter introduces the theme of this book—the social welfare system as a response to human need. It starts by considering human need as a part of the human condition and moves through how people meet their needs. In a complex technological society not all human need can be met through personal efforts. Thus, throughout history people in their collectives or social structures have created mechanisms or systems of organizing their responses to human need. This chapter gives us an overview of these mechanisms as they affect the system in the United States from three perspectives: first, approaches used in providing for human need, second, historical milestones that changed the structure and philosophy underlying the contemporary U.S. social welfare system, and finally, the motivations that influence decisions about how human need should be met. Later chapters will develop these themes in more depth.

## Human Needs

*Human needs* refers to those resources people need if they are to survive as individuals and to function appropriately in their society. No definitive list of needs can be given because people and situations vary both in terms of specific individuals and specific situations and in terms of different needs at varying stages of development. For example, a child with an enzyme deficiency has different nutritional needs from a child of a similar age who does not have that problem. The needs of young children for protection and care are very different from those of young adults. For individuals to develop self-esteem (a sense of self-worth that allows people to function comfortably in their environment),one culture may require considerable freedom of choice; another culture may require considerable conformity to societal expectations about roles and behaviors. Families with an unemployed breadwinner in densely populated cities do not have the means to raise a portion of their food while a rural family living in poverty may be able to. Every individual and family has needs that, if provided for, would enable the family and its members to function more adequately. But these needs differ, depending on the individual and the situation.

Human needs can include the following:

1. Sufficient food, clothing, and shelter for physical survival.
2. A safe environment and adequate health care for protection from and treatment for illness and accidents.
3. Relationships with other people that provide a sense of being cared for, loved, and belonging.
4. Opportunities for emotional, intellectual, and spiritual growth and development. This includes the opportunity for individuals to make use of their innate talents and interests.
5. Opportunities for participation in making decisions about the common life of one's own society. This includes being able to make appropriate contributions to the maintenance of life together.

Any specification of some need of any particular group of people must consider its life-style, culture, and value system. It must also consider the physical, emotional, cognitive, social, and spiritual attributes of the individual being helped. Need must also be considered in the light of issues of responsibility for self, others, and the general social condition.

In the context of the United States a theme of *rugged individualism* has influenced our thinking about social welfare—the belief that each person should be responsible for meeting his or her own needs. To truly live this life-style, one must be adult, a hermit, and live where the environment allows living off the land. This situation is neither possible in contemporary society nor desirable in terms of optimal human growth and development. Human beings have always depended on others to provide for their needs. These others may have been family, clan, tribe, neighbors, co-workers, or a part of some organized structure such as church, city-state, feudal systems, or governmental unit.

Human beings have always had some means for meeting human need. The means for meeting human need that serves the common good is known as *social welfare*. The network of services that result from custom and public policy forms what is known as the social welfare system.

This system is particularly concerned with individuals and families that cannot meet their needs with their own resources. Children, older people, and the handicapped are of particular concern. The system includes government programs, private nonprofit organizations, and informal helping endeavors.

Important questions within this social welfare system are: which needs should be met by individuals and families in caring for themselves and each other? Which needs should be met through relationships among people outside formal structures (the informal system)? And which needs are the responsibility of the formal social welfare systems (government and other formal organizations)? The search for this balance in meeting human need is an ever-present issue in the development of the contemporary social welfare system in the United States.

## Societal Responses

Society has evolved six different kinds of societal arrangements for meeting human need: mutual aid, charity-philanthropy, public welfare, social insurance, social services, and universal provision.[1] Each arrangement has developed from people's responses to societal structures and from beliefs about human needs; why people are unable to meet their needs and what society's responsibility is in meeting these unmet needs. Each arrangement has particular qualities that make it especially appropriate for meeting particular kinds of needs under differing circumstances. Each has advantages and disadvantages. Today's social welfare system makes use of all six arrangements. (See Table 1.1 for definitions of these arrangements.) Thus, in evaluating the U.S. social welfare system it is important to consider which arrangement is most appropriate to meet specific needs of a particular circumstance.

### Mutual Aid

*Mutual aid* is the oldest form of social welfare. It probably has been used ever since humans banded together in extended families or loose social groups. It is, however, the least recognized and documented in welfare literature. Mutual aid is the expression of the need of people to have responsibility for each others' well-being. Friends and neighbors have provided for children when family capacity for care has broken down. Social groups have cared for their own aged, weak, and deviant. Studies show mutual aid mechanisms are present in primitive societies. Imperatives for mutual aid are a strong part of the Judeo-Christian traditions. Mutual aid was present in the craft guilds of the Middle Ages when they provided funds for the burial of members and the support of their

Table 1.1   Arrangements for Delivery of Social Welfare Service

**Mutual Aid**

The expression of mutual responsibility for one another that occurs outside formal community structures. Helper and helpee are peers who may change roles, depending on the situation.

**Charity-Philanthropy**

Redistribution of wealth by some mechanism outside the government through voluntary giving. Usually givers have higher status than receivers. Benefits may be tangible or intangible.

**Public Welfare**

Provision of support (food, clothing, shelter, health care) for those unable to make such provision for themselves that uses the mechanisms of government (taxation, etc.).

**Social Insurance**

Required contribution to funds used for money-payments to individuals contributing to the program (or their beneficiaries) who meet the criteria for which the program is intended (over sixty-five, disabled, widowed). The program is governmentally administered.

**Social Services**

Intangible benefits provided by agencies and institutions (governmental and nongovernmental) that provide help in the area of social functioning.

**Universal Provision**

Provision of fiscal support or services by governmental units are available to everyone.

Based in part on work by Gerald Handel, *Social Welfare in Western Society* (New York: Random House, 1982). Definitions differ somewhat.

widows and children. It was present in various immigrant groups as they settled in ethnic enclaves in the United States and together provided for their own needs.

Ferdinand Tonnies (1855-1936), an early German sociologist, explored the relationships among people in the industrialization of society and used the terms *gemeinschaft* (a society using mutual aid to meet human need) and the contrasting term *gesellschaft* (individuals related through structures in the community).[2] Contrast the functioning of informal structures like families and neighborhoods with the formal structures of a bureaucracy and consider how informal functioning supports helping through mutual aid. In U.S. society this type of helping is still very apparent in rural communities. Farmers help each other during harvests. Neighbors in small towns often come to depend on each other during a crisis like a death or illness in a family.

Another good example of mutual aid is the self-help groups that have been particularly useful in meeting the needs of individuals in transition (Widow to Widow, for example), those who are isolated and lonely (Parents Without Partners), and those who share similar problems (Alcoholics Anonymous).[3] The recognition of natural helpers as a resource is another manifestation of mutual aid. In many communities (particularly rural communities and in some neighborhoods) there are individuals to whom people go for advice or for help in solving problems who have won the trust and respect of the community.[4] Another example of mutual aid is giving a benefit for someone who has been injured or who has lost property through a disaster.

Mutual aid seems to work most effectively when the people helping and being helped hold similar values, come from a similar culture, or have a similar life-style. The relationship between people can be one of sometimes being helper, sometimes being helped. It is egalitarian and reciprocal. It has the advantages of being relatively nonintrusive, culturally relevant, fiscally inexpensive, nonstigmitizing, and relatively autonomous. Mutual aid seems to be less effective among people of different cultures, life-styles, or ethnic groups. It is usually short-term and of limited financial commitment like pitching in to sandbag a rising river or providing shelter after a fire. It requires a situation in which the helper has sufficient motivation, energy, and enough resources to provide the needed help. It also requires that the helpee respond in a way that provides satisfaction to the helper. Mutual aid is not appropriate for meeting all human need. But it is a very important arrangement that has always been a part of human society and that deserves more understanding, attention, and appropriate use within the current U.S. social welfare system. Mutual aid is usually found within a single class or group. When stratification causes one group to acquire greater wealth and power, the mutual aid ethic is transformed into the belief that the richer should help the poorer—or *charity-philanthropy*.

## Charity-Philanthropy

When societies began to stratify and develop a class structure, new means of helping became necessary. With stratification came a differential distribution of power and resources. But the mutual aid ethic of being responsible for others' well being persisted. Two early European examples of this kind of social welfare are the feudal system and the Roman Catholic church. In feudal times the lord of the manor was responsible for the well being of his serfs. After the breakup of feudalism, the Roman Catholic church became the institution responsible for caring for those in need through hospitals, alm houses, schools. Gifts to the church were seen as gifts to the poor. The tithe (giving one-tenth of one's income to the church) became expected of all. Although this means of redistributing wealth was a way of carrying out society's social welfare function, it was also a means of social control. To receive help meant, at least in part, adhering to accepted norms and behaviors. For example, in response to help from the church individuals were expected to live by the teachings of the church and provide for their own needs as much as possible. They were not to waste resources by indulging in pleasure. It is important to note that the church's charity was not governmentally administered or controlled. It was a means for providing help based on the relationship of one social class to another social class. Thus the helper assumed a position of power over the helpee.

In the nineteenth century, the U.S. social welfare system developed institutions and organizations that laid the foundations for the use of charity-philanthropy. Individuals with wealth established and endowed schools and colleges, libraries, hospitals, orphanages, and homes for the aged. People believed that those who were privileged to have wealth should share with the less fortunate, particularly through the establishment and maintenance of institutions for the "uplift of the masses" or for those who needed care through no fault of their own. On the other hand, society made sure that no help was given that would in any way deter the able-bodied from working to provide for themselves and their families.[5]

Two organizations are particularly important in describing the charity-philanthropy arrangement in the United States. They are the Charity Organization Societies and the settlement houses. Though different in underlying philosophy, both originated in Great Britain in the latter part of the nineteenth century and were quickly copied in the United States.

The *Charity Organization Societies* (COS), forerunner of the present-day Family Service Association of America, originally functioned with friendly visitors, usually women of the upper class who carried out their charitable responsibility by visiting poor women in an attempt to motivate them toward better ways of living. The friendly visitor gave advice about such things as child rearing and housekeeping and warned against the evils of drink and idleness. The system was based on the belief that poverty came from wrong living, misuse of money, excessive drinking, and immorality. Money or other concrete aid was supplied only in exceptional situations and for very short periods of time. An extensive system of coordination and supervision developed. The individual or "case" was the focus of attention, with emphasis on finding out why the person was having difficulty. But the friendly visitor believed that the source of the difficulty rested within the individual's ways of functioning; that the poor had the means to overcome their problems and a friendly visitor, could help the needy find their own means for overcoming difficulty. This method of giving help became known as *scientific charity*. It provided the beginnings of social work as a profession—the friendly visitor evolved into the caseworker.

On the other hand, the *settlement house* was a place in the neighborhood of low-income families, usually immigrants, where wealthy and privileged people could live among the poor. Socially concious clergy and university women were also apt to be found living in settlement houses. They believed that by becoming a neighbor, they could bring about needed change and thus meet human need. Another method was to invite neighbors into the settlement house for clubs and classes (group activity) that helped immigrants adapt to the new country and its way of life. It was hoped that this would also demonstrate a caring attitude. The settlement house workers believed that through club activity people could find enrichment and education that would lead them to a higher quality of life. Rather than seeing the cause of problems originating in individuals and their life-style, the cause was seen as resting in the environment and stemming from a lack of understanding about how to cope in new surroundings. The settlement workers were also heavily involved in research to identify the factors causing need and in activity to eliminate those factors that caused the need.[6]

The COS and the settlement houses engendered numerous private agencies. This term emphasizes that the support and governance of such agencies comes from private citizens not government sources. Included in this group of agencies are those supported by religious groups. Today many of these agencies do receive support from governmental funds through grants and purchase of service contracts. Some examples of private agencies include those concerned with the welfare of children (Children's Aid Societies), family counseling agencies (Family Services), child guidance clinics and other mental health services, and community center and group service agencies (YWCAs). The advantages of the private agency are that it voluntarily redistributes resources and lets people carry out their responsibility for others in ways that are more personal than governmental mechanisms. This approach has more flexibility, focuses on particular cases, and provides relative autonomy for the helper. It has enjoyed an absence of governmental control, but as government has made its presence felt in many parts of our society so it also has developed regulations for *private agencies.*

There are, however, disadvantages to the charity-philanthropy arrangement. It does seem to reinforce class structure and thus can stigmatize the people receiving help. With limited funds and other resources it cannot meet all existing need. Because of its independent functioning, services coordination has been difficult to achieve. It also often seems to have difficulty responding to different cultural groups. Finally, it can lead to an overemphasis on professionalism and an elitism that can be dysfunctional.

Despite its limitations, the charity-philanthropy arrangement remains an important component of our social welfare system. Like mutual aid it cannot provide for all human need, but it can best provide for some needs such as counseling people with problems in interpersonal functioning and the development of new services that mutual aid and governmentally-controlled systems have difficulty providing.

## Public Welfare

The third arrangement used in meeting human need is *public welfare*. The essence of this component is the control of and the provision for the needy by governmental regulations, tax-supported financial aid, and institutional care. The arrangement uses local, state, or federal tax monies to provide minimal support for people unable to provide for themselves.

The U.S. public welfare system generally traces its roots to the *English Poor Law of 1601*. This law, discussed in greater detail later in this chapter, was a codification of laws that the British parliament had passed during the previous century to regulate begging and to establish governmental involvement in provision for the needy. It reinforced the notion that the local community was responsible for the care of its poor. The thrust of the English Poor Law was carried over to the American colonies and their provision for their own poor.

What became known as *indoor relief* or the care of certain persons in congregate-care institutions became popular in the seventeenth and eighteenth centuries. Poorhouses, hospitals, and orphanages were established. Although many of these were privately supported and thus fall within the charity-philanthropy arrangement, many were also partially government supported. State governments, in particular, became responsible for the care of some groups of people. States established separate institutions for the retarded, the blind, the deaf, and the mentally ill. In 1845 President Franklin Pierce vetoed a bill that would have provided support for the care of "indigent insane persons" by the federal government, saying the Federal Constitution did not provide power for this activity. Thus the principle of local and state responsibility for care of the poor remained operational until the 1930s.

The present U.S. public welfare arrangement began with the federal government's response to the Great Depression of the 1930s.[7] President Franklin Delano Roosevelt's New Deal policy, which provided work relief, reversed the thinking of the Pierce veto and established the involvement of the federal government in providing public welfare. The

*Social Security Act* of 1935 with its numerous amendments is the base for the U.S. public welfare system. This act was an important part of the New Deal. Certain categories of poor became the joint responsibility of state and federal governments. These include mothers (families in some cases) with dependent children (ADC, Aid to Dependent Children, and AFDC, Aid to Families with Dependent Children), the aged (OAA, Old Age Assistance), the blind (AB, Aid to the Blind), and the disabled (AD, Aid to the Disabled). This approach has come to be known as *categorical assistance*. More recently (1972) all but the aid to dependent children have become the responsibility of the federal government. General assistance, help given to those who do not fall in one of the categories, falls to state and local governments. Institutional care has been de-emphasized and for the most part also remains the responsibility of the state and often the local governments. In 1965, the Medicaid program (Title XIX) was added to the Social Security Act. This amendment pays for medical care for the poor. Fiscal responsibility for the program is shared by the federal government and the states.[8]

The public welfare system has two major strengths. First is its universal quality: anyone who meets stated criteria is covered. Mutual aid and charity-philanthropy do not have this quality. Thus, the public welfare approach provides more kinds of help to more people. This scope can only be possible with a relatively large and relatively stable fiscal base. However, the second major advantage of this arrangement, its dependence on a tax base, provides a large and stable source of funds.

Unfortunately, the federal government operates upon a system of bureaucracies. Such impersonal service delivery is not capable of responding flexibly to individuals in need. Bureaucracies often create a proliferation of rules, regulations, red tape, and paper work. All of this reduces the government's capacity to respond to human need and increases the costs of supplying needed services.

Another limiting factor of public welfare is the principle of *less eligibility;* that is, individuals should not be provided for at a level equal to or higher than the level an individual working for a living attains. This policy has developed for several reasons. One is society's need to maintain people in the work force so they can be hired for relatively low wages. Another is the belief that most people do not want to pay taxes to maintain others in a better life-style than they maintain themselves. This principle of less eligibility contradicts the idea that all basic human needs must be met. Thus, governmental support often remains at very low levels.

Another disadvantage of public welfare is the stigma the dominant culture attaches to receiving public assistance of any kind. This stigmatization is a major cause of the prejudice and discrimination that people who receive public assistance often experience. It in turn affects their feelings of self-worth and thus further increases their need for support.

Inflexibility in the government's response to the diverse populations and diverse needs is another important limitation. Thus, despite its mandate, public welfare does not serve all segments of U.S. society equally. For example, under some circumstances it is not responsive to middle-aged adults who are unable to work because of mental or physical handicaps.

Currently, and as throughout social welfare history, much discussion has centered on public welfare. These discussions often focus on the identification of who are the "worthy" or "deserving" poor. They reflect a concern that some poor should be able to help themselves or may not be victims of circumstances beyond their control. Behind this is an assumption that assistance for these "undeserving" poor should at best be minimal. Some of the questions involved include: Should such assistance be given to only certain particularly vulnerable categories, the aged, widowed, children, or handicapped persons? Does public welfare discourage the able-bodied from working? What should be the response to extensive unemployment caused by disruptions in the economic system? Should help be in the form of institutional care or should public welfare provide subsistence within the community? And if subsistence, should it be in cash payments to the poor or needy, provision of commodities like surplus food, or by paying selected caregivers? What level of care should be provided? What are the responsibilities of relatives and the local communities for the care of their own? Which level of government should be responsible for providing financial resources to support the disadvantaged? Despite many questions and limitations public welfare is the core of the current U.S. social welfare system for it provides the *income maintenance* segment of the system. Income maintenance provides financial assistance in the form of cash or a voucher given by government agencies to individuals and families when their incomes fall below a predetermined level.[9] Examples of income maintenance services are Aid to Dependent Children, food stamps, Supplimentary Security Income for the aged. Without income maintenance human need cannot be met in our contemporary American society.

## Social Insurance

The fourth arrangement used in the social welfare system is social insurance. *Social insurance* is a mechanism where citizens (or employers and employees) are required to contribute to governmentally administered funds. These funds then pay out when the insured condition or status is reached by any contributor. In the United States a group of insurance programs, including old-age and survivors insurance, disability insurance, and medicare (medical insurance for those over sixty-five years of age) are provided under the Social Security Act and its amendments. (The same act that provides for social welfare benefits.) Workers have a certain percentage of their paychecks deducted and employers are required to contribute; this money is paid into a fund which in turn pays benefits to qualified aged and disabled people.

This arrangement had its beginnings in Europe during the latter part of the nineteenth century when first Germany and then Great Britain introduced health, old age, and accident insurance. In the United States the first social insurance was Worker's Compensation. This developed in response to the rise of industrial accidents that disabled breadwinners and thus plunged families into poverty. Between 1910 and 1920 many states passed laws providing insurance and protection against the risk of income loss due to industrial accidents, and for the medical care needed as a result of the accident.

Other types of social insurance are also a part of the contemporary U.S. social welfare system. These are Old Age and Survivors Insurance, Unemployment Insurance, and Medicare. Old Age and Survivors Insurance, now referred to as Old Age, Survivors, Disability, and Health Insurance (OASDHI) provides three types of benefits: retirement income, income to families of deceased workers, and income to workers permanently and totally disabled. The benefits received depend in part on the worker's contributions to the fund: those who have worked little receive little. Since its inception in 1935 the program has gradually expanded to include more and more of the work force, but it is still not universal. Unemployment Insurance operates from funds collected by a payroll tax, with each state setting up its own program. Medicare, which came into being as a result of the 1965 amendments, provides health insurance for people over sixty-five. It is co-insurance; that is, the recipient pays a part of the cost of health care. The Medicare Program is federally administered.[10]

Social insurance has several advantages. Because individuals contribute to the funds they draw upon when they meet the requirements for obtaining benefits, social insurance does not carry the stigma that other arrangements do. This arrangement also has a universal quality, although it is somewhat limited since some people do not contribute and thus are not eligible for benefits. However, the extent of the coverage is now so broad that social insurance can be considered almost universal. It is also nonintrusive. There is no investigation to establish need and with relatively simple eligibility requirements.

There are, however, some disadvantages to social insurance. Of current concern is the shifting population pattern of many more older people on Social Security and fewer younger people contributing to the plan. Whether the OASDHI fund can continue to provide the present benefits without increasing the level of contributions or find new sources of funds is a real concern. Also, as noted before, the rules and regulations of bureaucracy are often unresponsive to human need in its individual and diverse forms. And the system has difficulty adjusting to these inequalities and to changing social patterns. The exclusion of the housewife from primary benefits is an example. Another limitation is that not everyone is a part of the system. Certain individuals "fall between the cracks." Housewives, some seasonal workers, some state and local government employees, and some agricultural workers do not have Social Security coverage. The program is not as universal as many would desire. But social insurance has, despite its limitations, become a very important part of the social welfare system by providing income at times when people might otherwise have to depend on public welfare income maintenance programs.

## Social Services

Not all the social welfare needs that people have can be fulfilled merely by providing money. Traditionally these non-monetary types of help have come from mutual aid and charity-philanthropy. Though mutual aid and private agencies have done a fine job, they have not been able to provide for all the needs nor universal coverage for even some of the needs.

The heart of social services is a wide variety of counseling services known as casework. However, it also includes other kinds of services such as information and referral, socialization and other group services and supportive services. In addition, services that increase the capacity of communities to meet human needs are included in this arrangement. *Social services* can then be defined as supplying non-money help that directly or indirectly increases people's abilities to function in society.[11]

The roots of contemporary social services lies in the work of the Charity Organization Societies (COS) and the settlement houses. From these origins many agencies, services, and other provisions have grown to meet a wide variety of needs. From the Charity Organization Societies came the concept of helping people through a one-to-one relationship. This has led to an emphasis on casework as the vehicle for the delivery of social services. COS also pioneered much of the community organization approach with its emphasis on coordinating services. The settlement house movement initiated services to groups and to communities, helping people change their environment. The many and varying uses of the social service model will become apparent in Part Three of this book, where the various fields of service are examined.

Until recently, social services tended to remain primarily within the charity–philanthropy arrangement. Then some services, especially in the areas of child welfare and mental health, began to be provided by governmental agencies. There was a gradual recognition that income maintenance programs alone could not fulfill everyone's needs. The 1967 Social Security Amendments allowed state governments to provide services to Aid to Dependent Children (ADC) recipients. Thus the Social

Security Act was broadened to recognize social services as a distinct arrangement. When Title XX of the Social Security Act was passed by Congress, this amendment broadened the kinds of services offered and the individuals who could receive such services. Services like family planning and information and referral could be provided to everyone regardless of income.

One of the advantages of social services is its individualized attention to the need and its specific response to the person in the situation. Thus, response to diversity is much more possible than with other arrangements. This arrangement also recognizes that needs exist that are not caused simply by inadequate income. Social services also place an emphasis on the need for voluntary acceptance of services.

There are, however, disadvantages to social service. It is a very intrusive kind of help in many instances, calling for delving into very personal aspects of people's lives. Professionalism has produced other negative spin-offs. One of them is that some social services tend to discourage the use of mutual aid or the informal helping system, professionalism has given helping an elitist flavor. It has made certain kinds of help very expensive. Sometimes it places a stigma on those who turn to it for help. Also help has not been available to all who need and can use it. It should be recognized, on the other hand, that the professionalism of social services has brought about a higher level of care and a greater capacity to help in circumstances that are beyond the capacity of the informal system.

## Universal Provision

*Universal provision* is fiscal support or services given by governments to enhance the social functioning of all the people within a society. Universal provision requires no means test, which means that no one has to show that they or their family fall below a predetermined income level to receive benefits. No eligibility requirements are necessary other than that recipients belong to a particular category of people (over sixty-five, children, etc.). This arrangement has not been used in the United States to the extent it has in other countries. It must, however, be recognized as an option when discussing how the U.S. social welfare system can be more responsive to human need.

Primary examples of universal provision in the United States are the public health services like Poison Control Centers or the Communicable Disease Center in Atlanta, particularly as they safeguard everyone's health. The Older American Act of 1965 provides planning, social, and nutritional services for anyone over sixty years old regardless of income. This program, however, has never been adequately funded and currently targets only those with income or social need.

Canada has three major universal provisions: Family Allowances, Old Age Security, and Medicare. Family Allowances pays a set sum for every dependent child in a family. Old Age Security pays a basic allowance to every person over sixty-five years of age. Medicare covers medical and hospital costs for everyone. These programs are supported from the federal and provincial general tax funds.

One advantage of universal provision is that everyone is covered. Administrative costs are cut because eligibility processing is minimal. Some of the cost is reclaimed since this income is taxable. No stigma is placed on those receiving these benefits; in fact, society recognizes that people through no fault of their own need subsidies. In many countries, these provisions have become rights.

The major disadvantage is, of course, cost. At issue is the question: Is it better to pay taxes and be protected or is it better to provide for need on an individual basis (both through each individual's personal effort and government programs)?

Each of the six arrangements with their strengths and limitations has developed within the U.S. social welfare system to deliver a particular set of benefits and services that meets certain needs within our society. Understanding each arrangement is necessary for understanding the total social welfare system. (See Table 1.2)

## Development of the United States Social Welfare System

The milestones set within the history of the social welfare system show how it has developed. The following material examines the major historical points at which the system changed in some significant way.[12] In Part Three, the development of fields of practice will be considered. *Fields of practice* are services to specific groups such as children or families, the aged, and services within specific settings such as health care or correction facilities. Although the study of fields of practice shows how the identification of a group (class) of people in need and the provision of resources and services to that group has been an important influence on the evolution of the overall social welfare system, a look at the general, historical background of the system is a necessary framework for understanding the *development* of the fields of practice.

Two historical milestones are the passage of specific social welfare legislation and the development of the institutions, agencies, and programs within the system. The first can be tied to specific dates, the latter cannot. Both, however, grew over time. With the institution/agency development, it is difficult to specify a precise date when the new service or philosophy was generally accepted throughout the system. Specific legislation of the type being discussed usually was preceeded by other

Table 1.2  Summary of Social Welfare Arrangements

| Arrangement | Government Involvement | Relationship | Stigma | Strength | Limitation |
|---|---|---|---|---|---|
| Mutual Aid | No | Reciprocal | No | Quickly available if given within cultural context | Limited to persons who are culturally similar |
| Charity-Philanthropy | No | Super-ordinant or subordinant | Yes | Individualization | Limited by scope of resources available Tends to be controlled by dominant groups' expectation |
| Public Welfare | Yes | Superordi-nant, sub-ordinant, or impersonal | Yes | Breadth of coverage | Controlled by dominant groups' expectations Bureaucratization |
| Social Insurance | Yes | Impersonal | No | Breadth of coverage Lack of stigma | Bureaucratization Some individuals left out |
| Social Services | Yes | Depends on situation | Probably in some cases | Breadth of coverage | Limited funding Bureaucratization |
| Universal Provision | Yes | Limited | No | Breadth of coverage | Cost |

legislation or by legislation at another level of government. The passage of this legislation was the climax of a process or movement toward a new way of providing for need.

In understanding how the system grew and changed it is important to note not only milestones but also the influences involved in the changes. There are two types of influences: situational and philosophical. Situational influences include the historic context of the economic, social, and political events in the country at the time. The philosophical influences are those values, beliefs, and prevailing philosophic constructs that influenced the process of change resulting in a milestone.

## English Poor Law, 1601

The English Poor Law is generally considered the first milestone because it was the basis of the social welfare system in both Colonial and Post-Revolutionary America. The sense of this law formed the foundation of the system until the passage of the Social Security Act in 1935. In fact, its philosophy influences attitudes toward social welfare even today. It regulated the poor and dealt with the many wandering beggars. This law became necessary as England changed from an agricultural society to an industrial one. The introduction of sheep raising and the enclosure of property had pushed people off the land and into a new life-style in the cities. Vagrancy became intolerable. The old system of the landholder being responsible for those who lived on his land was breaking down. Too, England had embraced Protestantism. The monasteries and other Roman Catholic institutions that had met the needs of the poor were abolished by the Crown. It was a time of unrest and uncertainty about responsibility for those in need.

The response was restrictive. Social control was the intent of the law. The poor were not allowed freedom to move around the country at will. Begging was controlled. People in need were returned or required to remain in the locality where they held residency. Residency was established by birth or by living and working in a locale for a period of time before becoming indigent.

*Local control* was another provision of this law; the poor and dependent were the responsibility of the local government unit. This unit was responsible for all who held residency or settlement in that area. The law also required that people be responsible for the care of their relatives in need; this is the principle of relative responsibility. There was some differentiation between the able-bodied poor, those able to work, and other poor. The able-bodied could be required to work. Categorical assistance, or the practice of providing assistance to different categories of people such as children, the aged, or disabled adults, has its roots in this provision.

This law continued the churches' involvement in caring for the poor. The churches were made responsible for administrating the welfare system. Funding came largely through tithes donated to the church. What was new was that the government now regulated the system. This change came about not from concern for poor people but from political expediency; the growing numbers of poor, and the unrest they created, had to be controlled.

In the new world, this system of social control and local control was culturally appealing. Puritan-Calvinism with its well-known work-ethic found the approach congruent with its beliefs. In the new environment everyone had to work. There was scarcity and a belief in equality. With little social stratification there was no concern about a class structure. The smallness and isolation of settlements made local control appropriate. The categorization of able-bodied versus the sick, disabled, and widows with children also fit the values and beliefs of the people. The major unsolved problem was the outsider who might require assistance. They were dealt with through residency laws. The needy strangers were sent back to their place of legal residence. The social welfare system of the old world fit the needs of the new situation, thus it was adopted and still influences the contemporary system.

## Institutional Care 1820–1850

As the nation of the United States grew out of the colonial period politically, it also grew geographically and economically. Its population increased. In 1790 the population of the United States was 3,929,000; in 1850 it was 23,261,000. During this period, immigration from Ireland and Germany were responsible for a substantial amount of the population growth. Vast amounts of new territory were opened for settlement. Roads, canals, and railroads opened the west. Cities expanded rapidly. The factory system became an important economic factor. No longer could subsistence economy and local care provide adequately for all human needs. People worried that the able-bodied poor were not being reformed (were not forced to be self-supporting) under the prevailing system. Also it was more difficult for local communities to provide care for their special classes of dependent people (the mentally ill, children, etc.) A belief was growing that these dependent people needed a special environment that would encourage them to grow or change. This, in turn, stemmed from a belief that people were perfectable. Few recognized that changes in society could be responsible for people being unable to provide for their needs. Instead, the causes of need were seen as lying within individuals and their own responses to changing conditions. The answer was institutions that would care for and train dependent persons so they could become self-supporting. Gradually, *institutional care* became an accepted means for helping needy people.

Originally all dependent people were placed in institutions, the local *alms house* or poor house. This practice became known as *indoor relief*, care in an institution, as opposed to *outside relief*, care within a community. It later became evident that some of the needy required more specialized care or, in the case of children, separate care from other dependent people.

In the beginning, great emphasis was placed on the institution being a place of refuge or asylum that would substitute for the family in providing needed socialization and protection for vulnerable individuals. It was for this reason that the institution was seen as a progressive development for the social welfare system. By the middle of the 1800s, however, most of the institutions lost this emphasis on protection and socialization and developed a custodial approach, concerned with protecting society by removing troublesome individuals.[13]

Local communities were often not able to provide specialized institutions. Thus, from the 1820s on, states began to establish institutions to care for children, the mentally ill, the blind, deaf, and the retarded. Correctional institutions were established to deal with criminals. Some of these institutions, particularly hospitals and those caring for children, were established by wealthy individuals as their charity work, thus falling under the charity-philanthropy category. Others, financed by the state tax base, fell under the public welfare arrangement.

In the development of the institutional care we see three additions to the social welfare system (still dominated by the principles of the English Poor Law):

1. the widespread use of the charity-philanthropy arrangement

2. the acceptance by state governments for the responsibility of caring for certain categories of needy people

3. the beginning of the recognition that a social welfare system developed for a subsistence economy could not meet human need in an industrial society.

The goals of social welfare in this era were expressed as helping people develop self-respect and dignity through self-support and by protecting vulnerable people from temptation. These goals were translated into the social control goals of "making people behave themselves and keep working."

The system in the United States was developing and taking on a unique character—responding not only to individual need but also to its citizens' beliefs about dependency. People were beginning to realize that the needs of some members of the society were not being met and that this was not due to these people's lack of moral character but to circumstances beyond their control. This was a response to the nation's unique social, political, and economic reality.

## *Charity Organization Society and Settlement Houses 1885-1900*

After the Civil War the movement toward industrialization and urbanization continued. Also, immigration continued to bring more and more people into the country. Many were from rural backgrounds and had difficulty adjusting not only to a new country but to a new, urban way of life as well. Some were now from southern and eastern Europe whose life-styles differed from the Northern and Western Europeans who had up to this time made up the majority of immigrants to the United States. In addition, a stratified class society had developed—with some people having considerable wealth and power and others having very little of either. The large city slums that housed the families of poorly paid workers, many of whom were immigrants, became the concern of the wealthy who saw it as their "Christian duty" to help meet the needs of the poverty-stricken. Two very different types of agencies, both imported from Great Britain, were founded to work with the residents from the slums. These were the Charity Organization Societies (COS) and settlement houses discussed earlier in this chapter.

Although the two systems were based on very different beliefs about the cause of unmet need and responded in very different ways, both were reacting to the same situation, the increasing number of poor and immigrant people struggling to adapt to life in large cities, suffering from a frightening range of problems. Both agencies also came into being because of the new stratified social class structure. They were expressions of concern by the wealthy for the well being of their fellow men and women. Generally, both agencies were an expression of a religious conviction that those who had should share with those who did not. They were new systems of helping, within the charity—philanthropy category, that formed a basis for an important segment of our social welfare system. They both furthered the dual system of private charity complementing public provision. Most important, they emphasized that need was more than financial need.

Both the COS and the settlement houses accomplished a great deal. From those working in these agencies came a concern about human need that, along with the progressive reform movement of the early twentieth century, gave rise to laws addressing such problems as child labor, mother's aid, widows pensions, the juveniles. The settlement house workers, concerned about the plight of labor, were involved in the formation of unions and labor legislation. From the settlement houses came the innovation of the working in groups. Most important the settlement house and the COS produced leadership for developing the profession of social work and for devising new approaches to meeting human need. From these agencies the private sector of the social welfare system came into being.

## The 1935 Social Security Act

This act and its subsequent amendments are the major source of United States public social welfare policy today. The passage of the Act in 1935 marked the beginning of a major shift in the social welfare system. The Act relates primarily to three of the mechanisms discussed in the last section: public welfare, social insurance, and social services. For a summary of its provisions and amendments see Table 1.3. After a time of relative prosperity following World War I, a severe economic depression heralded by the 1929 stock market crash plunged the nation into economic disruption. There had been other such periods but none so extensive as what has come to be known as the Great Depression. It affected all classes of society; the rich whose investments were now worthless, the growing middle class whose jobs disappeared and whose savings were lost when banks closed, and of course those with chronically low incomes suffered greatly. Their usual sources of income and other help, traditionally provided by the charity-philanthropy arrangement, dried up as these sources were financially overwhelmed by the extent of need. Everyone knew people who were considered moral and upstanding who were suddenly out of work, had no resources to fall back on, and were now among the needy. Thus, it quickly became apparent that individuals could be unable to meet basic needs for themselves and their families through no fault of their own.

The short-term response to this situation was a package of federal programs known as the New Deal. This overall program contained legislation to improve the economy and provide jobs for the unemployed. But the measure that permanently and basically changed the social welfare system was the Social Security Act of 1935.

This Act with its subsequent amendments provides the basic income maintenance structure still in use today. It provides two types of benefits, social insurance for people who are a part of the labor force and social welfare for people outside the labor force. These provisions were detailed earlier in this chapter and will be discussed more fully in Chapter 7. The Act represents unprecedented public involvement in the social welfare system and significant movement away from local control of and responsibility for those in need.

In 1935, workers were covered for old age benefits, and in 1939, survivors benefits were added. In addition, grants were made to the states for the partial funding of unemployment insurance programs.

Under the social welfare arrangement, grants were made to states to provide an income maintenance program for mothers of dependent children without fathers' support (ADC), for the blind (AB), and old age assistance for those over sixty-five with insufficient income from other sources (OAA). In 1956, a program for the totally and permanently disabled was added (AD). In 1961 further aid became available for needy

Table 1.3    Provisions of the Social Security Act and Its Amendments

| Year | Legislation | Category |
|------|-------------|----------|
| 1935 | Social Security Act passed | |
| | Title I   Grants to States for old age assistance (OAA) | Public welfare |
| | Title II   Federal old-age benefits | Social insurance |
| | Title III   Grants to states for Unemployment Compensation | Social insurance |
| | Title IV   Grants to states for aid to dependent children (ADC) | Public Welfare |
| | Title V   Grants to States for maternal and child welfare | Health and some social services |
| | Title X   Grants to states for aid to the blind (AB) | Public welfare |
| 1939 | Old age insurance expanded to include survivors and eligible family members. | Social insurance |
| 1950 | Aid to dependent children broadened to include relative with whom child is living; becomes aid to families with dependent children. (AFDC) | Public welfare |
| 1956 | Disability insurance added to the insurance package. | Social insurance |
| 1962 | Provision of social services to AFDC families. | Social services |
| 1965 | Title XVIII   Medicare providing federal health insurance for aged and disabled. | Social insurance |
| | Title XIX   Medicaid providing grants to states to use with matching funds for health care for public welfare recipients and the medically indigent. | Public welfare |
| 1972 | Title VI   Supplemental security income, federally administered means tested income maintenance program that supplants OAA, AB and AD. | Public welfare |
| 1975 | Title XX   Social services amendments, comprehensive social services program | Social services |
| 1981 | Social service block grant, amended Title XX, consolidates social service programs and gives greater state discretion | Social services |
| 1983 | Amendments affecting insurance making them more fiscally secure | Social insurance |

dependent children whose father was in the home (AFDC). All of these programs were state administered.

In addition, certain services were provided in the areas of child welfare and maternal and child health, through grants to state administered programs. The social service category really originated as a part of the provisions in the Social Security Act.

In 1965 amendments added Medicare and Medicaid and a provision for additional social services in 1962 and 1974. In 1974, Old Age Assistance, Aid to the Blind, and Aid to the Disabled were converted into a federal program called Supplementary Security Income (SSI). This is a federally funded and administered program that provides income to those with insufficient resources.

Though the Reagan administration has made many changes in social welfare programs, the basic structure set out in the Social Security Act remains. The federal government—through social insurance programs that are federally administered, through public welfare programs both federally and state administered, and through social service programs largely state administered—provides a basic system for social welfare in the United States. State governments are required to administrate programs within specified guidelines and to provide matching funds for most state administered programs. This system is supplemented and complemented by mutual aid and charity-philanthropy arrangements.

Although since 1960 many new and important programs such as low-income housing, food stamps, and so on have supplemented the social security programs none, except the limited program under the Older Americans Act that introduced universal provision, has changed the basic system.

The social welfare system then is a combination of six arrangements. Questions about the system, therefore, should not address which arrangement should be used to provide for all need or which level of government should be responsible for meeting need? Rather the question should be which arrangement and which level of government is appropriate for meeting specific needs?

## Motivators of Social Welfare Decisions

To understand how decisions affecting which type of program and which level of government should be responsible for meeting some particular need, one must first know what factors have influenced those decisions. To do this, one more analytical framework is useful. This framework has been developed by David Macarov of the Hebrew University of Jerusalem.[14] He identifies the motivators for social welfare programs as mutual aid, religion, politics, economics, and ideology. It should now be apparent that each of the arrangements and each of the milestones in the social welfare system came about in response to changes, not only changes in need but changes in our society's beliefs about the nature of need. For example, mutual aid is not only a way to meet human need, it is also a natural caring response that motivates the development of other services and programs. The formal social welfare system evolved because it became apparent that in a complex industrial or post-industrial society the collective needs of citizens are dependent on meeting at least minimal needs for everyone within society.

Mutual aid is an important motivator, though not the only motivator, permeating our social welfare system. Both the mutual aid and charity-philanthropy arrangements had a strong religious motivation. Like most of the world's religions, Christianity and Judaism have strong imperatives regarding responsibility for others. Most of the individuals involved in developing charitable and philanthropic institutions and agencies were in part satisfying their religious beliefs as they dedicated time and money to developing those responses to human need. The work of Charles Loring Brace, who founded the Children's Aid Society, is an example of social welfare work influenced by religious motivation. Brace first became aware of the plight of poor children in New York City when, as a student at Union Theological Seminary, he visited the Five Points area and conducted religious meetings and classes for street children. When he formed the Children's Aid Society he was supported by various Protestant denominations in his work.[15]

The prevailing political climate has a considerable influence on the social welfare system. For example, the political events in Europe that brought about the Protestant reformation disrupted the caring for the needy by the Roman Catholic Church. The creation of the social security system was politically expedient in the 1930s. Because of the immensity of the problems and the number of people affected, the political system had to devise some means for dealing with the effects of The Great Depression if a political party expected to remain in power.

Economic influences are often difficult to separate from political influences because the political scene is so responsive to economic factors. For example, in the early 1930s the serious economic condition of the country, caused by the Great Depression, the Dust Bowl drought, and the onslaught of immigrants from war torn Europe, set the stage for a political climate that in turn created a major change in the social welfare system. Currently, the economic situation—reflected in a growing national debt, and concern about taxes—has motivated a political program calling for major cutbacks in social welfare spending. At the same time, such economic factors as a continuous rise in the cost of living and mass unemployment have made it politically inexpedient to accept cuts in social security and unemployment programs.

American society has been built on a strong emphasis on individualism and free enterprise. Both of these ideologies have argued against the creation of universal provision arrangements. Some interpret universal provision as meaning that people won't have any incentive to provide for their own needs. From time to time, altruism and humanitarianism have been strong motivators for the development of new programs and services. The late 1960s was such a time. During this period, for example, many people marched and protested against laws and practices that discriminated against people of a different race, color, or religion. The Civil Rights Movement grew out of this concern and resulted in new legislation prohibiting discrimination in the workplace and in any public facility.

Thus, each of the five motivators: mutual aid, religious, political, economic, and ideological factors have influenced the development of the contemporary social welfare system. At any point in time, one or more of the these motivators may predominate. Usually several, if not all, are a part of any change in our social welfare system.

## Summary

The contemporary social welfare system has developed as our society's response to its unique forms of human need. To understand that system it is important to first understand the mechanisms created to deliver resources and services to the people who need them. Six mechanisms have been identified: mutual aid, charity-philanthropy, public welfare, social insurance, social service, and universal provision.

But how and why did these mechanisms develop? Certain milestones stand out as keys to understanding this evolution. These include the English Poor Law, the roots of institutional care, the Community Organization Societies and settlement houses, and the Social Security Act of 1935.

A third way of analyzing the system is to identify the factors in a society that motivate a particular kind of response to an identified need. Mutual aid, religious, political, economic, and ideological motivators seem to be the most influential.

## Key Terms

alms house
categorical assistance
charity-philanthropy
Charity Organization
  Societies

English Poor Law
fields of practice
human need
income maintenance
indoor relief

institutional care
less eligibility
local control
mutual aid
outside relief
private agencies
public welfare
rugged individualism

scientific charity
settlement house
social insurance
Social Security Act
social services
social welfare
universal provision

## Questions for Discussion

1. Which kinds of needs are most appropriately provided by which kinds of provision in contemporary American society?

2. How much should society rely on mutual aid and charity-philanthropy to provide for individuals in need?

3. What are the advantages and disadvantages of universal provision? Should Americans make more use of this provision?

4. Contrast the American social welfare system before the passing of the Social Security Act of 1935 and since 1935.

## Notes

[1] This formulation is based in part on material developed in Gerald Handel, *Social Welfare in Western Society* (New York: Random House, 1982). The interpretation of each component differs somewhat from that of Handel. One additional arrangement, universal provision, is added.

[2] Ferdinand Tonnies, *Fundamental Concepts of Sociology (Gemeinschaft and Gesellschaft)* trans. Charles P. Loomis (New York: American Books, 1940).

[3] For a good discussion of this development see: A.H. Katz and E.I. Bender, eds., *The Strength in Us: Self Help Groups in the Modern World* (New York: New Viewpoints, 1976). Also see: Phyllis R. Silverman, *Mutual Help Groups: Organization and Development* (Beverly Hills: Sage Publications, 1980) and Diane L. Pancoast, Paul Parker, and Charles Froland, eds. *Rediscovering Self-Help: Its Role in Social Care* (Beverly Hills: Sage Publications, 1983).

[4] For a discussion of the phenomena see: Alice H. Collins and Diane L. Pancoast, *Natural Helping Networks: A Strategy for Intervention* (Washington, D.C.: National Association of Social Workers, 1974). Also see: Charles Froland, et al., *Helping Networks and Human Services* (Beverly Hills: Sage Publications, 1981); David E. Biegel and Arthur J. Naparstek, eds., *Community Support Systems and Mental Health: Practice, Policy, and Research* (New York: Springer Publishing Co., 1982); and William J. Sauer and Raymond T. Coward eds., *Social Support Networks and the Care of the Elderly* (New York: Springer Publishing Co., 1985).

[5] For an excellent discussion of this development see: Robert H. Bremner, *American Philanthropy* (Chicago: The University of Chicago Press, 1960).

6 For further discussion of this development see: Robert Bremner, *From the Depths: The Discovery of Poverty in the United States* (New York: New York University Press, 1964), pp. 60–66.

7 These will be further discussed in Chapter 7.

8 For further discussion of this development see: June Axinn and Herman Levin, *Social Welfare: A History of the American Response to Need*, 2nd ed. (New York: Harper and Row Publishers, 1972).

9 For discussion of this provision, see: Norman L. Wyers, "Income Maintenance Systems," in *Encyclopedia of Social Work*, 18th ed. (Silver Springs, MD: National Association of Social Workers, 1987), pp. 888-898.

10 A good source for further study of the development of social insurance is James Leiby, *A History of Social Welfare in the United States* (New York: Columbia University Press, 1978), chapters 11, 12, 13.

11 For further discussion see: Alfred J. Kahn, *Social Policy and Social Services*, 2nd ed. (New York, Random House, 1979).

12 For in-depth treatment of the historical development of the American social welfare system the reader is referred to: Axinn and Levin, *Social Welfare;* Lieby, *Social Welfare;* and Walter I. Trattner, *From Poor Law to Welfare State* (New York: The Free Press, 1974).

13 An excellent discussion of this development is found in, David J. Rothman, *The Discovery of the Asylum* (Boston: Little, Brown and Co., 1971).

14 David Macarov, *The Design of Social Welfare* (New York: Holt, Rinehart & Winston, 1978).

15 Lieby, *Social Welfare*, p. 83. This development will be further discussed in Chapter 8.

## Suggested Readings

Axinn, June, and Levin, Herman. *Social Welfare: A History of the American Response to Need*, 2nd ed. New York: Harper and Row Publishers, 1972.

Bremner, Robert H. *American Philanthropy*. Chicago: The University of Chicago Press, 1960.

Compton, Beulah R. *Introduction to Social Welfare and Social Work: Structure, Function and Process*. Homewood, Ill.: The Dorsey Press, 1980.

*Encyclopedia of Social Work*. Silver Springs, Maryland: National Association of Social Workers, 1987. See particularly articles on "History of Social Welfare," "Settlements and Neighborhood Centers," and "Social Security."

Handel, Gerald *Social Welfare in Western Society*. New York: Random House, Inc., 1982.

Lieby, James. *A History of Social Welfare in the United States*. New York: Columbia University Press, 1978.

Lieby, James. "Social Security at 50," *Public Welfare*, 43 (Fall 1985), 4-12.

Macarov, David. *The Design of Social Welfare*. New York: Holt, Rinehart and Winston, 1978.

Ostrander, Susan A. "Voluntary Social Service Agencies in the United States," *Social Service Review*, 59 (September 1985), 435-454.

Trattner, Walter I. *From Poor Law to Welfare State*. New York: The Free Press, 1984.

# Chapter 2

## The Emergence of Professionalism within Social Welfare

Chapter 1 discussed the evolution of the U.S. social welfare system. One of the trends noted in that discussion was the emergence of social work as a profession. This chapter discusses the historical evolution of social work,placing an emphasis on the close relationship between the growth of social work as a profession and the historical development of our social welfare system.

## Roots of Social Work

The earliest signs of social work emerged when formal institutions and organizations replaced informal help provided through mutual aid. In Europe, the first institution to respond was organized religion. In the beginning, help was given on an individual to individual basis. The motivation to assist the needy was inspired by religious teachings that stated it was a person's duty to help those in need. This religiously inspired motivation was evident within many early societies, including those of the ancient Egyptians, Chinese, Babylonians, Hebrews, Greeks, and Romans, and persists throughout the world today.

   The two major religions that most influenced our system, Judaism and Christianity, placed considerable emphasis on mutual aid. Judaic scripture, particularly the Old Testament books of Leviticus and Deuteronomy, provided commandments calling for charity to the poor, sick, aged, and strangers. Later, a more formalized system of relief was created in the Talmud, a collection of Jewish laws and traditions. The

Talmud set forth directives on how resources should be gathered and distributed, and how much should be given. Thus, Jewish tradition was one root of a beginning institutionalization of social welfare.

These traditions continued with the development of Christianity. Christian teachings also emphasized charity and service to others. The parable of the Good Samaritan (Luke 10: 25-37) is an example of this teaching. At first Christian responses were in the form of mutual aid, but by the second century Christian charity became more formally organized. Granting relief had become a function of churches or church related groups. The clergy, particularly with the development of the monastery system in Europe, were charged with this responsibility. Clergy were seen as leaders in carrying out social welfare function of the churches. In a sense they became the first helping professionals. Their work was inspired by altruism, a sense of calling and commitment to serve the interests of people, and this altruism and commitment are still considered characteristics of a modern professional helping person. Within the Roman Catholic Church, Saint Vincent de Paul organized groups of volunteers to serve the needy that came to be known as the Ladies of Charity (1617), and eventually became the Society of Saint Vincent de Paul (1833). Protestants also made extensive use of their laity in carrying out charitable work. These groups of volunteers are also forerunners of modern day society workers.[1]

The organized church as the main pillar of social welfare eventually gave way to other systems of relief. By the seventeenth century, social welfare had become the responsibility of government. The shift of responsibility for social welfare from the church to government was exemplified by the establishment of the Elizabethan Poor Laws of 1601 in England. The government gradually evolved institutions and organizations whose major functions were the delivery of social welfare services. This in turn led to special job classifications for the employees in these organizations. These forerunners of the social work profession in England were transferred to the United States.

# The Beginning of Professionalism in the United States

The public poor relief system established during colonialization and the early days of the new nation created a system of direct relief provision and institutional care. Public officials, called the overseers of the poor, and the employees of the institutions, replaced clergy in the roles of caregivers. They too can be considered early forerunners of the professional social workers. As private philanthropy and charity developed in the late nineteenth century, a British model of poor relief caught the attention of philanthropists in the United States. The New York Society for the Prevention of Pauperism (1819) and the New York Association for Improving the Condition of the Poor (1843) were formed to assist the poor. Both served as models for the development of the Charity Organization Societies. The early forerunners of the Charity Organization Societies (COSs) experimented with a combination of volunteers and a few paid staff in investigating the needs of the poor and providing relief. These organizations employ a paid staff who performed administrative roles, but the volunteers who came to be called the *friendly visitors* provided direct services to people. The paid staff and the friendly visitors were the immediate predecessors of professional social workers in the United States. These pioneer efforts can be viewed as "a major step on the road to professionalization."[2]

*Settlement house workers,* as mentioned in Chapter 1, used different methods to help people than their friendly visitor counterparts. Their work style could be described as missionary, working hand in hand with neighbors in improving adverse social conditions. Gradually the settlement workers developed broader goals of social reform, often acting through legislation and social policy change. These workers assisted in bringing about changes in child labor laws, in women's labor laws, in the institutional care of the disabled and the mentally retarded, and were involved in the development of child welfare services and the establishment of juvenile courts. The success of the efforts provided considerable

impetus to the movement toward professionalization.

## The Search for Professionalism

At the beginning of the twentieth century the friendly visitors, through their experiences in working with people, had begun to see the complexities of human needs and problems. Their original philosophies of poverty being caused by moral defects gave way to a new understanding of the interaction between people and their immediate environment and the problems that arise from that interaction. No longer could they place the locus of the problems within the individual. Environmental factors such as crowded housing, disease, unemployment, discrimination and prejudice, and problems within the family had to be taken into consideration when assessing an individual's needs and in developing plans for assistance. Additional knowledge and skills assessment and intervention techniques were called for to mitigate the complex human problems that helpers were called upon to deal with. Society began to understand that assisting people involved far more than simply providing financial aid, and that love in one's heart for people was not the sole qualification for a person engaged in charity work. If social work was to grow beyond the concept of mutual aid, it needed to become scientific through the development of knowledge, problem-solving procedures and methods, and professional skills. Professional schools with authoritative entrance standards were being called to provide leadership in this effort. With these changes of philosophy, the movement toward professional charity work, later called social work, further developed.

A step toward making charity work more scientific was taken when the Charity Organization Societies began to identify the needed knowledge base and established specified methods and procedures for doing their work. These were formalized into what was later called *case work.* Case work methods and processes call for a careful investigation and diagnosis of problems in the interaction between people and their immediate social environment. Charitable relief was redesigned to meet needs based on these new perceptions and techniques.

Friendly visitors and paid agents alike needed to be trained to use these procedures appropriately. At first the training consisted mainly of apprenticeship. New volunteers and staff simply observed the work of experienced staff and thus learned the methods and processes of charity work. In addition to apprenticeships, agencies gradually began to use more formal training, which consisted of lectures, reading, and discussing literature. Another opportunity to broaden the understanding of charity work and to learn new methods and techniques was provided by the Conference of Charities. Founded in 1870, and expanded in 1894, its name was changed to the National Conference of Charities and Corrections. This annual conference acted as an exchange, where the ideas and work experiences of charity workers were shared and taught, for the benefit of all involved in helping people.[3]

The settlement houses also recognized the need for training their resident workers. They began to organize in-house training, often inviting sociology, economics, and political science professors from nearby colleges and universities to lecture to staff on various topics.

By the end of the 1900s, the Charity Organization Societies and the settlement houses realized that formal education, perhaps even higher education, was needed to professionalize what eventually was to be known as social work. Charles Kellog, the general secretary for the New York Charity Organization Society, frequently commented on the need for more "intelligent agents."[4] His intent in saying this was that agents' abilities to perform their duties depended on how well educated they were. The education thought to be needed was some kind of special social work education. Leaders in the field began to publicly voice this concern. The first formal plea came in 1893 from Anna L. Dawes, who presented a paper at the National Conference on Charities and Corrections, "The Need for Training Schools for a New Profession."[5] In this paper, Dawes presented the case for the establishment of formal training schools for charity workers. Although she did not provide much detail about how this could come about, she did suggest that those who had retired from charity work could become teachers, passing on the knowledge they had gained in their work. The use of the words "new professional," in Dawes's paper, clearly demonstrates the extent to which the early leaders in charitable work were concerning themselves with moving toward professionalization.

Four years later in 1897, Mary Richmond of the Baltimore Charity Organization Society, presented a paper at the National Conference, "The Need for a Training School in Applied Philanthropy."[6] Richmond argued that there was a need to attract educated young people into charitable work. She expressed the view that if these young people were willing to commit themselves to a life of charitable work, they needed opportunities for education and professional development. Calling attention to the fact that providing these opportunities would have to be limited, since charity work was not an established profession, she argued that professionalization could not be established without the development of a professional school. Richmond urged that "we should begin to move without delay in the direction, at least, of some definite system of training." She also set forth the conditions under which she felt a school should be established, which included what curriculum should be taught, by whom, and where a school should be located. Most importantly, Richmond felt that course work should consist of both theoretical and practical field training. The timely impact of this presentation provided the impetus for the establishment one year later of what was to become the first school of social work.

## The Emergence of Training Schools

The New York Charity Organization Society in 1898 organized a six week annual training course in applied philanthropy. Twenty-seven people attended the program, most of whom were college graduates and already working in the field. This first course work consisted of lectures and practical field work. Some years later the curriculum was expanded to an academic year, with emphasis on training college graduates without experience.

In the early 1900s other training schools came into existence. In 1901 in Chicago, cooperative effort between the University of Chicago and Chicago settlement houses created a series of courses that were later organized into an independent *training school*. Training schools were also organized in Boston (1904), Philadelphia (1908), St. Louis in (1908), Cleveland (1913), and Houston (1916). At first, these schools functioned independently of institutions of higher learning.

With the emergence of all these new training schools, came a need to establish standards for common curriculum among the schools. There was a great deal of argument between the schools concerning the appropriate curriculum content. Many schools were committed to teaching casework: this had received considerable impetus from Mary Richmond's book, *Social Diagnosis.*[7] The Chicago School of Civics and Philanthropy had established a broader curriculum with emphasis on research, social policy, and administrative issues. Western Reserve University had begun to teach courses in group work. Standards for common curriculum often became a topic of conversation between the directors of these schools when they met each year at the National Conference of Charities and Corrections. It became clear that some sort of curriculum standardization was needed. In 1919, under the leadership of Porter R. Lee, then director of the New York School of Social Work, the Association of Training Schools of Professional Social Work (ATS) was established. The creation of this organization was a giant step forward in the professionalization of social work. The Association of Training Schools, which in 1952 became the *Council on Social Work Education*, was and remains today the official accrediting and standard-setting body for social work education in the United States.

The early training schools remained for many years under the auspices of the social agencies that supplied the instructors and the fieldwork apprenticeship training experiences. Even though the Association of Training Schools attempted to set curriculum standards, disagreement continued among the schools over what should be taught. Gradually, beginning in the late 1920s, a movement toward including professional social work education in the higher education systems began. The Chicago School of Civics and Philanthropy was a leader in this effort. This school eventually became part of the University of Chicago.

Edith Abbott in *Social Welfare and Professional Education* [8] stressed that social work methods needed to consist of more than casework. She felt that social workers needed a much broader knowledge base that included the biological sciences, sociology, anthropology, economics, psychology, research, and the law. Abbott also advocated that social work education be housed in a university setting.

The Association of Training Schools provided further impetus for this in 1935 when it began to require any school desiring membership to be a part of an institution approved by the Association of American Universities. The ATS also developed minimum curriculum standards for its member schools, and mechanisms for reviewing the schools to insure compliance. Originally both graduate and undergraduate programs were eligible for membership. However, in 1939 the ATS set further standards by requiring that member schools wishing to be accredited must establish a two-year graduate program. Thus, the first professional degree in social work the Master of Social Work (MSW) was established. Since the 1940s the education and training of social workers has been solidly rooted in the mainstream of higher education at the masters level.

Although professional social work education was thus mandated to be graduate education, undergraduate programs continued to exist in land grant and liberal arts colleges and universities. Many schools were offering baccalaureate degrees in sociology with an emphasis in social welfare or social work. These programs, although not eligible for membership in the Council on Social Work Education (CSWE), continued to have a relationship with CSWE by attending CSWE national meetings. At these national meetings, specific educational sections were made available to undergraduate educators. Later, associate level programs in human services and doctoral programs in social work also emerged. But neither of these two levels of training and education were eligible for *accreditation* and membership in CSWE.

# Further Professionalization:
# The Establishment of Professional Organizations

Informal interest among social workers in developing professional organizations began around 1900. This was a frequent discussion topic among social workers at the National Conference of Charities and Corrections. At the same time, due to an increase in the number of paid social work positions, the National Social Workers Exchange was formed in 1917. The exchange provided placement of social workers in paid and volunteer positions, and offered vocational counseling. For a number of years the exchange accepted both paid and volunteer social workers as members. In 1921 the exchange responded to interest in moving from its informal structure to the creation of a formal professional organization. It became the American Association of Social Workers (AASW).

Membership in the AASW was limited to paid social workers. In the years from 1917 to 1949, social workers from specific fields of practice began to talk about organizing themselves into professional organizations. In the beginning, these social workers organized what were called discussion clubs, which were located in a few large cities, including Boston, Philadelphia, New York, Milwaukee, and St. Louis. Medical social workers were the first to do this. These discussion clubs soon gave way to structured professional organizations. Organizations that came into existence included:[9]

the American Association of Medical Social Workers (AAMSW), 1918

the National Association of School Social Workers (NASSW), 1919 the American Association of Psychiatric Social Workers (AAPSW), 1926

the American Association of Group Workers (AAGW), 1946

the Association for the Study of Community Organization (ASCO), 1946

the Social Work Research Group (SWRG), 1949

These groups emerged as the specific fields of social work practice developed within the profession. By 1949, there were seven separate professional organizations, the largest being the AASW. In the early 1950s strong interest and new leadership unified the profession, leading to the merger of the seven separate organizations in 1955 into what is known today as the *National Association of Social Workers* (NASW). NASW is recognized as the official social work professional organization in the United States with fifty-five chapters in all fifty states and Puerto Rico. Membership in the NASW is now open to professional social workers holding either a bachelor's or master's degree in social work from a program accredited by the Council on Social Work Education. The NASW has as its purposes: the promotion of the "quality and effectiveness of social work practice in the U.S.; to further the broad objective of improving conditions of life in our democratic society through the utilization of knowledge and skills of social work; to maintain and promote high standards of practice and preparation for practice, to work toward alleviating or preventing sources of deprivations, distress or strain by utilization of social work methods and social action."[10]

## Is Social Work a Profession?

This question has been raised since the 1900s when the charity workers first sought professional status.

As early as 1915, social work's professional status came into question. Dr. Abraham Flexner, an authority on graduate education who had intensively studied the medical profession, presented a paper at the National Conference on Charities and Corrections, "Is Social Work a Profession?"[11] In this paper Flexner concluded that social work had not yet achieved professional status. His basis was that social work lacked a specific and unique knowledge base of its own. Flexner believed that the proper provision of resources to those in need did require specific knowledge, and that resembled mediation. That is, the social worker acts as a mediator between the needy person and the resources provided by the charity agencies. Although Flexner agreed that social work did meet some of the criteria of professions, he denied it was a profession in "the same sense in which medicine and law are professions." Efforts began shortly thereafter to address Flexner's criticism that social work lacked a knowledge base and specific practice methods.

One of the first efforts in conceptualizing practice methods came in 1917 with the publication of Mary Richmond's *Social Diagnosis*.[12] The book established guidelines and norms for professional practice, greatly needed at the time. It also provided impetus for an ongoing development of literature about social work practice. The book was a pioneer in developing the unique methods that Flexner had stated social work lacked.

In the 1920s social workers became very interested in psychological theory. The writings of Sigmund Freud and others reshaped the thinking of social workers and provided new understandings of human behavior. This resulted in a change in direction in case work, considered the main method of social work at this time. Social workers began to focus on working with people in the area of psychological functioning and individual adjustment, as contrasted with the earlier concerns about poverty, environmental factors, and social reform. This change has been referred to as social work's estrangement from the poor.[13] It resulted as much from the social and political climate of the times as it did from the new understandings about human behavior. In the early 1900s, social reform was considered a legitimate function of social workers as evidenced in the efforts of the settlement workers. However, in the aftermath of World War I, social reform became an unpopular activity, largely due to a popular reaction to perceived radical influences in political and social structures such as the rise of facism and communism. Social reform was seen as radicalism. Case work, now influenced by psychological theory, seemed a safer and more legitimate approach for assisting people. Social workers also felt that movement in this direction would increase the prestige of the new profession in the eyes of the general public.[14]

Periodically, the question of whether or not social work was a profession continued to be asked. Ten years after Flexner's position was given, William Hodson, then president of the American Association of Social Workers, reopened the debate. He delivered a paper at the 1925 National Conference of Social Work in which he re-examined social work's professional status. He argued that Flexner's position was no longer valid because social work had developed a knowledge base, expanded methods of education and training, and increased the number of trained persons in the field. Hodson maintained that in most ways social work was a profession, saying that the final test would come in public acceptance of the profession. He hoped that the American Association of Social Workers would provide the leadership needed to bring this about.[15]

In 1932, Esther Lucille Brown compared social work with other professions in a paper read at the National Conference of Social Work.

In this comparison, Brown concluded that social work needed to increase its professional prestige by continuing to fill social work positions with trained people, by increasing the salary levels of social work positions, by maintaining the quality of field work in education, and by obtaining graduate-level status in the educational process. This would, in her estimation, further legitimize social work's claim to being a profession.[16]

The most widely circulated article about social work's professional status was by Ernest Greenwood, published in 1957. This article described what Greenwood believed to be the major attributes of a *profession*:

1. *A Systematic Body of Theory.*    Professions have general and specific knowledge and understandings that underlie and guide the professional's use of technique in the performance of duties.

2. *Professional Authority.*    The professional possesses authority based on expertise gained from an extensive education, knowledge, and use of technique. The consumer or client of the professional's services gains a sense of security by the professional's use of authority.

3. *Community Sanction.*    The professional's authority is sanctioned by the community in informal and formal ways. Informally, the community sanctions the professional's authority and expertise, and the profession's regulation of itself through accreditation or licensing. Formally, sanction is given to some professions through law or the police powers of the community.

4. *Code of Ethics.*    Professions possess formal and informal codes of ethics that its members must uphold. Formal codes are written, and professionals affirm their intention to uphold the provisions of the code. Informal codes are unwritten and exist in the context of mutual relationships among professionals. A code of ethics protects the clients from unethical conduct in the provision of services by the professional. A code of ethics also performs a self-regulatory function within the profession itself.

5. *Professional Culture.*    Professions possess a professional culture that has both formal and informal aspects. Formal aspects of professional culture include the settings in which professional and client come together for their work and the professional-client relationship. The informal aspects of professional culture are the values, norms, and common symbols to which the professional is socialized and must adapt.

In his analysis, Greenwood examined how well and to what extent social work had acquired these attributes. He concluded that "social work is already a profession; it has too many points of congruence with the model to be classified otherwise."[17]

Although social work's status as a profession continues to be a subject of debate, it is currently recognized by the United States Census Bureau, the public, and its practitioners, as a profession.

## Who Are Professional Social Workers?

With most of the arguments about social work's status as a profession laid to rest, a recent issue of the profession has been who are professional social workers? The recognized professional social worker prior to 1970 was someone holding a master's degree in social work (MSW). In 1970, the bachelor's degree in social work (BSW) became recognized as the first professional degree. Several events led to this recognition. Undergraduate programs in social welfare had been preparing people for direct social work practice positions for many years. Workers holding the bachelor's degree were considered preprofessionals or semiprofessionals. As early as 1951, when the Hollis-Taylor report, *Social Work Education in the United States,* was published, the elitism of graduate social work education began to be seriously questioned. The Hollis-Taylor report affirmed the legitimacy of undergraduate education in preparing people for professional tasks. It states, "In view of this report social work education will be in a sounder position when the profession officially recognizes that the area of undergraduate concentration (major and minor) offered prospective social workers is an organic part of professional education and should not be characterized by the nondescript term 'preprofessional.' "[18]

During the 1960s, serious questions arose about the graduate schools of social work's capacity to supply sufficient professionals for the social welfare system. With increased recognition of social problems and human needs it became evident that the supply of trained workers was inadequate. This was particularly true in the public sector where the social service arrangement was expanding in size and importance. It was hoped for a time that the manpower needs of these agencies could be met by graduate-level workers. Even though the number of graduate-level workers doubled from 1950 to 1967, the needs for trained workers increased at a faster rate, causing a shortage in the supply. In addition, public agencies could not compete with the private social service sector in attracting MSWs for employment, due to inadequate salary levels and undesirable working conditions. In 1965, public agencies began to abandon efforts to employ people with master's degrees and started using baccalaureate-level workers in direct service delivery positions.[19]

During this same period several organizations began to concern themselves with manpower issues. The Council on Social Work Education, the National Association of Social Workers, the Department of

Health, Education, and Welfare, and the Southern Regional Education Board all studied how to effectively utilize social services manpower.

For example, in 1960, the CSWE completed a study of the curriculum structure in social work education that considered whether undergraduate social work programs should be recognized as capable of producing professionally trained personnel for the social services.[20] In 1965, the Task Force on Social Work Education and Manpower of the Department of Health, Education, and Welfare published a report, *Closing the Gap in Social Work Manpower*. In this report the task force made the following recommendation: "There is a critical need for the advancement of undergraduate education in social welfare both for direct entry of graduates into practice and as preparation for graduate education."[21]

In 1968, another manpower study was published by the National Association of Social Workers, *Differential Use of Social Work Manpower*.[22] The study concluded that there was an inefficient use in the delivery of social services of what is called subprofessional manpower, including workers trained in baccalaureate social welfare programs.

Also strengthening the position of baccalaureate education in social work was the work of the Southern Regional Education Board Task Force. In 1971, it published, *A Core of Competence for Baccalaureate Social Welfare and Curricular Implications*.[23] The recognition by these studies of the ability of undergraduate programs to produce graduates capable of performing professional social work tasks and functions brought pressures on NASW and CSWE to change their positions on the baccalaureate-level worker. These pressures led to a decision by NASW, as a result of referendum, to allow graduates of baccalaureate programs approved by CSWE to join the association with full membership entitlements. In the spring of 1970, as a result of NASW's action, CSWE made the decision to develop guidelines for the approval of undergraduate programs. These two actions brought full recognition of the baccalaureate degree as the first professional degree in social work. This position was further strengthened when the CSWE in 1973, as a result of further study of the approval process, developed stringent accreditation standards for undergraduate programs. The focus of the accreditation standards was on preparing students for professional practice. The accreditation standards and accreditation process were fully implemented in 1974. Schools that had since 1970 been approved constituent members of CSWE were now eligible for accreditation and full membership in the CSWE.

Accreditation standards set forth by CSWE are designed to provide authoritative guidelines on educational goals and minimum standards of quality for both Baccalaureate and Masters degree programs in social work. Their purpose is to maintain quality and to stimulate improvement in professional education for social work that will prepare graduates to meet the demands of professional practice.[24]

Social work now is a profession with two points of entry, the bachelor's (BSW) and the master's of social work (MSW) respectively. But argument continues over whether the bachelor's degree should be considered the first professional degree. Some authorities have suggested that recognizing the BSW as such has taken social work down the road toward deprofessionalization.[25] They question whether social workers with only a BSW are prepared to function at the same level of professional expertise as their MSW counterparts. There are conflicting viewpoints about this issue. Brennan states, "Not only do BSW and MSW social workers occupy similar positions in many agencies, but there is no valid evidence to show that the MSW performs at a higher level."[26] Another view is that the BSW performs with no more expertise than the agency-trained worker who holds a college degree in something other than social work. A study in 1977 relative to this issue concluded that when comparing BSW level workers with agency-trained workers, the BSWs were found to be no less efficient in their work than the agency-trained workers. The study also concluded the BSW workers appeared to be more career-oriented, have a greater identification with the norms of the profession, and are a more stable work force than agency-trained workers.[27] Arguments on this topic undoubtedly will exist for sometime within the profession, until more agreement has been reached about the issue. However, the recognition of the BSW as a professional degree has and will continue to influence and shape the nature and course of social work education and practice.

# Summary

In this chapter, discussion has focused on the emergence of social work as a profession within the social welfare system, showing that its emergence is closely tied to the evolution of that system. In tracing social work's historical development as a profession several key points were addressed. Training for the profession began with apprenticeship and developed further with agency-based training schools that eventually became part of the system of higher education. Schools of social work and accreditation standards set forth by CSWE laid the foundation for professionalism. As social work grew it began to take on the attributes of a profession suggested by Greenwood and lay to rest earlier criticisms. Finally, in today's world social work is a profession in which there are two points of entry, the beginning professional who possesses the BSW and the advanced professional who possesses the MSW. Social work remains a young and growing profession, yet possesses a long history of service to society. It is diverse and reflects the ever changing context of society. As social change and the economic and political climate within society have given rise to human need, social work has attempted to respond. The responses and the conditions that necessitated them will be further discussed in subsequent chapters of the text.

## Key Terms

accreditation
CSWE (Council on Social
  Work Education)
case work
friendly visitors

NASW (National Association of
  Social Workers)
profession
settlement house workers
training schools

## Questions for Discussion

1. Discuss what the forerunners of modern day social workers did to contribute to the overall development of the profession.

2. What do you consider the most significant milestones in the development of education and training for social workers?

3. How did the structure of early education and training for social workers differ from today's structure? What do you see as the strengths and limitations of each type of structure?

4. Explain why social work is considered a profession.

5. What do you see as important in bringing about recognition of the BSW as a professional degree? What seems to be hindering its recognition by some agencies?

## Notes

[1] See Ralph Dolgoff and Donald Feldstein, *Understanding Social Welfare* (New York: Harper & Row Publishers, 1980), pp. 32-33, and Walter I. Trattner, *From Poor Law to Welfare State* (New York: The Free Press, 1974), pp. 1-6.
[2] See Dolgoff and Feldstein, *Understanding Social Welfare*, pp. 223-250.
[3] See Trattner, *Poor Law*, pp. 190-207.
[4] Dorothy G. Becker, "Adventures in Social Casework: The Charity Agent 1880-1910," *Social Casework* 44 (May 1963): 255-262.

[5] Anna Dawes, "The Need of Training Schools for a New Profession," *Lend-A-Hand* 2 (1893): 90-97.

[6] Mary E. Richmond, "The Need for Training Schools in Applied Philanthropy," *Proceedings of the National Conference of Charities and Corrections* (Boston: George H. Ellis, 1890), pp. 181-188.

[7] Mary E. Richmond, *Social Diagnosis* (New York: Russell Sage Foundation, 1917).

[8] Edith Abbott, *Social Welfare and Professional Education* (Chicago: The University of Chicago Press, 1931).

[9] See Roy Lubove, *The Professional Altruist: The Emergence of Social Work as a Career* (Cambridge, MA: Harvard University Press, 1965), pp. 124-125.

[10] Purposes of the National Association of Social Workers, as printed in: Rex A. Skidmore and Milton G. Thackeray, *Introduction to Social Work* (Englewood Cliffs, NJ: Prentice-Hall, 1982), p. 378.

[11] Abraham Flexner, "Is Social Work a Profession," *Proceedings of the National Conference on Charities and Corrections* (Chicago: Hildman Publishing Co., 1915), pp. 576-590.

[12] Richmond, *Social Diagnosis.*

[13] Elizabeth A. Ferguson, *Social Work: An Introduction* (New York: J.B. Lippincott Co., 1975), p. 13.

[14] Herman Borenzweig, "Social Work and Psychoanalytic Theory: A Historical Analysis," *Social Work* 16 (January 1971): 7-16.

[15] William Hodson, "Is Social Work Professional? A Re-examination of the Question," *Proceedings of the National Conference of Social Work,* (Chicago: The University of Chicago Press, 1925), pp. 629-636.

[16] Esther L. Brown, "Social Work against the Background of Other Professionals," *Proceedings of the National Conference on Social Work* (Chicago: The University of Chicago Press, 1932), pp. 520-553.

[17] Ernest Greenwood, "Attributes of a Profession," *Social Work* 2 (July 1957): 45-55.

[18] Ernest V. Hollis and Alice L. Taylor, *Social Work Education in the United States* (New York: Columbia University Press, 1951), p. 175.

[19] Ferguson, *Social Work*, p. 9.

[20] Herbert Bisno, *The Place of the Undergraduate Curriculum in Social Work Education* (New York: Council on Social Work Education, 1959).

[21] U.S. Department of Health, Education, and Welfare, The Departmental Task Force on Social Work Education and Manpower, *Closing the Gap in Social Work Manpower* (Washington, D C : The U.S. Government Printing Office, November 1965), pp. 80-81.

[22] Robert L. Barker and Thomas L. Briggs, *Differential Use of Social Work Manpower* (New York: National Association of Social Workers, 1968).

[23] Harold L. McPheeters and Robert M. Ryan, *A Core of Competence for Baccalaureate Social Welfare and Curricular Implications* (Atlanta: Southern Regional Education Board, 1971).

[24] Harry Specht, "The Deprofessionalization of Social Work," in Paul E. Weinberger, ed., *Perspectives on Social Welfare* (New York: Macmillan Publishing Co.), pp. 490-505.

[25] Commission on Accreditation-CSWE, *Handbook of Accreditation Standards and Procedures* (Washington, D.C.: Council on Social Work Education, 1984).

[26] Earl C. Brennan, "Professionalization and the B.A. Practitioner," in Weinberger, *Perspectives*, p. 321.

[27] Preston M. Dyer, "How Professional is the BSW Worker?" *Social Work* 22 (Nov. 1977): 487-492.

## Suggested Readings

Brennan, Earl C. "Professionalization and the B.A. Practitioner," in Paul E. Weinberger, ed., *Perspectives on Social Welfare*. New York: Macmillan, 1974.

Dinerman, Miriam, and Geismar, Ludwig L. *A Quarter Century of Social Work Education*. Silver Springs, MD: National Association of Social Workers, 1984.

Dolgoff, Ralph and Feldstein, Donald. "Social Work: The Emergence of a Profession," in *Understanding Social Welfare*. New York: Harper & Row, 1980, pp. 223-250.

Flexner, Abraham. "Is Social Work a Profession." *Proceedings of the National Conference on Charities and Corrections*, Chicago: Hildman Printing Co., 1915. P. 576.

Greenwood, Ernest "Attributes of a Profession." *Social Work* 2 (July 1957): 45-55.

Hollis, Ernest V., and Taylor, Alice L. *Social Work Education in the United States*. New York: Columbia University Press, 1951.

Lubove, Roy. *The Professional Altruist*. Cambridge: Harvard University Press, 1965.

Trattner, Walter I. "The Quest for Professionalization," pp. 190-207, in *From Poor Law to Welfare State: A History of Social Welfare in America*. New York: The Free Press, 1979, chapter 11. U.S. Department of Health, Education, and Welfare, *Closing the Gap in Social Work Manpower*. Washington, D.C.: U.S. Government Printing Office, 1965.

# Part Two

## Conditions that Give Rise to Human Need

This section discusses human need and the reasons why individuals, families, and personal networks cannot always meet the needs of individuals and families. Social change and an increasingly complex society with a monetary economy are shown to be basic reasons why there must be societal provision of social welfare programs and services. It will help the student understand why some people are unable to provide for all of their own needs and their family's.

There are four chapters in this section. Chapter 3 considers change that has taken place in society in the United States and how that change has affected people who live in that society. Chapter 4 examines poverty as one of the major contributors to people not being able to meet their own or their family's need. Chapter 5 considers the resources people need to function in contemporary society. Chapter 6 looks at racism and discrimination as they affect individuals and interfere with meeting human need.

# Chapter 3

## Social Change

The contemporary social welfare system is a response to social changes surrounding the development of modern society in the United States. This society has been heavily influenced by the industrial revolution and scientific technology. This chapter explores some important areas of change and how those changes have affected our society and the individuals in it. It develops the theme that problems in meeting human need and societal responses to human need increase during times of accelerated social change. The chapter presents the viewpoint that social control and provision for human need are inextricably related in our social welfare system's development. *Social Control* is the use of legal means to control actions of people that are perceived as undesirable by the larger society. As social change takes place, economic and political change usually results. This in turn is a motivating factor for change in the ways human needs are met. Religious and ideological responses are often slower to respond to change. Conflicts develop in thinking about what responses should be made to the change. This hesitation and conflict places further stress on those who find it difficult to meet their needs because they have been caught in the "winds of social change."

Chapter 1 pointed out that the English Poor Laws were, in part, a result of the movement away from an agricultural society to a society based on factory production, a result of industrial revolution. It also noted that the Poor Laws developed out of the need for social control, control of vagrancy, and the need for a stable labor force in the new economic system.

Institutional care in the United States grew out of changes in population patterns and the change from a subsistence economy to a monetary economy. In a *subsistence economy* people meet their basic needs by hunting, fishing, farming, or through other efforts directly tied to the natural resources that surround them. A *monetary economy* on the other hand, uses currency in exchange for food, clothing, and shelter. Institutional care also involved concern for not only human need but also for an element of social control. The Charity Organization Society and settlement houses were responses to change brought about by massive immigration to the United States from Europe. Although they were concerned about the problems faced by these immigrants, there was also a social control component related to fear of cultural differences.

Social change and resulting political and economic conditions also influenced the development of the Social Security Act. The conversion from a subsistence economy to a monetary economy made it necessary to provide monetary support for those unable to provide for themselves. The Depression with its massive unemployment made it very difficult for many citizens to provide for the needs of their families. A governmental program that provided at least a minimal income became economically necessary and politically expedient.[1]

In this chapter *social change* will be considered from three perspectives:

1. Society as a social system, the nature of change in systems, and the effect of such change on the functioning of the societal system.
2. Change as it has had an effect on the societal system in the United States with emphasis on changes brought about by industrialization, scientific, and medical advances.
3. Change as it has affected individuals in our contemporary society.

## Society as a Social System

Considering *society as a social system* allows a view of social change that includes understanding how change in one part of a system calls for change in other parts of that system. A social systems approach gives a framework for discussing how social change affects both the society as a whole and individuals within that society. In other words, as change takes place in a part of society, some of the mechanisms developed to maintain that society also must change. Some individuals find it very difficult to change or discover that their customary ways of functioning no longer are acceptable or provide the resources they once did. Thus a farm worker may realize he no longer has the skills needed for working in a highly mechanized agricultural system. Or even if he upgrades his skills, his services may no longer be needed in the new system. He then becomes unable to support himself and his family. His customary way of life is severely disrupted and his capacity to function as a productive member of society is threatened. In addition, because his family members are not having their needs met, they too may be vulnerable to serious problems in social functioning. Change in one part of the system—say the introduction of mechanized farming methods—brings about change in other parts of the system—many farmworkers lose their jobs.

Contemporary social work has adopted a social systems approach for understanding individuals, families, small groups, agencies and institutions, and communities. This approach reveals not only the internal functioning of a system but the interaction between the system and its environment in the broadest sense of the term. In the broadest dimension, society is seen as the environment; however, it too can be considered as a social system.

Definition of this system level can be problematic. Anderson and Carter define society as, "a group of people who have learned to live and work together" and "culture [as] that which binds a particular society together."[2] They further indicate that society includes all human beings. This definition is too broad for the present discussion. The political entity of the United States is a more useable definition of the society *boundary* when referring to the society to which our social welfare system belongs. In fact, this entity as a system is almost too large and unwieldy, containing many subsystems of varying size and complexity. However, because of the important relationship between the federal political system and the social welfare system, we will find it useful for our discussion here.

A social system consists of a whole (the United States); its parts (states, communities, agencies, institutions, groups, families, and individuals); the functional subsystems (economic, political, health, social welfare, etc.); the relationship of the parts to each other; and of the whole to its environment (the world and other political entities). For the system to function, its parts must relate to each other in a *steady-state* condition. *Steady state* denotes a balance or sense of equilibrium where the various parts work together to complement, counteract, enhance, and support each other. Steady state also implies a degree of movement and change that a system can tolerate and thus remain functional, given that change in one part of the system requires change in other parts. When the amount of change is so great that some other parts of the system cannot absorb it without excessive stress or crisis, then the system is not in steady state.

For example, in contemporary U.S. society, change in the family functioning is taking place because many women are being forced into the labor market to meet their families' needs. In addition, many other women are also choosing to enter the labor market because of opportunities for advanced education and because of their desire for equal status.

This change in family life calls for new approaches to the care of young children. Society has been able to tolerate alternatives to maternal child care as long as they do not threaten the deeply held notions about the importance of the family in the life of the young child. However, if under the new kinds of child care, children seem to be suffering from unmet needs for love, discipline, or attention some people are very quick to claim the "destruction of the family." When the degree of change moves beyond the tolerance of the system, people are quick, sometimes too quick, to locate the cause.

Relationships among individuals in a system are defined by role structures, behavioral expectations, and class and status designations. Relationships among groups of individuals and functional subsystems are more difficult to identify and define. For example, the employer-employee relationship arises from expectations about behaviors on the part of both parties. The employer expects employees to carry out specified tasks, to adhere to work rules, and to work cooperatively with others. Employees expect the employer to pay them at the specified time and to provide a work environment that supports their endeavors. Implied in this relationship are the assumptions that the employer is the authority in the work situation, thus giving the person filling that role status. Some of these relationships are set by the individuals involved. Others are defined by and carried out through a variety of formalized structures (government, business associations, etc.) where the relationship is set by tradition or law. These formalized relationships are thus less flexible and respond slowly to change.

In large systems, specialized forms of organization exist to carry out the functions necessary for maintenance. Warren has identified these functions in communities as production, distribution and consumption (the economic subsystem), socialization, social control, social participation, and mutual support.[3] His conceptualization is also applicable to the societal system. Each subsystem has its own means of decision-making that in one way or another is validated by the larger system. Communication among subsystems is another important function. Each system also must create some means of allocating resources and energy to its various subsystems for the carrying out of assigned tasks. In times of great change when decision-making processes and communication are threatened, there is a tendency for systems to try to stabilize by increasing social control measures.

This brief description of a social system, with specific application to the U.S. societal system, can only be considered cursory at best. It does, however, provide a sense of how social change or change in any of the functional subsystems (political, economic, etc.) demands change in other parts of the system. Furthermore, change often pushes societal systems to a greater degree of organization (bureaucratization) by developing new mechanisms for social control and for the provision for human need.

For example, as government takes over social welfare functions new ways of carrying out these functions have developed. Neighbors no longer make decisions about who deserves to be helped. To insure that help is not arbitrarily given it has been necessary to formalize requirements for receiving help, which has led to a complex structure for administering social welfare programs.

The so-called cultural lag that often exists in times of change causes some parts of the system to operate under old rules while other parts have made the adaptation needed to accommodate the change. This lag causes confusion about how individuals are expected to function. The confusion that exists today about women's roles is an example. Societal change (economic and other) has made it necessary for many women to join the labor force. Yet women are also expected to continue to fill traditional roles in the home. The result is often a role overload. The confusion in turn can reduce people's capacity for social functioning. The impact is felt not only by the societal system but by the parts that include individuals and their capacity to meet their own human needs.

Understanding how the societal system functions from a social systems point of view is one way of understanding the relationship between provision for human need and provision for social control as they operate in the social welfare system. It helps us appreciate the complexity and the interrelationships of the mechanisms that have been developed to provide for the well-being of individuals and their society.

## Change as It Affects the Societal System

To show how societal change affects the societal response to human needs, three changes will be highlighted: (1) population shifts in size, urban-rural residence, and age distribution; (2) growth in dependence on a monetary economy; and (3) changes in family structure and functioning.

### Population Shifts

Changes in the population can best be seen by examining census data. Table 3.1 shows the population growth of the United States from 1800 to 1980—220,578,142 new people. Table 3.2 shows the shift of the U.S. population from a rural to an urban society. In 1800 only 6 percent of the U.S. population lived in urban areas. In 1970 this had risen to 73.5 percent. This growth has been steady, slowing only during the 1930–1940 Depression years. Table 3.3 shows the shift in age distribution between 1900 and 1980. Of particular note is the dramatic rise in the number of elderly. The 55-65 age group has almost doubled as a percent-

Table 3.1    Population and Area of United States 1800–1980

| Census Date | Number | Number per square mile of land area | Increase over preceding census | |
|---|---|---|---|---|
| | | | Number | Percent |
| 1800 | 5,929,483 | 6.1 | 1,379,269 | 35.1 |
| 1810 | 7,239,881 | 4.3 | 1,931,398 | 36.4 |
| 1820 | 9,638,453 | 5.5 | 2,398,572 | 33.1 |
| 1830 | 12,866,020 | 7.4 | 3,227,567 | 33.5 |
| 1840 | 17,069,453 | 9.8 | 4,203,433 | 32.7 |
| 1850 | 23,191,876 | 7.9 | 6,122,423 | 35.9 |
| 1860 | 31,443,321 | 10.6 | 8,251,445 | 35.6 |
| 1870 | 39,818,449 | 13.5 | 8,375,128 | 26.6 |
| 1880 | 50,155,783 | 16.9 | 10,337,334 | 26.0 |
| 1890 | 62,947,714 | 21.2 | 12,791,931 | 25.5 |
| 1900 | 75,994,575 | 25.6 | 13,046,861 | 20.7 |
| 1910 | 91,972,266 | 31.0 | 15,977,691 | 21.0 |
| 1920 | 105,710,620 | 35.6 | 13,738,354 | 14.9 |
| 1930 | 122,775,046 | 41.2 | 17,064,426 | 16.1 |
| 1940 | 131,669,275 | 44.2 | 8,894,229 | 7.2 |
| 1950* | 151,325,798 | 42.6 | 19,161,229 | 14.5 |
| 1960 | 179,323,175 | 50.6 | 27,997,377 | 18.5 |
| 1970 | 203,302,031 | 57.6 | 23,978,856 | 13.4 |
| 1980 | 226,504,825 | 64.0 | 23,202,794 | 11.4 |

*Reflects inclusion of Alaska and Hawaii

Source: U.S. Department of Commerce, Bureau of the Census. *Statistical Abstract of The United States, 1981,* p. 5.

age of the total population. The 65 and over age group is almost three times greater in 1980 than in 1900. The percentage of people under 14 years old has continued to drop, except for the baby boom years of the 1950s and 1960s.

These facts indicate an enormous change in the characteristics of the population of the United States. Now it is important to identify how those changes have affected human need. The growth in the population and the shift from a rural, agriculture society to an urban, industrial society brought many people into new and unfamiliar environments. Many immigrants were from rural areas. Often both the immigrant and the migrant from rural areas in the United States were driven to the new urban life by harsh economic and political conditions. They came to the new situation under stress and were not prepared for the further stresses caused by many people (often strangers) living very close together. They had little knowledge of the sanitary measures required by overcrowding.

Factory jobs called for long hours doing monotonous tasks under close supervision, very different from life in an agriculture setting. These people not only suffered from poverty and hazardous health conditions, they suffered from disruption of family life and from not understanding what they needed to do to survive in their new surroundings. The immigrants often could not speak English and thus had additional trouble understanding how to use those resources and opportunities available to them. Once social change had disrupted their usual pattern of functioning, the newly urban poor had difficulty meeting their needs, and their social behavior often did not adhere to the norms of the established society in which they found themselves. The dominant classes of society were pressed to find ways to meet migrants and immigrant's needs and to control their misunderstood behavior.[4]

Table 3.2    Urban-Rural Population in the United States 1800–1970

| *Census Date* | Urban | | Rural | |
|---|---|---|---|---|
| | *Number* | *Percent* | *Number* | *Percent* |
| 1800 | 322,000 | 6.0 | 4,986,000 | 93.9 |
| 1810 | 525,000 | 7.2 | 6,714,000 | 92.7 |
| 1820 | 693,000 | 7.2 | 8,945,000 | 92.8 |
| 1830 | 1,127,000 | 8.7 | 11,739,000 | 91.2 |
| 1840 | 1,845,000 | 10.8 | 15,224,000 | 89.2 |
| 1850 | 3,544,000 | 15.3 | 19,648,000 | 84.7 |
| 1860 | 6,217,000 | 19.9 | 25,656,000 | 80.2 |
| 1870 | 9,902,000 | 25.7 | 28,656,000 | 74.3 |
| 1880 | 14,130,000 | 28.2 | 36,026,000 | 71.8 |
| 1890 | 22,106,000 | 35.1 | 40,841,000 | 64.9 |
| 1900 | 30,160,000 | 39.6 | 45,835,000 | 60.3 |
| 1910 | 41,999,000 | 45.6 | 49,973,000 | 54.3 |
| 1920 | 54,158,000 | 51.2 | 51,552,000 | 48.7 |
| 1930 | 68,955,000 | 56.2 | 53,821,000 | 43.8 |
| 1940 | 74,424,000 | 56.5 | 57,245,000 | 43.5 |
| 1950* | 96,468,000 | 64.0 | 54,479,000 | 36.0 |
| 1960 | 125,269,000 | 69.9 | 54,054,000 | 30.1 |
| 1970 | 149,325,000 | 73.5 | 53,887,000 | 26.5 |

*From 1950 a slightly different definition has been used.

Source: 1800–1940. U.S. Department of Commerce, Bureau of the Census. *A Statistical Abstract Supplement, Historical Statistics of the United States, Colonial Times to 1957*, p. 8. 1950–1970. U.S. Department of Commerce, Bureau of the Census. *Statistical Abstract of the United States, 1981*, p. 14.

Table 3.3    Age Distribution of Population of the United States 1900–1980

| Census Year | Total Population | Under 14 | % | Population by Age 14–24 | % | 25–34 | % |
|---|---|---|---|---|---|---|---|
| 1900 | 76,094,000 | 24,581,000 | 32.3 | 16,514,000 | 21.7 | 12,162,000 | 16.0 |
| 1910 | 92,407,000 | 27,806,000 | 30.0 | 20,024,000 | 21.7 | 15,276,000 | 16.5 |
| 1920 | 106,466,000 | 31,756,000 | 29.8 | 28,858,000 | 19.6 | 17,417,000 | 16.4 |
| 1930 | 123,077,000 | 33,638,000 | 27.3 | 24,852,000 | 20.1 | 19,039,000 | 15.5 |
| 1940 | 132,122,000 | 30,521,000 | 23.1 | 26,454,000 | 20.0 | 21,446,000 | 16.2 |
| 1950 | 151,683,000 | 38,605,000 | 25.5 | 24,458,000 | 16.1 | 23,926,000 | 15.8 |
| 1960 | 179,323,000 | 55,786,000 | 31.1 | 24,020,000 | 13.3 | 22,818,000 | 12.7 |
| 1970 | 203,235,000 | 57,936,000 | 28.5 | 35,467,000 | 17.5 | 24,923,000 | 12.3 |
| 1980 | 226,505,000 | 51,282,000 | 22.6 | 42,475,000 | 18.5 | 37,076,000 | 16.4 |

It was on this group of unadapted, newly urbanized people caught in the turmoil of a changing society that the Charity Organization Society and settlement houses focused their concern. Both had a goal of helping these people establish a life-style congruent with the needs and demands of living in urban American society. Their goal spoke not only to the concern for the individual and the family but to the larger needs of society.

Social change due to population change has not only been related to the size of the population and urban-rural change. The length of the life span has also increased. In 1900 a person could expect to live 48.2 years. In 1959, this rose to 69.9 years; and by 1976 to 72.8 years.[5] With this aging of the population has come pressures to develop new support systems for this elderly population. If elders remain in the work force, they fill jobs needed by younger workers. If they are removed from the work force, then they can no longer support themselves and some societal provision must be made for their support. The Social Security Act provides the major mechanisms used since 1935 to support those over 65 years of age. It provides monetary and health care support for meeting individual need and while providing for societal need by allowing the older workers to leave the work force.

In recent years as medical advances have further lengthened the life span, we now have a new group of elderly, those over 75 years of age known as the *"frail elderly."* This population increased 52 percent between 1960 and 1965. Persons reaching 65 now can expect to live sixteen more years.[6] This group often needs more than income support. They may need other services either in the home or in institutions: help with

| | | Population by Age | | | | | |
|---|---|---|---|---|---|---|---|
| 35–44 | % | 45–54 | % | 55–65 | % | Over 65 | % |
| 9,271,000 | 12.2 | 6,439,000 | 8.5 | 4,027,000 | 5.3 | 3,100,000 | 4.0 |
| 11,761,000 | 12.7 | 8,454,000 | 9.1 | 5,101,000 | 5.5 | 3,985,000 | 4.3 |
| 14,383,000 | 13.5 | 10,503,000 | 9.9 | 6,620,000 | 6.2 | 4,929,000 | 4.6 |
| 17,270,000 | 14.0 | 13,096,000 | 10.6 | 8,477,000 | 6.9 | 6,706,000 | 5.4 |
| 18,422,000 | 13.9 | 15,555,000 | 11.8 | 10,694,000 | 8.1 | 9,031,000 | 6.8 |
| 21,569,000 | 14.2 | 17,413,000 | 11.5 | 13,424,000 | 8.8 | 12,287,000 | 8.1 |
| 24,081,000 | 13.4 | 20,485,000 | 11.4 | 15,572,000 | 8.7 | 16,560,000 | 9.2 |
| 23,101,000 | 11.4 | 23,235,000 | 11.4 | 18,602,000 | 9.2 | 19,972,000 | 9.8 |
| 25,336,000 | 11.2 | 22,797,000 | 10.1 | 21,700,000 | 9.6 | 25,544,000 | 11.3 |

Source: 1900–1950. U.S. Department of Commerce, *Historical Statistics of the United States, Colonial Times to 1957*, p. 6.
1960–1980. U.S. Department of Commerce, *Statistical Abstract of the United States, 1981*.

many tasks of daily living such as self-care and care of the home; considerable health care and often opportunity for social contact with others. One of the challenges of the 1980s is the development of mechanisms that respond to the needs of this growing group of frail elderly. Again, change in one aspect of society, the population, calls for change in its social welfare system.

## Growth of a Monetary Economy

With the movement from rural to urban living came the movement for a *subsistence economy* to a monetary economy. Most people no longer had land available to use to provide a major portion of their food supply. A family could not "take in" individuals in unfortunate circumstances as live-in servants or apprentices. Often families could not even provide for a relative who has no means of support. Costs of essentials, such as food, shelter, clothing, and medical care rose dramatically. The availability of money became essential for survival in our contemporary, money-based society. Since older traditional means of taking care of self and others are no longer possible in today's social system, social welfare mechanisms must provide monetary means for needy people. Thus the social welfare system has had to change because of social and economic changes.

Another important change in the U.S. related to changes in the economy has been the development of what is now being called a *service society*. A service society is one in which the majority of the labor force is engaged in providing services (intangibles) as opposed to producing material goods (tangibles).[7] This in part has contributed to the professionalization of helping. Paid helpers are a part of the service sector. Salaries of paid helpers (professionals) and the supporting administrative structure are major expenditures in the social welfare budget. Thus economic changes affect not only how people provide for their own basic needs, but how society provides for the needs of those who cannot provide for themselves.

The growth of a governmental social welfare system is related to the growth of the necessity of monetary provision for human need. That means the system must be set up not only to provide for human need but also to control costs and to control the decision of whose needs and which needs are provided for.

An important contemporary issue is how much income and how many services can be provided through monetary mechanisms by the various supporting political entities. This can be translated: How much tax money is available for providing for the welfare of individuals in U.S. society? A related question is how much of a contribution through taxes and other means are citizens willing to make to help meet the needs of others? A third question is who are to be helped—those who are unable to meet basic needs (the poor) or those who are concerned about social control (all citizens)? In other words how much welfare must be provided to prevent riots, uprising, and other civil strife? Economic change has disrupted an earlier steady state. Society is using the social welfare system to bring about a new balance by providing for new areas of human need, some of which are a result of the economic change. At the same time, society is using that system as a form of social control, social control that is needed if a steady state is to be maintained.

It is thus apparent that changes in the economic system have brought about changes in how people meet their needs both individually and collectively. During the process of change, old means for meeting need become either unusable or ineffective. Until new means are developed some people, through no fault of their own, are unable to meet their individual or family need.

## Changes in Family Structure and Functioning

Another question that should be raised about social change is whether a particular change is desirable or whether change should be resisted in an effort to achieve a steady state? The conservative political stance is usually to minimize change. The more liberal or progressive stance is to work for change. When political power rests with those who are comfortable with the current situation the pull is for minimal change. When a significant group in the country is being adversely affected by social and economic conditions, the push is for change. Societal change has affected not only the population distribution and the economy of our society, but it has affected the ways families function. Large families are no longer as desirable as when the economic base was the family farm or small family business. Many children were then an asset, providing extra hands to carry out the work to be done. Today with an economic base that requires many women to work outside the home, children are often an economic liability. Advances in maternal and child health have resulted in more children surviving their early years and fewer women dying in childbirth. Thus we find many families choosing to limit the number of children they produce. For women this has led to a shorter period of child care and a greater opportunity to enter the labor force outside the home.

Women enter the labor force for more than just economic reasons. Women have more opportunity for education and thus more of the skills needed in the labor market. Laborsaving devices have freed women of much of the drudgery of caring for the home and have provided them with time for other activities. These women also contribute to family change as they develop new mothering patterns and new patterns of sharing household tasks.

The changed economic system also has a need for a mobile work force. As a result of this, family members often find themselves relocated at some distance from their extended family. These families must often seek new means for help once given by extended families, such as a grandmother's care of a sick child when the mother is employed outside the home, or the support of a caring network in times of stress.

It is not the purpose of this discussion to note all the changes in family life. Rather the point is that social change has brought about change in the functioning of families and thus altered their capacity to meet some of the needs of family members through mutual aid. It has led to more dependence by the family on the functioning of the economic marketplace to meet most of their needs. For some families changes have forced an increased reliance on social welfare services to meet the needs of its members.

Some families are more vulnerable than others to problems in meeting their members' needs: those with the least capacity and opportunity to function in the job market, those with single parents, minority group families, those composed of aging people (sixty-five years of age or older), and those containing individuals with special medical and other needs. These families often cannot earn enough money to meet their basic needs. They are also the families that have been affected the most by social change—the ones whom social welfare must assist.

Some would find the solution for these problems as a return to an idealized family of some earlier day. They should remember that such an idealized family never existed for more than a few people, even in other times. The history of social welfare provides many situations in which the family by itself was insufficient to meet human need. The families of the poor, the widow and orphaned, the sick, and aged, the immigrant often could not provide for all their members needs. So the social welfare system developed mechanisms to meet at least some of their needs, first through institutions, then through settlement houses and the COS, and finally through some provisions of the Social Security Act. The solution for today's family in stress does not lie in return to an outdated, idealized family structure but in seeking new ways to balance the role of the family and the role of the social welfare system.

The major theme of this portion of this chapter has been that social change brings about change in the way human need is met. Social change also affects society's capacity to respond to human need. This in turn calls for change in the social welfare system.

## Social Change as It Affects Individuals

As a society changes, individuals in that society must also make changes. These changes involve the way a person provides for personal needs, such as earning a living, the kind of formal education a person obtains, and the roles and norms for functioning in the family and other social systems. In other words, a change in life-style may be necessary. Often the social change is gradual enough to allow a series of small personal changes within the coping capacity of an individual, with minimal disruption to how that individual functions. At other times the required change is sudden or outside the capacity of the individual. Automation of an industry may cause individuals to lose essential employment. In a day of intensive job specialization, skill obsolescence can come swiftly and unexpectedly. In the early 1980s, auto industry workers found themselves in this kind of situation. Hardworking and productive people found themselves no longer needed by their society. With outdated skills and knowledge, people may have little opportunity for learning new ones. Change may require moving to a new, strange environment. Cultural patterns of behavior, developed in a different time and place, may hinder a person's ability to easily adapt to change. An individual may feel tension between a need to adhere to the patterns of their cultural group and a need to develop new and different ways of functioning with other societal institutions. Some individuals will be caught by change and find themselves unable to meet their needs or their family's.

For example, family farmers are finding they can no longer provide for their families' needs from a farm income. They are often forced to leave their farms and seek other employment. But they need training to enter the skilled labor force, and they must leave the culture of farming and the environment they have known all their lives. Like other displaced workers, these people then may find themselves dependent on social welfare arrangements.

It is important to consider what happens to people left behind by change, victims of progress. These people often feel alienated from others. They feel powerless to deal with the impact of the negative circumstances and see no way to meet their need. They are often resentful. Perhaps they believe they have lost that which is most meaningful for them. With no job or with little opportunity to participate in a meaningful human enterprise, they seem to "drop out" or isolate themselves from people and activities that would give them a sense of self worth. Their new social milieu provides them with few indicators of expected behaviors. They have a sense of normlessness. With their low self esteem and hopelessness comes a lessened ability to adapt. Thus they feel caught in a vicious cycle. These people need more than income maintenance from the social welfare system. They need social and educational services to be helped to reenter the mainstream of society. With this kind of assistance these people may be able to break out of their poverty cycle—to the betterment of themselves and of society.

Disruption in the family system and its capacity to provide for its children's needs gives the children few opportunities to develop into adults who can adequately participate in the economic system and in other aspects of the society to meet their own and society's needs. Thus a poverty life-style is created. This in turn encourages discriminatory practices. Poverty and discrimination are results of social change; they contribute to individual dysfunctioning.

## Summary

Social change is a necessary ingredient of any society's growth and development. Change does, however, disrupt the functioning of a society's institutions, families, and individuals. The customary methods of meeting human need become inadequate or dysfunctional and new mechanisms need to be created. When individual lives are disrupted, this can lead to deviant behaviors that threaten society. The social welfare system has developed mechanisms for providing for unmet need that also have built into them mechanisms of social control.

One way of understanding the contemporary social welfare system in the United States is to study the effect social change on the development of that system. In this chapter a social systems perspective has been used to discuss how social change has affected both the societal system and its functioning and the individual who is a part of the societal system.

## Key Terms

boundary
frail elderly
monetary economy
service society
social change

social control
society as a social system
steady state
subsistence economy

## Questions for Discussion

1. What changes in U.S. society since 1800 have brought about changes in thought about the government's responsibility for its citizens?

2. What kinds of provisions for human need resulting from social change should government provide?

3. Should social welfare provision be used as social control?

4. How does changing family structure and functioning affect the need for social welfare services?

## Notes

1 For discussion of social control and social welfare see: Walter I. Trattner, ed., *Social Welfare or Social Control? Some Historical Reflection on "Regulating the Poor"* (Knoxville, TN.: The University of Tennessee Press, 1983).
2 Ralph E. Anderson and Irl Carter, *Human Behavior in the Social Environment: A Social Systems Approach*, 2nd ed. (Chicago: Aldine Publishing Co., 1978), p. 35.
3 Roland L. Warren, *The Community in America* (Chicago: Rand McNally & Co., 1963), particularly Chapter 6.
4 For further discussion of this social development see: Leonard Dinnerstein, Roger L. Nichols, and David M. Reimers, *Natives and Strangers* (New York: Oxford University Press, 1979).
5 Anita Harbert and Leon H. Ginsberg, *Human Services for Older Adults: Concepts and Skills* (Belmont, CA.: Wadsworth Publishing Co., 1979), p. 4.
6 Louis Lowy, *Social Work with the Aging* (New York: Harper & Row Publishers, 1979).
7 Carl Gersuny and William R. Rosengren, *The Service Society* (Cambridge, MA.: Schenkman Publishing Co., 1973), p.2.

## Suggested Readings

Anderson, Ralph E., and Carter, Irl. *Human Behavior in the Social Environment: A Social Systems Approach*, 2nd ed. Chicago: Aldine Publishing Co., 1978.

Gersuny, Carl, and Rosengren, William R. *The Service Society*. Cambridge, Mass.: Schenkman Publishing Co., 1973.

Piven, Frances F., and Cloward, Richard A. *Regulating the Poor: The Functions of Public Welfare*. New York: Pantheon Books, 1971.

Trattner, Walter I., ed. *Social Welfare or Social Control? Some Historical Reflections on "Regulating the Poor."*, Knoxville, Tenn.: The University of Tennessee Press, 1983.

# Chapter 4

## Poverty, Human Needs, and Social Welfare

*Poverty* is a serious social problem that contributes to the inability of individuals to meet their basic needs. According to the United States Census Bureau, in 1983 thirty-four million people had incomes below the poverty line. This represents 15 percent of the United States population. No single social problem has been more troublesome in its effects on the social system.

Throughout history, numerous attempts have been made to reduce or eliminate poverty in the United States. The social welfare system has been the primary mechanism for doing this since it is designed to assist those persons in society whose needs exceed their means to satisfy them. Yet poverty persists, despite public welfare and other antipoverty programs and services. Poverty is amazingly difficult to destroy. Like a cat, poverty seems to have at least nine lives.[1] Poverty is a complex and destructive social problem, deeply rooted in the total social structure of our society, a disgrace that distorts our nation's image as the land of plenty and promise.

This chapter is devoted to an extensive discussion of the phenomenon of poverty, with the aim of helping the reader understand the relationship between poverty and human needs and the societal responses made through the social welfare system to deal with the effects of that relationship. This chapter examines the definitions of poverty, who the poor are, the causes of poverty, the discovery and rediscovery of poverty, and professional responses to poverty. This chapter examines the different definitions of poverty and identifies the poor and the causes of poverty, as well as the response to poverty from both society and social workers.

# What Is Poverty?

To define poverty is difficult. It can be defined loosely by mass culture or it can be defined more strictly by government laws and regulations. Poverty can also be defined by the individuals or groups who experience it. Furthermore, poverty can be described by the use of selected economic, sociological, or political definitions. Some of these definitions are discussed below.

## Individual

Some individuals consider themselves poor, even though by established economic measures of poverty they may not be. These individuals base their perceptions of being poor on comparison of themselves to others. Conversely, other individuals considered poor by standard measures do not consider themselves poor. This suggests that poverty and deprivation are relative, depending on individual perceptions. But this self-definition of poverty is not very useful. If this were accepted as the sole definition of poverty, almost everyone might consider themselves poor which adds nothing to our understanding. Therefore, individual definitions are not used much for describing poverty.

## Societal

Some people's view of the poor is based on stereotypical perceptions or value judgements. They categorize the poor as people from the "wrong side" of town, or simply as recipients of public assistance, or even solely as members of racial or ethnic groups. Sometimes the poor are lumped together by society into one large homogeneous group without considering the diversity that in fact exists among the poor. All that is seen is the poverty life-style, without considering the true causes of the conditions under which poor people live. To define poverty on the basis of stereotypes, without considering the causes, distorts our understanding of poverty.

## Institutional

American society has provided official definitions of poverty. The federal government was charged with this responsibility and first offered a definition of poverty in 1964, when the President's Council of Economic Advisors in its annual report stated, "By the poor we mean those who are now not maintaining a decent standard of living; those whose basic needs exceed their means to satisfy them." An alternative definition also offered by the Council of Economic Advisors was, "Poverty is the inability to satisfy minimum needs."[2] These two definitions are sufficiently vague to have provoked a great deal of debate about what constitutes a decent standard of living, or what should be considered a person's minimum needs. Nevertheless, these definitions provided the impetus for establishing an official poverty line used to distinguish the poor from the non-poor. The *poverty line* acts as the official measure of poverty in considering the incomes of individuals or families. Since 1965, the responsibility for establishing the official poverty line has rested with the Social Security Administration. The original 1964 poverty line was set at an annual income of $3,000 for a family of four, and $1,500 per year for an individual. The poverty line has risen steadily since 1964. In 1984 it stood at $10,609 for a family of four.[3]

## Economic

Poverty has been most often defined in economic terms, using personal or family income as a determinant. It is often classified as a problem of low income. It is best understood as a lack of the necessary income for people to meet their needs for food, clothing, shelter, energy, transportation, and medical care. In a monetary society like ours a family's ability to meet these needs is dependent on the structure and functioning of the economic marketplace and not on their own ability to produce food and goods. But as the monetary society attempts to achieve a balance between meeting human needs and providing for social control, as discussed in the previous chapter, it has made it difficult for some families to meet their daily needs for survival.

## Sociological

Poverty can also be viewed from a sociological perspective. One viewpoint is that poverty exists as a more or less permanent fixture of the social structure. That is, the poor occupy and are assigned special status by society through a system of social stratification.[4] This view assumes that social benefits—such as wealth, power, and status—are not equally distributed throughout the social strata, thus creating a clear distinction between the "haves" and the "have nots."

Two other points of view that help to define poverty are the concepts of *absolute* and *relative deprivation*. Absolute measures of deprivation are based on established fixed standards of living.[5] Those individuals or families whose resources fail to meet the minimum standards are considered deprived. One problem with absolute measures of deprivation is that the standards are fixed, and no adjustments are made to account for increases in the costs of living. In addition, the terminology about what is considered minimum standards of living is confusing. Absolute measures of deprivation also fail to make judgements about whether the distribution of income and resources is adequate or not.

Relative measures of deprivation is the view that poverty is a problem of unequal distribution of resources within the population, rather than a problem of inadequate resources. In this viewpoint, the poor are those whose incomes fall below the poverty line, established by comparing all incomes and then selecting a point in a range of incomes as the poverty line. (This is the measurement of poverty that the Social Security Administration uses each year to derive the official poverty line.) This measurement of deprivation is flexible, adjusting the poverty line as incomes increase. Although the poverty line is determined using the concept of relative deprivation, the line actually is treated as an absolute measure and is frequently used to determine an individual's and family's eligibility for public social welfare programs and services.[6] Absolute and relative measurements of poverty are useful in offering insight into what poverty is. But they, along with other sociological viewpoints, are only pieces of the puzzle of understanding the complexities of poverty.

## Political

Poverty can be studied as a political problem. The poor in the United States have not been sufficiently mobilized to exert their political influence and their power to make known and bring about changes in the economic system that would provide the income resources they need. The poor are placed in a difficult situation. With economic affluence comes social status. With social status comes the power to use society's resources for one's own goals. Today's poor have the potential to become a powerful political constituency if they could be collectively organized. This was demonstrated in the 1960s when they became powerful forces for change. The involvement of poor blacks was a turning point in the civil rights movement, adding both numbers and a *raisons d'etre*. More recently the voter registration activity associated with Jesse Jackson's 1984 bid for the Democratic presidential nomination was an attempt to organize the poor and other disenfranchised groups so that they could exert political influence. (Unfortunately, these efforts have not brought about any significant change in the political status quo.) This was again attempted in the national election of 1984, when a voter registration movement was tied to Jesse Jackson's candidacy for president.

## Cultural

Poverty can be defined in cultural terms. One such theory was the concept of the *culture of poverty*. Oscar Lewis, an anthropologist, was a proponent of this view. According to this view, poverty forms the basis for a separate and distinct culture. Lewis contended that in the groups he studied, mainly Mexican Americans and Puerto Ricans, poverty served as a foundation for their culture. The poor, according to this theory, have developed norms, values, attitudes, and life-styles different from the rest of society's.[7] The culture of poverty theory is not as well accepted today as it once was. Defining poverty in cultural terms today is seen as a narrow view. Poverty is now defined in a more comprehensive manner, which includes the influence of economic, social, and political factors.

## Who Are the Poor?

For poverty to be more fully understood in terms of its relationship to human needs, it is necessary to come to grips with who the poor are. Societal ignorance and insensitivity have created stereotypic perceptions of the poor. Quite often the poor are thought of as a homogeneous group, perhaps varying with geographic location. (We go into this in more depth in Chapter 6.) Poverty is often seen as confined to specific ethnic groups, blacks, native Americans, and Hispanics, or as mainly an urban problem, like a ghetto in a large city. If it is perceived as a rural problem at all, it is thought to be restricted to western Indian reservations, Appalachia, the rural south, or to migrant farm workers. But what people do not understand is that the poor are quite a diverse group.

Although racial and ethnic minorities make up a significant proportion of the poor, there are also over twenty-three million poor whites in the United States today. Stereotypes also ignore the aged, women, children, and the working poor. To gain full awareness of who the poor are, the effects of poverty on each of these groups must be examined.

### Racial Minorities

BLACKS   All racial minorities are overrepresented in the ranks of the poor, a result of longstanding racial discrimination in our society toward these groups. Among them, blacks represent the largest group classified as impoverished. In 1984 nearly ten million black Americans or 35.7 percent of all blacks had incomes below the poverty line.[8]

In the last twenty years, some blacks have gained some economic affluence, primarily as a result of civil rights legislation that opened doors to schools and jobs. However, societal discrimination continues to handicap their efforts to achieve economic equality.

NATIVE AMERICANS   In 1980, 27.5 percent of all native Americans had incomes below the poverty line. In addition poverty rates among native Americans who live in particular geographic locations is higher than the national rate. For example, in South Dakota 45.8 percent of native Americans had incomes below the poverty line in 1980.[9] Three factors are important in discussing causes of their poverty. One is unemployment. Unemployment rates on native American reservations are high because most reservations were placed in geographically undesireable, economically depressed areas, with little or no industry to provide employment. Therefore, native American people are heavily dependent on assistance from the U.S Bureau of Indian Affairs and other local and state public welfare agencies. Their dependency has come as a result of one-hundred-plus years of paternalistic practices by the federal government sanctioned by laws passed in the 1800s that forced, and continue to force, dependency today. Despite this rather gloomy scenario, the economic situation is rapidly changing for many tribes. Native American tribes in the southwestern United States, for example, have been successful in industrial development, which has somewhat improved their economic situation. Native Americans are also handicapped in their efforts to rise out of poverty by the lack of educational opportunities and job-related skills, both on and off the reservations. Lastly discrimination against native Americans contributes to the perpetuation of their impoverishment.

HISPANICS  Spanish-speaking people, or Hispanics, include Mexican Americans, Puerto Ricans, Cubans, Filipinos, and others. Hispanics are significantly represented among American poor. Almost five million Hispanics, representing 28.4 percent of this population are living in poverty and face much of the same type of discrimination in the employment market as do other minorities. One group, the migrant farm workers of the southwestern and western United States, is particularly at risk of living in poverty. Because their employment is seasonal and requires a transient life-style, their lives become disorganized and chaotic. They are often exploited by unscrupulous growers. Adaptation to the migrant life-style creates a subculture with special problems of access to the social and health services that would interrupt the poverty cycle.

## The Aged

According to 1984 United States census data, 12.1 percent of all persons aged sixty-five or older live below the poverty line.[10] Several factors are associated with poverty and the aged. Generally, the elderly have limited or fixed sources of income, which may consist of social security benefits, supplemental security income, veterans benefits, some form of pension or retirement benefits, or a combination of those sources. In many instances the income is near or below the poverty line. Programs to help the elderly have imposed limits on additional earned income as eligibility standards for participation. Thus they cannot legally bolster their income in any way if they depend on those programs. This limited income curtails their purchasing power, forcing many elderly people into a poverty life-style. Other problems the aged face as a result of inadequate income are poor housing, lack of medical care, poor nutrition, and lack of transportation.

## Women

Women are also a diverse group who experience the detrimental effects of poverty. They make up a large percentage of those who are considered poor, particularly in families where they are the heads of household. More than three million or 36 percent of U.S. families headed by a woman had incomes below the poverty line, according to the 1983 United States Census Bureau.[11]

Chief among the causes of this situation is unemployment, significantly higher for women heads of household than for men. Working women earn less than their male counterparts, which also accounts for their difficulty in rising above the poverty level. But the real culprit operating here is gender discrimination. Women have been discriminated against in the educational system, and therefore often lack the education or job skills necessary to earn an adequate living. Women have also been discriminated against in the labor market, even though laws prohibit it. Lastly, for some families headed by women, the embarrassingly low amount of public assistance payments often keeps the family living at or below the poverty level.

## Children

One of the largest diverse groups among the poor are children. It is estimated that 22.1 percent of all persons considered poverty-stricken are children.[12] What is tragic about this is the children do not have a choice in the matter. They are trapped in poverty due to their status as children and are unable to break away from its destructive effects. Poverty affects children in physical, social, psychological, and emotional ways. It predisposes children to the risks of mental illness, juvenile delinquency, alcoholism and drug abuse, child abuse, and family violence in addition to nutritional and health problems associated with poverty's deprivation. These effects cause them to function inadequately in the educational system. Often a cycle of generational poverty develops. Children in families in which the cycle of poverty is not interrupted carry the deprivation into adulthood, continuing the cycle with their own children.

## The Working Poor

The working poor also feel the grip of poverty. The *working poor* are those individuals and families who are employed but earn insufficient wages to meet their basic needs. In 1984, 30.1 percent of heads of households in families having incomes below the poverty level work fulltime.[13] A most distressing factor unique to this group is that although they work hard and earn an income, however insufficient, they usually are not eligible for any sort of public assistance because eligibility standards for most assistance programs are based on income. This sadly perpetuates the poverty life-style for the working poor. Also some of the working poor do not apply for programs that are available such as food stamps, to avoid the stigma connected to receiving financial aid.

Some farmers comprise another group of people who might be considered working poor. The current farm crisis has severely affected the ability of farming families to meet even their most basic human needs as they struggle to maintain their farms, some of which have supported their families for several generations. Since these people own land, they are considered to have resources: however, if they dispose of the resources, then they no longer can farm and are thrown into the ranks of the unemployed, often with no saleable skills.

## Geography of Poverty: Urban? Rural?

Lastly, in identifying the poor, it is useful to become aware of the geography of poverty. Is poverty mainly an urban phenomenon, or is it prevalent in rural areas? Poverty is commonly thought to be more prevalent in urban than rural areas because it is more readily seen in metropolitan areas, due to high concentrations of population. In rural areas, where people live at considerable distances from one another, poverty becomes more difficult to observe. Contrary to popular belief, poverty is proportionately more common in rural areas than in urban. Twenty-seven percent of the United States population lives in rural areas. Within that population, 15 percent of individuals and families have incomes below the poverty threshold. Compare this to urban areas that comprise 73.4 percent of the population but where only 11.1 percent of the population is considered impoverished by official standards.[14] Yet rural poverty remains largely unseen due to the fact that "The rural population, widely dispersed, racially and culturally heterogeneous, socially and politically incohesive does not compete well for attention."[15]

# Causes of Poverty

The definitions of poverty are complex and the causes even more so. To try to understand this complexity, three broad areas of causation will be discussed: economic, social, and political.

## Economic Causes

The economic causes of poverty, as agreed upon by most authorities, are income distribution, inadequate income supports, unemployment, underemployment, and inflation. Too often, poverty is thought of merely as a result of low or inadequate income, but to identify this as the only economic cause of poverty is too simplistic. It is more meaningful to examine why large proportions of the U.S. population have low or inadequate incomes, and thus are considered poor.

INCOME DISTRIBUTION   The chief factor is income distribution. The *Gross National Product* (GNP) roughly defined as the total income of the country and the indicator of a nation's wealth, is divided among a number of economic units. (One economic unit is the personal household, either an individual or a family household.) These units contribute to the GNP through production and consumption of goods, services, and resources. The *distribution of income* is subject to influence by the marketplace, society at large, and through political process, and the way that income is distributed is what causes poverty. One writer boldly states that we have a dual economy in the United States, an economy of affluence and an economy of poverty.[16] Although a minority of U.S. households are poor, those that are "are poor not because of inadequate total output or Gross National Product, but because of inequalities in the distributing of income and wealth."[17] (See Table 4.1.) Although the U.S. Gross National Product has steadily increased since World War II, the distribution of wealth throughout the population has not changed very much, demonstrating the perpetuation of poverty.

An economic measure that redistributes wealth to the poor is income transfers through public income maintenance programs and other social programs. The source of the income transfer payments is revenue from personal and corporate income taxes collected by the federal government. But this measure has not provided sufficient redistribution of wealth to move large numbers of people out of poverty. Contributing to

Table 4.1   Changes in the Distribution of Income 1947–1980

| Income Class | Percentage of National Income 1947 | 1980 |
| --- | --- | --- |
| Lower | 5.1% | 5.1% |
| Upper-Lower | 11.8% | 11.6% |
| Middle | 16.7% | 17.5% |
| Upper-Middle | 23.2% | 24.3% |
| Upper | 43.3% | 41.5% |
| Top 5 Percent | 17.5% | 15.3% |

this failure is the fact that the philosophies that have influenced income transfers have not changed. Those who hold the wealth are affluent, not only in wealth, but also in social and political influence. The affluent exercise their influence in the marketplace and in political spheres, thus dominating decision making on national social policy and social programs for the poor. A capitalistic economy does not place a high value on sharing wealth, or equally distributing income: competition and self-sufficiency are held more valuable. The United States is a prosperous nation yet poverty abounds.

INADEQUATE INCOME SUPPORTS   The unequal distribution of wealth and income is largely responsible for the continuation of this contradiction. Inadequate income supports as a cause of poverty occurs as a side effect of our economic system, where the emphasis is placed on production and consumption.

The ability to produce and consume goods and services is related to levels of personal and family income. Production of goods and services stimulates the economy and thus employment, which in turn produces wealth and income. Production, however, is only one side of the picture. It must be balanced with adequate levels of consumption. People must be able to buy the goods and services produced, otherwise an imbalance or disequilibrium in the economy results. The poor generally are not producers or consumers.

Within our economic system the ability to obtain goods and services is called *purchasing power*.[18] If a person's purchasing power is too low due to a low personal or family income he or she has an inadequate income support. The poor have very low incomes thus their purchasing power is negligible or nonexistent. Most of their income, in whatever form it is received, is spent on necessities. They are unable to invest or save money or purchase non-essential goods as most other people in our society are able to do.

Income supports for some of the poor are provided through income maintenance assistance (the public welfare arrangement). In theory these programs should increase purchasing power as they provide recipients with additional cash. However, these programs, because of the low levels of income assistance they provide, fail to significantly increase the purchasing power of the poor, thus contributing to the perpetuation of a poverty life-style for many poor people.[19]

UNEMPLOYMENT AND UNDEREMPLOYMENT   Temporary or seasonal unemployment, although they may cause short-term poverty, are only a small part of the problem. Chronic or permanent unemployment and underemployment are the biggest contributors to poverty. *Underemployment*, working at a job that provides insufficient income is a particular cause of the working poor.

*Unemployment* has always been a feature of the U.S. economy. There are several views on this matter. One view is that unemployment exists because some people do not desire to be employed, despite available employment opportunities. Related to this is Schiller's concept of the flawed character. This assumes that individuals are in control of their destinies and choose to live in poverty. In opposition to this view, Schiller presents the viewpoint known as the restrictive opportunity argument, which states that individuals are not in control of their economic status. He argues that therefore, poverty life-styles are caused by factors outside the realm of control of the individual. Schiller states, "the poor are poor because they do not have adequate access too good schools, jobs, and income, because they are discriminated against on the basis of color, sex, or income class, and because they are not furnished with a fair share of government protection, subsidy or services."[20] Although both arguments may be somewhat valid in explaining unemployment, the restrictive opportunity argument better describes the realities of poverty today.

This view holds that unemployment exists because the economy fails to meet the market's demands for goods, services, and resources. More jobs would be created if production were able to keep pace. Poverty due to unemployment results in part from a lack of jobs particularly during times of economic recession. However, the lack of access to employment is a more important cause.

INFLATION    Lastly, another economic cause of poverty is *inflation.* A simple definition of inflation as used here would be increased costs of living equal rising costs in the basic necessities of life, as well as nonessential goods and services. Although inflation erodes the quality of life for all Americans, its effects on the poor are even more devastating. With limited purchasing power due to inadequate income, inflation lessens even further their ability to buy the necessities of life. Inflation is an economic reality that the poor have little means to control. Inflation is a result of the functioning of the marketplace, which the affluent, due to their economic, social, and political influence, control. It is the poor who disproportionally suffer the consequences of inflation.

## Social Causes

Poverty can also be described as a social phenomenon. Various social and environmental factors can be identified as causes of poverty. Among these social factors, negative societal attitudes towards the poor stand out as important contributors to the incidence of poverty. High value placed on self-sufficiency and society's infatuation with the Protestant work-ethic have played a part in this. This virtue of self-reliance in U.S. society has as its core the philosophy that: "Society does not owe anyone a living; people make their own living."[21] Success and making one's own way is measured in terms of hard work. Many wrongly believe that poor people have low income not because of membership in an economic class, or from other circumstance beyond their control but because they are not useful to society, are less hard-working, frugal, and responsible. Poverty then becomes a failure to adhere to the values about work and self-sufficiency. This sort of thinking also affirms the flawed character argument of poverty discussed earlier. These attitudes and values operate in social interaction and form the basis of prejudice and discrimination toward the poor. We are not just referring here to discrimination on the basis of race, ethnic origin, or sex, although that is undoubtedly involved, but to a more structural or institutional discrimination, tied specifically to the status of being poor. The poor are discriminated against throughout the whole structure of society, restricting and even denying them opportunities for living a satisfying life. While it is true that certain groups are overrepresented in the ranks of the poor, no one can deny that societal discrimination has had a devastating effect on all poor. Discrimination perpetuates the vicious cycle of poverty that the poor struggle daily to escape. This issue of discrimination will be more fully examined in Chapter 6.

In addition to societal values and attitudes, individual and environmental factors breed and sustain poverty. Seldom discussed is the fact that poverty can be caused by physical or mental handicaps, poor health, age, or the feelings of defeatism and impaired self-worth. Although downplayed as a significant type of poverty, John Kenneth Galbraith, a noted economist, has referred to this as "case poverty," which recognizes that some people are poor due to circumstantial factors.[22]

Alan Little has described two types of poverty with relevance to individual social factors. He identifies *crisis poverty*, caused by a catastrophic traumatic event, such as injury, illness, divorce, that renders the person unable to work for a living, thus causing poverty. He also describes *life-cycle poverty*, which results from changes associated with stages of life, for example, a person who is too old to work and may lack adequate retirement resources. Although these factors might be considered only temporary causes of poverty, they nonetheless contribute significantly to its incidence.[23]

Along with individual factors, environmental factors also are among the social causes of poverty. Environmentally caused poverty can best be described by discussing the effects of poverty upon families. One's immediate social environment influences and shapes one's future. The family in U.S. society services as the primary system of socialization. Children are taught attitudes, values, and skills that are later used by them as adults to survive. Poor families which often lack these appropriate values, attitudes, and skills transmit instead attitudes that are self-defeating, and tend to perpetuate the poverty cycle. Some poverty, then, appears to be caused by being socialized into a dysfunctional environment or culture, as Lewis's culture of poverty theory contends. This view is also supported by what Galbraith spoke of as an "insular poverty."[24] Insular poverty refers to islands or pockets of poverty where almost everyone is poor. The forgotten poor of Appalachia, whose plight was so often described during the 1960s, is an example of this type of poverty. Little also has described *inherited poverty*,[25] inheritance, not in the sense of genetics, but inheritance of the poverty life-style through family socialization.

Poverty is a complex social phenomenon with many social causes. These causes are as important as the economic causes when developing an understanding of the roots of poverty.

## Political Causes

The poor are politically disadvantaged, as was discussed earlier in this chapter. Their deprivation is caused not only by their lack of participation in the mainstream political processes, but also as a result of years of unjust and inadequate social policies that by their nature were designed to be mechanisms of social control.

As Michael Harrington, the author of *The Other America*, put it some years ago, "the poor are politically invisible."[26] The poor are disenfranchised from the political institutions that determine social welfare policy. Therefore they are not represented and have little or no voice in the determination of social welfare policy at the local, state, and national levels. This has contributed to the maintenance of the status quo. Changes in or the creation of new social policies more favorably affecting the poor have not occurred as often as they might if the poor themselves were more involved in the decision-making process.

Politicians are influenced by many interest groups. It has been suggested that "political leaders must obviously strive to accommodate groups that will provided them the votes to win elections."[27] Therefore, knowing that the poor often do not vote, nor can they contribute very much to campaign funds, some political leaders feel no particular obligation to represent their interests. Politics and politicians can also become self-serving. The rise of interest in poverty issues during the 1960s, some believe, was not a result of a public outcry, but because poverty became a popular political issue.[28] Even though the poor gained some political influence as a result of the antipoverty movement during the 1960s, it was not sufficient to bring forth any lasting changes or improvements in social policies that affect the poor. Poverty is not a significant political issue today. It has given way to concerns about the general economic well-being of the nation. With the swing of the political pendulum toward the conservative side, politicians are unwilling to vote for expensive social welfare programs. The efficiency and efficacy of the social welfare system is being seriously questioned by politicians. Questions about who the poor are, and whether they are truly needy, and what the response of government should be to their needs are reemerging. Although efforts to respond through transfer payments or legislatively mandated social programs have generally benefited the poor over the last two decades, the number of people remaining in the depths of poverty has actually increased. This is due to poverty's relationship to the U.S. economic, social, and political systems. To be effectively dealt with, the nature of poverty must be understood within these three realms.

## Discovery and Rediscovery of Poverty: Societal Responses

At the turn of the current century (late 1800s, early 1900s) poverty was discovered as a significant social problem. Several factors influenced that discovery. The United States was a country in transition, experiencing rapid social change. The industrial revolution was making an impact, driving a surge of population growth in the large industrial cities that brought with it a host of social ills—overcrowding, disease, unemployment, crime, and poverty. In addition, the nation was experiencing an influx of immigrants, many of whom were poor, and all involved in a life-style change. Society became stratified, with a more definite class structure than had previously existed in the United States. Poverty became a threat to society's equilibrium, an unavoidable social problem that had to be dealt with. Societal responses to poverty up to this time had largely consisted of mutual aid, some forms of local assistance, and institutions. But these responses proved insufficient as the nation grew. The Charity Organization Societies and settlement houses emerged and assumed responsibility for some of the human needs caused by poverty. As prosperity increased and a feeling of balance returned, the social welfare system seemed adequate to deal with the needs of the poor. However, this all came to halt during the early part of the 1930s.

### First Rediscovery

In 1929, the stock market crashed, followed in the next few years by banks failing, industries and businesses shutting down. Millions of Americans lost their sources of livelihood, including farmers who lost their farms and land. The country was thrown into the depths of an unprecedented economic depression. Poverty then became not a problem for a few, but instead for millions. What the Great Depression clearly demonstrated is that poverty is not solely a problem of the individual, as had been earlier thought. It is instead a social and economic problem with the potential for affecting large numbers of people.

Responses to the poverty caused by the depression were slow to come. The social welfare system was overwhelmed by the massive extent of need. Sentiment in support of federal intervention and assistance grew. However, Hoover administration officials, believers in *laissez-faire economics*, were reluctant to intervene, convinced that the economy by itself would reactivate, stabilize, and return America to prosperity. Americans were reluctant to wait for this to occur, and in the 1933 presidential election, Franklin D. Roosevelt was elected. During the early years of Roosevelt's presidency, federal intervention of the economy was accomplished through legislation designed to ease the burdens of the depression. First came the *New Deal* programs, which provided unemployment relief and public works employment, in hopes that the economy would quickly recover. By 1935, it became evident that, despite federal intervention, a more long-term solution to poverty was needed, and that year Congress passed the Social Security Act. It provided both social insurance and public welfare programs designed to be permanent responses to poverty. Despite these programs, comprehensive solutions to the Depression-based poverty have remained elusive. By 1939, the United States was on the verge of entering World War II. The demand for war goods by our European allies stimulated some economic recovery, which was fully realized in 1941 when the country entered the war. Spurred by the war effort, the economy improved vastly, and prosperity returned for most Americans.

From the time the United States entered the war in 1941 to the end of the decade of the 1950s poverty slipped away into obscurity. Not that poverty didn't exist, but with the general economic well-being of the nation, poverty was thought to be limited. This view was widely supported in the literature of the day, an example of which is Galbraith's *Affluent Society*,[29] published in 1958. Galbraith contended that America had become an affluent nation. In his view, poverty was again deemed a matter of individual circumstances and not the general mass problem it had been during the depression. Although conceding that some poverty existed, people assumed it was geographically isolated. By the end of the decade, the poor had for all practical purposes become invisible. This view was to change and change rapidly. The beginning of the new decade of the 1960s brought with it a sense of restlessness among the American people, particularly among youth and black Americans. What was to follow was the second rediscovery of poverty.

## Second Rediscovery

In 1960, John F. Kennedy was elected President. He brought to the job an awareness of the unrest among the people, and the impending change it was about to bring. He had become popular with youth and blacks during his candidacy because of his humanitarian concerns. Continuing in this spirit, in his inaugural address Kennedy urged the United States to rise up and fight the common enemies of humankind—tyranny and poverty. This sparked renewed interest in poverty as a significant social problem and political issue. Literature emerged that called attention to the seriousness of the poverty problem. Michael Harrington's book, *The Other America*,[30] was especially important and caught the interest of the Kennedy administration, which was seeking new ways to approach the problem of poverty. Unfortunately, Kennedy's aspirations to find solutions were not realized during his lifetime, but the Johnson administration was able to carry out the spirit of his aspirations.

Other realities and events also began to shape renewed interest in poverty issues. The civil rights movement called attention to racism and poverty. Other events, such as Martin Luther King's Poor People's March on Washington, did likewise. After his reelection to the presidency in 1964, Lyndon B. Johnson, in a message to Congress on March 3, 1964, unveiled a plan to declare a national *War on Poverty*. In this message, Johnson asked Congress to consider a piece of legislation entitled the *Economic Opportunity Act of 1964*, which he stated "strikes at the causes, not just the consequences of poverty."[31]

The Economic Opportunity Act called for the creation of new programs to combat poverty, under the direction of a new separate federal agency, the *Office of Economic Opportunity* (OEO). This agency would in turn be under the direct administration of the president. The Economic Opportunity Act became law on August 20, 1964. New programs created under this act were: the Job Corps, a work training and work study program for youth; *Community Action Program*, an opportunity given to local communities to design *antipoverty programs* suited to their needs, with primary funding from the OEO; VISTA, or Volunteers in Service to America, a volunteer group that works in areas of the country where poverty is prevalent. As the programs developed, particularly the community action programs, many local antipoverty programs came into existence. The basic underlying premise on which the whole war on poverty and its programs were based was maximum feasible participation. What this basically meant was it is not government's role to do for the poor, but the role of the poor, with governmental assistance, to do for themselves. The poor then were to be involved in the planning, administration, and delivery of the antipoverty programs. With the funding provided by the Office of Economic Opportunity, and the planning and development of programs by state and local community action programs, the war on poverty machinery was set in place in both urban and rural areas across the country.

The success, or failure, of the antipoverty programs of the 1960s is a subject of debate. Several factors detracted from its success, most importantly inadequate funding. During these years the Johnson administration and Congress faced dilemmas over priorities in spending. The United States by this time was heavily involved in the Vietnam War.

The philosophy of "guns versus butter," that is, the nation's ability to engage in a war and still provide for its citizens, was the source of this dilemma. The result was that the war on poverty took a back seat to the war in Vietnam in priorities in funding. Sundquist, in evaluating the antipoverty efforts states, "Hardly had its central theme, the War on Poverty, been accepted by Congress and enacted into law than funds, attention, and leadership were diverted to the morass of Vietnam."[32]

Another problem with the administration's war on poverty programs was eventually the program became administratively top-heavy. More dollars were spent administrating the programs than in actual serving the impoverished. There was also no uniformity in administrative models, particularly among the local community action programs. Some were controlled by the local political power structure. Others were dominated by professionals, with no semblance of the philosophy of maximum feasible participation by the poor. The programs were prone to political infighting that produced chaos in their administration. It has been pointed out, that, "No single appraisal of community action is possible, because the one thousand CAA's include all kinds—the militant, and the tame, the rigorously managed, and the sloppily managed, and professionally dominated and the poor dominated, and centralized, the decentralized, the respected, and the disdained, and all shadings in between all these poles."[33]

In an overall evaluation of the war on poverty, one point on which most agree on is that "the expectations engendered by the promises were far beyond anything the program had the capacity to deliver."[34]

With the change in presidential administration in 1968, Richard Nixon declared an end to the War on Poverty. The end was not abrupt, but a gradual piece-by-piece dismantling of the programs. Some parts of the Office of Economic Opportunity and its programs (e.g., Headstart, Job Corps) had proven their viability and were transferred into other structures of the federal government.

The War on Poverty did leave some positive contributions that seem to have become permanent features of the societal response to poverty through the social welfare system. One of these is the right of the community and of the service consumer to have input into decisions made about community service delivery. Consumers' awareness of their rights and of access to information about services has also grown. And educational, job training, and legal services, now readily available to the poor, resulted from the antipoverty programs. This second rediscovery of poverty, and the programs developed in response to it, still goes on, and in the future may provide valuable lessons for developing sound national policy towards the eradication of poverty in the United States.

From the beginning of the 1970s to the present time, national interest in poverty as a social problem has declined. Little has changed in the social welfare structure since the passage of the Social Security Act of 1935. Poverty persists, just as alive and well as always. Although change is needed, attempts to overhaul the system have been made in two out of the last three presidential administrations without success. Recently, the Reagan administration has attempted to restructure the social welfare system through what it calls the New Federalism, whose prevailing philosophy is that the federal government needs to lessen its responsibility for social welfare and transfer major responsibility back to the individual states. It remains to be seen whether this will be accomplished.

## Professional Responses to Poverty

Historically, formal responses to poverty in the 1800s brought forth the development of social work as a profession. Until the 1920s, social workers remained committed to the poor. But as knowledge of psychological and social functioning expanded, the profession slowly began to move away from exclusive work with the poor. During the 1930s, the demands of the Depression, and also again in the 1960s, the War on Poverty, again involved some social workers with the poor.

Although not directly related to the War on Poverty, but perhaps influenced by it, a great deal of emphasis was placed on deploying trained social work manpower within the public social welfare system. The system continues to be the largest employer of professional social workers, though many workers in this system still do not have professional education.

Professional organizations, such as the American Public Welfare Association, the National Conference on Social Welfare, and the National Association of Social Workers (NASW), all have prioritized the issue of poverty. A large proportion of the membership of these organizations, particularly NASW, are professional social workers. Yet, today a great deal of argument concerning what social work as a profession is and is not doing about poverty issues continues. Some accuse social work of abandoning the poor, though recent professional journals do contain articles about the impact of the New Federalism on those living in poverty. Some feel that to fulfill the ideals and aspirations of the professions's founders, the profession must rededicate itself to work with the poor. Leadership in the development of social policy and programming to deal with poverty must come from dedicated professionals. Daniel Moynihan suggested that the war on poverty resulted not from civil unrest or the demands of the poor but from "professionalization of reform."[35] Professionals again need to assume leadership roles in the development of a sound national policy on dealing with poverty.

## Summary

Poverty remains a complex and destructive social problem in the 1980s. This chapter has focused on the development of understandings of the poverty situation, and its effects and consequences for our society. What we have not been able to show are solutions to poverty. Those solutions remain elusive and complicated. Some argue that a complete overhaul of the existing social welfare system is in order, calling for the elimination of categorical eligibility and provision, and instead providing universal provision or guaranteed annual income. Others believe that a combination program of income maintenance and work experience (workfare) would be a viable solution. Regardless of which arguments are used to justify solutions to the poverty problem, a major step would be the rearrangement of our national priorities, with a concerted effort on the part of the general citizenry, the government, and the helping professions to take whatever steps are necessary to remove the barriers preventing those who live in poverty from obtaining employment and/or sufficient income to live a personally satisfying life.

## Key Terms

| | |
|---|---|
| absolute deprivation | life-cycle poverty |
| antipoverty programs | New Deal |
| Community Action Program | Office of Economic Opportunity |
| crisis poverty | poverty |
| culture of poverty | poverty line |
| distribution of income | purchasing power |
| Economic Opportunity Act | relative deprivation |
| Gross National Product | underemployment |
| inflation | unemployment |
| inherited poverty | War on Poverty |
| laissez-faire economics | working poor |

## Questions for Discussion

1. Explain why poverty is difficult to define. Which of the numerous views of poverty seems to you to be most relevent in understanding the nature of poverty?

2. Who are the poor in the United States today? Should society be held accountable for the needs of all poor people, or do certain groups of poor warrant more attention than others?

3. Discuss the economic, social, and political causes of poverty in the United States today. What do you think can be done to assist in their elimination?

4. Discuss, from your own viewpoint, what society's responsibility is for dealing with the effects of poverty on individuals. How can the social welfare system become more responsive to the needs of the poor?

5. Explain what social work's responsibility for serving the interests of the poor should be. How can this be done on an individual level and on a collective level?

# Notes

1 Sidney Lens, *Poverty: Americans Enduring Paradox* (New York: Thomas Crowell Co., 1969). p. 2.
2 Harry Haxlitt, *The Conquest of Poverty* (New Rochelle, NY: Arlington House Publishers, 1973). p. 33.
3 U.S. Department of Commerce, Bureau of the Census, *Money Income and Poverty Status of Families and Persons in The United States: 1983*, Series P-60, No. 145, (Washington, D.C.: U.S. Government Printing Office, 1983).
4 Louis Coser, "The Sociology of Poverty," *Social Problems* 13 (Fall 1965): 140–148.
5 Robert Plotnik and Felicity Skidmore, *Progress against Poverty: A Review of the 1964-1974 Decade* (New York: Academic Press, 1975).
6 For a discussion on measurements of poverty see: Mollie Ovshansky, Harold Watts, Bradley Schiller, and John Karbel, "Measuring Poverty: A Debate," *Public Welfare* 36 (Spring 1978): 46-55. Also see: Joseph M. Dukert, "Who is Poor? Who is Truly Needy?" *Public Welfare* 41 (Winter 1983): 17-22.
7 Oscar Lewis, *La Vida* (New York: Random House, 1966).
8 U.S. Dept. of Commerce, Bureau of the Census, *Money Income.*
9 U.S. Dept. of Commerce, Bureau of the Census, *Money Income.*
10 U.S. Dept. of Commerce, Bureau of the Census, *Money Income.*
11 U.S. Dept. of Commerce, Bureau of the Census, *Money Income.*
12 U.S. Dept. of Commerce, Bureau of the Census, *Money Income.*
13 U.S. Dept. of Commerce, Bureau of the Census, *Statistical Abstracts of the United States: 1985*, (Washington D.C.: U.S. government Printing Office, 1984) 105th edition.
14 U.S. Dept. of Commerce, *Statistical Abstracts of the United States: 1985.*
15 Varden Fuller, "Rural Poverty and Rural Area Development," in *Poverty in America*, ed. Margaret S. Gordon, (San Francisco: Chandler Publishing Co., 1965), p. 390.
16 Dale A. Tussing, *Poverty in a Dual Economy* (New York: St. Martin's Press, 1975), p. 16.
17 Tussing, *Poverty,* p. 16.
18 Bradley Schiller, *The Economics of Poverty and Discrimination* (Englewood Cliffs, NJ: Prentice-Hall, 1976), p. 13.
19 David Macarov, *The Design of Social Welfare* (New York: Holt, Rinehart & Winston, 1978), pp. 113-120.
20 Schiller, *Economics.*
21 Tussing, *Poverty,* p. 85.

22 John Kenneth Galbraith, *The Affluent Society* (Boston: Houghton Mifflin Co., 1958), p. 325.
23 Alan Little, "Poverty Types," *Encyclopedia of Social Work*, (Washington, D.C.: National Association of Social Workers, 1971), p. 929.
24 Galbraith, *Affluent Society*, p. 326.
25 Little, "Poverty Types."
26 Michael Harrington, *The Other America: Poverty in the United States* (New York: Macmillan Publishing Co., 1962).
27 Richard Cloward and Frances Fox Piven, "Politics in the Welfare System and Poverty," in *Poverty in America*, ed. Louis A. Ferman, et al. (Ann Arbor, MI: University of Michigan Press, 1969), p. 223.
28 Elinor Graham, "The Politics of Poverty," in *Poverty a Public Issue*, ed. Ben B. Seligman (New York: The Free Press, 1965).
29 Galbraith, *Affluent Society*.
30 Michael Harrington, *UX (The Other America)* (New York: Macmillan Publishing Co., 1962).
31 Lyndon B. Johnson, "Message to Congress," in Hanna H. Meissner, ed., *Poverty: The Affluent Society* (New York: Harper & Row Publishers, 1966), p. 204.
32 James L. Sundquist, ed., *On Fighting Poverty* (New York: Basic Books, 1969), p. 235.
33 Sundquist, *Fighting Poverty*, p. 239.
34 Robert J. Lampman, "What Does I Do For the Poor?—A New Test for National Policy," *The Public Interest* 34 (Winter 1974): 66-82.
35 Daniel P. Moynihan, "The Professionalization of Reform," *The Public Interest* 1 (1965): 6-16.

## Suggested Readings

Dolgoff, Ralph and Feldstein, Donald. *Understanding Social Welfare.* New York: Harper & Row Publishers, 1980.

Galbraith, John K. *The Affluent Society.* Boston: Houghton Mifflin Co., 1958.

Gordon, Margaret S. *Poverty in America.* San Francisco: Chandler Publishing Co., 1965.

Harrington, Michael. *The Other America: Poverty in the United States.* New York: Macmillan Publishing Co., 1962.

Plotnik, Robert, and Skidmore, Felicity. *Progress against Poverty: A Review of the 1964–1974 Decade.* New York: Academic Press, 1975.

Schiller, Bradley. *The Economics of Poverty and Discrimination.* Englewood Cliffs, N.J.: Prentice-Hall, 1976.

Sundquist, James L. *On Fighting Poverty.* New York: Basic Books, 1969.

Tussing, Dale A. *Poverty in a Dual Economy.* New York: St. Martin's Press, 1975.

# Chapter 5

## Social Welfare Resources

Human beings have a variety of needs that must be filled if they are to live functional, satisfying lives, including food, shelter, health care, safety, opportunity for emotional and intellectual growth, relationships with others, and spiritual fulfillment. Usually many of these needs are met through an individual's personal resources, or within family and friendship networks. But when an individual's resources are inadequate, these needs must be met through societal mechanisms. The social welfare system is one such mechanism. The lack of financial resources to provide for basic needs is known as poverty and was examined in the previous chapter. This chapter looks at the resources and services not directly related to financial provision that individuals and families need in order to be functioning members of society. This chapter explores different ways of classifying these resources by function and through life span frameworks. It will address conditions and attitudes that influence availability and that may block the use of resources and services for those who need them. Issues of accessibility and acceptability and resource usability by groups with diverse characteristics will also be discussed.

## Need for Resources

Within contemporary U.S. society the mechanisms used for meeting human need can be categorized as:

> personal: self, family, friends, work colleagues

informal: natural helpers in the community, self-help groups, community grassroots groups, clubs and other groups that function informally

institutional: schools, churches, and other formal organizations

societal: services, agencies, and institutions set up to meet specific human needs.[1]

Usually, people first attempt to meet their need within the personal system and, if that is not possible, move to the informal, to the institutional, and finally to the societal system. For example, if a father is seeking information about how to deal with his child's discipline problem, he will probably first discuss the problem with a family member or a friend. If no solution to the problem is found, he may seek an informal source such as a group of like-minded parents. If that is either not possible or does not yield a solution, he may then discuss the problem with a teacher or a minister. Finally, after all else has failed, he may seek out a social agency that offers counseling services to parents.[2]

Social change has moved our society from a subsistence economy to one highly dependent on money to purchase food, shelter, clothing, and other necessities. This same change has also changed how people satisfy their needs for socialization, for intellectual and emotional growth, and for satisfying relationships—from depending on self and family (mutual aid) to depending on a broader social network and on societal provision. For example, once families were largely responsible for the socialization and education of their children: now they depend on not only the societal provision of public education but on many informal and formal community resources to carry out this function. Anthropological studies have shown how individuals depend on family and close associates to provide help, support, and other resources. These studies also show how change disrupts these patterns of survival and weakens the individuals coping capacity.[3]

The need for resources or services to assist people facing problems of social functioning keeps growing. *Resources* are what individuals and families need so they can carry out the roles and tasks assigned to them by society and can lead reasonably satisfying lives. *Services* are those resources requiring the activity of a person employed within the social welfare system. One factor that has increased the need for such services is the mobility of the population and the breakdown of personal resource networks. For example, a family with two young children moves two thousand miles to a large city, where the only people they know are work colleagues of the husband and the wife, none of whom have young children. One of the children becomes seriously ill and requires hospitalization. The family is faced with not only the problems of the ill child but with the need for some kind of child care for the other child. The family may not yet have developed a personal friendship network through neighbors, clubs, or churches upon whom they can depend for support. Both parents are already emotionally stressed in adjusting to the new jobs and living arrangements. This family may need some help from a social agency in coping with this situation, since they have an inadequate personal network and few if any contacts with informal or other resources.

When adequate resources and services are not available to such families there is danger that impaired social functioning can result in the form of inadequate parenting, marital dysfunctioning, or inability to function in the workplace to name but a few. This can then lead to a need for expensive resources, such as income maintenance, psychological counseling, or other long-term services. And such problems can result in further deterioration of both individual and family social functioning.

The range of services and resources needed by a person or a family to gain an optimal level of social functioning within U.S. society is vast. The specific needs change from time to time and from community to community, depending on a wide range of circumstances. Far too many services and resources exist to be specified in this discussion. What will be presented is a formulation that provides a means for determining the range of needed resources.[4] Areas of need include the following:

1. Financial. This area includes job training, career counseling and employment searches, counseling around work-related problems, training in money management and retirement planning, and information about where and how to receive financial assistance. In other words, this area covers those services and resources that either enable individuals to become economically self-sufficient or which enable them to find and use alternate means of providing for their economic needs.

2. Parenting. This area includes parent-child counseling; supportive services for parents of children with special needs, or for parents who are not able to independently carry out the parenting role; educational services focused on the parenting role; substitute child care (day care or foster care) for children needing part-time or full-time care outside the family setting. In other words this area includes those services that help parents fulfill their parenting responsibilities or that provide alternate child care.

3. Marital Relationship. This area includes premarital counseling, marital counseling, services for divorcing persons. Services in this area include all those aimed at strengthening the marital relationship or that help people recover from the negative consequences of a break-down in a marital relationship.

4. Interpersonal and Community Relationships. This area includes resources that teach people how to meaningfully participate in group activities; services to help newcomers become acquainted with the community; activities that provide participation opportunities in religious, cultural, political, and educational events; socialization activities for children and youth. This area includes those services that provide education for and experience in working with others, in activities that are both personally satisfying and that enhance the functioning of the environment.

5. Physical and Mental Disabled Persons. These include support services, training, transportation, special housing, as well as specialized care and health services. This area includes services that enable handicapped people to lead a satisfying life and to participate as much as they can in mainstream activities.

6. Schools, Hospitals, and Institutions. These services enable individuals to make maximum use of the institutions, their facilities, and personel. These services include counseling services in the schools and social workers in medical settings. They are ancillary to the primary service of the institution in which they are housed.

7. Community Organization. These services include coordinating existing services, modifying services not effectively responding to the needs for which they are responsible, and developing new services when necessary.

8. Other Services. These include information and referral services that link persons to a wide variety of resources, supportive services, problem-solving services for coping with personal and environmental problems, crisis services and counseling and therapy services for people experiencing severe social functioning problems. These services are aimed at preventing the need for more expensive services, such as income maintenance, institutionalization, or long-term therapeutic intervention.

While this classification and the examples given do not include all the resources a complex society provides for its members, it does illustrate the variety of resources that can be provided. Many people can purchase these services, if they have sufficient income, but people living near or below the poverty line do not have the money to obtain this kind of help. These services must be provided to them if they are to avoid even greater problems than simple poverty.

A single-parent mother with two elementary school-aged children takes a job in an accounting firm in a city some distance from the place she has always lived and from her family and friends. She is immediately faced with finding substitute child care during after-school hours and school vacations. She also needs to find social outlets for herself. She may have difficulty dealing with the loss of the familiar and supportive environment she has left behind. She may need problem solving or counseling services. Without these needed services, she may not function adequately as either a parent or at work. She might even lose her job, the sole economic resource for her family. Even more importantly, she might lose the capacity to function as a self-sufficient person and a role model for her children. Not every single parent moving to a new community will have trouble finding needed resources or will risk more serious problems. However, some individuals may, and an information and referral service for single parents can meet their special needs before problems develop.

# Life Span Needs

Another way of categorizing resources is to identify the resources that are often needed at various stages in a person's life span. These stages are early childhood (birth to age 5), late childhood (ages 6 to 12), adolescence (ages 13 to 19), young adulthood (ages 20 to 35), middle adulthood, (ages 36 to 60), and older adulthood, (ages 61 and up). This classification is not rigid, and some people may need the services listed at particular stages at their life, either when younger or older.

1. Early Childhood: Services for young children may include services to their parents that develop and enhance parenting skills, services for handicapped children that help overcome or compensate for the handicap and encourage maximum social functioning, alternate child care services for families who cannot or will not give full-time care, including day-care, foster-care, and adoption services.

2. Late Childhood: Services for elementary school-age children include the services listed above plus services that help children maximize their use of important educational opportunities, services that develop socialization skills and constructive use of leisure time, after-school and vacation day-care when needed by families with working parents, therapeutic counseling and other psychological services needed by children displaying behavior problems. Foster care, adoption, or residential treatment may be needed for a few children.

3. Adolescence: Services needed by adolescents may include remedial teaching and counseling to help kids remain in school, locating appropriate educational or vocational programs, services that prevent and treat problems of delinquency, alcohol and drug abuse, that help adolescents deal with and make needed deci-

sions about sexuality, and career planning. Some adolescents need help with out-of-wedlock pregnancy and single parenting. Some adolescents cannot live with their own families and these individuals need alternate living opportunities, foster homes, group homes, or institutional care. Handicapped adolescents need special services to help them cope with their changing bodies and social lives.

4. Young Adulthood: Services in this category are those that help individuals take on adult roles and tasks in a competent and satisfying manner, such as finding a mate and developing a satisfying marriage, parenting, evolving a work role or career, participating in their community and in decision-making. Handicapped people need special resources and services to participate as fully as possible in all aspects of their lives, like specialized transportation, barrier-free housing and workplaces.

5. Middle Adulthood: Services needed by individuals in this category include those that enable them to deal with mid-life changes of a physical, cognitive, and emotional nature. These would include such concerns as living with adolescent children, children leaving home, mid-life physical and emotional changes, career changes, loss of employment, severe or disabling illness or disability. People in this category also often have to take care of aging parents—a responsibility that requires some support. Also services are needed that enable pre-retirement planning.

6. Older Adulthood: Services for older adults help them adjust to the changes that come with old age, such as physical change and disability and retirement from the work force, services that provide satisfying use of leisure time and continued participation in community life, supportive and protective services that allow older people to remain in the community, transportation services and housing adapted to elderly needs, services that maximize use of health services, including home health and institutional services.

Obviously, living in contemporary U.S. society often requires resources from outside a personal network, a community's mutual aid network, or the available institutional resources. However, these services are neither universally available nor always adequate. Not all of these services can or should be the responsibility of the government. Some can and should continue to be provided by personal networks, community mutual aid, or community institutions.[5] But so far, no one can agree on what resources and which individuals the social welfare system is responsible for. It is important that the social welfare system provide resources and services appropriately available to the people who need them; when such services are missing people develop more severe problems that drive them into income maintenance and expensive long-term care. It makes sense for the social welfare system to support personal, natural, and community systems or networks of resources and services.

# Availability of Resources

If a wide variety of resources, which includes service, are needed to support people with their social functioning then these resources must be available for use. *Availability* means that the resources are present in sufficient quantity for all who need them. However, quantity is not the only factor in defining availability. Distribution, accessibility, usability, and coordination must also be considered.

*Distribution* of the resources within the social welfare system remains a difficult problem. Resources are usually more readily available in large metropolitan areas, and less available in rural or sparsely populated areas. They are more readily available in affluent cities and states, and less available in areas with lower tax bases or poorer populations. They are more likely to be present where citizens have a high level of social consciousness, less where citizens believe strongly in "rugged individualism." People who need resources and services usually are too poor to travel long distances to receive services. They may find it difficult to take time off from work or from child care responsibilities. They may be physically unable to travel.[6] All of these circumstances contribute to the problems of distribution of resources within the U.S. social welfare system.

A second and related factor in resource availability is *accessibility*. Resources may be located fairly near to the people needing them and still not be accessible. If needy people do not know about them, they are not accessible. If they cannot be reached by public transportation, then they are not accessible to people without cars. If there is a fee for the use of the resources, then they are not accessible to people on limited income. If the hours when the resource or service is available are those when some people needing the service must be at work, school, or taking care of children, then the service may not be accessible to them.

Another factor in availability is *usability*. Resources are not usable if the people needing the resource and the people responsible for its distribution do not speak the same language. A Spanish-speaker with a limited knowledge of English needs to have access to a Spanish-speaking resource person. Resources need to be congruent with the culture of the people needing them. For example, in native American culture, it is important that family members share what they have; the nutrition programs for older people are unusable. Traditional native Americans would rather go without than break their cultural mores of sharing.

Resources and services delivered from outside the user's frame of reference are often not easily used by people of other economic groups. For example, blue-collar families may avoid using resources in white-collar, downtown settings because they feel uncomfortable outside their own neighborhood or environment. The attitudes and approaches of those who deliver the resources also can make recipients uncomfortable thus keeping them away from needed resources. For resources and services to be available they must be in a form usable by the people needing them.

A final element of availability has to do with *coordination* of resources. People often need several different resources that may not all be available in one place or agency. Conflicting information or conflicting demands may confuse people needing resources. This can add an additional burden to already burdened people, for it may call for some sorting out, finding ways to deal with the conflicting information or demands, and places additional responsibility on the resource user. Resource providers also can do a better job and avoid duplicating service if they are aware of the involvement of other resources within the community or through other people or family members. Also, fragmentation of the resource delivery system, having to go to a number of different agencies to use a resource, or the duplication of the services (the same service being delivered by several agencies), and people not knowing which resource would be best for them present problems in the coordination of resources. For resources to be available, they must be coordinated efficiently.

For resources to be available, they must be appropriately distributed, accessible to, and usable by those who need them. And someone must coordinate them. Resources and services are important in supporting and providing for human needs in contemporary society, but attention must be paid to distribution, accessibility, usability, and coordination within the social welfare system.

## Discontinuity of Needs and Services

Our current social welfare system is biased toward the culture and value systems of middle class people. It makes assumptions about individuals' and families' needs based on middle class perceptions. The resources and services are structured to conform to middle class preferences. But contemporary U.S. society contains diverse cultures and lifestyles.[8] Mizio and Delaney have pointed out the need for differential resources and service delivery strategies for minority people.[9] They note that cultural life-styles and values must be considered, along with experiences of prejudice and discrimination. For example, Spanish-speaking clients may not be able to find services available in Spanish. They may not find a professional helper who not only understands the language but who also understands the Hispanic family structure or their use of folk medicine and healing. If family structure or the traditional healing methods are not considered when developing a service plan, that plan may be incongruent with the client's life-style and unusable. This gap between what is needed and what is provided for people outside the middle class, particularly ethnic minorities, creates a discontinuity of availability that the social welfare system must remedy if the needs of all our citizens are to be met.

## Summary

This chapter discussed the wide range of resources and services that individuals and families may need. These services and resources can be categorized by functions or tasks or they can be categorized by life span stages.

Factors affecting availability of resources were also discussed: these include distribution, accessibility, usability, and coordination. Discontinuity between the culture and life-style of ethnic minorities and the way resources and services are delivered is another problem of availability.

## Key Terms

| | |
| --- | --- |
| accessibility | resources |
| availability | services |
| coordination | usability of services |
| distribution | |

## Questions for Discussion

1. What range of resources and services do you think the social welfare system should provide to individuals and families?

2. How can those working within the social welfare system make sure that resources are available to all individuals or families?

3. What can be done to correct problems in distribution of services in the United States?

4. What should be done to resolve the discontinuity between cultural and life-style considerations and the delivery of resources?

# Notes

1 Allen Pincus and Anne Minahan, *Social Work Practice: Model and Method* (Itasca, IL: F. E. Peacock, 1973), Chapter 1, has a similar formulation.

2 See David Landy, "Problems of the Person Seeking Help in Our Culture," in *Social Welfare Institutions: A Sociological Reader*, ed. Mayer N. Zald (New York: John Wiley & Sons, 1965), pp. 559-574.

3 Michael Young and Peter Willmont, *Family and Kinship in East London* (London: Routledge & Kegan Paul, 1957) and Carol B. Stack, *All Our Kin* (New York: Harper & Row Publishers, 1974).

4 A very complete discussion of the range of services is found in Shelia B. Kamerman and Alfred J. Kahn, *Social Services in the United States* (Philadelphia: Temple University Press, 1976).

5 See David Macarov, in "Mutual Aid," in *The Design of Social Welfare* (New York: Holt, Rinehart & Winston, 1978), pp. 43-75.

6 These observations are based on one of the author's continuing study of service delivery systems.

7 For further discussion of the issues raised in this section see Robert Perlman, *Consumers and Social Services* (New York: John Wiley & Sons, 1975).

8 See Robert L. Berger and Ronald S. Federico, *Human Behavior: A Social Work Perspective* (New York: Longman, 1982), pp. 65-98.

9 Emelicia Mizio and Anita J. Delaney, *Training for Service Delivery to Minority Clients* (New York: Family Service Association of America, 1981).

# Suggested Readings

Berger, Robert, and Federico, Ronald S. in "Human Diversity and Human Needs," *Human Behavior: A Social Work Perspective*. New York: Longman, 1982, pp. 65-98

Gottlieb, Benjamin H., ed. *Social Networks and Social Support*. Beverly Hills: Sage Publications, 1981.

Kamerman, Shelia B., and Kahn, Alfred J. *Social Services in the United States*. Philadelphia: Temple University Press, 1976.

Macarov, David. *The Design of Social Welfare*. New York: Holt, Rinehart & Winston, 1978.

Mizio, Emelicia, and Delaney, Anita J. *Training for Service Delivery to Minority Clients*. New York: Family Service Association of America, 1981.

Perlman, Robert. *Consumers and Social Services*. New York: John Wiley & Sons, 1975.

Whittaker, James K., and Garbarino, James. *Social Support Networks: Informal Helping in the Human Services*. New York: Aldine Publishing Co., 1983.

# Chapter 6

## Racism and Discrimination

Chapter 3 discussed social change, how social change influenced the development of the U.S. social welfare system, and how social change, at various points in American history, has brought about special social conditions and problems to which our social welfare system has had to respond. In Chapter 4, poverty was discussed as one of those special social problems. Two other social problems, racism and discrimination, which this chapter examines, have had powerful effects on the course of social welfare. Racism and discrimination have denied many Americans access to the resources of our nation. This, of course, leads to a host of economic, psychological, and social needs. Furthermore, the needy of our country's diverse minority groups are sometimes even denied the social welfare resources that could help them overcome the problems caused by racism and discrimination. Developing an understanding of the cause and effect relationship between racism and discrimination and meeting human needs is important for everyone who is trying to understand the U.S. social welfare system. This chapter focuses on developing that understanding. Particular emphasis will be placed on the responses of the social welfare system to racism and discrimination. This will include discussion of the human diversity perspective, a framework for analyzing the functioning of diverse groups within our society.

## Racism, Prejudice, and Discrimination—Definitions

Racism, prejudice, and discrimination are often used interchangeably to describe social conflict between majority society and minority groups, but little attention is usually paid to their individual meanings.

Racism is the belief that a certain race or races are superior to all others. In the United States, racism becomes the belief that Northern European caucasians are superior. Brieland, Costin, and Atherton state, "color becomes the determinant for classifying people as insiders or outsiders."[1] Therefore, racism in the United States is a kind of white racism, based on the concept of *ethnocentrism*, the belief that one's own group is superior and preferred over other groups.[2] Two forms of racism exist in the United States, *individual racism* and *institutional racism*. These are described by Carmichael and Hamilton:"Racism is both overt and covert. It takes two closely related forms; individual whites acting against individual blacks, and acts by the total white community against the black community. We call these individual racism and institutional racism."[3] Although these two forms of racism are discussed in their relation to the black experience, they have application in analyzing racism and its effects on all racial groups in U.S. society.

The terms discrimination and prejudice are often confused when they refer to the actions of the majority society towards racial and other minority groups. But these two terms do not mean the same thing. *Discrimination* is the overt and deliberate *act* of behaving or acting toward some group, affording them differential treatment.[4] Discrimination describes the actions of dominant white society toward a particular minority group. *Prejudice*, on the other hand, refers to a set of negative *beliefs* that are held about someone or something. Prejudice is defined as "any set of ideas and beliefs that negatively prejudge groups or individuals on the basis of real or alleged group traits or characteristics."[5] Prejudice then is beliefs or cognitive thoughts about a particular group, not behaviors or actions, as is the case in discrimination. These two concepts are sometimes difficult to separate because they can both exist independently of one another. It is possible, for example, for someone to be prejudiced toward a group of people without discriminating against them, and it is also possible to discriminate against these groups without being prejudiced toward them. In either case, it is a matter of individual motivation. The white business owner who claims not to be prejudiced against minorities may try to discourage them from entering his establishment for fear that his other customers may stay away. Conversely, the employer whose business is dependent on funding from governmental sources, who admits to prejudice toward minorities, may be forced to hire such individuals, to be in compliance with equal opportunity employment policies, thus avoiding discrimination. Of course, it is also possible for both prejudice and discrimination to be dual motivators of actions taken against people from racial or minority groups. With a clearer understanding of these terms, attention will now be focused on discussing the factors associated with the causes of racism and discrimination.

# Causes of Racism and Discrimination

Racism has always existed in the United States. Our nation's image as the land of the free, its values of respect for human rights and dignity has always been tarnished by the forces of racism. Some form of white supremacy, both ideologically and institutionally, existed from the first day English immigrants arrived on the North American continent. Negative attitudes, for example, toward native Americans appeared at once, but prejudice toward other races and ethnic groups began centuries before the discovery of the New World. The causes of racism are many. Factors contributing to racism range from individual attitudinal factors to collective societal attitudinal and ideological factors.

## Individual Factors

Individual attitudes certainly contribute to racism; many individuals within U.S. society hold prejudicial attitudes toward racial groups. It is important to understand how individuals come to hold such attitudes. Recalling the definitions of racism and prejudice is helpful. Racism is the belief that certain races are superior to others. Prejudice is a set of beliefs that negatively evaluate and judge individuals or groups on the basis of their characteristics. Social scientists agree that the formation of racially prejudiced attitudes occurs as a result of social learning. "Prejudice, like all culture is learned, taught and transmitted through the process of socialization into one's group and society."[6] Preference for one's own group, ethnocentrism, is learned through socialization, and it forms the basis for prejudice toward groups different than one's own. It must be made clear that socialization does not always cause prejudice: prejudicial attitudes must be present in social structures that perform the socialization function, such as the family, for prejudice to be transmitted. But unfortunately, when prejudice is present, it sustains and spreads prejudice from generation to generation. However, engaging in discrimination toward particular groups is a matter of individual choice, based on the perceived rewards or negative consequences of such action. While individual factors contribute to racism, it is also a consequence of societal attitudinal and ideological factors.

## Societal Attitude Factors

Prejudice and discrimination occurs on a collective level, that is, on a societal level. Although prejudice is an irrational prejudging, it can be based on a person's experience. For example, if someone rents an apartment to a young college student and that person doesn't pay the rent or destroys the property, the landlord may believe that all college students are irresponsible. The specific groups targeted for prejudice and discrimination vary, depending on geographic location. In certain parts of the United States, blacks are targeted; in other parts of the country, native Americans and Hispanics are targeted. Prejudice and discrimination are a part of a learned response toward people. This learned response is a result of socialization that has occurred in a geographical and cultural sense. Some whites in the southern United States have been taught prejudice toward blacks. People in the Dakotas are sometimes socialized to be prejudiced against native Americans. The list of examples could go on and on. Although some might view racism as a problem isolated within specific geographic areas, this view is too simplistic. Racism is deeply embedded within the total U.S. social structure. It has become institutionalized. Racism is a collective response from many parts of society. It can be best explained in this way: "When white terrorists bomb a black church and five black children are killed, that is an act of individual racism. But when in that same city, five hundred black babies die each year because of the lack of proper food, clothing, shelter, and medical facilities, that is a function of institutional racism."[7]

Societal institutions were created and designed to meet human needs through structured distribution of goods, resources, services, and other social benefits. The means by which they are distributed by the institutional structure is influenced by political, economic, and social forces. As discussed in the chapter on poverty, the distribution is inequitable and unjust. Minority groups, like the poor, are discriminated against and denied equal opportunity to a share of the resources. And they are often denied a voice in the policy decision making affecting the control of the distribution of goods and services. However unintentional or unconscious it may be, society, through its institutional structure, rewards and penalizes certain groups: majority groups tend to be rewarded in society's political, economic, educational, legal, medical, and social welfare institutions. Minorities tend to be penalized by being denied fair and equitable treatment from these same institutions.

In institutionalized racism, race determines who is rewarded and who is punished. Any person or group who permits race to affect the distribution of social welfare benefits is racist. The U.S. social welfare system as a societal institution is no more exempt from racism than any other institution. Social welfare programs and services, delivered in a white cultural mode and based on social policies developed from a middle-class bias have maintained the status quo position of minority racial groups.

## Some Solutions to the Problems of Racism

The questions of why racism has continued to exist in the United States may be answered in part by examining the ideologies that form the basis of racism. Ideology is the system of beliefs and assumptions of a group or culture. Concerning racism, two ideologies are prevalent in our society. One group believes the culture of a predominantly white world is desireable. This ideology conflicts with another that feels that all racial groups must share equally in the overall framework of society.

The first ideology assumes that racism can be eradicated by the process of *assimilation*. This belief "holds that the existing culture or civilization, or the majority is desirable, and other groups must change themselves to become like the existing majority group."[8] In this view, all minority groups are expected to assimilate into the majority culture. If this occurred, racism, or white supremacy, would likely cease to exist since the differences between cultures within our society would fade away. The ideology of assimilation is in direct conflict with the ideology that believes all groups should share in society while still retaining their own cultural patterns. In reality, total assimilation is not possible, since racial and ethnic groups have little desire to give up their distinctive life-styles. But if total assimilation is unrealistic, a compromise between the two major ideologies might be possible. In the last two decades, society has moved away from the assimilation ideology toward a recognition of the value of diversity, as evidenced by the civil rights movement, civil rights legislation (e.g. the Equal Opportunity in Employment laws), and in the efforts of ethnic groups to maintain pride in their ethnic identity. Two other solutions to the problem of racism have been put forth as more desirable than either unilateral assimilation or total unassimilation. These are mutual assimilation and cultural pluralism.[9]

*Mutual assimilation*, or the melting pot concept, "holds that each group must give up part of its heritage, while another part is absorbed by and becomes integral to the remainder of society—in short, that from an amalgam of all groups a new entity arises."[10] Here, each group is expected to give up part of its heritage while sharing other parts of its culture with the total society. It has been argued that this view represents the situation in our country today. To some extent, the United States has become a melting pot for ethnic and cultural groups, for example Afro and Hispanic Americans have given us unique forms of music and many Asian groups have served-up a feast of exotic foods.

However, there are cracks in the melting pot. Racial groups face a skin color barrier when it comes to mutual assimilation. While certain cultural characteristics held by ethnic groups are sometimes more acceptable to society at large, white society has been slow to realize that all Americans, regardless of their complexions, accents, or behavior are going to have a part in shaping our culture; they have not done their part in mutual assimilation. Blacks, native Americans, Mexican Americans, and other groups continue to be victimized by the forces of racism and discrimination. It has been pointed out that "the melting pot has just as often been a boiling cauldron of conflict in which the vehement fury of racism and discrimination has never stopped bubbling."[11]

A fourth view related to the belief that all groups should fully and equally participate in society is *cultural pluralism*. In this view, each group retains desirable and essential parts of its cultural heritage, while actively taking full part in the total society. In cultural pluralism, diversity and difference is accepted and rewarded, not punished. Society has made some movement toward acceptance of this perspective in recent years. Most minority groups see this as the most desirable solution to racism and continue to press for its adoption.

Although it is true that no single ideology totally represents the relationship between majority society and minority groups in contemporary U.S. society, these proposed solutions are useful in illustrating racism and discrimination in our country. Attention will now be given to discussing the effects of discrimination on specific groups and how these groups have responded to it.

## Discrimination toward Blacks

Discrimination, prejudice, inequality, and injustice are just a few terms that describe the historical relationship between majority white society and blacks. Although the first blacks were free men, by the end of the 1700s, most were trapped in the chains of slavery. Blacks overcame this injustice, only to become trapped again in the snares of a racist society that has never afforded them equal status.

### From the Civil War to World War II

At the end of the U.S. Civil War, blacks' long journey to achieve integrity, dignity, and equality began, a journey that today is not fully realized. Although blacks were freed from slavery after the Civil War by the Thirteenth Amendment to the Constitution, they were ill-prepared to deal with their newfound destiny as free citizens. During Reconstruction (1865-77), the federal government for a short time attempted to prepare blacks for their new status. But blacks, lacking in education, land, and other resources, fell once again into second-class citizenship. In the aftermath of Reconstruction, despite guarantees of civil rights—such as equal protection under the law and the right to vote, as provided in the Fourteenth Amendment of the Constitution—the South returned to "home rule." State-passed laws, referred to as the Jim Crow laws, called for the segregation of blacks and whites in schools and public places. Blacks in all southern states were denied the right to vote under amendments to state constitutions. In the North during this time, they were also not accepted as equals, a further denial of their civil rights. From the turn of the century through the 1940s, blacks were trapped in the forces of racial prejudice and discrimination in both the South and the North. In the South, the Jim Crow laws legitimitized their inferior status. Any attempts to press for basic civil rights were dealt with harshly, even by lynching. White supremacy groups like the Ku Klux Klan effectively kept blacks from collective action. In the North, blacks were subject to stereotyping and denied equal opportunities in education and employment. For a long time, blacks had no alternative but to accept the inferior status society had so unjustly imposed.

During World War II, the status of blacks did not improve significantly, with widespread discrimination toward employing blacks in defense industries until in response to pressures brought by black leaders, President Franklin Roosevelt signed into law Executive Order 8802. This executive order forbade discrimination in the defense industries' employment policies on the basis of race, color, creed, or national origin. As with most laws, loopholes were found that weakened its effectiveness: this law did not significantly improve the situation, and employment opportunities for blacks continued to be restricted.

## Growth of the Civil Rights Movement

Up till this point in history, the struggle for black civil rights had consisted of constitutional change and court battles; during the 1950s this effort continued. One of the turning points in this struggle, which set the course for several events to follow, was the 1954 Supreme Court case *Brown v. Board of Education*. This case dealt with the issue of whether black students should be admitted to predominantly white public schools. It arose out of similar situations in several states. The Supreme Court ruled that segregation in the public schools, permitted by state laws, was unconstitutional. Although states had been permitted to segregate blacks and whites in the public schools—based on the 1896 Supreme Court decision of *Plessy v. Ferguson* that allowed separate but equal facilities for black students—the *Brown v. Board of Education* case essentially voided this decision and is considered to have been an important step toward improving the quality of education for blacks.

This victory added much fuel to the fire by fostering a growing awareness among blacks that aggressive action toward achieving equality could be successful. Other major victories were won in the 1950s, in particular, the confrontation at Little Rock, Arkansas; black students were admitted to high school under a federal court order and with protection of federal troops. These events set the tone for the development of new pride among blacks, and the emergence of new civil rights leaders. At the beginning of the 1960s, the black civil rights movement entered what has been termed its protest phase.

Black protests consisted of both violent and nonviolent actions. Both kinds of protest had significant effects on the civil rights movement. The nonviolent movement led by Dr. Martin Luther King, Jr. of the Southern Christian Leadership Conference promoted the causes of the nonviolent protest groups such as the Congress of Racial Equality (CORE), Student Nonviolent Coordinating Committee (SNCC), and the National Association for the Advancement of Colored People (NAACP). Many nonviolent protest demonstrations were held throughout the South and were frequently marked by violent actions by the white power structure. The most noted event was the 1963 Poor Peoples' March on Washington D.C. Blacks and whites alike participated in this march. Martin Luther King's famous and influential "I have a dream" speech was given there. His work captured the imagination of both blacks and whites and inspired leadership and action in the nonviolent civil rights movement.

The protest phase also had a violent side. Some black leaders were not satisfied with the relatively slow gains of the nonviolent movement and believed that aggressive, violent action was necessary to achieve the aims of equality. Rioting by blacks in Detroit, Michigan, and the Watts area of Los Angeles, California, were examples of this violent side. The Black Power movement, characterized by radical, revolutionary militant groups like the Black Panthers, and cultural nationalist groups like the Black Muslims, was another component. The widespread racial unrest encouraged by Black Power groups, as well as the nonviolent protest, prompted President John F. Kennedy in 1963 to introduce new civil rights legislation. In the aftermath of Kennedy's assassination, President Lyndon Johnson urged Congress to proceed with this legislation and the Civil Rights Law of 1964 was passed. This law guarantees everyone equal protection under the law.

Another victory for desegregation occurred in 1965 when the Voting Rights Act was signed into law. This brought an end to the practice of "home rule" engaged in by the southern states for many years. Blacks as a collective group now had the potential to become a political force.

The protest phase of the 1960s, if nothing else, brought to the forefront a public awareness of the social conflict bred by racism. In 1967 President Johnson authorized the President's Commission on Civil Disorders, the so-called Kerner Commission, to study the issues and problems of civil unrest in the United States. Overwhelmingly, the Commission stated as its number one finding the fact that white racism was at the heart of civil and racial unrest. Shortly after the assassination of Martin Luther King, Jr., the protest phase of the black civil rights movement waned. The decade of the 1970s up to the present time has been characterized by a number of positive gains in equality for blacks. Political gains have been made. Black politicians have been elected mayors of cities, legislators, congressmen, and senators. The Equal Opportunity Act has also provided increased opportunities for blacks in employment and education. Despite these gains blacks continue to be overrepresented in the ranks of the poor. This indicates that a more subtle type of institutional discrimination continues to exist.

# Discrimination toward Native Americans

Racism toward native Americans has a long-standing history, but it has its roots in different issues. The European quest in the New World for land and for control of its resources was the first act of discrimination. The values held by the white settlers were very different from the values of the people they found in the new land. White colonists did not appreciate native Americans' love for their land nor the high value that their society placed on sharing resources. The colonists believed that expansion, claiming new land and controlling its resources were their God-given rights. They believed it was their duty to "convert the savages" to Christianity. Unfortunately, native Americans also believed their use of the land was *their* God-given right. These two world views soon came into conflict.

As the colonist population grew and expanded its territory, whites and native Americans could no longer live in harmony. Native Americans became pawns in the wars between France and Great Britain, and later between the American Colonies and Great Britain. Following the American Revolution, the United States government continued its earlier practice of entering into treaties with various tribes. Although these treaties recognized Indian tribes as sovereign nations with land entitlements, they were systematically broken, provoking further conflict.

Pushed further and further west by the European's greed for land and willingness to use force to get it, native Americans stopped cooperating and began to strike back. From the mid-1800s to the turn of the century whites and native Americans fought over land rights.

During the 1830s, the federal government authorized the forced resettlement of Indian tribes to lands west of the Mississippi River. Thousands died of illness and exposure. In 1834, Congress created the United States Indian Service, which eventually became the U.S. Bureau of Indian Affairs. White agents located on military outposts were charged with carrying out the programs and policies of the federal government. The real test of the government's control over the tribes came in 1862 when the Homestead Act was passed by Congress. This opened up the West to white settlement and broke the treaties made with the tribes that gave them all the land west of the Mississippi River. After another series of battles, the vanquished native Americans were forcibly confined to reservations under the control of the Bureau of Indian Affairs.

By the end of the nineteenth century, native Americans had become a conquered people, far removed from their original homes. With a great deal of their land gone and their cultural heritage threatened or destroyed, native Americans were forced to accept and begin to live in the shadow of the dominant culture.

This is yet another vivid example of institutional racism. Native Americans have been driven into dependency on the government as their major source of means for survival. Uprooting entire cultures and relocating them far away from their usual sources of food, shelter, and trade forced the abandonment of their original cultures. To survive, they had little choice but to more or less live within the expectations of the dominant white culture. In recent years, renewed cultural pride and a sense of heritage has allowed some native American people to return to traditional values and life-styles, to the extent possible in a highly technological world. But reservations, despite the many and varied human services programs offered, remain economically depressed areas, where poverty, disease, crime, alcoholism, and other social problems continue to exist. Open discrimination toward native Americans exists outside the reservations. Native Americans who live in these areas are subjected to the same forces of prejudice as other minority groups.

Prior to the 1960s, the native American struggle for equality and civil rights was a quiet one, largely jurisdictional and legal. But in the late 1960s, influenced by black protests, the struggle went through a protest phase, marked by both nonviolent and violent efforts. Nonviolent protests included the 1972 takeover of the Bureau of Indian Affairs building in Washington, D.C. and the occupation of Alcatraz Prison in San Francisco. Violence broke out in 1973 when militant American Indian Movement members occupied a building on the Pine Ridge Indian reservation at Wounded Knee, South Dakota and a riot took place at the courthouse in Custer, South Dakota, over the alleged murder of a native American by a white.

Gains have been made by native Americans in their struggle for equality in recent years. Landmark victories have been won in terms of ownership of land and mineral rights. Changes have also occurred in the relationship between native American tribes and the U.S. Bureau of Indian Affairs (BIA). The BIA has lessened its control over Indian affairs and is now moving toward a policy of Indian self-determination. It has been long in coming, however, and the struggle still goes on.[12]

## Discrimination toward Hispanics

A third minority group experiencing significant societal discrimination and prejudice are Spanish-speaking Americans. Included in this group are the two largest subgroups, Mexican Americans and Puerto Ricans, plus Cuban Americans, as well as other smaller Spanish-speaking groups.

### Mexican Americans

The majority of Mexican Americans are concentrated in the southwestern United States. Some seventy-five thousand Mexicans were residents of the Southwest when this area became part of the United States in the aftermath of the Mexican-American War in 1848. While sharing and participating in the cultural history of this area, they were never afforded equal status and opportunity as U.S. citizens. Large-scale Mexican immigration to the United States began at the turn of the century, as a result of civil wars and economic chaos in Mexico, and the attractive employment opportunities in the United States. Efforts to curtail immigration began in the 1930s and have continued since that time. However, each year large numbers of Mexicans continue to enter the United States as illegal aliens.

Life for Mexican Americans in the towns and cities of southwestern United States was filled with the harsh and bitter realities of prejudice and discrimination. Excluded from the mainstream of community life, Mexican Americans were shunted into ghettos called *barrios,* which became pockets of poverty and a host of social problems. In many places in the Southwest during the 1940s and 1950s, Mexican Americans, like blacks, were faced with public, institutionalized segregation. The lifestyle foisted upon them demonstrates that "the experience of discrimination is not an academic concept, rather it forms an integral part of their life experiences."[13]

The effects of prejudice and discrimination on Mexican Americans is vividly portrayed by examining their lack of equal opportunity within the social mainstream over the last two decades. They have suffered from unequal opportunities in employment and inadequate incomes. Many are employed in a "secondary labor market, characterized by relatively dead-end jobs paying low wages, offering little security, and providing limited choices of economic advancement."[14] It is not surprising, then, that large numbers of Mexican American families have incomes below the poverty line. There is a large income gap between the median income for Mexican American families and for all families in the United States.

Through a form of institutional racism, Mexican Americans have been denied equal educational opportunities. They compare unfavorably to other groups in terms of numbers of years of school completed. It should be noted, however, that some improvement has been made among younger Mexican Americans. Language barriers have been at the heart of this struggle. Many Mexican American students still attend segregated schools, and schools are failing to provide youngsters with incentives to complete their education. Thus the vicious cycle continues; lack of education in turn results in fewer employment opportunities and reduced incomes.

Mexican Americans also had been denied their civil rights and equal protection under the law. In 1970, the United States Commission on Civil Rights stated that "American citizens of Mexican descent in five southwestern states are being denied equal protection of the law in the administration of justice."[15] They were being arrested more often, subjected to verbal and physical abuse, and being denied due process of law. They were also receiving maximum penalties under the law more consistently than individuals from other groups.

The civil rights movement for Mexican Americans has essentially been a nonviolent effort, characterized by political mobilization rather than violent protest. However, some nonviolent protest did occur. In the 1960s a migrant farm worker, Ceasar Chavez, led a nonviolent movement to unionize migrant workers in the southwestern United States. The agribusiness system that employed thousands of Mexican Americans had victimized and taken advantage of them for years. Through the efforts of Chavez and his followers, plus successful boycotts across the country, the United Farm Workers, an affiliate of the AFL-CIO, became a reality. Today, the members of this union enjoy collective bargaining rights as a way of improving their quality of life.

In the political arena, Mexican Americans have become a highly mobilized entity and have made significant gains during the decade of the seventies. This has come about through the efforts of local, state, and national coalitions and organizations. Such groups as the Mexican Political Organization, Community Service Organization of Los Angeles, The Mexican American Legal Defense and Education Fund, and the National Council of La Raza have spearheaded this political movement. As a result, Mexican American individuals have been elected to local and state public offices, although not at the national level. The Mexican American vote is a powerful force that serious politicians must deal with. Although some gains have been made in the struggle for equality for Mexican Americans, particularly in politics, prejudice and discrimination against them continues today.

## Puerto Ricans

Other Hispanic groups, such as the Puerto Ricans and Cuban Americans, also share in suffering the brunt of racism and discrimination from the dominant society. The case of Puerto Ricans is a special one. As citizens of the United Sates, they enjoy the freedom to move back and forth from the island to the mainland without immigration restrictions. However, "they come from an area that has its own strong cultural background and language. As a result the problems of cultural uprooting, intercultural misunderstanding, prejudice and discrimination affect them as they have affected most newcomers before them."[16] The resulting outcomes of discrimination such as poverty, unemployment, inequitable education, and unequal protection in the U.S. justice system are problems of life which are also faced by this group.

# Discrimination toward Asian Americans

Asian Americans are a group who have seemingly assimilated into the mainstream of society more than the groups previously discussed. However, Asian Americans were subjected to prejudice and discrimination in the earlier days. To some extent this is also true today and should not be ignored. Large numbers of Asians, particularly Chinese, began to enter the United States in the 1850s. The United States was a prospering nation that needed an inexpensive labor force to work in the construction of railroads and new industries.

Conflict between the Chinese immigrants and white society became a significant problem shortly thereafter. Acts of violence against Chinese people occurred in 1854, in the aftermath of a decision made by the California Supreme Court in *The People v. Hall.* The court ruled that Asians could not testify either for or against whites charged with a crime. The court's decision provided the impetus for abuse toward the Chinese. Murder, lynching, destruction of property, and robbery were common acts of violence against the Asian community. In the 1880s, the efforts of the Chinese Americans to improve their status through employment and property ownership was met with legislated exclusionary measures. In 1883, Congress passed the Chinese Exclusion Act that brought an end to the immigration of Chinese into the United States and prevented the naturalization of Chinese already in residence.

Japanese immigrants, who began to enter the United States in the 1880s, found their situation no better. The Immigration Act of 1924 created a quota system that favored the immigration of white ethnic groups from Europe and excluded Asians.

In the aftermath of the Japanese attack on Pearl Harbor in 1941, Japanese American citizens and legal aliens on the West Coast were taken into protective custody by the federal government and confined in "relocation camps." Japanese Americans became targets of suspicion. This is another example of how discrimination based on race has dictated social responses to racial groups since the same practices were not employed in relation to German Americans during World War II, even though several German Americans were convicted of spying while no Japanese Americans had ever been accused of disloyalty.

During the war years, two events eased the plight of Asian Americans. In 1943, all Asians residing in the United States were finally permitted to become naturalized citizens. This opened the door for further Asian immigration.

The second event occurred in 1944, when the U.S. Supreme Court ruled that the policy of confining Japanese citizens should be revoked. Japanese citizens who were forced to abandon their possessions and property during the period of confinement were faced with the task of beginning their lives over again. Recovery from this injustice was a slow and difficult process for Japanese citizens.

Since the end of World War II, efforts to improve the social status and quality of life for Asian Americans has been met with varied results. Like other minorities in the United States, some Asian Americans have been able to achieve a satisfying quality of life, while others have continued to experience the disadvantages associated with prejudice, discrimination, and disenfranchisement from dominant society. Many Asian Americans continue to suffer from poverty, inadequate housing, inadequate education, poor health care, and unemployment and underemployment. Language and cultural barriers often prevent Asian Americans from taking advantage of human services that could help them. Second and third generation Asian Americans struggle with the dilemma of adhering to traditional cultural values while adopting the values of mainstream society. In recent years, immigration of Asians to the United States has been on the increase, particularly large numbers of Vietnamese, Cambodians, Laotians, Thais, and Koreans. The social welfare system has responded to the needs of these people. The Refugee Act of 1980 allows eligible refugees to receive income maintenance assistance, including medical care for a period of three years. Considerable debate ensued in 1982, when this legislation was reviewed with concerns about the refugees' possible dependence on this assistance. This is still a problem, but concern has been tempered by the awareness that resettlement requires more time than was originally anticipated.[17] Social service agencies and other organizations, particularly churches, have helped with aid in the resettlement of these refugees. Many of them are children, some of whom have special needs, which has stimulated the development of specialized adoption programs. The struggle for equality for Asian Americans, although not readily observed by most, continues as it has since the 1800s.

Prejudice and discrimination, as can be seen from the previous discussion of its effects on all minority groups, has always been an integral part of the U.S. social and cultural structure. They have blighted and distorted our nation's image as the champion of human dignity and human rights. Leon Chestang, a black social worker, in response to this says

> The realities are that the society stands for human dignity while at the same time it disrespects Blacks and other minorities; the society stands for human mutuality while it shuns integration for all its citizens. Few individuals reared in a society such as this can escape incorporating its practices; none can escape being touched by them. Each of us—all of us—shares or is affected by American racial attitudes.[18]

Although minorities have made some gains toward equality, the consequences of prejudice continue to affect the meeting of human needs of those belonging to these minorities. Discussion in this chapter has largely focused on discrimination on the basis of race or ethnic heritage, but other forms of societal discrimination exist within society. These issues also must be considered.

# Discrimination toward Other Groups

Among the many "isms" that label the process of discrimination are "ageism" and "sexism." Discrimination based on age and sex are perhaps the most obvious and readily seen forms of discrimination besides racial discrimination. Of course, societal discrimination is not limited to just these groups. Other groups such as the mentally ill, the physically and mentally handicapped, homosexuals, and certain other ethnic groups often bear the burden of societal prejudice and discrimination. These groups are denied opportunity in some way within U.S. social, economic, and political structure.

## Ageism

*Ageism* is defined as the "process of systematic stereotyping and discrimination against people because they are old, just as racism and sexism accomplish this with skin color and gender."[19] Discrimination against the elderly occurs in the marketplace, on the streets, in the institutional structures of society, in social policy and programs, and within the whole fabric of society. U.S. culture is characteristically youth-oriented and has left no meaningful function, role, status, or place for the aged person. Their wisdom is not valued as it is in many cultures. Society has developed stereotypes of the aged such as: the aged are less intelligent, senile, rigid and conservative in thought, unable to learn, and risky as employees. These false images justify the lack of societal responses to the needs of aged people. The consequences of these social attitudes about the aged are vividly seen when viewing their collective status. They are over represented among the poor, stripped of dignity and purpose through forced retirement, are easy targets of crime, and generally are not provided meaningful social roles within society. It is only within the last few years that society has even begun to become concerned about the plight of the aged. These problems will be discussed in greater detail in a later chapter.

## Sexism

Women have also been disadvantaged through social discrimination. *Sexism*, a term that describes discrimination based on gender (this could include both men and women) has been most often used to describe discrimination against women. What is involved is that: "Women have been singled out for differential and unequal treatment, and have been excluded from full participation in society on the basis of their sex."[20] Sexism occurs throughout the structure of society, particularly in the marketplace where they suffer unequal opportunities for employment, career advancement, and personal income. Discrimination also occurs in the educational system, where women have been socialized through educational processes to believe that they are incapable of pursuing certain careers, particularly those deemed socially acceptable for and dominated by men.

In large part, sexism is caused by societal attitudes, norms, and values that have fostered the illusion that women are inferior to men. These social attitudes are readily transmitted into messages that have become part of the socialization process where, "Women have been taught and have learned behaviors that have led them to assume positions of powerlessness and disrespect."[21] Men are socialized to believe that they are dominant and superior to women in all respects, and therefore have perpetuated the forces of sexism operating within U.S. society. Through the efforts of the women's movement and change in the structures of society, particularly in the family, the public is aware of the destructiveness of sexism. Women in contemporary society have made some gains towards achieving equality. The Equal Rights Amendment (ERA), despite the fact that it has not been ratified, brought about a greater public awareness of inequality among the sexes, and represents a positive step in the direction of achieving change.

Other groups within the United States face the effects of discrimination: Included are the developmentally disabled, the mentally ill, homosexuals, some other ethnic groups, and people from certain religious groups.

Developmentally disabled people, those with either physical or mental handicaps often bear the brunt of discrimination. The physically handicapped experience a subtle form of institutional discrimination, as evidenced by the fact that society does very little to accommodate their special needs in many parts of their daily lives. For example, the physically handicapped, especially those in wheel chairs need to have special facilities in public buildings. This often is ignored, despite the laws and regulations that mandate ramps, parking places, larger doorways for them. The mentally retarded are quite often ridiculed and taken advantage of. Mentally ill people face painful stigma and harmful stereotyping that often prevents them from enjoying full opportunities for employment and education.

There are many other reasons why people are discriminated against. Some are discriminated against because of their sexual preference, others because they or their parents came from a different country, and thus, in some people's mind, automatically throwing their national allegiance into doubt.

Prejudice and discrimination against diverse groups affects the responses made by the social welfare system towards human need. It also has made it difficult for minorities and other groups outside the mainstream to take advantage of the resources of the social welfare system, since these tend to be structured by and for the majority culture and are not particularly responsive to the diversity that exists in contemporary U.S. society.

## Social Welfare Responses to Racism and Discrimination

An early response by the social welfare system was that of the settlement houses in the late 1800s, which helped immigrants to adjust to their new status as U.S. citizens. Settlement houses supported the Immigrant Protection League and other reform efforts. Jane Addams, for example, worked with reform groups that eventually developed into the National Association for the Advancement of Colored People (NAACP). This arose out of her long-standing relationship with Dr. W. E. B. DuBois, a black sociologist, and the founder of this organization. Other social reform efforts by the settlement workers in areas of prejudice and discrimination included advocating education for the mentally retarded and physically handicapped and laws to protect women and children in the labor market.

As the social work profession took shape within the social welfare system, it developed professional responses to prejudice and discrimination. Philosophically, social work as a profession has always been concerned with these issues, but in fact, concrete attempts to deal with the problem from the early 1900s through 1950 were largely indifferent, limited, and uncoordinated.[22]

In the 1960s, during the social upheaval and civil unrest of that decade, the profession became increasingly aware of its need to change its practices and develop greater understanding and sensitivity to the unique needs of minorities. The civil rights movement and the development of pride in minority people pushed social work to develop a knowledge base and skills aimed at the minority client. Until then, the state of the art in social work knowledge, methodology, and skills had not dealt directly with the problems of discrimination or the special needs of minorities. It became evident during the 1960s and early 1970s that this would no longer be acceptable, and that new approaches to working with minorities must be developed. As a result, the profession committed itself to positive change in this area.

Providing the leadership in this effort was the National Association of Social Workers (NASW), and the Council on Social Work Education (CSWE). In 1960, NASW adopted a formal Code of Ethics that expressed the commitment of the profession to work against the forces of discrimination. In 1967, the code was amended and included the following statement: "Social work is based on humanitarian and democratic ideals. Professional social workers are dedicated to the service of mankind, to the disciplined use of a recognized body of knowledge about human beings and their interactions, and to the marshalling of community resources to promote the well-being of all without discrimination."[23]

Even though NASW took a stand on these issues, the association continued to be criticized for its reluctance to acknowledge that many of its own members continued to hold racist attitudes and continued to be a part of a human services system that perpetuated institutional racism and social control over minority groups. Much of the criticism came from within the profession itself, from minority practitioners, especially blacks. The militancy that characterized the black civil rights movement found its way into the profession. Black practitioners were dissatisfied with what they perceived as the status quo position that NASW was assuming on issues of racism. In 1966 this led to the formation of the National Association of Black Social Workers (NABSW). The NABSW from its inception in 1966, to 1969 when it eventually split away from the main body of NASW, protested the lack of response to understanding the black experience. The NABSW continues today as a separate professional social work organization.

In the 1970s, NASW intensified its efforts to develop new understanding and improvement of the quality of practice with minority groups. One of the efforts was to encourage the publication in its journals of articles dealing with how to work with minority clients. Before this, little had been written on these issues. But since that time, a wealth of literature dealing with social work practice and minorities has been published. NASW has, on a number of occasions, devoted entire issues of its journal, *Social Work,* to these topics. In addition, social work books written by minority practitioners have filled a void that existed in the knowledge base of the profession.

In 1979, NASW revised the Social Work Code of Ethics. The new code is divided into several parts. One part of the code addresses the social worker's ethical responsibility to the client. It states: "The social worker should not practice, condone, facilitate or collaborate with any form of discrimination on the basis of race, color, sex, sexual orientation, age, religion, national origin, marital status, political belief, mental or physical handicap, or any other preference or personal characteristic, condition or status."[24] The expanded Code of Ethics reflects the profession's interest in working against discrimination.

Leadership in combating prejudice and discrimination and in developing a more viable response to them has also come from the Council of Social Work Education. CSWE, since the 1970s, has improved social work education and training on these issues. Their effort has focused on three issues: the recruitment of minority students, the recruitment of minority faculty, and curriculum development and curriculum content that prepares social workers to engage in practice with minority clients. Accreditation standards for both graduate schools and undergraduate programs in social work have been developed that call for content in the curriculum on ethnic groups and women. Schools have made a concerted effort to recruit minority students and faculty, and enrollment of minority students in these programs has steadily increased since 1970. Social work programs at both levels have supported minority students by offering financial aid and scholarships. There also has been a significant increase in the numbers of minority faculty teaching in these schools and programs. In addition, considerable effort has been expended to improve the ability of nonminority faculty to teach minority students and minority content. The development of curriculum in both graduate and undergraduate schools in the area of ethnic and cultural diversity has improved significantly in the last several years. Specific courses in social work practice with diverse groups have been added to the curriculums of the schools.

One of the more recent curricular developments has been the adoption by many schools of the *human diversity* perspective, a framework useful in organizing knowledge and skills needed to intervene with diverse groups. Human diversity refers to "the continuum of differences between people and groups resulting from biological, cultural, and social factors."[25] The human diversity perspective emphasizes viewing the range of human differences, which form the basis of diversity, as normal and acceptable, as opposed to making judgements about people's characteristics as abnormal or unacceptable—like race, ethnicity, or any other human characteristic or preference. The social worker is then freed from the trap of viewing human behavior and difference in a normalcy framework. This framework also rejects stereotyping human characteristics that so often form the basis for the oppression, domination, control, and discrimination directed against diverse groups. In this view, the unique characteristics that people possess are considered strengths rather than weaknesses. Social workers are encouraged to use the strengths that people bring with them from their racial, ethnic, cultural, and social backgrounds. These are the basic resources that should be used in intervention with anyone.

Despite the fact that social work in recent years has adopted the human diversity perspective, the systems in which they work have not. The current system of social welfare and social services has ignored individual differences among the people whom they serve. The decisions about what social welfare benefits and which social services programs will be provided to meet human needs remains largely in the hands of majority groups, and others have little or no voice in these decisions. Social work in recent years has taken the lead and continues to push for change in the system through the efforts of NASW, CSWE, and other professional organizations concerned with social welfare and social services responses to human needs.

## Summary

In this chapter, prejudice and discrimination against the many subgroups within U.S. society have been presented as destructive and complex social issues that have interfered with meeting human needs. An effort was made to bring about a clearer understanding of racism, prejudice, and discrimination, and to discuss phenomena such as ethnocentrism, societal attitudes, and ideologies that cause them to occur and perpetuate their existence. Discussion also focused on the effects of prejudice and discrimination on specific groups, and how these groups have attempted to achieve equality and a sense of social justice. The responses made by social work as a profession to prejudice and discrimination were also highlighted showing how the profession has dealt with these social problems both within its own ranks, and also within the larger society. Several unanswered questions remain as to what will be the continued effects of these problems on meeting human needs in our society. It is hoped that the understandings developed in this chapter will stimulate thinking about what should be done in response to the issues raised.

## Key Terms

ageism                          ethnocentrism
assimilation                    human diversity
cultural pluralism              mutual assimilation
prejudice                       racism (individual
discrimination                      and institutional)
sexism

## Questions For Discussion

1. Discuss the differences between racism, discrimination, and prejudice. How have each impacted on the meeting of human needs in society?

2. Identify and discuss the multiple causes of racism. Which cause or causes do you believe are the most difficult to eliminate?

3. The American Civil Rights movement has consisted of both nonviolent and violent actions and events. What are examples of each? Why has the movement over the past two decades been primarily a nonviolent one?

4. What has social work as a profession done, historically, to work against the forces of racism and discrimination? What from your point of view remains to be done?

5. Discuss the human diversity perspective. Why does this perspective serve to guide the approaches that social work makes to diverse groups within American society?

## Notes

[1] Donald Brieland, Lela B. Costin, and Charles Atherton, *Contemporary Social Work: An Introduction to Social Work and Social Welfare* (New York: McGraw-Hill Book Co., 1980), p. 395.

[2] Roger Daniels and Harry Kitano, *American Racism* (Englewood Cliffs, NJ: Prentice-Hall, 1970).

[3] Stokely Carmichael and Charles V. Hamilton, *Black Power: The Politics of Liberation in America* (New York: Random House, 1967), p. 4.

[4] Raymond W. Mack, *Race, Class and Power* (New York: Van Nostrand Reinhold, 1968).

[5] William M. Newman, *American Pluralism: A Study of Minority Groups and Social Theory* (New York: Harper & Row Publishers, 1973), p. 196.

[6] Newman, *American Pluralism*, p. 197.

[7] Carmichel and Hamilton, *Black Power*, p. 4.

[8] David Macarov, *The Design of Social Welfare* (New York: Holt, Rinehart & Winston, 1978), p.134.

[9] Macarov, *Design* p. 134. Also see: Wynetta Devore and Elfriede G. Schlesinger, *Ethnic-Sensitive Social Work Practice* (St. Louis, MO: C.V. Mosby Co., 1981), pp. 17-18.

[10] Macarov, *Design*.

[11] Melvin Steinfield, *Cracks in the Melting Pot: Racism and Discrimination in American History* (New York: Glencoe Press, 1973).

[12] William Cingolani, "Acculturating The Indian Federal Policies, 1834-1973," *Social Work* 18, (Nov. 1973): 20-29.

[13] Harry Pachon and Joan Moore, "Mexican Americans," *Annals of the American Academy of Political and Social Science*, 454 (March 1981): 117.

[14] Pachon, "Mexican Americans," p. 118.

15 United States Commission on Civil Rights, *Mexican Americans and the Administration of Justice in the Southwest* (Washington, D.C.: U.S. Government Printing Office, 1970).

16 Joseph P. Fitzpatrick, and Lourdes Ravieso Parker, "Hispanic Americans in the Eastern United States," *Annals of the American Academy of Political and Social Sciences* 454 (March 1981): 106.

17 K.S. Kerpen, "Refugees on Welfare," *Public Welfare* 43 (Winter 1985): 21-25.

18 Leon W. Chestang, "The Issue of Race in Social Work Practice," in *Perspectives on Social Welfare: An Introductory Anthology,* ed. Paul E. Weinberger, (New York: Macmillan Publishing Co., 1974), p. 393.

19 Robert N. Butler and Myra I. Lewis, *Aging and Mental Health: Positive Psychological Approaches* (St. Louis, MO: C.V. Mosby Co., 1973), p. ix.

20 Louis Wirth, "The Problem of Minority Groups" in *Minority Responses,* ed. Minako Kurokawa, (New York: Random House, 1970), p. 34.

21 Sharon B. Berlin, "Better Work With Women Clients," *Social Work* 21 (Nov. 1976): 497.

22 Fred M. Cox et al., *Strategies of Community Organization,* 3rd. ed. (Itasca, IL: F.E. Peacock Publishers, 1979).

23 National Association of Social Workers, *NASW Code of Ethics - Amendments, April 1967* (Washington, D.C.: National Association of Social Workers, 1967).

24 National Association of Social Workers, *NASW Code of Ethics - July 1980* (Washington D.C.: National Association of Social Workers, 1980), p. 4.

25 Rex A. Skidmore and Milton Thackeray, *Introduction to Social Work* (Englewood Cliffs, NJ: Prentice-Hall, 1982).

## Suggested Readings

Berlin, Sharon B. "Better Work with Women Clients," *Social Work* 21 (Nov. 76): 492-497.

Brieland, Donald; Costin, Lela B.; and Atherton, Charles. "Racism," in *Contemporary Social Work.* New York: McGraw-Hill Book Co., 1980, pp. 394-520.

Carmichel, Stokely, and Hamilton, Charles V. *Black Power.* New York: Random House, 1967.

Cingolani, William. "Acculturating the Indian Federal Policies, 1834-1973", *Social Work* 18 (Nov. 1973): 24-29.

Knowles, Louis L., and Prewitt, Kenneth. *Institutional Racism in America.* Englewood Cliffs, NJ: Prentice-Hall, 1979.

Newman, William N. *American Pluralism.* New York: Harper & Row Publishers, 1973.

Macarov, David. *The Design of Social Welfare.* New York: Holt, Rinehart & Winston, 1978).

Pachon, Harry, and Moore, Joan. "Mexican Americans," *Annals of the American Academy of Political and Social Science* 451 (March 1981): 111-124.

Skidmore, Rex A., and Thackeray, Milton. *Introduction to Social Work.* Englewood Cliffs, NJ: Prentice-Hall, 1982.

Steinfeld, Melvin. *Cracks in the Melting Pot.* New York: Glencoe Press, 1973.

# Part Three

## Fields of Practice

Service delivery in the U.S. social welfare system is organized around problem areas (child welfare or health care), or around population groups (the aged, families). More recently, fields of practice have developed around a particular environment such as rural or industrial. This part of the book will examine what is known in social work as *fields of practice* or practice focused on specific problems or population groups. By looking at individual fields of practice in some depth, the complexity of service delivery in the social welfare system is easier to understand. Such study provides a historical perspective on why and how today's services are organized. It also is a good way to learn about the scope of practice and the differences between the fields.

Fields of practice to be considered include: income maintenance, services to children, services to families, health care, mental health care, corrections, and services for the elderly, plus a chapter on two developing fields of practice, industrial social work and rural social work. Each chapter will first define the field by identifying the population and/or problem it serves. Then, within that field the history of the social welfare system's response to need will be discussed. Contemporary practice in the field will be examined, using case examples. Issues and current concerns will then be explored. The final chapter of this section, looks at what makes a field of practice develop.

In addition, this part of the book will identify how the various fields of practice make use of the six arrangements discussed in Part One. It will also note how poverty, racism and discrimination, resource distribution, and social change have affected the population involved.

# Chapter 7

## Income Maintenance as a Response to Human Need

Chapter 1 discussed the arrangements that the U.S. social welfare system uses to provide for human needs, including the major societal values, philosophies, and historical changes that shaped its response. That introduction clearly indicated that one important function of any social welfare system is to provide for those who are, temporarily or permanently, without sufficient income to meet their basic needs—to provide income maintenance.

This chapter focuses on income maintenance services as an essential part of the social welfare system. It will define income maintenance and give a brief overview of income maintenance programs and services, and their historical development, including influential societal values, philosophies, economic, and social changes. Then it will take a look at programs and some alternatives. Social work's involvement in income maintenance will be considered from both historical and contemporary perspectives.

## Definitions of Income Maintenance

The concept of *income maintenance* can be more easily understood by separating and studying the terms, income and maintenance separately. Income, in a monetary society like the United States, simply defined, means the inflow of money necessary for people to purchase life-sustaining resources, material goods, or services. The term maintenance means to continue, hold, preserve, or perpetuate the existence of something at some level. Combining these two terms, income maintenance is a method of maintaining and controlling income. Our society has defined income levels necessary for the social good and to maintain social order. A program of income maintenance is designed to keep income at a level that will at least provide people with human needs, while controlling the extent and means of satisfying those needs.

The concept of helping people who cannot support themselves is a very old concept, as we shall see later, but the government institutionalized program of income maintenance is fairly new to the United States. The Social Security Act of 1935, with its subsequent amendments, is responsible for shaping current income maintenance programs. Prior to 1935, the concept of charity prevailed, more as a privilege than as a human right. But now individuals are guaranteed by law the right to receive income maintenance assistance if they are eligible.

Income maintenance's primary goal is to ensure that people are able to live at a minimum level of subsistance and satisfaction,[1] creating a safety net of resources for people without adequate income.

## The Structure of Income Maintenance Programs

The structure of income maintenance is a direct reflection of societal values and philosophies.[2] Income maintenance programs are based on two sets of diametrically opposed values. One set of values stems from society's concern for human suffering and calls for mechanisms that provide fair and equitable means for eliminating such suffering. The charity and philanthropic movements of the late 1800s are examples of this. And to some degree, the government's response, represented by the Social Security Act of 1935, also reflects this value. Other values that have influenced income maintenance hold the view that poor, deprived, or disadvantaged people in some way are responsible for that condition.[3] U.S. society tends to blame the victim. This victim is then punished by providing him or her with a very minimal maintenance income.

Another way to analyze the structure of income maintenance programs and services is to examine the extent to which U.S. society assumes responsibility for them. Harold Wilensky and Charles LeBeaux have offered two approaches in their book *Industrial Society and Social Welfare*. The first is called the *residual approach*. In this, assistance should only be offered when the normal means by which people obtain income, for example, from the family or workplace becomes inadequate or nonexistent.[4] Society in this view has only minimal and limited responsibility to provide income maintenance and would do so only when the customary channels are blocked. But when the usual income channels again become available, income maintenance would be withdrawn. One example of the residual approach is the case of the factory workers who have been laid off. They might receive unemployment compensation and food stamps while not working. When they return to work, these income resources are withdrawn. In this case, the assistance is offered only for a limited time and is categorical in that the recipient must meet defined eligibility requirements.

The second view they present is the *institutional approach.* The provision of income maintenance is recognized as the legitimate and first-line responsibility of a modern industrial nation,[5] recognizing that unmet human needs exist as a consequence of living in any industrial society. Therefore, income maintenance is a permanent and necessary part of the social structure.[6] Assistance is then based on universal, rather than categorical, need. Assistance for the aged who, because of their age and social status, are in considerable risk of lacking sufficient income, is an example of the institutional approach.

There is a third way to conceptualize societal responsibility for income maintenance, called the *developmental approach.* This takes the position that most income maintenance programs and services have been developed to solve the problems of unmet human needs. Thus it is possible, and perhaps desireable, to use income maintenance to provide a better quality of life and to promote and enhance human development. A program based on this philosophy would be universal and would embrace human need from a preventive and growth potential perspective.[7]

None of these approaches are totally accepted as guiding principles. Each, however, has influenced the development of the income maintenance response. The result is a compromise containing something from all three approaches. The actual structure of the delivery system consists of both private and public agencies. Public agencies make up by far the largest part of the delivery system. In this chapter, discussion of income maintenance will be limited to financial assistance programs, including General Assistance Programs, Aid to Families with Dependent Children, Supplemental Security Income, Food Stamps, government pensions, and private financial assistance programs.

# Historical Development of
# Income Maintenance Programs and Services

## *Europe and England*

As we learned in Chapter 1, people have come together to help others who are less fortunate or who encounter misfortune since the dawning of organized human society. With the exception of the Greeks, early western societies did not have formal, organized mechanisms for meeting human needs. Rather responses were largely based on mutual aid—person to person, family to family.

More formal forms of income maintenance began to emerge by the eleventh century (see Table 7.1). Feudalism, a complex social class and political system that existed from about the tenth to the sixteenth century, could perhaps be considered one of the earliest forms of income maintenance in Europe and England. Feudalism's economic underpinnings depended on serfs who were attached to the land and who supplied the ruling class with a stable labor force. Under the control of the lord of the estate, serfs essentially traded a large measure of their individual freedom for protection against sickness, unemployment, and old age.[8]

People who were not serfs and who lived in cities could look to the social, craft, and merchant guilds for help in time of need. These guilds not only helped their own members but they also lent assistance to others. According to historian Walter Trattner, "they distributed corn and barely yearly, fed the needy on feast days, provided free lodgings for destitute travelers, and engaged in other kinds of intermittent and incidental help."[9]

Two of the most critical sources of aid to the poor and needy were the medieval hospital and church. Early hospitals were attached to monestaries and located along roadsides and served a much wider function than they do today. Not only did they care for the sick but they "housed and cared for weary travellers, for orphans, the aged, and the destitute."[10] The church's role was, of course, pivotal at this time to society's ability to care for the poor and needy. Trattner explains that, "The bishop in each diocese was charged with the duty of feeding and protecting the poor within his district. He was directed to divide the total revenue of the diocese, which came from the church tithe, and to distribute a fixed portion—from a third to a fourth—to those in need."[11]

Throughout the fourteenth and fifteenth centuries several factors and events began to wear away these forms of income maintenance. The economic and political system of feudalism began to be replaced with a monetary economy. While rampant corruption and general decline weakened the role the church played in people's lives, civil forms of government began taking on more responsibility for organizing and protecting society. Natural disasters—most notably the bubonic plague (1334–1354) and several crop failures—further compounded the economic confusion and added greatly to people's insecurity and hardships. This period of social and economic upheaval "resulted in a tremendous increase in unemployment, poverty, vagabondage, begging, and thievery, especially in the growing commercial centers to which many of the needy gravitated."[12]

According to Trattner, "it was in this context that the modern institution of social welfare emerged."[13] One of the first organized or govern-

Table 7.1   Important Dates: Income Maintenance

| | |
|---|---|
| 1350–1530 | Series of statutes, the laborers laws forced able-bodied people to work, provided relief assistance to the worthy poor, e.g. children, aged, handicapped. |
| 1536 | Act for the Punishment of Sturdy Beggars and Vagabonds imposed severe penalties for begging |
| 1601 | Elizabethan (English) Poor Law |
| 1621 | Act for Settlement |
| Late 1600s to 1840s | Colonists dealt with human needs by mutual aid initially. Later, Colonial Poor Laws became the response to human needs. Several religious groups, and ethnic societies also provided charity to the poor. State Poor Laws replaced Colonial Poor Laws after the revolution. |
| 1843 | New York Association for Improving Conditions of the Poor |
| 1870s through 1900 | Charity Organization Societies emerged |
| 1935 | Social Security Act |
| 1956 | Amendments to Social Security Act added an income maintenance program to the physically and totally disabled |
| 1962 | ADC changed to AFDC, income maintenance and social services were separated |
| 1964 | Food Stamp Act |
| 1969 | Family Assistance Plan (FAP) |
| 1972 | Supplemental Security Income (SSI) |
| 1973 | WIN Program |
| 1977 | Jobs and Income Security Program (JISP) |

mental efforts to deal with these problems, and a forerunner of the 1601 English Poor law, was the Statute of Laborers passed in England. Actually a series of laws first passed in 1350, they were essentially aimed at getting able-bodied people to work and beggars off the streets, with restrictions placed on the granting of charitable aid to these people. By the early 1500s more laws were enacted that made the practice of begging by any able-bodied person a punishable offence. The Act for the Punishment of Sturdy Vagabonds and Beggars was passed by Parliament in 1536. It imposed even greater penalties for begging by able-bodied people, but it also made public officials responsible for obtaining and distributing resources collected by various means to the needy. Public jobs were also made available, and later amendments imposed a system of compulsory taxation to support the relief efforts. This law further expanded the government's role in social welfare and reflects two values that have continually influenced the social welfare response: society is responsible for helping people that are in distress and for providing social control and social order."[10]

With the passage of time it became quite evident that punishment was not an effective deterent to poverty. While still feeling a need to maintain the social order, Parliament embarked upon a course of action designed to apply public resources to human needs. To keep social order it imposed strict limitations on granting of assistance. Only certain categories of people were eligible for certain kinds of assistance. This action culminated in the passage of the Elizabethan Poor Law of 1601, commonly referred to as the English Poor Law. The able-bodied were given public jobs or "outdoor relief" as it was called. ("Indoor relief," or assistance, was provided to the aged, sick, and handicapped, either in their own homes or in institutions.) Dependent children were either indentured (an arrangement in which a dependent child would be given to a family where he or she could learn a trade and become self sufficient) or put into an institution.[14]

Vagrancy was controlled under the law by the concept of "settlement," whereby individuals could only receive assistance in the parish in which they were born.[15] Settlement is the direct forerunner of modern day residency requirements for eligibility for income maintenance assistance. Local control and responsibility was perhaps one of the most outstanding features of this law. With assistance from the churches and a system of local taxation, local government carried out the provisions of the law.

The English Poor Law of 1601 serves as the foundation of the American system of social welfare and income maintenance. Its philosophies and practices, which were brought to the new land by those who colonized America in the 1600s, have heavily influenced the scope and direction of social welfare in the United States.

## United States

The American colonial response to human need was based on mutual aid. It was expected that all colonists would work together for everyone's mutual benefit. Their religious beliefs supported this response. They were mainly protestants who believed strongly in the work ethic.[16]

As the population increased in the colonies so did the human need. One factor that contributed to this pressure was England's practice of sending people they considered to be undesirable to the colonies. Some of these people were political enemies of the state, others were sick, old or handicapped, and still others had criminal records. The colonial government was faced with meeting the needs of these people as well as developing a mechanism that would maintain social order. As a result, poor laws began to be implemented that were patterned after the English Poor laws.[17] Such features as "indoor relief" (institutional care) and "outdoor relief" (care in the community) began to emerge in the colonies. Compulsory taxation to fund the relief effort, as in England, was also a part of the colonial poor laws. Local communities were responsible for the administration of the laws. As this became increasingly difficult, the colonial treasury began the practice of reimbursing the local community for expenditures for providing relief. This practice is much like the modern day practice of state aid.[18]

Although political, economic, and social discontent with England culminated in the American Revolution, the country's system of social welfare remained unchanged. Individual states, fearing the investment of too much power in the federal government, assumed responsibility for social welfare. They developed state poor laws based on the models of the colonial and English Poor Laws. This arrangement of "public welfare" relief remained virtually unchanged until 1935, except for the development of the private charity and philanthropy movement in the late 1800s.

From just before the American Revolution until the late 1800s, several religious organizations made relief or assistance available to the needy. These forerunners of the philanthropy movement included the Quakers, who first organized relief efforts in the late 1600s and the Episcopal Charity Society of Boston. Other non-religious organizations were involved in extending a helping hand to the poor during this period as well. Many were associated with nationality or ethnic groups. The Scot's Charity Society, German's Society of New York, and the French Benevolent Society were all involved in the relief granting efforts.[19] The immediate forerunners of the Charity Organization Societies were the New York Association for Improving the Condition of the Poor and the New York Society for the Prevention of Pauperism. Both emerged in the middle 1800s. These were only two of many benevolent charity societies that sprang up in various locations throughout the country.

Social and economic values that said society has responsibility for providing assistance to those in need influenced the development of the system of income maintenance in late 1800s. Humanitarian values, in part based on Judeo-Christian beliefs, promoted assistance to the needy as a means of distributing society's benefits. The rise of the charitable and benevolent organizations reflects this set of values.

In direct conflict with the humanitarians were the economic and social philosophers who held different views on the issue of assisting the poor. They questioned the right of society to protect people in need of assistance. The poor laws came under serious attack in both England and the United States. In 1798 Thomas Malthus, a clergyman and social and economic philosopher, published his famous *Essay on the Principle of Population*. In this work, Malthus argues that the poor laws caused over-population by allowing dependent people to continue to exist through public assistance. In his view public assistance represented a violation of the natural order of things and caused a lower standard of living for everyone. Other enemies of the poor laws were the classical econo-mists, such as Adam Smith, David Ricardo, John Locke, and Thomas Locke. Each argued in their own way that the poor law system was not economically sound, as it interfered with the functioning of the mar-ket economy. They believed in a laissez-faire, or natural functioning, market economy with no interference or regulation by the government. Public assistance, which was supported by taxes on property, was seen as an unjust and immoral interference in the lives of those who held wealth.[20]

In much the same vain, another group of social philosophers held a philosophy based on Charles Darwin's law of natural selection. This adaptation of Darwin's biological theory holds that certain individuals, particularly those who had affluence and wealth, had proven their right to exist. Poor or dependent people, according to this view, should cease to exist as being poor demonstrates their unworthiness. Herbert Spencer, an English social philosopher, was the main proponent of this so-called Social Darwinism. He believed that granting of public assis-tance would allow the poor to exist contrary to the processes of natural selection. His view was that the poor were unfit and should be elimi-nated.[21] The opponents of public aid, seemingly had no malice against private charity and philanthropy. This is understandable as it fits nicely with their thinking about a laissez-faire economy. Those with wealth were given the freedom of choice in deciding whether or not they would like to assist the poor.

These rather pessimistic views, although influencing public senti-ment against what we now call income maintenance, never were com-pletely accepted in American society. Americans have always been concerned with moral obligations to assist people in need and to elimi-nate human suffering. Nevertheless, the philosophy of laissez-faire eco-nomics, Social Darwinism, and the work ethic have continued to influence social welfare and income maintenance policy in our society.

As noted in Chapter 1, permanent change in the structure of social welfare and income maintenance services occurred in 1935 with the Social Security Act. The Social Security Act changed the notion that the States should be solely responsible for the providing of income mainte-nance assistance. It moved the Federal government into public welfare arena, into a partnership arrangement with the states. The programs created by the Social Security Act of 1935 are the basis for income maintenance in the contemporary American social welfare system.

# Current Income Maintenance Programs

Income maintenance programs are designed to distribute or transfer income to people whose income is insufficient to meet their needs. They are often referred to as *income transfers*, that is, income is transferred through taxes from the more affluent to recipients of income maintenance.

All levels of government, local, state, and federal, are involved in providing these programs. The involvement of each will be discussed separately, though it will soon be apparent that the interrelationship of the three levels of government is necessary and inherent in the U.S. social welfare system.

## *Local Income Maintenance Programs*

The major local program of income maintenance assistance is what is known as *General Assistance (GA)*, in some parts of the country it is called "poor relief." This program closely resembles the old poor law.[22] General assistance is noncategorical; to be eligible, people do not have to possess certain characteristics (i.e., age, marital status) or be in a certain life situation. The main eligibility requirements for general assistance are income deprivation and residency in a particular county or state.

Various modes of administration exist in these programs. Some are under city, county, or parish administration, others are state-regulated. Most, if not all, are funded with some form of local, country, or state tax revenues. Assistance comes in a variety of forms. In some programs, recipients receive a direct cash grant. In many other programs, assistance is given in-kind, by providing tangible resources such as food, clothing, shelter, energy costs, and medical care. Food stamps may also be provided. Another feature of general assistance programs is that often they require recipients to work off their assistance in public work projects or, in some cases, pay back the assistance received. In some programs, liens are placed against the property of those who receive this type of assistance.

Many criticisms and problems are associated with general assistance programs. One of the most important is that no guarantee is given to the recipient that assistance will be ongoing. On the contrary, in most programs the assistance is supposed to be temporary or for an emergency. The aid may be cut off at anytime, subject to the discretion of the administration, often because some of these programs have no formal written eligibility requirements and policies, or no common eligibility standards. Another problem is that people from minority backgrounds are sometimes discriminated against by these programs and may be denied assistance; blacks in the southern states often face this. Often these programs are administered by people without adequate qualifications; many have no training in social work or any other helping profession.

## Federal and State Income Maintenance Programs

Several income maintenance programs or public assistance programs came into existence with the Social Security Act of 1935. They were originally created as a societal safety net, to insure a basic subsistence level for families and individuals not covered under two other provisions of the act, unemployment compensation and insurance for the aged. These programs were implemented as *grants-in-aid* programs, that is, a partnership relationship between the states and the federal government. The programs were to be administered by the states, subject to federal regulation and policy, funding provided on a matching basis from both the states and the federal government.

Three original income maintenance programs were created:

1. *Aid to Dependent Children (ADC)*—cash assistance provided to children in families that become dependent and deprived of income resources, due to parental absence through separation, divorce, or death.
2. *Old Age Assistance (OAA)*—cash assistance to poor people sixty-five years of age or older not covered by Social Security benefits. The creators of the Social Security Act realized that many older Americans would not be covered under the provisions of the social insurance for the aged program. Old Age Assistance was created to bridge that gap.
3. *Aid to the Blind (AB)*—cash assistance to blind people, who qualified under income eligibility criteria.

In 1956, the Social Security Act, was amended and expanded to add the program Aid to the Physically and Totally Disabled (APTD). Of these programs, only Aid to Dependent Children, now known as *Aid to Families with Dependent Children (AFDC)* remains solely under the administration of the states. The others were combined in 1972, into a federally administered program called Supplemental Security Income, which will be discussed later in this chapter.

AID TO FAMILIES WITH DEPENDENT CHILDREN   Since this program remains under state administration, no uniformity or consistency in its structure exists among the programs. In 1962, the original ADC program was restructured and renamed Aid to Families with Dependent Children. This change reflected a concern for the family, and a perceived need to assist AFDC recipients to become more self-supporting through social services and employment services.[23]

Families who apply for AFDC must meet two main eligibility criteria. The first is verification that minor children (those under eighteen years of age and attending school) are deprived of parental support as a result of at least one parent being deceased, incapacitated, or being absent through separation or divorce. The second criteria is income verification. A means test is used to determine financial eligibility. This test consists of determining total family need, depending on family size, including shelter (rent and utilities) on a predetermined formula that varies from state to state. Total family needs are then compared with family income resources, within defined limits, including salary, wages, savings accounts, and other liquid assets (such as stocks and bonds, cash value life insurance, trust accounts, or any other source that can be readily converted to cash). If determined needs exceed financial resources, the family is then eligible for the program.

Another feature of the AFDC program is that unless there are preschool children in the home, adult recipients, including children sixteen years of age who are not attending school, must register for work with their local Job Services office. This requirement was added in 1973, with the creation of the *Work Incentive program*, (WIN). The WIN program was designed to prepare or train AFDC recipients for employment or return to employment, by providing on-the-job training and support services like day care and other social services, so recipients eventually would become self-sufficient and no longer need public assistance. From its inception in 1973 until 1980, the federal government required that states participate and offer the WIN program. It has now been reduced to an option for the states. The WIN program is an example of the continued influence of the work ethic in public welfare and income maintenance programs.

Another variation of AFDC provided by some states is Aid to Families with Dependent Children—Unemployed Parent. This provides income to families in which both parents are present but one or both are chronically unemployed. Another variation of very recent origin is *workfare*. Many states have begun demonstration programs that require AFDC recipients to work for their income assistance, through work experience programs. Workfare is an example of the influence of the work ethic. Workfare will be discussed later in this chapter as an alternative to the current income maintenance programs.

No single program of income maintenance assistance has been so widely criticized by the general public and policymakers as the AFDC program. Some of the criticism is valid, but some is based on myth. Among the valid criticisms is the fact that there is no uniformity to recipients' payments among the states. Southern states have traditionally provided exceedingly low payments. The state of Mississippi in 1982 provided an average monthly cash grant of only $89.00, while more populous eastern states provide the highest average monthly cash payments to AFDC families: in 1982, New York paid an average of $385.00

a month, Connecticut averaged $395.00 a month, and Vermont, $383.00 a month.

Several societal myths have brought this program under attack. Chief among them is the belief that AFDC encourages large families because recipients, who are mainly women, have additional children so they can receive larger monthly incomes. This is highly unlikely when one considers that the addition to the family's assistance payment would probably not exceed $35.00 to $40.00 a month per child. Another myth is that many AFDC recipients are able-bodied people who would rather live on welfare than work. In reality, approximately 60 percent of all AFDC recipients are children. Only 40 percent are adults, many of whom are women single heads of household. Most recipients would rather not be on the program and would prefer to be self-sufficient. They are handicapped in their efforts by having to care for small children, by long-term disabilities, by their lack of education and training, and by sexual discrimination in the employment marketplace.[24]

Some people believed that AFDC recipients are cheaters who have defrauded the government into providing them with assistance. Repeated studies have shown very little fraud among recipients. More significant are the errors made by program officials working within the massive bureaucratic structure; they are responsible for ineligible families being on the program. Another myth is that most AFDC recipients are from minority groups. In fact, most AFDC recipients are white. Discrimination, however, causes minorities to be overrepresented in the AFDC programs.

FOOD ASSISTANCE PROGRAMS    Food assistance programs are a cooperative effort by the states and the federal government. These programs are relief-in-kind rather than direct cash benefit programs. They also are more universal than categorical, with the primary eligibility criterion being low-income.

The major food assistance is *food stamps*. This program is administered by the states with assistance and matching funds from the United States Department of Agriculture (USDA). (Since the 1930s, the USDA has distributed surplus food to needy families.) In 1964, Congress passed the Food Stamp Act that created food stamps, which low-income people can purchase for a portion of their face value to be used to buy food items. Generally, the program has been quite successful and has, in many ways, achieved its aims. However, like the other programs, it has had its share of problems. The primary problem is that policies and administrative procedures have constantly changed, causing confusion among recipients and a significant error rate in the program.

Federally aided school breakfast and lunch programs that help meet children's nutritional needs have been provided in some states. Other food assistance programs, such as Meals on Wheels for the elderly, are also being administered by private social service agencies with assistance from the states and federal government.

SUPPLEMENTAL SECURITY INCOME (SSI)    *Supplemental Security Income (SSI)* is a major, federally funded and administered income maintenance program. In 1971, the federal government, through an amendment to the Social Security Act, assumed responsibility for cash assistance to the aged and to any blind or disabled person of any age. SSI "federalized" the categorical assistance programs the states had been providing under earlier provisions of the Social Security Act. The program is administered by the Social Security Administration, and funded out of general tax revenues, with additional supplements from states that offer them. Financial eligibility for the program is determined by a means test for income. Eligibility for blind and disabled persons may require additional medical documentation of the extent of disability.

Although the program has the advantage of more equitable treatment of recipients nationwide, through a federally guaranteed uniform level of payment, it also has some disadvantages:

1. Too much time is needed to determine eligibility and to process applications.
2. Even though income levels are federally guaranteed, these still may not meet the high costs of living in certain areas, particularly where the state does not provide supplemental assistance.
3. The separation of SSI from state administration has caused duplication of administration and has increased the administrative costs since the states must still administer the AFDC program.

While no income maintenance program has existed without some degree of opposition, the advantages of the SSI program outweigh its disadvantages.

OTHER FEDERAL PROGRAMS    Veterans' pensions and other forms of relief-in-kind assistance to veterans of the armed services are provided by the Veterans Administration. Eligibility for a veteran's pension is based, in part, on the extent to which a person's disability is related to their military service. As a result, there is less stigma associated with receiving a veteran's pension than with other forms of income maintenance.

The United States Bureau of Indian Affairs (BIA) administers income maintenance programs and other social and rehabilitative services for native Americans residing in reservation areas. These programs are federally funded. The main program provided by the BIA is general assistance, which is temporary. Recipients are encouraged to apply for other, permanent programs, such as AFDC or SSI. General assistance is provided only until the person becomes eligible and begins to receive assistance from other programs.

Current income maintenance programs have both positive and negative aspects. On the positive side, these programs transfer income to people in need, as well as provide social and economic stability within society. However, because the various programs were developed at different times, they have different objectives and divergent eligibility criteria and are administered by different governmental jurisdictions. They are inconsistent in their missions, and do not form a well integrated system. Many overlap in their coverage but at the same time exclude many people who are in need, creating gaps in coverage.

Although many income maintenance programs are small, particularly local programs, many are not as scrutinized by policymakers as are the larger programs—AFDC, Foodstamps, Medicaid, and SSI.[25] Beginning in the 1960s and up to the present time there has been interest in changing existing income maintenance programs. Several proposals for change in these programs have emerged in recent years.

## Looking Ahead: Alternatives to Income Maintenance

For the last twenty-five years, alternatives to the current income maintenance programs have been a topic of discussion for both the general public and those who formulate social policy. Rapid social change, economic fluctuations, and continued debate concerning who should be helped at what level and at whose expense, have pushed the nation toward welfare reform. The work ethic continues to influence program direction: two recent proposals for restructuring the system called for work or employment. In the 1960s, a presidential commission on income maintenance recommended a universal type of system, but said that it should not provide financial disincentives to work."[26]

### Some Proposals that were Rejected

Although there have been numerous welfare reform proposals, two are noteworthy. The first was the *Family Assistance Plan* (FAP) introduced to Congress in 1969. This plan would have replaced the existing structure of income assistance with an entirely new plan under the complete control and administration of the federal government. This program's primary feature was that it would have provided a minimum guaranteed annual income to every U.S. household. In addition, the program would have provided incentives for working and penalties for not working. Unemployed persons in families of four or more would have received at least a minimum of $2,400 per year. Employed persons in families would have been guaranteed a minimum of $1,600, which would be allowed to rise to nearly $4,000 through earned wages before penalties would be imposed. Eventually the program was to be turned over to the states, in what was called the *New Federalism.*[27] Proponents of this program saw it as a positive step in the direction of improving the conditions of the poor. Critics of the proposal labeled it inadequate, costly, and a step in the direction of socialism. In the early 1970s, after much consideration in congressional committees, the proposal died from lack of support.

A second proposal for welfare reform was introduced in 1977. The Carter administration, based on several months of study, determined that the existing income maintenance system was complicated, unfair, and inequitable. They responded by introducing to Congress the *Jobs and Income Security Program* (JISP). Again, this program would totally have replaced the existing system. The main features of this plan were a jobs program for people capable of working but currently unemployed and income maintenance for individuals unable to work for specified reasons. Under the plan, unemployed people would have been placed on jobs in the private sector of the economy and earned at least the minimum wage guaranteed by law. They also would have received generous earned-income tax credits that, in theory, would have increased their gross income. For people unable to work because of parental responsibilities, disability, or age, a generous income maintenance was proposed. Under this plan, each household was guaranteed an adequate level of income. Families of four would have received $4,200 per year, aged couples $3,750 a year, and single persons at least $2,500 per year. Incentives to work were also provided that allowed for a substantial increase of income without penalty. The major drawback to this proposal was that it would have been far more costly than the existing system. Although congressional reaction to the JISP was favorable, Congress adjourned without taking action on it.

## Current Proposals

At the beginning of the present decade, discontent with the existing social welfare and income maintenance structure, which had been festering for sometime, surfaced again. In 1980, a trend toward political, economic, and social conservatism also emerged. A number of alternative proposals that would drastically change the existing system have been generated. These proposals are supported by a number of economic issues.

Enormous federal budget deficits have forced Congress to rethink the federal governments spending in many areas. Actions were taken to reduce the levels of government expenditure, with the belief that this would reduce inflation, and consequently stimulate the economy so that incentives would be created for increased production, leading to a rise in personal income resources.[28] One target for reduction of government expenditures has been social welfare and income maintenance. A laissez-faire attitude to the role of the federal government in this area has returned, based on the belief that expenditures for social welfare have undermined the natural functioning of the economy. The residual approach discussed earlier supports this view: government's role is to create a safety net of income maintenance for the "truly needy." But this naively asserts that someone knows who the "truly needy" are. However, "truly needy" has never been adequately defined. What has happened is a plan of action was set in motion, with congressional support, to eliminate or drastically cut federal expenditures in the basic income maintenance programs such as AFDC, SSI, food stamps, and Medicare.

The use of the term "New Federalism," coined by the Nixon administration, has emerged again within current welfare reform proposals. People feel strongly that responsibility for social welfare ought to be transferred back to the states. In this vein, Congress recently proposed to "federalize" Medicaid and transfer total responsibility for the AFDC program to the states. The resultant gains and losses of such a plan were reviewed by Congress and the governors of the individual states and was determined to be inequitable and unworkable. However, political support within Congress has allowed some cuts and changes in the structure of income maintenance and social services programs. In addition, cuts were made in unemployment insurance, employment, and child nutrition programs. However, the cuts were not as deep as originally anticipated. Recently political support for new welfare reform proposals has waned, or become sidetracked by foreign policy issues. It is difficult to predict the outcome of these new initiatives in welfare reform, and what changes in the existing structure of income maintenance programs and services will occur in the future.

Movement toward welfare reform, and the generation of alternatives to the present system has been slow to come. Although a number of proposals have been offered, none have been implemented this far. Recently there appears to be renewed interest in welfare reform. Although no formal proposals have surfaced in Congress, politicians, and professional organizations, such as the NASW and the American Public Welfare Association, are drafting proposals that would overhaul the present system. What directions or changes that will be offered in these proposals is not clear at this point.

## Work Experience Programs

Our society's ideology and the value it places on work has always had an impact on every aspect of income maintenance programs in the United States. Because the value of work is so integral to the American way of life, no alternative program of income maintenance that did not address work could be supported. Welfare has often been criticized as a deterrent to work. Thus, great efforts have been made in the structure of income maintenance to provide incentives for work; sometimes, in fact, to force people on assistance to work. Work is a primary determinent for eligibility for most income maintenance programs.[29] Others, such as general assistance, AFDC, and SSI, have been made available because recipients, for many reasons, are not working. In recent years, even these programs have reflected the work ethic. The WIN program attached to AFDC is one example. An experimental workfare program has been added to the AFDC program on a national scale. It calls for some AFDC recipients to work a predetermined number of hours a week to receive continued assistance. Proponents of this program believe that work experience helps recipients become more self-sufficient, by restoring personal confidence and self-pride. Critics counter that the program is demeaning, dehumanizing, rigidly controlled and lacking in necessary in-kind support systems like day care. If this program is to become a permanent feature of the AFDC program, it will need to insure adequate in-kind support systems, and adequate educational or on-the-job training provisions to maximize its success.

Other work experience programs not specifically tied to income maintenance have come into existence over the years: beginning in the 1930s with the New Deal; the Manpower Development and Training program and the Office of Economic Opportunity programs of the 1960s; and the Public Service Employment (PSE), Emergency Employment Act (EEA), and the Comprehensive Employment and Training Act (CETA), of the 1970s have all provided work experience to the unemployed poor. In addition the proposed Family Assistance Plan and the Jobs and Income Security Program had strong work incentive features. But no single comprehensive work-related income maintenance program has emerged.

Work experience programs have the advantage of congruence with our society's belief in the value of work. They may increase self-confidence and pride, which motivates individuals to move away from dependence on income maintenance. But a major disadvantage of these programs is cost. They may be more expensive to implement than the traditional programs, particularly if in-kind supports like day care, medical assistance, and education and training features are added. The future of the relationship between work and welfare seems inevitable. However, it remains to be seen what the exact nature of the relationship will be.

## Guaranteed Income Programs

The second alternative to the current income maintenance system is *guaranteed income programs*. Very simply, a guaranteed income program would provide a specific level of personal income to each family and individual in the United States. There are several ways that this might be accomplished. It might be provided through a system of cash grants. Families and individuals whose income is below a certain level would be provided a cash grant to bring their income up to a determined minimum standard. Or a combination of cash grants and work experience, or a combination of cash grants, work experience, and in-kind supports such as food stamps, medical assistance, and housing allowances could be used. A guaranteed income program would be designed to distribute income in a more equitable way to all people, and it would be more universal than present programs.

The advantages of guaranteed income include eliminating the stigma of welfare, creating a system based on actual income need rather than on categorical need, and allowing a more adequate distribution of income. A guaranteed income program would provide income maintenance to the entire population rather than selected categories of people. The biggest disadvantage is cost. Depending on the structure of such a program, implementation costs would exceed current levels of spending. The increased tax rate required to support a guaranteed income program has to be considered as a disadvantage. But the primary disadvantage of this kind of program is that it runs counter to the ideologies of rugged individualism and self-reliance. This is perhaps why such proposals are not politically acceptable and thus have not become reality.

## Negative Income Tax

Taxes on personal and corporate income essentially redistribute income throughout the population; these are called *income transfers.* Income maintenance programs are income transfer programs. Income maintenance recipients generally pay little, if any, personal income taxes; even if they work, their incomes are often so low they are exempt from paying. Middle and upper income level households in the United States carry the tax burden that supports income maintenance. However, due to income tax exemptions, and "loopholes," these households are sometimes able to avoid paying taxes, thus increasing their levels of personal income. The public assistance recipient has no such opportunity.

One income maintenance program that would deal with this phenomenon that has been proposed several times is called the *negative income tax.* Under this proposal, people with incomes below a certain level would not pay taxes on that income. Families with no taxable income would receive a cash grant equal to the amount of their personal exemptions if they had filed an income tax return. For example, under the current personal income tax structure that allows $1,000 exemption for each person a family of four would receive a cash grant of $4,320.00. This allows the family to take advantage of the same tax exemptions offered to middle and upper income families. A negative income tax program is a form of guaranteed income, even though it would probably be administered by the Internal Revenue Service instead of traditional welfare agencies.

Several advantages of the negative income tax exist. They include avoiding "welfare stigma;" eliminating categorical assistance; increasing administrative efficiency and cost effectiveness, since a single agency would be involved in administering the program; and universal provision. But of course there are also disadvantages to such a program. The assistance provided might be inadequate and in-kind support programs provided along with current programs may be withdrawn, causing new hardship. This type of program seems to have been more politically acceptable.

## The Role of Social Work in Income Maintenance Services

The financial assistance provision was motivated by humanitarian concern for human needs. One of the mechanisms developed to meet human need in the U.S. at the turn of the century, the private charity movement, was responsible in part for the emergence of social work as a profession. The charity workers' (later to be called social workers) primary responsibility was to assess the needs of the poor and to provide financial assistance to them. As professional education evolved (1900–1950), many social workers were educated in the social casework method, which enabled them to better serve their clients. They were better prepared to assume positions in private relief granting agencies, but also in the public welfare agencies that were created by the Social Security Act of 1935. A variety of roles were performed by professional social workers in these agencies, including child welfare positions, and caseworkers in public assistance, now called income maintenance. Schools of social work throughout the 1930s, 40s and 50s, focused on educating social workers for employment in the public welfare field.[30]

Although social work continued to evolve and move into other areas of need, it has remained involved in public welfare. Today large numbers of social workers are employed in public social agencies or have been at one time. But direct involvement by professionally educated social workers in income maintenance services has declined over the years, particularly since the 1970s when income maintenance was separated from social and rehabilitative services in public welfare agencies. Prior to this time, workers involved with income maintenance recipients were also offering social services that assisted in solving problems associated with economic needs. Many people needed income maintenance as a result of social or psychological problems that interfered with their attempts to be self-supporting. Social work placed an emphasis on utilizing the knowledge and skills of professionally educated workers who could effectively interact with recipients, with the goal of reducing or eliminating their need for economic assistance. This model of service to public assistance recipients was created through the 1962 amendments to the Social Security Act, which required that recipients of AFDC be offered a broad array of social services in addition to income maintenance. In the 1970s, people in the system started to realize that this pattern of service delivery had not achieved the desired results. Some believed that services should not be imposed on income maintenance recipients. Consequently, income maintenance and social services are officially separated in public social agencies today. Many professionally educated social workers, as a result of the separation, became involved in social services delivery in the public agencies and are no longer involved in the income maintenance services. Some professional social workers, usually MSWs, remain in income maintenance services, mostly as administrators, supervisors, researchers, and program planners.[31]

In recent years, some BSWs have begun to assume direct service positions in income maintenance services. A recent study reported that over one-half of the administrators surveyed would prefer to have direct service positions in income maintenance filled by the baccalaureate-level social worker.[32] The administrators feel that many recipients do indeed have additional needs, and that professional knowledge and skills are needed by direct service workers to establish the relationship with clients, to discern both their economic and social needs, and to link them with appropriate social services.

## A Case Study

Pamela M., a twenty-two year old woman, with two preschool age children, recently separated from her husband, came into the agency to apply for Aid for Families with Dependent Children (AFDC). Her case was assigned to Mr. B., a BSW social worker employed as an economic assistance caseworker. During her initial interview with Mr. B., he assisted Pamela in completing the necessary AFDC eligibility applications and determined that she was eligible. In discussing her situation and her need for AFDC, Mr. B. learned that Pamela's husband had abandoned the family, leaving them without economic support. Pamela seemed to be distraught and stated that the family had been having difficulties, including some abuse of her and the children by the husband. One of the children had a genetic disorder and special medical needs. She had

*continued*

no friends or extended family on whom she could call for assistance or support. In addition, Mr. B. learned that while Pamela had a high school education, she had no particular employment or vocational skills. Because she had been left totally responsible for the care of the children, she said she felt overwhelmed and was beginning to lose her temper with them, and was afraid she might abuse them. She also stated she had been thinking about having the children placed in foster care or possibly giving them up for adoption.

Using the knowledge and skills he had received in his professional education, Mr. B. assessed Pamela's situation and concluded that she was experiencing problems that would certainly require additional social services in addition to AFDC. He referred her to the county general assistance office and explained that they would help her with her immediate financial needs until her AFDC check arrived. He made an appointment for her to apply for food stamps. He asked the community's Easter Seal Society about assistance for the child with special medical problems. He also referred her to the family services unit of the AFDC office so that a family service social worker could help her sort out her feelings about her children and discuss her parenting skills.

Social workers in the income maintenance field of practice have done much to improve public social welfare policy affecting the delivery of income maintenance services. Much of this has been done through the work of professional organizations such as the National Association of Social Workers (NASW), the American Public Welfare Association (APWA), and the National Conference on Social Welfare (NCSW). These organizations, whose membership is largely social workers, have advocated, endorsed, and supported increases in AFDC and SSI assistance grants to insure an adequate standard of living for recipients, alternative proposals, such as guaranteed income programs, national health insurance, and other programs that would provide additional income to those in need and plans that would allow humane, dignified delivery of the economic assistance programs.

# Summary

Income maintenance has been influenced not by one predominent value and philosophy, but by several, including humanitarian concerns and societal responsibility, the work ethic and "blaming the victim." The current income maintenance programs meet some needs, but they are far from perfect. Answering the question "Where do we go from here?"

involves considering alternatives to the current system. Social work has always been a part of this field of practice, but the professionals should recommit themselves to this crucial area of service. The exact structure or direction that income maintenance will take in the future is unknown. However, some alteration in the structure is inevitable.

## Key Terms

Aid to Families with Dependent Children (AFDC)
developmental approach
Family Assistance Plan (FAP)
fields of practice
food stamps
General Assistance (GA)
Grants-in-Aid
Guaranteed Income Programs
income maintenance

income transfer
institutional approach
Jobs and Income Security Program (JISP)
negative income tax
residual approach
Supplemental Security Income (SSI)
workfare
Work Incentive program (WIN)

## Questions for Discussion

1. Discuss the term income maintenance. What are income maintenance programs designed to do?

2. Discuss the values, philosophies, and motivations which influenced the structure of income maintainance services historically? Which ones currently do this?

3. Of what importance are the English Poor Laws in the development of income maintainance services in the United States? Do they continue to influence these programs today? How?

4. Discuss the reasons why the American colonists developed responses to human need patterned after the English Poor Laws?

5. What is general assistance? How does it differ from the state-federal programs of AFDC and SSI?

6. Discuss why the AFDC program is the most often criticized welfare program in the United States today. Do you think these criticisms are valid? Why do you think so?

7. Why were the categorical programs serving the aged, blind, and disabled combined into the general program of Supplemental Secur-

rity Income? Are the needs of recipients better met through SSI than through the old categorical programs?

8. Discuss the reasons welfare reform has been a source of concern in the United States during the last two decades? Are the current programs adequate or inadequate in your estimation?

9. Discuss welfare reform proposals that have emerged in the last two decades. Why were they not accepted? What direction do you think the alternatives to the present system should take?

10. Discuss the roles and functions that social workers have in income maintenance. Should social work make a stronger commitment to this field of practice in the future?

# Notes

1. Donald Brieland, Lela Costin, and Charles Atherton, *Contemporary Social Work: An Introduction to Social Work and Social Welfare* (New York: McGraw Hill Book Co.; 1980). p. 173.
2. Ralph Dolgoff and Donald Feldstein, *Understanding Social Welfare* (New York: Longman, 1984), pp. 18–20.
3. Dolgoff, *Social Welfare*, pp. 3–8.
4. Harold L. Wilenksy and Charles LeBeaux, *Industrial Society and Social Welfare* (New York: The Free Press, 1958).
5. Wilenksy, *Industrial Society*.
6. Wilenksy, *Industrial Society*, p. 106.
7. Based on the writings of Alfred Kahn and John Romanyshyn, Ralph Dolgoff and Donald Feldstein have offered the developmental conceptualization of social welfare. See *Understanding Social Welfare*, p. 107–133.
8. Walter Trattner, *From Poor Law to Welfare State* (New York: The Free Press, 1979), p. 4–5.
9. Trattner, *From Poor Law*, p. 5.
10. Trattner, *From Poor Law*, p. 5.
11. Trattner, *From Poor Law*, p. 5.
12. Trattner, *From Poor Law*, p. 7.
13. Trattner, *From Poor Law*, p. 7.
14. Walter Friedlander and Robert Z. Apte, *Introduction to Social Welfare* (Englewood Cliffs NJ: Prentice-Hall, 1980), p. 15.
15. Beulah R. Compton, *Introduction to Social Welfare and Social Work* (Homewood, Ill.: The Dorsey Press, 1980), p. 156–157.
16. June Axinn and Herman Levin, *Social Welfare: A History of the American Response to Need* (New York: Harper & Row Publishers, 1982), p. 19.
17. Trattner, *From Poor Laws*, p. 14–15.
18. Trattner, *From Poor Laws*, p. 20.
19. For detailed discussion of the forerunners of charity and philanthropic movements see Trattner's *From Poor Laws*, chapter 3, and Compton, *Social Welfare*, chapter 11.
20. Compton, *Social Welfare*, chapter 9.

21 A detailed discussion of Social Darwinism may be found in Dolgoff, *Social Welfare*, pp. 77–78, Compton, *Social Welfare*, chapter 15, and Macarov, *Design* (New York: Holt, Rinehart & Winston, 1978), chapter 9.

22 H. Wayne Johnson. *The Social Services: An Introduction* (Itraska, IL: Peacock Publishers, 1982), p. 61.

23 Skidmore and Thackeray, p. 208.

24 Skidmore and Thackeray, p. 209.

25 Norman L. Wyers. "Income Maintenance System," *Encyclopedia of Social Work*, ed. (Silver Spring MD: National Association of Social Workers, 1968), p. 888–898.

26 Andrew Doblestein. *Politics, Economics, and Public Welfare*. Englewood Cliffs, NJ: Prentice Hall, Inc., 1980, p. 121.

27 Trattner, *From Poor Laws*, p. 261

28 Ronald C. Federico, *The Social Welfare Institution: An Introduction* (Lexington, MA: D.C. Heath and Co., 1984), p. 123–124.

29 Doblestein, *Politics*, p. 122.

30 Irving Weissman and Mary R. Baker, *Education for Social Workers in the Public Social Services* (New York: Council on Social Work Education, 1959).

31 Ginsberg, *Practice of Social Work*, p. 16.

32 Norman L. Wyers, "Income Maintenance Revisited: Functions, Skills, and Boundries," *Administration in Social Work* 5 (Summer 1981): 20.

## Suggested Readings

Axinne, June, and Levin, Herman. *Social Welfare: A History of the American Response to Need*. 2nd ed., New York: Harper & Row Publishers, 1982.

Compton, Beulah R. *Introduction to Social Welfare and Social Work*. Homewood, IL: The Dorsey Press, 1980.

Dolgoff, Ralph, and Feldstein, Donald. *Understanding Social Welfare*. 2nd ed., New York: Longman, 1984.

de Schweintz, Karl. *England's Road To Social Security*. Philadelphia: University of Pennsylvania Press, 1943.

Federico, Ronald C. *The Social Welfare Institution*. Lexington, MA: D.C. Heath and Company, 1984.

Skidmore, Rex A., and Thackeray, Milton G. *Introduction to Social Work*. Englewood Cliffs, NJ: Prentice-Hall, 1982.

# Chapter 8

## Services for Children

Statements such as "the future of America lies in its young," and "children are America's most precious resource," attest to the strong value our society places on children. The well-being of children is a source of social concern; the protection and care of children is one of the oldest forms of charity. In today's world, the social welfare arrangements that respond to children's needs are organized under the broad term *child welfare services*. This encompasses the programs and services provided both by public social service agencies and by private and voluntary service agencies.

*Child welfare*, like social welfare is a broad concept and can be defined in broad terms. Two definitions are provided here to demonstrate this breadth. Child welfare is a "series of activities and programs through which society expresses its special concern for children and its willingness to assume responsibility for some children until they are able to care for themselves."[1] Child welfare is further broadly defined as "whatever is considered essential for the child to develop fully and to function effectively in society.[2] Child welfare can also be defined narrowly. Much of the focus in child welfare services has been on the needs of children and families when family functioning, particularly parental functioning, has broken down, or when children's developmental, emotional, or behavioral functioning has made it impossible for them to remain within the family setting.[3] This definition narrows the perspective on child welfare by considering the relationship between family functioning and the well-being of children. It has been suggested that the key to maintaining the well-being of children is to support and strengthen the family. Traditionally, formal social welfare structures have ignored this idea. Only within recent times has the social welfare delivery system and the profession of social work begun to recognize the importance of the family for the child.[4] Child welfare, then, is our society's way of acting out the high value it places on the well-being of its children.

# The Scope of Child Welfare Services

The child welfare service system has traditionally provided two broad areas of service. First, it has provided services to insure the child's maintenance within the family setting. Second, it has provided services to children who are unable to remain in their own homes. Services in the first area include: day-care services, homemaker services, protective services, health services, nutrition services, income maintenance, mental health services, family counseling services, educational services, and services to unmarried parents. Services in the second area include: foster family care, institutional care, group homes, and adoption services. These two service areas have become linked together in a service delivery network or system. The system engages in services activities designed to prevent, deal with the consequences of, or otherwise provide solutions to problems potentially jeopardizing the welfare of children. In recent years, much effort has gone into developing and providing services to children in their natural homes, which is consistent with the recently renewed interest in and value placed on preserving families and providing permanency for children. When this is not possible, children have been provided with a permanent family arrangement, such as placement with relatives or adoption.

# The Historical Development of Services to Children

The emergence of services to children in the United States can be traced to colonial times. The development of formal social welfare arrangements and services to children have taken many forms since then, each influenced by the economic climate of the times, and by on going social movements and social change. To attempt to understand today's structure and systems of services to children, it is necessary to understand the events and trends from the past that have shaped its development.

## Colonial Times to 1880: Mutual Aid and Poor Law Arrangements

The early colonists, inspired by the sense of freedom gained by being in a new land, emphasized self-sufficiency. Families were the basic social and economic unit within colonial society. Children were afforded no special status or role within the family as they are today. They were

Table 8.1  Important Dates: Services for Children

| | |
|---|---|
| 1727 | Ursuline Convent, first established orphanage in the United States |
| 1853 | New York Childrens Aid Society was formed |
| 1874 | New York Society for the Prevention of Cruelty to Children was founded |
| 1909 | First White House Conference on Children |
| 1912 | U.S. Childrens Bureau formed |
| 1920 | Child Welfare League of America (CWLA) was founded |
| 1921 | Sheppard-Towner Act |
| 1972 | Stanley versus Illinois Supreme Court Decision |
| 1975 | Title XX Amendments to the Social Security Act were passed by Congress. Also P.L. 94-142 Education of all Handicapped Children Act |
| 1978 | Indian Child Welfare Act |
| 1980 | Adoptions Assistance and Child Welfare Reform Act |
| 1981 | Omnibus Reconciliation Act reorganized some Title XX services for children |

expected, along with all members of the family, to contribute to everyone's maintenance and well-being. Children's individual needs were superceded by family needs. When problems arose that overwhelmed the family's abilities to solve them, mutual aid was the mechanism for assistance. Formal social welfare structures were nonexistent. Colonists were expected to have a sense of duty, to lend a hand, to assist others in the struggle for survival. As the population grew, however, mutual aid became impractical for some situations and was supplemented by formal means influenced by the English Poor Laws.

The harsh and bitter realities of daily living in the colonies resulted in high infant and adult mortality rates. As a result, many children became orphaned and dependent. Colonial officials became concerned about the children from poor, dependent families, or the "children of paupers" as they were called. They feared that these children were inevitably destined to a life of pauperism if they were not taught to become self-sufficient.[5] Thus, dependent and orphaned children were cared for within the traditions of the poor laws. Several measures of care were employed. Some children were maintained within their own families through provision of outdoor relief, that is, assistance provided directly to the family. Some families and children were actually auctioned off to individuals or families who had agreed to care for them.

One common practice was to apprentice children to families in which they could be taught a trade or skill and thus become self-sufficient. The practice of *apprenticeship* reflected the belief that all individuals should be a part of a family. On a more practical level, it provided a useful way to control and discipline children, reduce unemployment, provide skilled workers to meet the needs of the growing colonies, and to relieve public officials from the responsibility of directly caring for needy children. Other children were placed in the care of relatives. Many other families and children were placed in almshouses by the authorities. Some religious groups cared for children within their group by placing them with members of that faith in either institutions or private homes. During this period, a few special institutions were created for the care of orphaned or dependent children via the charity-philanthropy arrangements. These *orphanages* were homes that provided care for children whose parents had died or abandoned them. The Ursuline Convent, established in New Orleans in 1727, was the first formally established orphanage in the United States. After the American Revolution, the same patterns of care for children continued virtually unchanged until recent years. Emphasis was placed on low-cost care, and on the teaching of virtues of industry and self-sufficiency.

## The 1800s: Private Charity-Philanthropy Arrangements

Social change in the latter part of the 1800s fostered the development of formal structures in social welfare, including the care of dependent children. Although earlier patterns of response to children's needs continued, some changes occurred that shaped the direction for the future.

One of the most striking changes was the creation of special child care institutions for dependent and truly orphaned children, under the auspices of the states and private and religious organizations. The impetus for their creation came from a reaction to the evils of almshouses. Children placed in almshouses received no special care and were treated no differently than the adults placed there. Society began to worry about the effects of placing children in institutions with the sick, physically disabled, mentally retarded, mentally ill, delinquent, or criminal. Conditions were deplorable. Treatment was often harsh and brutal. As a result, dependent and orphaned children began to be placed in orphanages rather than almshouses. Since economics was uppermost in the minds of public officials, change was slow to come. It was cheaper and more economically efficient to invest public funds in almshouses rather than to subsidize child care in private institutions. Toward the end of the nineteenth century several states passed laws prohibiting the placement of children in almshouses. Other practices, such as apprenticeship and indenturing, also came under a great deal of attack. *Indenturing* was beginning to be considered a form of slavery. This had become a sensitive issue in the aftermath of the U.S. Civil War.

Concern over these issues created a climate for additional reforms in formal child welfare structures. The first of these reforms was the emergence of *Childrens Aid Societies*. These organizations were concerned with "child saving," rescuing children from the harsh realities of urban life and the insensitive practices of the public poor law system. In 1853, the New York Childrens Aid Society, was founded primarily through the efforts of a young minister named Charles Loring Brace. Brace and his followers, although sensitive to the needs of dependent children, were far more concerned with the protection of property and the city from what he considered the "dangerous classes, which included homeless and delinquent children."[6] Although he created programs within the city for dependent youth, Brace's main priority was to remove dependent and orphaned children from the city. He rounded up children off the streets and sent them by train to family homes far away in the rural areas of the west and midwest in the belief that such children needed a family upbringing in a clean, moral home, away from the evils of the city life. Over the next twenty-five years (1854–1880), the New York Childrens Aid Society placed more than fifty-thousand children in such homes. This was heralded as a major innovation in the care of dependent children, but also was criticized as nothing more than a form of indenturing. Another problem with Brace's program was that, in some instances, siblings were separated. Some families overworked the children, failed to properly educate them, physically abused them, and poorly fed them. Nevertheless, this program is considered to the forerunner of the *foster care* service as we know it today.[7]

In the years that followed, Childrens Aid Societies in other states developed similar practices, but much more care was taken in recruiting and selecting the family homes. Placements were also followed and reviewed periodically. In the beginning, the homes were free homes; families would take in children out of the goodness of their hearts. Gradually, public officials in several states began to place children in foster homes at public expense: Massachusetts in the late 1800s was one of the first states to begin to actually pay foster parents for child care. This started a new era in child welfare and in some states replaced institutional care as the primary method of dealing with dependent children.[8] Institutional care for children with special needs continued to be supplied by both public and private child care organizations.

In the latter half of the nineteenth century two additional formal structures for the care of children emerged. These were the Charity Organization Societies (COS) and the settlement houses. COS indirectly contributed to children's well-being by focusing on their maintenance within the family. And the friendly visitors understood well the effects of poverty on children. Casework services were designed to preserve the integrity of family life. Likewise, but through different approaches and means, some of the settlement workers' social reform efforts focused on child welfare issues, (e.g., child labor legislation, education of immigrant children, and the creation of the first juvenile court). The work of these two private charitable groups furthered the cause of protecting and caring for dependent children.

Toward the middle of the nineteenth century, the United States began to experience the effects of the industrial revolution, with its massive social change. The family's functions as a social institution changed and society began to assume some of the responsibilities for the socialization of children that families had held exclusively before. The passage of compulsory education laws is one example. With a new understanding of child development came the recognition that children had certain rights that parents were responsible for protecting. If these rights were not protected, states reserved the right to intervene on behalf of the child. States passed legislation providing for legal guardianship and adoption. This principle not only formed the foundation for the juvenile justice system, but was also applied to cases of child mistreatment. Reform in this area came first from the private sector, eventually spreading into the public sector. In 1874, the New York Society for the Prevention of Cruelty to Children was founded. Its purpose was to advocate on behalf of abused children, to insure their ongoing protection from harm. Although their aims centered on the prosecution of individuals suspected of child abuse and not on rehabilitative services, their work brought about a public awareness of the child abuse problem.

By the end of the 1800s, formal structures for child care had been created. Although these structures have changed substantially through the years, much remains that can be traced to the developments of this era. The changes of the 1800s were instrumental in preparing the way for new innovations that followed.

## 1900s: Public Welfare and Social Services

In 1909, the first White House Conference on Children was held, marking a shift in child welfare priorities, philosophies, and policies. The delegates to the conference went on record as promoting and supporting the principle that children need stable home environments. At all costs, resources and services should be directed toward maintaining them in their own homes. They recognized that children's basic needs usually could be met through the natural family—if adequate resources, supports, and services were provided. No longer should child welfare systems remove children from their homes solely on the basis of inadequate family income. These new philosophies recognized federal responsibility in this area. In 1912, Congress provided legislation to authorize the development of the *Children's Bureau*. Spearheading the effort to create the bureau were early social workers Jane Addams and Lillian Wald. Julia Lathrop was appointed as the first bureau chief. In the beginning, the Children's Bureau activities were restricted to broad responsibilities, such as investigating and reporting all matters related to the well-being of all children, including economic, health, child placement and labor concerns, and activities of the juvenile courts and state legislation affecting children.[9]

In 1921, the efforts of the Children's Bureau were substantially bolstered by the passage of the *Sheppard-Towner Act*. This legislation gave the Bureau the responsibility for administering a grants-in-aid program to the states for maternal and child health services. By 1929, when the program was discontinued, almost three thousand child and maternal health programs had been established in forty-five states, primarily in rural areas. The Children's Bureau, however, for many years continued to be the guiding force in the child welfare system. Its roles and missions have changed over the years, but it remains today as a separate office within the U.S. Department of Health and Human Services.

The Social Security Act of 1935 launched the federal government into a joint partnership with the states in responsibility for broad social welfare programs and services, like the widow's pension or mothers aid movement and later Aid to Families with Dependent Children (AFDC). In addition, the Social Security Act's social insurance program gradually provided benefits to survivors (widows and dependent children). In 1971, the Supplemental Security Income (SSI) program extended income maintenance assistance to families of permanently or totally disabled children. Other forms of federal financial and income maintenance assistance are provided through veterans pensions. Native American children receive some aid through the U.S. Bureau of Indian Affairs.

The Social Security Act also made funds available on grants-in-aid basis to the states to develop social and rehabilitative services. Beginning in the late 1930s, the states created child welfare programs within their public welfare agencies. Public welfare departments at first focused on traditional child welfare services, such as child protection, foster care, institutional care, and adoptions. In the 1960s, the Department of Health, Education, and Welfare mandated the separation of social and rehabilitative services that previously had been combined with income maintenance services. Child welfare services, which had always been a separate function, were reorganized under this structure. Additional funding fostered growth in child welfare services. New service programs like day-care, family homemaker services, services to unmarried parents were added. In the late 1960s, public social service agencies were permitted by amendments to the Social Security Act to purchase services from private child welfare agencies, family service agencies, and mental health centers. This solidified the overall delivery system and linked the public social service system with the private system.

Private child welfare agencies, as outgrowths of the private-charitable organizations, had for many years provided many of the same types of child welfare services as public agencies. The movement to organize the system of private agencies received its major impetus from the Child Welfare League of America (CWLA) founded in 1920. The mission of the CWLA is to set standards, coordinate, and accreditate child welfare agencies. In addition, the CWLA has expanded its roles to include research, information-sharing, and the education of social workers working in the field. The CWLA is a powerful force, shaping the direction and future of child welfare services.[10]

## Current Trends, Issues, and Concerns

Although many positive developments occurred in the 1970s, several trends and issues continued to be discussed within the field. In 1975, Congress passed the Title XX Amendments to the Social Security Act, which reorganized public social services by shifting some administrative, planning, and policy decision-making back to the individual states. The impact of Title XX on child welfare services was minimal. Most states continued to provide a complete program of child welfare services, despite the fact that Title XX created ceilings of federal funding for social services. Perhaps the most controversial aspect of Title XX was its gradual shifting of responsibility for social welfare from the federal government to the states. This has become more of a source of concern in recent years because less populated, rural states find the federal funding reductions make it difficult to maintain the services they are now providing to children.

In 1981, Congress passed the Omnibus Reconciliation Act, which again reorganized the social services program created by Title XX. Under this new act, funding for some programs, including some child welfare programs, were consolidated into *block grants* with annual reductions in funding. These grants consolidate many service programs into a single source of funding as opposed to funding each program. Under block grants single services may receive less funding. Advocacy and lobbying efforts were somewhat successful in keeping many child welfare programs out of the block grants, but some programs experienced recent cuts in federal funding. Most of the cuts have been in programs such as AFCD, Medicaid, child nutrition programs, school lunch programs, and others. Traditional child welfare programs, such as protective services, foster care, or adoption, appear to be holding their own at the present time. But current economic and political trends cause some concern for the future of even these.

The effects of poverty on children also remains an issue and a source of current concern. In a recent publication, the American Public Welfare Association reported that the current poverty rate among children is at its highest level since 1965.[11] Cuts in AFCD and Medicaid funding do not paint a bright picture for the future.

Prejudice and discrimination are still big problems in the field of child welfare. The treatment and services afforded to minority children remains inadequate.[12] For example, only within the last fifty years have the needs of black children been considered. Prior to this time, the black community cared for its children. Even though laws require that minority children receive the same standards of care given to white children, such is not the case; widespread discrimination continues to exist within the system.[13]

In recent years, the picture for native American children has become brighter, thanks to the passage by Congress of the *Indian Child Welfare Act of 1978*. Under this act, native American tribes are afforded the right to intervene in child welfare matters that affect a tribe's children. They have the right to assume legal jurisdiction over Indian children and provide plans for their ongoing care. This has given native American people a voice and a measure of self-determination in the care of their children.

Another current issue is the problem of children remaining in foster care or some form of institutional care for long periods of time. Priorities in child welfare have shifted from out-of-home care to serving children in their own homes. For children in need of placement outside their natural homes, the emphasis is now on short-term placements. The family is given help in the form of counseling, and eventually the child is returned to the home. Because thousands of children have remained in care for extended periods of time, Congress in 1980 passed the Adoptions Assistance and Child Welfare Reform Act. This act provided funding incentives for the states to develop mechanisms for *permanency planning* for children. Plans are to be developed in cooperation with the courts, by reviewing the legal status of children, by providing services that return children to natural families, or by making permanent arrangements for children through placement with relatives or through adoption. As an attempt to create a stable environment for children, permanency planning has become the core of all child welfare services provided by both private and governmental agencies.

As can be seen, child welfare services historically protected and provided alternative care for dependent and orphaned children. As time passed, new social welfare structures and arrangements have come into play as responses to the overall economic, social, and emotional needs of children. In today's world, a well-established delivery system provides child welfare services.

# Current Child Welfare Services

The current emphasis in child welfare services is on the blending together into one framework the two traditional areas of service—those designed to maintain the child in natural family settings, and those that offer substitute care outside the natural family—called a permanency framework. All child welfare services today primarily focus on creating conditions of permanency in the lives of children.

## Protective Services

Recent developments have demonstrated that children can be protected from harm, through supportive efforts designed to remedy the social conditions and problems in family functioning that would otherwise result in children being removed from their homes. *Child Protective Services* (CPS), a broad area of service within the child welfare field, is specifically designed for this purpose. The basic aims of child protective services are as follows:

> To guard children from further detrimental experiences or conditions in their immediate situations, bring under control and reduce the risks to their safety and or well-being, prevent further neglect or abuse, and restore adequate parental functioning whenever possible or, if necessary, take steps to remove children from their own homes and establish them in foster situations in which they will receive more adequate care.[14]

In recent years, protective services has placed primary emphasis on modifying social conditions and problems in parental functioning, to allow children to remain with the family. Removing children from their homes usually is done only if a child is in immediate danger due to parental or family circumstances (for example, because of abuse or neglect), or, if after an extensive period of intervention, circumstances and problems within the family have shown no improvement. In either case, efforts are made to insure that the child's placement in foster care is of short duration. Intervention is focused on preparing the family and the child for the child's eventual return to her or his natural home.

Child protective services are mainly involuntary, that is, they are imposed on families. (In rare instances, a family will make a request for such services.) In most states, public social service agencies are mandated by law to protect children. In some states these functions are performed by special protective service providers such as units within family or juvenile courts, private child welfare agencies, law enforcement agencies, or child protection teams composed of public social service, medical, mental health, and law enforcement personnel. Whatever the arrangement, the agency or team is responsible, by legal sanction, for receiving referrals, investigating, and intervening with families to insure that children receive their rights to adequate care and protection from harm.[15] Physical abuse, parental neglect, and sexual exploitation and abuse are the most common family problems requiring the attention and intervention of child protection authorities. No social problem in recent years has brought forth such an outpouring of public outrage and concern as has that of *child abuse*. Increased attention in the media and rigorous public education campaigns have brought the plight of victimized children into a national focus.

CHILD ABUSE    Concern for protecting children is exemplified by the *child abuse and neglect reporting laws*, present in all fifty states. These laws usually require selected professionals to report suspected child abuse situations to child protection authorities. The general public is also encouraged to report child abuse and neglect.

The physical abuse of children may be defined as physical injury, or anything that threatens or jeopardizes the well-being or life of a child. These include violent methods of discipline, including beatings that cause lacerations, abrasions, bone or skull fractures, or intentional burning.

Parental neglect appears to be on the increase and is perhaps more damaging to children because of its subtle nature and the fact that it occurs over extended periods of time before being called to the attention of the authorities. The neglect of children involves deprivation of the physical necessities of life, as well as emotional security and affection, or education, or medical care. It may also involve inadequate supervision, abandonment, or providing an environment injurious to the child's welfare.

Sexual exploitation and abuse has most recently received a great deal of media exposure. Consequently, child protection agencies, law enforcement, and the courts have focused attention and effort on this problem. The sexual abuse of children may include parent-child incest initiated by either or both parents; forcing a child into sexual activity by stepparents, relatives, or family friends; the rape of a child by a stranger; and sexual exploitation of children, such as prostitution or pornography. Child victims range in age from infants to adolescents.

The incidence of physical and *sexual abuse*, and parental neglect is thought to be extensive, yet no accurate measures are available to fully document their existence. If accurate measures were available, physical abuse might become the leading cause of death among children. Within the last ten years research has focused on documenting the incidence of child abuse. In 1974, Kempe estimated that 60,000 children were victimized by abuse each year.[16] The National Humane Society in 1978 reported 614,000 confirmed cases of child abuse in the United States. By

1979, the figure had risen to 711,000 confirmed cases.[17] A study conducted from 1974 through 1980 by the National Center on Child Abuse and Neglect estimated that the number of children being mistreated in some way was 10.5 children per 1,000. This included estimates of unreported cases as well as reported cases. Their estimate for physical abuse was 3.4 children per 1,000. Studies on the incidence of sexual abuse, including incest and other types of abuse, report varying rates of child abuse. In 1981, the National Center on Child Abuse and Neglect estimated an annual incest rate of 100,000 cases per year. A study in 1982 estimated the annual rate of incest to be nearly 250,000 cases per year. Some recent estimates indicate that close to one million children annually are victims of physical and sexual abuse.[18]

CAUSES OF CHILD ABUSE AND NEGLECT   The causes that precipitate physical child abuse and neglect cannot be isolated into separate, specific factors. Physical abuse and neglect results from multiple and interacting events, conditions, and circumstances that vary with the family situation.[19] Much research has focused on identifying contributing factors and causes. In the 1960s, Kempe and Helfer engaged in research stemming from their work with physically abused and neglected children. Several years later, their findings were organized into a theory that they termed "the battered child syndrome."[20] Their conclusion was that a multitude of interacting factors appear to predispose certain families to develop abusive relationships.

Other research concluded that three broad areas of interacting situational factors seem to precipitate physical abuse and neglect. They are (1) environmental and situational stresses, (2) characteristics of the parent(s), and (3) characteristics of the children that make them vulnerable or prone to physical abuse or neglect.[21]

Again it must be made clear that none of these factors alone is sufficient to produce abuse or neglect: it is the interaction between them that does so. Environmental and situational stresses may include economic stress resulting from loss of income caused by unemployment, or social isolation, or physical illness, or dysfunction in the marital or parent-child relationships. Predisposing characteristics of parents include abuse by their own parents; ignorance; poor training of parenting skills; poor socialization of parenting roles; impulsive behavior; inability to resolve frustrations and control anger; psychological disturbances such as depression, personality disorders, and mental illness; unrealistic expectations of child behavior; and the abuse or dependence on alcohol or other chemical substances. Abused and neglected children may also possess characteristics—such as demanding and unacceptable behaviors, rejecting the parents gestures of love and affection—that lead to episodes of child abuse.

The causes of sexual abuse include poor parental self-concepts and sexual identification, unsatisfactory sexual relationship within the marriage, intimate situations between parent and child, an older, sexually attractive child seeking attention through covert or overt seductive behavior, a child's exposure to adult sexual behavior, and parents who may have also been victims themselves.[22]

In all forms of child abuse and neglect, cautious assessment of causative factors is imperative to avoid stereotyping. Each case needs to be approached with respect for its individual nature. (See the case study provided later in this chapter for an illustration of how child abuse and neglect might be treated by a protective services worker.)

## Role of Social Workers in Protective Services

The treatment approaches used and the roles assumed by social workers in protective services vary from situation to situation, depending on the needs and problems present within the family. However, social workers in protective services generally assume two primary roles. First and foremost, they must be primarily concerned with the ongoing protection of the child. Secondly, they must prepare an intervention plan that will help the family remove the conditions or resolve the problems that have caused the intervention and placed the child at risk. Serious cases, or cases where parental cooperation is not assured, may require the further intervention of family or juvenile courts to insure the child is protected from parental abuse or neglect.

Intervention may involve direct counseling with the family and extensive use of agency and community resources, such as homemaker services, foster care, medical and health care services, mental health services, economic assistance resources, nutritional services, parent education services, and drug and alcohol treatment services. Treatment approaches and arrangements will vary from community to community.

## Day-Care Services

*Day-care services* for children is an area of service within child welfare. Today it is very common for both parents in a family to be employed, creating a dependence on alternative child care arrangements. Other family circumstances may also require day-care services. Children from families with parent(s) involved in educational or vocational training, or children from troubled families are placed in day-care facilities to give the parents needed respite. Children with special needs (the physically, mentally, emotionally, or behaviorally handicapped) may also make use of specialized day-care services.[23] Many day-care centers, preschools, and other such agencies receive federal funding to support the costs of child care. Family day-care (day care of children in a family or home setting) is another form of this service, and again, depending of family eligibility, may be subsidized by federal or state funding sources. Most states require that child-care agencies, organizations, and family day-care homes be licensed to provide such services. Day-care services for children perform a vital function by providing a substitute for family care that focuses on the health, educational, social, and recreational needs of children.

## Homemaker Services

*Homemaker services* to children and families are provided by both public social services and private agencies. They are designed to care for children within their own homes, when they cannot receive adequate parental care. Homemakers are assigned to families to help with overall family maintenance. Homemakers, usually women, are trained in child care, home management, and in some instances home health care tasks. They may be assigned for a few hours a week or on a full-time basis, depending on family need.

Family situations that may require homemaker services include protective service cases, the absence of one parent, the physical or mental incapacitation of one or both parents, or the death of one parent. Homemakers may also teach home management skills, child care skills or home health care skills to parents whose immaturity or ignorance may have placed family welfare in jeopardy. Homemaker services are most often provided to low-income families; however, at times, almost any family may find them useful. Recent funding to support such services has declined, causing their curtailment.

## School Social Services

An integral, crucial part of a child's life are his or her educational experiences. Much of a child's future is dependent on the opportunity to receive a successful education. In the last century, educators and professional social workers have combined efforts to insure that the educational needs of children are met. Large numbers of trained social workers have been employed in community schools throughout the country. In the early 1970s, the Education of All Handicapped Children Act (PL-94-142) intensified and broadened the tasks and roles of social workers in the schools.[24] School social workers mediate among students, parents, schools, and the community. Problems that arise from the interaction among these groups or have the potential of jeopardizing the child's education are focused on by the social worker. [25] School social workers provide individual and family counseling, group counseling for children with special needs, act as advocates with the school or community for educational services, act as a liaison between the home and school environments, help teachers understand the needs of children, assist school administrators with policy formation and planning for educational needs, and act as a liaison between the school and community social service agencies.

Nutrition services are also provided by public and private agencies and organizations supported by federal, state, and local funding. For many years federal funding has supported nutritional services in public and private schools. Nutritional services are also available under the auspices of state and county public health agencies and county extension programs.

## Services to Unmarried Parents

Child welfare and family services agencies have regularly provided services to *unmarried parents*. Although some may question why it is included in a chapter on child welfare services, the rationale lies in the fact that the majority of unmarried parents are adolescents.

Intervention with unmarried parents usually begins at pregnancy. These young people need assistance in many areas of their own lives, as well as in planning for their child. For some time it has been agreed that unmarried parents are a population at risk. They face many potential problems as parents. Services for them focus on the prevention of such problems. The most difficult task facing the social worker is helping the parents decide what they should do about their unborn child. Options usually discussed with unmarried parents are abortion, giving up the child for adoption, or keeping it. This is a difficult decision for unmarried parents. Both the father and mother should make the decision. The social worker needs to take special care in supporting whatever decisions are made through counseling. Services may include economic assistance for prenatal medical care, delivery, and postnatal care; support counseling for unmarried parents and other family members; child management and parenting skills services; foster care services; preadoption release services, and follow-up services.

## Additional Services for Children in Their Own Homes

Other services that help maintain children in natural family settings include health care services, nutrition services, mental health services, and family counseling. Children in AFDC and SSI households are automatically eligible for Medicaid health care services. Health-related services are also available to developmentally disabled children and are provided by both public and private agencies. These services are supported by both federal and state funding. Education and health care services are provided to children with various conditions, including physical and mental handicaps, blindness, and deafness. Public Law 92-142, passed in 1975, substantially bolstered health care services to this population within recent years. Private benevolent community service organizations like the Shriners, Lions Clubs, Elks Clubs, Jaycees, and Rotary Clubs, have developed and made significant contributions for disabled children.[26]

A full range of services are provided by community mental health centers to families and children, including psychological and psychiatric evaluations, child guidance services, and family counseling and therapy. These services are also provided by private family service agencies. The purpose of these services is to strengthen and support families who are experiencing difficulties and to preserve the family unit. Many of the services provided by these agencies are designed to assist with troubled parent-child relationships.

As can be seen, a large number of services are made available to assist children in their own homes. For those children unable to remain in their family settings, the child welfare system provides a multitude of services with an emphasis on permanency planning for the child.

## Substitute Care Services for Children

Every child requires care in order to survive. The process of emotional bonding to other human beings enables the child to develop physically, socially, intellectually, and emotionally. In today's world, many families struggle to perform the child-care tasks and functions expected of them. Social changes that have occurred in this century have placed a considerable burden on the family's independence and self-sufficiency. Lacking supports and under stress, some families find it hard to provide a suitable home for their children.[27] When a child, for whatever reason, is unable to remain in the care of his or her natural parents, *substitute care* is provided to insure that the child's basic needs are met, and that he or she has opportunities for successful growth and development in a nurturing environment.

Why, when, and for what reasons do children need substitute care? The major reason is a breakdown in family functioning, or parental incapacity brought on by environmental stresses.[28] Children needing substitute care may also have special needs that the parents cannot meet, due to their own inabilities to cope, the lack of family resources, or a lack of community resources to meet the child's needs. Children who are afflicted with medical, physical, intellectual, or emotional disabilities also sometimes need substitute care services. Children may need substitute care due to the temporary or permanent loss of one or both parents as a result of death, abandonment, desertion, hospitalization, incarceration, or a parent's decision to surrender the child for adoption. However, children also sometimes need such services in families where both parents are present because of chronic physical or mental illness, physical disabilities, mental retardation, ignorance, emotional immaturity, chemical dependency, neglect, and child abuse.[29]

To avoid the trap of placing blame entirely on family and parental functioning, remember that children may require substitute care services because of the conflict between expected family social roles and environmental conditions that make those roles difficult to perform. This attitude emphasizes how important it is to look closely at the deficiencies in a family's social role performance, and the environmental pressures and stresses that contribute to those deficiencies.[30] Decisions to remove children from their homes and place them in substitute care are not made lightly, and require much careful assessment and planning. Placing children temporarily or permanently also involves the judicial system, where the best interests of children, and due process of law, and the rights of all involved are protected.

## Family Foster Care

Most children needing substitute care need a stable family environment in which to live. *Family foster care* homes often meet that need. Both public social service agencies and private child welfare agencies are authorized to provide family foster home placements for children. Family foster care is the placement of choice whenever possible, and it is the most often used form of substitute care. Family foster homes give children a chance to experience family living with substitute parents and other family members, in a stable environment that meets their physical and emotional needs.[31] Foster families should be harmonious and cohesive family units, so foster children can learn appropriate behavior, roles, and responsibilities. A sincere desire to help troubled children should be the main motivation for families willing to become foster parents—not financial reward.

SELECTING FOSTER PARENTS   The procedures used to recruit and select foster parents vary, but they are usually selected through some form of home study or investigation. In the last several years, a number of states have begun to train foster parents, as a way of professionalizing their services. Training also promotes the concept that foster parents are team members, working hand in hand with agency staff to provide services to children. In most states, foster homes must be licensed to accept children for placement. The biggest problem that remains is that the number of children needing foster home placement exceeds the number of foster homes available.

Recently, much effort has gone into recruiting foster parents from various racial and ethnic groups. Child welfare professionals have become increasingly sensitive to the fact that children need homes that maintain their cultural and racial integrity. Despite efforts to increase the number of minority foster homes, a critical shortage remains.

Some foster children may also have particular educational, medical, or emotional needs, that must be addressed in the placement. Child welfare agencies have begun to develop specialized foster care programs for these children. In the past, many of these children were institutionalized. But now, professionals recognize that some special needs children benefit from family foster home placements, backed up by supportive community services. Agencies have begun to train foster parents to provide the necessary specialized care.

The cost of providing family foster care services is extremely high. The number of children entering foster care placements has increased significantly in recent years, as it has replaced institutionalization as the placement of choice, putting additional burdens on social agencies. Family foster care services are financed both by federal and state funds and by other private funding sources, but the main funding mechanism is Title IV of the Social Security Act, combined with matched state funds. Children placed in foster homes supported by this funding in most states are also eligible for Medicaid services.

Child welfare professionals have recently recognized that children stay in foster care for unneccessary long periods of time, and federal policy in foster care services has focused on shortening the duration of foster care placements. Agencies have emphasized returning children to their natural homes as quickly as possible, or placing them in other alternative permanent placements. The federal government has offered financial incentives to the states, through the *Adoptions Assistance and Child Welfare Reform Act of 1980*, to engage in permanency planning services in the hope that such planning will not only provide cost savings, but more importantly, reduce the time that children spend in temporary placement.

SOCIAL WORK ROLE IN FAMILY FOSTER CARE    Social workers in family foster care have a dual role. One, they are responsible for helping foster parents and children adjust to the placement, and for providing other support services. Second, they must engage in permanency planning for the child's future. This includes intervening with the natural parents so the child can be eventually returned to them. If this is not realistic, the workers must explore alternative resources for the child, such as placement with relatives or adoption. The following case example illustrates the roles assumed by social workers in intervention with a troubled family, including the protective service and substitute care roles.

## A Case Study

Billy and Jody, ages 4 and 3, were removed by the juvenile court from the care of their mother, Elise, due to a long history of both physical and emotional neglect, despite extensive intervention on behalf of the child protective unit (CPU) of the state's social services agency. Elise lacked an adequate income and had many emotional problems, including alcohol abuse. She had established a neglectful pattern of child care that failed to provide adequate food, clothing, and medical care. She left her children unsupervised for extended periods of time and verbally abused them. The CPU considered the home environment one that jeopardized the children's well-being, and they worked with the mother for eight months before they removed the children and placed them in family foster care. Intervention with Elise had included providing homemaker services, involving the county public health nurse and nutrition specialist from the state maternal care health agency, interpersonal counseling at the community mental health center, and services (income and employment assistance and supportive counseling) by the CPU social worker assigned to her case. Elise, for a short time, attended Alcoholics Anonymous meetings. Despite this eight month intervention, the social worker saw little improvement. Thus, the CPU petitioned the court for temporary removal of the children from Elise's care. At the time or removal, the court made it clear that Elise would be given six months to improve her situation to regain custody of her children, or the court would permanently remove them.

The removal of her children did seem to motivate Elise to make the necessary changes to improve her situation. The social worker, realizing that this might not last, also developed alternative plans for permanent ongoing care of the children; placement with relatives or the possibility of adoption was considered. However, during the six months, Elise was able, with the help of the worker and other community services, to alleviate the undesirable situation. She found a regular job and kept it for four months; she became actively involved in Alcoholics Anonymous and remained sober; and she located better housing and made arrangements for good child care while she was working. The children were returned to her care. Subsequent follow-up intervention through supportive CPU services and other community services, made it possible for this mother to regain full custody of her children.

## Institutional and Residential Care Services

Institutions continue to care for and treat children with special needs who cannot benefit from placements in family foster homes. Children needing institutional care range in age from preschoolers to adolescents. Most of these institutions, residential treatment facilities, and group homes care for older children and adolescents. These facilities are operated by public, private, and religious agencies. Currently over 2,000 community-based group homes serve an estimated 20,000 dependent, psychologically disturbed, and socially maladjusted youths.[32] Group homes provide a wide variety of services, including ongoing care, and educational, psychological, emotional, social treatment, and recreational services. Most utilize the community's resources and services. Many also provide services to the families of children placed with them. Children with physical, emotional, and intellectual disabilities, blind or deaf children, children with psychological disorders, delinquent children, and chemically dependent children are all served through these institutions, treatment centers, and group homes. The funding for these services comes from federal, state, and local public tax dollars, and private sources. Although most children placed in such facilities are there because of special needs, they may also require permanency planning services. Social workers in these facilities perform direct service roles, such as individual, family, and group counseling. They also provide indirect services, involving staff coordination and supervision, program planning, advocacy, and staff training.[33]

## Adoption Services

The *adoption* of children by people not related by blood ties is a legal process. Families are created or expanded when the ties between biological parents and children are severed by the courts and legally reestablished with adoptive parents. Adopted children become the legal children of the adoptive parents and are entitled to all the rights and benefits that a biological child would have. Adoption serves a number of purposes. Most importantly, it enables children who are legally free for adoption to have a permanent home that they otherwise might lack. Adoption provides a way for couples who are unable to biologically produce children to become parents. Adoption is a way for children, whose parents cannot or are unwilling to care for them, to be insured an adequate home in which to grow up. Adoption, unlike other forms of substitute care, is permanent and gives children much-needed stability. Over extended periods of time, adoption is also the most cost effective form of substitute care.[34]

New trends and issues have appeared within the field of adoption services over the past fifteen years. Most noteworthy are new methods of evaluating which children are adoptable, and which potential families should be eligible to adopt them. An adoptable child is defined as any child who needs a permanent home, who can benefit from family relationship, and who is—or should be made—legally free for adoption. Essentially, any child regardless of age, sex, race, and despite physical, intellectual, or emotional disabilities should be considered an adoptable child.

New thinking about the kinds of families that should receive adoptive placements has also influenced adoption agencies. Emphasis is now being placed on the needs of the child. Large families, single-parent families, foster families, relatives, and families from the child's racial group are now considered potential resources for adoption.

The scarcity of infants available for adoption is another trend that has brought about new developments in adoption services. In the past, most families wanted to adopt infants, but in the last twenty years the numbers of infants available for adoption has declined markedly. This has been caused by the increased availability of birth control, and the fading social stigma against unmarried parents keeping their children. Adoption services provided by public and private child welfare agencies have shifted focus within the last ten to fifteen years to older children who now, by new definition, are considered adoptable. Much time and effort has gone into developing adoption services for older children. The Child Welfare League of America, child welfare agencies, and other child interest organizations have contributed greatly to the development of adoption services for older children and children with special needs. The adoption of minority children by adoptive families from the same groups has been substantially bolstered by the efforts of the CWLA, the National Association of Black Social Workers and through the *Indian Child Welfare Act of 1978.*

There are a number of ways that children become available for adoption. First, remember that children being placed must be legally free for adoption. The most common way that infants become available for adoption is when parents choose to voluntarily surrender their parental rights to their child so it may be adopted. And the parental rights of both biological parents must be considered: the 1972 Supreme Court Case of *Stanley* v. *Illinois,* firmly established the parental rights of biological fathers. Younger children who continue to be at risk from abuse or neglect can be permanently removed from their parents' care by the courts and be placed for adoption. Older children who are legally free for adoption, who have been in the care of the same foster parents for a long time, can be adopted by those foster parents. This type of adoption is on the increase and has contributed much toward the success of permanency planning.

TYPES OF ADOPTION   The two primary types of adoption are agency and independent adoptions. An *agency adoption* is arranged by a child welfare or social service agency sanctioned and authorized by law or license to do so. These agencies match as best they can the child available for adoption with an approved family that investigation has shown will be able to meet the needs of the particular child. Supportive services, including legal services, and counseling, are also provided to the new family to promote the success of the placement. In situations involving special needs children, some agencies engage in what is termed a "subsidized adoptive placement," which involves placing the child with a family that without financial assistance could not provide for the child's on-going care: in these instances, agencies provide the necessary money that makes the adoption possible.

*Independent adoptions* can also occur. In most states, families can adopt a child through arrangements made by a third party acting independently of a social agency. This person acts as a facilitator between the biological parents and the adoptive parents and makes the necessary legal arrangements for the adoption. Children, again, must be legally free, and this usually occurs by biological parents voluntarily releasing them for adoption. This type of adoption has been called a "gray-market adoption." A "black market adoption," the sale of infants or children, is illegal in most states. In recent years, independent (gray market) adoptions have increased greatly, often as a way of avoiding the lengthy study process in agency adoption and the sometimes very long waiting period.

A variation of an independent adoption involves the legal adoption of children by their stepparents or by a relative. Again, the parental rights of the absent biological parent must be terminated legally.

SOCIAL WORK ROLES IN ADOPTION SERVICES   Working in the field of adoption services is one of the most rewarding areas of social work practice. Social workers assume many roles in adoption services, including preparing children and families for adoptive placement, finding adoptive home, and completing adoptive home studies. Beyond this, social workers are responsible for providing support services to families with adopted children to insure the success of the placement. This is especially crucial when the adopted child is older or handicapped. In these cases, the social worker can direct the new parents to such resources as a child psychologist or physical therapist who can make the transition for both child and parents smoother. Occasionally, when placements experience difficulties, social workers must also be prepared to provide ongoing services to the family. Some placements may require extensive work, particularly those involving special needs children. Social workers in adoption services may also become involved in community development, public education advocacy, program policy and planning, and administrative roles.

# Summary

Child welfare services are dedicated to protecting and promoting the well-being of children, and to insuring that their needs are met during this vulnerable time in their lives. Formal service delivery structures in child welfare, and the policies that have influenced their purposes and missions, have changed over time, in response to social changes that have affected American society as a whole. The two broad areas of child welfare services, those dedicated to maintaining children in natural family settings, and those for children at risk and unable to remain within their natural homes, have been organized into a permanency framework. Service today is based on the assumption that all children are entitled to a stable, nurturing family home environment. It is believed that for most children, with support and assistance, natural families can provide the best environment in which children can live and grow. Child welfare services, homemaker services, school social services, day-care services, and other forms of assistance to families can bring this about. When these efforts fail, for whatever reasons, and children cannot remain in their natural homes, they must be guaranteed permanent substitute care. Permanency planning mechanisms, such as placement with relatives or adoption, can provide that. Services to children that protect their well-being and socialize them for living within our society should be viewed as an investment in our nation's future.

# Key Terms

adoption
Adoptions Assistance and Child
   Welfare Reform Act of 1980
agency adoption
apprenticeship
block grants
child abuse
child abuse and neglect
   reporting laws
child neglect
Child Protective Services (CPS)
Children's Bureau
Childrens Aid Societies
child welfare
child welfare services

day-care services
family foster care
foster care
homemaker services
indenturing
independent adoption
Indian Child Welfare Act of 1978
orphanage
permanency planning
school social services
sexual abuse
Sheppard-Towner Act
substitute care
unmarried parents

## Questions for Discussion

1. The term *child welfare* can be defined both broadly and narrowly. What is the narrow definition of child welfare? What is the broad one? Which view do you think should take precedence?

2. The child welfare system has traditionally focused on two broad areas of service. What are these two areas? How are they currently organized?

3. In recent years, much attention has been focused on developing and providing services to children in their own homes. What has brought about this change?

4. Prior to the present century, children were afforded no special status and were treated as "mini-adults." When did this perspective begin to change? What circumstances caused the change?

5. What does the term *child saving* mean? How did it influence the institutional care of children in the late 1800s? When did this concept fall out of favor and what factors brought about the change?

6. How has the Indian Child Welfare Act of 1978 influenced and changed the practices of child custody and the adoption of native American children?

7. How has the Adoptions Assistance and Child Welfare Reform Act of 1980, impacted and influenced the development of permanency planning services for children?

8. Experience has demonstrated that children can be protected from abuse and neglect through effective child protection service. What are the basic aims of this service to children? Do you think more emphasis should be placed on protecting children? Why?

9. What causes child abuse and neglect? What are some contributing factors? Which factors contribute to the incidence of sexual abuse? What can be done to eliminate sexual abuse of children?

10. What treatment roles do social workers assume in child abuse and neglect situations? In sexual abuse situations?

11. What roles and services do social workers perform and provide in the community school systems?

12. Why is it important, when working with unmarried parents, that service delivery focuses on both the unmarried mother and the unmarried father?

13. In recent years, federal policy has focused on the necessity of permanency planning for children in foster care. Why has this come about?

14. Discuss the concept that any child is adoptable. What has influenced this new way of thinking?

15. All children are entitled to a stable and nurturing home environment. How do child welfare services bring this about?

# Notes

1 Juvenile Rights Project of the American Civil Liberties Union Foundation, *Childrens Rights Report* (New York: American Civil Liberties Union Foundation, Feb. 1977), p.1.
2 Child Welfare League of America, *A National Program for Child Welfare Services* (New York: Child Welfare League of America, 1971), p.2.
3 Brenda G. McGowan and William Meezan, *Child Welfare: Current Dilemmas and Future Directions* (Itaska, IL: F.E. Peacock Publishers, 1983).
4 Lela B. Costin and Charles A. Rapp, *Child Welfare: Policies and Practice* (New York: McGraw-Hill Book Co., 1984).
5 McGowan, *Child Welfare.*
6 Walter I. Trattner, *From Poor Law to Welfare State: A History of Social Welfare in America* (New York: The Free Press, 1979), p. 99.
7 Ibid.
8 McGowan, *Child Welfare.*
9 Jacqueline K. Parker and Edward M. Carpenter, "Julia Lathrop and the Childrens Bureau: The Emergence of an Institution," *Social Service Review* 55 (March 1981).
10 McGowan, *Child Welfare.*
11 American Public Welfare Association, "Poverty Reaches Highest Level Since 1965, Hits Young Hardest," *Washington Report* 18 (September, 1983): 1.
12 Walter Friedlander and Robert Z. Apte, *Introduction to Social Welfare* (Englewood Cliffs, NJ: Prentice-Hall, 1980).
13 Andrew Billingsley and Jeanne M. Giovannoni, *Children of the Storm: Black Children and American Child Welfare* (New York: Harcourt Brace Jovanovich, 1972).
14 Costin, *Child Welfare*, pp. 271-272.
15 Donald Brieland, Lela B. Costin, and Charles R. Atherton, *Contemporary Social Work: An Introduction to Social Work and Social Welfare* (New York: McGraw-Hill Book Co., 1985).
16 Henry C. Kempe and Roy E. Helfer, eds., *The Battered Child* (Chicago: University of Chicago Press, 1974).
17 Sources from which statistics were extracted include: Nagi Saadz, "Child Abuse and Neglect Programs: A National Overview," *Children Today* 4 (May 1975): 13–18; Richard J. Gelles, "Violence toward Children in the United States," *American Journal of Orthopsychiatry* 48 (October 1978): 580–592; American Humane Association, *National Analysis of Official Child Neglect and Abuse Reporting* Washington D.C.: U.S. Department of Health and Human Services, Childrens Bureau, DHHS Publication No. (SRS) 81-30232, 1979; and Costin, *Child Welfare.*
18 These statistics were extracted from the following: U.S. Department of Health and Human Services, *Study Findings: National Study of the Incidence and Severity of Child Abuse and Neglect* (Washington, D.C.: U.S. Government Printing

Office, DHHS Publication (OHOS) 81-30325, 1981; and Ruth S. Kempe and C. Henry Kempe, *The Common Event: Sexual Abuse of Children and Adolescents* (New York: W.H. Freeman Co., 1984), pp. 14–15.

[19] Alfred Kadushin, and Judith A. Martin, *Child Abuse: An Interactional Event* (New York: Columbia University Press, 1981).

[20] Kempe and Helfer, *The Battered Child.*

[21] Sources discussing interacting factors include: David G. Gill, *Violence against Children: Physical Abuse in the United States* (Cambridge, MA: Harvard University Press, 1970); Norman A. Polansky, *Damaged Parents: An Anatomy of Child Neglect* (Chicago: University of Chicago Press, 1981); Kadushin, *Child Abuse;* Costin, *Child Welfare;* and Jeanne M. Giovannoni, "Child Abuse and Neglect: An Overview," in *A Handbook of Child Welfare: Context, Knowledge, and Practice*, eds. Joan Laird and Ann Hartman, (New York: The Free Press, 1985), pp. 193–212.

[22] Costin, *Child Welfare.*

[23] Friedlander, *Social Welfare.*

[24] For a complete discussion of school social work see: Robert T. Constable and John P. Flynn, eds., *School Social Work: Practice and Research Perspectives* (Homewood, IL: The Dorsey Press, 1982).

[25] Flynn, *School Social Work.*

[26] Friedlander, *Social Welfare.*

[27] Erva Zuckerman, *Child Welfare* (New York: The Free Press, 1983).

[28] Zuckerman, *Child Welfare.*

[29] Zuckerman, *Child Welfare.*

[30] For a discussion on family social roles see: Alfred Kadushin, *Child Welfare Services* (New York: Macmillan Publishing Co., 1980). Also see Zuckerman, *Child Welfare.*

[31] Brieland, *Contemporary Social Work.*

[32] Martha M. Dare, "Comparison of Basic Data for the National Survey of Residential Group Care Facilities: 1966–1982," *Child Welfare* 63 (November-December, 1984): 479–490.

[33] Tom Rey, "Social Work in Community-Based Group Care Facilities," in *Social Work in Juvenile and Criminal Justice Settings*, ed. Albert R. Roberts (Springfield, IL: Charles C. Thomas, Publishers, 1983), pp. 181–197.

[34] Elizabeth S. Cole, "Adoption Services Today and Tomorrow," in *Child Welfare Strategy in the Coming Years: An Overview*, ed. Alfred Kadushin (Washington, D.C.: U.S. Department of Health, Education, and Welfare, DHEW Publication No. COHDS 78-30158, 1978.

## Suggested Readings

Constable, Robert T., and Flynn, John R., eds. *School Social Work: Practice and Research Perspectives.* Homewood, IL: The Dorsey Press, 1982.

Costin, Lela B. and Rapp, Charles A. *Child Welfare: Policies and Practice.* New York: McGraw-Hill Book Co., 1984.

Kadushin, Alfred, and Martin, Judith A. *Child Abuse: An Interactional Event.* New York: Columbia University Press, 1981.

Kadushin, Alfred, ed. *Child Welfare Strategy in the Coming Years: An Overview.* Washington, D.C.: U.S. Department of Health, Education, and Welfare, DHEW Publication No COHDS78-30158, 1978.

Kempe, Ruth S., and Kempe, C. Henry. *The Common Secret: Sexual Abuse of Children and Adolescents*. New York: W.H. Freeman and Co., 1984.

McGowan, Brenda G., and Meezan, William. *Child Welfare: Current Dilemmas and Future Directions* (Itaska, IL: F.E. Peacock Publishers, 1983).

Zuckerman, Era. *Child Welfare*. New York: The Free Press, 1983.

# Chapter 9

## Services to Families

Although the family is the primary social unit, it takes on many forms within our society. In light of this, the American Home Economics Association offers a broad definition of the *family* as it exists in the United States today:

> . . . two or more persons who share resources, share responsibility for decisions, share values and goals, and have a commitment to one another over time. The family is the climate "one comes home to," and it is this network of sharing and commitments that most accurately describes the family unit regardless of blood, legal ties, adoption, or marriage.

Within the family, individuals are socialized, protected, and nurtured so they can develop the skills necessary for their well-being and survival. The well-being of children is dependent on the well-being of the family, as was discussed in Chapter 8. To meet the needs of individuals, the family unit in whatever form must first have its needs met.

The mechanisms for meeting family needs have changed as society has changed. In the past, most family needs were taken care of by the immediate or extended family network. But as social change altered traditional family structures, responsibility for families who cannot function on their own has shifted to the U.S. social welfare system, and public and private social service agencies which are a part of it. The focus of this chapter is on how the family in contemporary society takes care of the needs of its members; the past and current economic and social changes that have affected the structure, roles, and functions of families; the social conditions that influence families and that give rise to changing needs, and that can lessen family stability; and the development and scope of social services available to families, and the role of social work in their delivery.

# The Contemporary United States Family

Rapid social, economic, and technological change—particularly in the latter half of this century—has challenged the contemporary family. Some authorities argue that the family as the primary social unit is rapidly disintegrating. Some evidence does suggest that this is true: for example, it is estimated that one in two marriages end in divorce. A slightly more positive viewpoint is that the family's ability to adjust and cope with social expectations and demands have simply not kept pace with the social changes that have occurred; this has placed stresses on the family, and, for some, has threatened their stability.[1] Family stability and cohesiveness are, in part, dependent on the degree to which individuals in a family feel connected to each other. Social change and technological advancement have given individuals more opportunities and choices about family life-style, including types of career, marriage partners, and whether or not to have children. Values about the importance of the family to the individual have also changed as a result of this. Society currently places a high value on individual growth and self-actualization, the self-oriented individual, as opposed to the group-oriented individual who has a sense of connectedness to the family. The focus of socialization within the family has been on preparing family members for participation in a society that emphasizes the individual more than the family unit.[2] Within some families, this has led to a feeling of detachment and weak emotional bonding, undermining their solidarity.[3] The problems individual family members experience as a consequence of this have not gone unnoticed. The social welfare system has responded to family situations where children need protection from abuse or neglect, and has provided assistance to aged family members. However, these efforts have often been designed to assist individuals, rather than to strengthen the family as a social unit.[4] A system of response directed at maintaining the family unit has not been developed. This is due largely to the absence of a national family social policy that clearly demonstrates society's responsibility to support families by providing resources and services aimed at ameliorating the social conditions and problems that jeopardize their well-being.

## Changes in Family Structure

Prior to the turn of the present century, the family was the primary social and economic unit within society. The basic family structure was the *extended family system*. Families were large, with several generations, which included brothers, sisters, cousins, great aunts and uncles, all working closely together, all living in close proximity to one another. People, more often than not, were raised, lived, and died close to their birthplace. Most needs were met within the family system. Families needed to be large; the larger the family, the more producers available, and the better off the family became. When family problems occurred, they were responded to by mutual aid within the extended family structure. But the industrial revolution brought about vast changes. The changeover from an agricultural economy to a monetary industrial economy meant families did not necessarily produce all their necessities (food, clothing, shelter) on the family farm or in the local community. Large families were no longer an asset. Extended families broke up when the younger generations relocated to the large industrial cities in search of new opportunities and higher wages. This resulted in the eventual change from the extended family to a new form of family structure the *nuclear family*, usually consisting of only the two parents and one or more children.

The nuclear family remains the predominant family type today, and little suggests that it will be completely replaced by any other family form.[5] However, in contemporary U.S. society, particularly since the beginning of the 1970s, several alternative family forms have emerged.

A common variant family form is the *single-parent family*, where only one parent is present in the home. A number of circumstances have brought about its appearance: out of wedlock births, desertion, separation, divorce, death, or incarceration. Single-parent families have also resulted from adoptions of children by individuals. These families are growing in number. In 1983, there were approximately six million single-parent families compared with five million in 1980.[6]

The *step-family*, or what has been recently been termed the blended or *reconstituted family*, is another variant. A step-family occurs when either one or both partners in a marriage bring with them children from a former relationship. There are approximately ten million of these families in the United States and they too are growing in number. For some of these families, the process of blending together as a single, cohesive family unit has been difficult, giving rise to relationship problems among family members. In recent years, professional helpers have begun reaching out to reconstituted families who are experiencing difficulties, to help them with their problems or obstacles that prevent them from achieving harmonious relationships and family cohesiveness. A growing body of professional literature on service delivery to these families has resulted.[7]

The childless family is another family form. Many couples in recent years have chosen this as a family life-style. Cohabitation without marriage, with children present is another form, as is the homosexual family arrangement.

Changes in the structure of the family have affected the ways families seek and receive help with needs and problems. The shift from the extended family system to the nuclear family and other family forms has reduced the availability of family mutual aid as a resource. For families with problems, their extended family usually cannot be called upon to provide immediate help because of geographical distances that separate so many families from their relatives. In contemporary society, families needing help often must turn to public and private social welfare agencies.

## Changes in Family Roles and Functions

The family is supposed to provide its individual members with opportunities for growth and development, and to teach them the physical, social, intellectual, and emotional skills necessary to prepare them for membership in the larger society. That process of growth and development for individual family members depends on the growth and development of the family itself. Just as individuals grow and develop through predictable phases in their life cycle, so does the family (e.g., marriage, birth of children, children reaching adolescence, and the separation of the children from the family unit). Each phase of family development brings new tasks, different societal demands and expectations. The family's ability to perform its roles and functions depends on its successful transition through the developmental life cycle.

Effectiveness in performing roles and functions is also measured by the extent to which the family is able to meet its needs as a unit and the needs of its individual members.[8] Social and technological advancements that have occurred during this century have affected the family's ability to do this. The family's roles and functions have changed as have the ways in which they perform them.

In the past, the family—whether immediate or extended—was responsible for meeting the total needs of its members. These needs included protection and safety, physical (food, clothing, shelter), emotional, health, education, religious, and leisure and recreation. Today it is no longer necessary for families to assume total responsibility for these needs. Societal structures have assumed many of these responsibilities of which education and health care are just two examples.

Despite changes, the family has retained some of its traditional roles and functions: these include reproduction, meeting the basic physical and emotional needs of family members, and early socialization of children.[9] However, even some of these family roles are now being challenged: changes in family values, technological advancement, and economic pressures have brought this about. For example, parenting roles have changed. Traditionally, women had major responsibility for the care and socialization of preschool children. Many women, either out of economic necessity or the desire to pursue a career, are now employed. This has resulted in role-sharing, not only in providing for the family's economic needs, but in child rearing responsibilities. Responsibility for child care has shifted to individual child care providers or other community arrangements such as day-care centers and preschools. Even the role of reproduction is now being challenged by surrogate parenting. Advancements in medical technology have made it possible for reproduction to occur in laboratory test tubes. These new phenomena have the potential to further alter the family's responsibilities.

The family structure and functioning has changed in response to societal change. Whether these changes will bring about further deterioration of the family's influence on the individual remains to be seen. If the family, despite the continuing erosion of its roles, can continue to effectively meet the needs of its members, it has a reasonable chance of remaining the primary social unit in society.

## Economic Impacts on the Family

The industrial, money-based economy operating in contemporary society has sometimes caused economic stress on families. Economic security for families has always been tied to the functioning of the marketplace. Since 1900, the U.S. economy has fluctuated with cycles of depression, recession, inflation, and relative prosperity. With each fluctuation, families have had to find ways to protect their own economic stability. Not all have been successful. In 1983, eight million families in the United States had incomes below the poverty level. Almost four million of these are single-parent families headed by females.[10] Poverty complicates the problems experienced by these families in coping with economic fluctuations. This is not to say that poor families are different from all other families; their problems differ in degree of impact, rather than in the kinds of problems that all families experience.[11] Adequate income and economic supports are essential to successful family functioning. In families where there is not enough money, much family energy is spent in securing the resources necessary to sustain life. What can result is *role-overload*, where more energy is spent in just making ends meet than in providing emotional support to family members. Families headed by single parents are particularly vulnerable to this since the single parent is required to fulfill all expected family roles with limited energy and time. Inadequate economic supports, and the role-overload associated with it, often leads to tension and conflict within the family and to possible family dysfunction.

For many families, economics demand that both parents work. In some families, this has led to a weakening of family cohesiveness. If both parents spend most of their energy and time in obtaining financial supports, the emotional and socializing roles may suffer. In many dual-career families, this does not become a problem because parents make a conscious effort, through role-division and role-sharing, to insure that the needs of family members are met. But when this does not occur, family stress and conflict may result in weakened family relationships and eventual problems in family functioning. Stressed families are those that most often come to the attention of the social welfare system, and they are in need of supportive help.

## Family-Centered Problems

In 1980, *White House Conferences on Families (WHCF)* were held in three locations, Baltimore, Minneapolis, and Los Angeles. Among the thousands of issues raised and recommendations made concerning family problems or conditions, four broad areas of concern were defined:

1. families and economic well-being, including economic pressures on family functioning and income support problems
2. family challenges and responsibilities, including family-centered relationship problems like divorce, family violence, substance abuse, juvenile delinquency, and the special problems of handicapped, disabled, and aged family members
3. families and human needs, including education, health, housing, and child care
4. families and major institutions, including the family's relationship with government, the media, community institutions, and the law and judicial system.[12]

### Families and Economic Security

At the heart of adequate economic security of families is income. The three primary sources of family income are employment, social insurance, and public assistance.[13] Employment income is the most socially acceptable. Unemployment and underemployment undermine both the economic and social well-being of the family. For some families, racial or gender discrimination has been an obstacle to finding adequate employment. The WHCF addressed this issue by making the recommendation that, "It is imperative that all branches of government strengthen and enforce existing legislation on programs of full employment. Each person should have the opportunity to obtain a job which provides a feeling of usefulness and dignity at wages sufficient to support a decent standard of living.[14]

As discussed in previous chapters, Old Age Survivors Disability Health Insurance (Social Security) provides benefits to individuals upon retirement, to spouses, widows, and dependent children of deceased or permanently disabled insured workers, and to disabled workers. For survivors, the families of deceased workers, it provides a much-needed

supplement to other income sources. For families without income supports, public assistance becomes the alternative. Aid to Families with
Dependent Children (AFDC) and its supplementary programs is the
primary source of public assistance for these families, providing a
monthly cash assistance grants to eligible families. Nonmonetary, in-
kind, assistance is also provided through food stamps, subsidized housing, fuel assistance, and Medicaid. For aged, disabled, or blind family
members, the federal government also offers cash assistance through
Supplemental Security Income.

On the other hand, families that accept such aid often face welfare
stigma, which is demeaning and only adds to their problems. Recognizing that the current system of public assistance fails to adequately
strengthen and support economic security for families, the WHCF recommended that, "The Federal Government must insure a minimum
living standard for all citizens in the United States and territories. AFDC
and other public assistance programs should be combined into a Family
Assistance program, fully funded by the Federal Government."[15]

Many families in today's world continue to struggle with economic
security. Recommendations made by the WHCF on social and economic
policies have not been acted on. Therefore, the status quo in economic
security for the family has been maintained. Serious questions need to be
asked about whether society can reasonably expect troubled families to
maintain themselves as independent and self-sufficient units without
adequate help from societal support mechanisms. Decisive action must be
taken to insure adequate supports for these families if we want them to be
stable and productive members of our society.[16] What the future holds,
however, for the economic security of all families remains to be seen.

## Family Relationship Problems

Two family relationship problems need to be looked at closely: they are
divorce and family violence. While these two problems by no means
reflect all family relationship problems, they have received considerable
attention from professionals concerned about family maintenance.
Other family problems, such as juvenile deliquency, the special needs of
handicapped, disabled, and aged family members are also important
and will be discussed in other chapters.

DIVORCE    Although the divorce rate in the United States has increased since the end of World War II, it is expected to stabilize in the
near future.[17] The causes of divorce are many. Some suggest that our
highly technological society has brought about the attitude that almost
anything is replaceable, including a marriage. If it doesn't work, throw
it out. If the marital relationship does not meet the partners' expectations
or satisfaction, a divorce is quick and easy to obtain.[18] The emergence of

liberalized divorce laws, particularly the concept of no-fault divorce, reflects these attitudes. Incompatibility in the marital relationship perceived by one or both partners can also contribute to the breakup of the relationship. These include incompatibility in sex roles, excessive life and marriage demands, unmet emotional needs of marital partners, the inability of the marriage to satisfy the individual, individual conflicts about personal fulfillment, and incompatible social roles for both partners. When such incompatibility exists in a marriage, tension and conflict often leads to marital difficulties and even divorce, unless the couple makes conscious efforts to resolve them.[19] In recent years, the stigma surrounding divorce has faded, making it a much more attractive alternative than it had been in the past.

It is unnecessary to argue whether divorce causes family problems, or whether family problems causes divorce. It is more important to consider the consequences of divorce on the emotional well-being of family members, and how divorce affects family functioning. Children are particularly vulnerable to emotional problems as a consequence of divorce. Children experience divorce as a terrible and confusing loss in their lives, in much the same way that they experience the death of a loved one. This sense of loss can give rise to many emotions within the child, grief, guilt, depression, anxiety, confusion, and bewilderment. The effects of these feelings on the child can be severe and can last well into adulthood. Studies show that emotional problems and behavioral disturbances in adolescents and adults—including depression, alcoholism, anxiety disorders, and suicide—are often linked to unresolved feelings associated with loss experienced in childhood.[20]

The effects of divorce can be just as severe for adults. They also experience divorce as a loss, with many of the same accompanying emotional reactions as children experience. What is of central concern here is that divorce impairs adults' capacity and ability to parent. While this impairment is usually only temporary, it can sometimes extend over long periods of time.

In recent years, social workers and other professional helpers have focused a great deal of attention on helping families cope with the consequences of divorce. Social service agencies have developed specific programs designed to address those needs including: crisis intervention, divorce mediation, family therapy and counseling, support groups for divorced parents, children's support and treatment groups, and parenting skills groups.[21] The legal system has also joined this effort. Family and domestic courts, in recognition of the consequences of divorce on the family, have begun the practice of divorce mediation. Crisis intervention services and family counseling have begun to be offered by professionals employed by the courts with the goals of either preventing divorce or insuring that the needs and problems of all the family members will be dealt with if divorce occurs.[22]

FAMILY VIOLENCE    Violence in the family encompasses many broad areas, including abuse of spouses, children, and aged family members. This discussion is limited to spousal abuse, more specifically wife-abuse, or wife-battering. Violence toward spouses ranges all the way from verbal abuse and minor physical assaults to homicide. It has been estimated that 15 to 25 percent of all homicides are linked to episodes of spousal abuse.[23] Most family violence is limited to verbal and physical abuse. A combination of factors are associated with the development of violent behavior patterns within the family: unstable family relationships, parents' childhood experiences with violence, current situational stresses, both internal and external, poor impulse control, inner rage, alcohol or drug abuse, jealousy, sexual conflict, poor communication skills, feelings of personal inadequacy, and fear of intimacy.[24] Patterns of family violence have the potential of being passed on from generation to generation. Children who experience, witness, or are somehow exposed to violent relationships within their families, appear to be predisposed to developing the same patterns of abuse relationships in adulthood. This appears to hold true for both men who batter, and women who become victims of abuse. Violence perpetrated toward one family member can set up abusive patterns toward other members. In some abusive families, the husband physically abuses his wife, then the wife abuses the children.

Violence within families has always existed. Only within the past two decades has a greater awareness of this social problem developed within society at large, the helping professions, and the judicial system. Prior to the 1970s, they saw the problem of spousal abuse as an unfortunate but nevertheless private matter within families, requiring only individual responses to its victims, as opposed to a conscious and deliberate large-scale response to family violence as a legitimate social problem.

Societal attitudes about women and spousal abuse were largely to blame for the lack of attention to this problem. Beliefs—such as a woman being the property of her husband, or that it is the husband's right to abuse the wife, or that some women have a masochistic desire to be punished, or that women provoke the abuse—prevailed and handicapped society's efforts to adequately respond.

Since the 1970s, awareness of spousal abuse as a national problem has come to the forefront. Sociological, social work, and feminist research and literature has struck a responsive chord and has forced society, the helping professions, and the legislative and judicial systems to reexamine their beliefs and practices toward abused women.[25]

In recent years, specialized programs for abused women have been created. Crisis-emergency shelters for battered women and their children have been one such development. The services provided by these shelters include individual counseling, support and self-help groups, legal services, and referral services to social service agencies for economic assistance and educational and vocational training.[26] Services are also provided to the entire family by both public and private agencies. Public agencies are called upon when the violence seems to be caused by situational stresses (unemployment or inadequate income, drug or alcohol abuse). Private social service agencies, family service agencies, and mental health agencies provide more intensive treatment and counseling services to violent families, family therapy, marital therapy, and treatment for abusive men. These services help control or eliminate the violent and abuse patterns and keep the family together.

The judicial system is starting to concern itself with the legal aspects of family violence. Laws have been passed in several states that protect victims of spousal abuse. The laws have helped law enforcement agencies respond to family violence by spelling out, in clear-cut terms, what their roles and responsibilities are. Law enforcement agencies have begun employing professional social workers to work with its officers as a team in investigating and intervening in situations of family violence. It is hoped that this concerted effort by society, the helping professions, and the judicial system will break the destructive cycle of family violence in the near future.

## Social Services Agencies Serving Families

Both public and private social service agencies provide services to strengthen families. The history of service to the family is extensive and dates back to the turn of the century, when formal but private social service structures began to appear. The Charity Organization Societies (COS) generally focused on financial security for families, but they began to recognize the importance of the relationship between the individual and the family and shifted their focus to improving family functioning. In the years following the Depression, the COS underwent reorganization and many branches became *private family service agencies*. These agencies assist families to function better socially and psychologically. In 1946, many of these private agencies became affiliates of the *Family Service Association of America (FSAA)*. The FSAA states that it "is dedicated to the purpose of strengthening family life through detecting, correcting, and preventing those conditions that tend to have an adverse affect on family functioning."[27]

Today the FSAA, through its affiliates, assists troubled families, by providing a host of therapeutic services, including family therapy and counseling and marriage counseling. In addition to therapeutic services, many family service agencies focus on preventing problems in family functioning by offering programs of *family life education*. These programs are designed to improve family relationships by providing educational groups or classes that teach skills in family communication, family problem solving, and parenting that will better equip members for family living. The FSAA itself, and many of its affiliate members, also have focused recently on advisory services that promote legislative and community change that will help families carry out their expected roles and functions.[28] Most of these family agencies are funded by charging fees and by a variety of other private and governmental sources, including the United Way. These agencies were forerunners in using new methods of family therapy that developed in psychiatry, psychology, and social work in the 1960s. Now, families from virtually all socio-economic backgrounds have enjoyed access to the services provided by these agencies.

Other private agencies available to families include community mental health centers, where assistance focuses on, but is not limited to, the mental health problems of family members. And many religious or church-affiliated agencies (e.g., Jewish Family Services, Lutheran Social Services, Catholic Family Services, and others) also offer a great deal of assistance to families. While some provide services only to families of their own religion, others are available to all families. The bulk of the services to families are provided by private agencies, but *public social service agencies* also work with troubled families. Public agencies usually help low-income families with economic security needs, with family violence problems, and with other family relationship problems.

## Social Work and Family Services

Work with troubled families has always been a key task of the profession. Graduate schools of social work, from their beginning, have provided substantial specialized curriculums to prepare practitioners with the knowledge and skills necessary for working with families. And undergraduate social work programs that educate beginning practitioners include family content in their generalist framework. Although social work is not the only helping profession that works with troubled families, it is probably the predominant one. The following case example illustrates service provisions to a family by a social worker employed in a family service agency.

### A Case Study

The J family made a request for services from the child guidance clinic. Mr. and Mrs. J were worried about the violent and destructive behavior being exhibited by their ten-year-old son Eric. According to Mr. and Mrs. J, in recent months Eric appeared sad and generally unhappy. On several occasions, these episodes were fol-

*continued*

lowed by violent and destructive behaviors in which he physically assaulted his sister and damaged or destroyed his own personal possessions and other items in the J home. The Js were at a loss to understand what was causing these "temper tantrums," as they called them. The measures they had employed to control his outbursts had failed. They stated that they were at their "wit's end" and were considering placing Eric in a foster home or institution. Eric had also begun to have problems at school with poor academic performance and physical aggression toward his peers.

The social worker assigned to their case spent the initial session and part of the second session gathering information from Mr. and Mrs. J and Eric. During the session with Mr. and Mrs. J, the social worker discovered that the Js were experiencing marital conflict, associated mostly with Mr. J's reluctance to spend time with Mrs. J and the children—caused, according to Mrs. J, by his excessive work schedule and other interests outside the family. The worker also learned that Mr. and Mrs. J's sexual activity had been reduced to "almost never." They both said that they had tried to keep their conflict hidden from the children, but Eric's recent misbehavior had "pitted them against each other even more," causing them to fight openly in front of the children. They also discussed their relationships with the children with the social worker. From their perspective, their daughter was a "good girl," who had never caused them any trouble. She was a straight A student, involved in school activities, and well-liked by her peers. Concerning Eric, they had often thought that they had failed in their parental roles since he was so different from his sister. The Js felt they had a right to expect the same behavior from Eric as they did from his sister.

In the initial session with Eric, the social worker realized that Eric was concerned about his parents fighting because "they're fighting about me, it's my fault." He also expressed anger about being constantly compared to his sister, which he stated his parents did frequently and openly with him. He said, "They're probably going to get a divorce, and it's my fault." Eric admitted that he would get so mad at his parents and himself, he would "lose control and beat on people or things."

The social worker, in the third session with Mr. and Mrs. J and Eric present, shared his assessment of their situation. He explained that Eric had been feeling disenfranchised by his family, due to the marital conflict and the excessive expectations placed on him by his parents. His violent and destructive behavior came from his anger toward his parents and himself, and his attack on his sister resulted from Eric seeing her as part of the problem since he was constantly being compared to her. The social worker made the following recommendations:

*A Case Study . . . continued*

1. The Js should receive marriage counseling
2. Mr. J should realign his priorities and spend more time with his wife and children.
3. They all should continue in family therapy, to work on their excessive expectations and other relationship problems.

After several months of counseling, Eric's violent behavior subsided and his school performance improved. The Js agreed that they "felt much better about their marriage and family than they had for years." The case was closed shortly thereafter.

## Summary

The family remains the central social unit in U.S. society. Due to social and technological change, family structure, roles, and functions have changed over time. The change from the extended family structure to the nuclear family has resulted in changes in the ways that family needs are met and family problems are dealt with. This chapter discussed how family mutual aid was replaced by a formal social welfare system that works toward the goal of strengthening and preserving the integrity of the family.

Changes in roles and functions since the turn of the century have created problems in many families. The recommendations that emerged out of the White House Conference on Families (WHCF) clearly show the need for a strong and unified national social policy on behalf of the family. The lack of economic security and family-centered relationship problems, such as family violence and divorce were addressed in this chapter, as well as how public and private social service agencies and the judicial system have responded to them. Since professional social work is needed to assist troubled families, undergraduate programs and graduate schools need to prepare practioners. A case study was provided to illustrate how a social worker would intervene to assist a family experiencing problems.

Finally a key point emphasized throughout the chapter is that a society must continue to strengthen and protect the family as the most important societal institution.

## Key Terms

divorce
extended family
family
family life education
Family Service Association
    of America (FSAA)
family violence
nuclear family

private family service agencies
public social service agencies
single-parent family
step-family
role overload
reconstituted family
White House Conference on
    Families (WHCF)

## Questions for Discussion

1. Is the American family rapidly disintegrating? What evidence seems to point to this? What evidence contradicts this belief?

2. How has social and technological change in this century brought about changes in family structure, roles, and functions? In what ways has this caused instability in some families?

3. What new variant family forms have emerged since the turn of the century? What new problems and what new responses by the social welfare system have these new forms created?

4. How has the absence of a unified national policy on families affected the maintenance of the integrity of family life?

5. What accounts for the alarming rate of divorce in U.S. society? How has divorce affected the stability of the family?

6. What concerns do helping professionals have about step families or reconstituted families? What have they done to assist them?

7. What are the causes of family violence in contemporary U.S. society?

8. Should the judicial system play more of a role in protecting victims of family violence? What roles should the system assume?

9. What factors have caused few of the recommendations of the White House Conference on Families to be implemented?

10. How would a sound national policy on the family enhance the efforts of Family Service Agencies to provide purposeful assistance to the family?

# Notes

1  Rae Sedgwick, *Family Mental Health: Theory and Practice*, (St. Louis, MO: C.V. Mosby Co., 1981), p. 115.
2  Erva Zuckerman, *Child Welfare* (New York: The Free Press, 1983).
3  Sedgwick, *Family Mental Health*, p. 113.
4  Robert Morris, *Social Policy of the American Welfare State: An Introduction to Policy Analysis* (New York: Harper & Row Publishers, 1979).
5  John Turner, ed., *Encyclopedia of Social Work*, 12th ed. (Washington, D.C.: National Association of Social Workers, 1971), p. 361.
6  U.S. Department of Commerce, Bureau of the Census, *Statistical Abstract of the United States, 1985* (Washington, D.C.: U.S. Government Printing Office, 1985).
7  Two of many recent sources are James E. Hunter and Nancy Schuman, "Chronic Reconstitution of Family Style," *Social Work* 25 (November 1980): 446–453; and Harriet Johnson, "Working with Step Families: Principles of Practice," *Social Work* 25 (July 1980): 304–308.
8  Irene Goldenberg and Herbert Goldenberg, *Family Therapy: An Overview* (Monterey, CA: Brooks/Cole Publishing Co., 1985), pp. 16–22.
9  Elizabeth Ferguson, *Social Work: An Introduction* (New York: J.B. Lippincott Co., 1975), p. 12.
10  U.S. Department of Commerce, Bureau of the Census, *Characteristics of Persons and Families below the Poverty Level* (Washington, D.C.: U.S. Government Printing Office, 1983).
11  Ferguson, *Social Work*, p. 115.
12  See: *Listening to America's Families: Actions for the 80s: Final Report of the White House Conference on Families* (Washington, D.C.: U.S. Government Printing Office, October 1980), and John J. Demsey, *The Family and Public Policy: The Issue of the 1980s* (Baltimore: Brooks Publishing Co., 1981), pp. 141–153.
13  National Conference on Social Welfare, *Families and Public Policies in the United States* (Washington, D.C.: National Conference on Social Welfare, 1978), p. 19.
14  Dempsey, *The Family*, p. 141.
15  Dempsey, *The Family*.
16  See: Zuckerman, *Child Welfare*, and Patricia Spokes, "Family Impact Analysis: Its Promise for Social Welfare," *Social Casework* 64 (January, 1983): 3–10.
17  Sar Levitan, *What's Happening to the American Family* (Baltimore: Johns Hopkins University Press, 1981).
18  Sedgwick, *Family Mental Health*, p. 113.
19  James M. Henslin, "Why So Much Divorce," in *Marriage and Family in a Changing Society*, ed. James J. Henslin (New York: The Free Press, 1985), pp. 424–428.
20  Claudia L. Jewett, *Helping Children Cope with Separation and Loss* (Boston, MA: The Harvard Common Press, 1982), pp. ix–x.
21  Judith S. Wallerstein, "The Overburdened Child: Some Long-term Consequences of Divorce," *Social Work* 30 (March–April, 1985): 116–123.
22  Robert M. Counts and Anita Sacks, "The Need for Crisis Intervention during Marital Separation," *Social Work* 30 (March–April, 1985): 146–150.
23  Jeffrey L. Edleson, "Working with Men Who Batter," *Social Work* 29 (May–June, 1984): 237–242.
24  R.J. Gelles, *The Violent Home* (London: Sage Publishers, 1972); and B. Justice and R. Justice, *The Abusing Family* (New York: Human Services Press, 1976); and J.P. Martin, *Violence and the Family* (New York: John Wiley & Sons, 1978).

[25] See: Mary A. Jansen and Judith Meyers-Abell, "Assertiveness Training for Battered Women: A Pilot Program," *Social Work* 26 (March, 1981): 164; Jane H. Pfouts and Connie Renz, "The Future of Wife Abuse Programs," *Social Work* 26 (November, 1981): 451–455; and Cathy Costantino, "Intervention with Battered Women: The Lawyer-Social Worker Team," *Social Work* 26 (November, 1981): 456–461.

[26] Albert R. Roberts, *Sheltering Battered Women: A National Study and Service Guide* (New York: Springer Publishing Co., 1981).

[27] Family Service Association of America, *Requirements for Membership* (New York: Family Service Assn. of America, 1979).

[28] Patrick V. Riley, "Family Services," in *Handbook of the Social Services,* eds. Neil Gilbert and Harvey Spect (Engelwood Cliffs, NJ: Prentice-Hall, 1981), pp. 92–94.

## Suggested Readings

Demsey, John J. *The Family and Public Policy: The Issue of the 1980s.* Baltimore: Brooks Publishing Co., 1981.

Levitan, Sar. *What's Happening to the American Family.* Baltimore: Johns Hopkins University Press, 1981.

Martin, J.P. *Violence and the Family.* New York: John Wiley & Sons, 1978.

Roberts, Albert R. *Sheltering Battered Women: A National Study and Service Guide.* New York: Springer Publishing Co., 1981.

Wallerstein, Judith, and Joan Kelly. *Surviving the Breakup: How Children and Parents Cope with Divorce.* New York: Basic Books, 1980.

White House Conference on Families. *Listening To America's Families; Actions for the 80s.* Washington, D.C.: U.S. Government Printing Office, October 1980.

Zuckerman, Erva. *Child Welfare.* New York: The Free Press, 1983.

# Chapter 10

## Health Care and Social Welfare

Social welfare and health care are usually seen as two different systems. The health care system is generally responsible for the area of sickness and disability, but there are areas where health care and social work overlap, have common concerns, and common themes. One of the areas of overlap between the two systems is the practice of social work.

Before proceeding to discuss these overlapping, common concerns it is important to define health. Health is usually considered to be freedom from disease. But this definition fails to consider the relative nature of health. Is the person with a well controlled chronic disease unhealthy? Is a frail elderly person with minimal health problems other than the fraility of old age unhealthy? What about the differing cultural definitions of illness and disease, are individualized definitions of illness to be considered? Carel Germain, author of one of the major texts on social work in health care setting, defines health as "a multidimentional process involving the well being of the whole person in the context of his [or her] environment."[1] The *health care system*, then, must by necessity be broadly defined. This system consists of institutions and professionals, including those in private practice, who have as a primary focus the care of the physically ill and the physically disabled, and who are engaged in activity that prevents physical illness and disability. This definition excludes the area of mental health, though it is often included in the health care field. However, the social welfare response to mental health is extensive and has followed a somewhat different course. Social welfare and mental health will be considered separately in the next chapter.

After discussing common concerns of the social welfare field and the health care field, a review of the historical development of social legislation relating to health care and of social services in health care is presented. Next, the contemporary role of the social worker in the health care system is considered. Finally, some of the current issues in health care services affecting the social welfare system are discussed.

## Health Care and the Social Welfare System

One of the common themes of health care and social welfare is the nature of human functioning. Both systems, are *holistic*, that is, they are concerned with the whole person. This includes the biological, psychological, social, and spiritual aspects of living and functioning. Social functioning, the concern of the social welfare system, cannot really be separated from the other functions. Illness and disability are important reasons why people have difficulty providing for their needs and functioning well in society. They strongly influence a person's self-image and social behavior. The reactions of spouses, children, co-workers, and friends to illness or disability affect how a patient responds to the condition and functions socially. Medical treatment also has psychosocial effects on the individual and on the family. For example, when a mother with young children is hospitalized, plans must be made for child care, children may be upset by the absence of their mother, the husband may have concerns about his wife and children that may in turn affect his functioning in the work place. The financial cost of hospitalization adds another concern. The mother's response to treatment would very likely be affected by her worry about her children and husband and perhaps feelings of guilt for causing their distress. And of course, the social welfare system must be concerned with the health of the individuals they are serving.

On the other hand, the health care system must be concerned with the psychological, social, economic, and spiritual aspects of patients, since these aspects have considerable effect on their physical status. For people to comply with prescriptions and recommendations from health professionals, they must have enough money to purchase the health care and to buy the prescribed food and medications. Culture, religious beliefs, and family patterns also affect how a patient responds to medical advice. The emotional or psychological state of an individual has a considerable influence on the capacity of the physical body to respond to medical treatment. It is the individual in a holistic sense with whom both the social welfare system and the health care system are concerned.[2]

Another area of overlap is related to environmental factors. Public health and social welfare have had a long partnership in this area.[3] Public health workers seek to "prevent disease, prolong life, and promote physical and mental health . . . through community efforts."[4] The same could be said of social workers. Both fields have social reform and social control approaches to social problems.

A third overlapping area is concern for the family. The family can be a resource or an obstacle during an illness. In turn, illness affects the family's capacity to function. The health care system must be concerned with the effect family members have on the sick person and the effect of the illness on the family. The social welfare system is concerned with how illness and disability influence the social functioning of not only the ill or disabled individual but the family, the various institutions that serve the individual and family, and the community at large. Illness can place the family at risk of not being able to meet its needs, either because of the energy that must go into supporting or caring for an ill member, or because the illness makes it impossible for a vital role (financial support, parenting, marital, etc.) in the family to be filled. Epidemic illness can put entire communities at risk. When the individual, the family, or the community risks not being able to meet social functioning needs through the usual mechanisms and resources, the health care system depends on the social welfare system to develop means for meeting unmet needs.

## Arrangements Used to Deliver Health Care

Another way of looking at the relationship of health care and social welfare is to note the arrangements that have been used to deliver health care. As with social welfare, mutual aid has always been a primary resource. Most individuals depend on family, friends, and neighbors in times of illness. Most minor illnesses are handled by self-care methods, which often are used after consulting other people. In places where medical care was not available (e.g., the frontier, isolated areas) medical care was provided by family and neighbors with special experience or skill in the care of the sick. Mutual aid was and continues to be an important component of health care.

Hospitals were among the early institutions created under the charity-philanthropy arrangement. Often these institutions were developed by religious groups. Early hospitals were sometimes set up to separate the sick from the general population in the poorhouses. They were meant to be places where these people could get adequate treatment and where, it was hoped, the indigent could be restored to health and thus to be able to again provide for their own needs. Gradually, hospitals came to be places where all sick people could receive the care they needed. Two levels of care evolved. Those who could pay were cared for in private hospitals or in the private services of large hospitals. Those who could not pay, the *charity patients*, were cared for in *charity hospitals* or on charity wards. The care of charity patients was often given to physicians in training, while care of the private patient was given by personal physicians.

Charity patient care was not only a part of the health care system but also of the social welfare system. When that care was paid for by government funds, the care given in charity hospitals and on charity wards was seen as public welfare. Many city and county hospitals were created to care for charity patients. Bellevue Hospital in New York City and Cook County General Hospital in Chicago are examples of hospitals supported by local government funds. Such hospitals provide not only inpatient care (patients stay in the hospital) but outpatient clinics (patients don't stay overnight) as well. People who are unable to pay for the services of private physicians use these outpatient clinics as their primary medical care provider. These medical services are clearly within the public welfare arrangement.

A contemporary public welfare mechanism that covers medical services for those who cannot afford to pay is *Medicaid,* which is provided under the Social Security Amendments of 1965. By 1971, Medicaid benefits had been extended to not only the aged and families on AFDC but also to the disabled, the blind, and to most individuals suffering from end-stage renal disease. Medicaid is available to people in income maintenance programs and, in some cases, to those who are known as medically indigent, that is, who are not eligible for income maintenance but whose incomes are too low to pay for adequate medical care. Medicaid is jointly funded by state and federal governments and administered by the states. The states are given considerable latitude over which services to provide. But all programs must provide outpatient and inpatient care, laboratory and X-ray service, skilled nursing home care, and physicians' care. A major criticism of the Medicaid programs implemented by the states is their almost exclusive focus on treating illness, with little concern for prevention and rehabilitation.

Social insurance, in the form of national health insurance, has been a topic of discussion in the United States since at least 1912, when the Progressive Party under Theodore Roosevelt had a proposal for national health insurance in their party platform.[5] To date, despite numerous attempts to provide universal coverage through a national health insurance plan, the United States remains one of the few major nations without such a plan. Only one segment of our population is covered by a universal health care social insurance plan—the elderly (those over sixty-five years of age). In 1965, amendments to the Social Security Act provided the *Medicare* program, (passed at the same time that the Medicaid program was established.) All persons over sixty-five are covered by Part A, which is financed through the payroll taxes, commonly known as Social Security, paid by workers and employers. Part A pays primarily for inpatient hospital care. There are deductibles (an amount to be paid before the insurance payments begin) and co-payments (the insurance only covers a percentage of the costs). Part B is optional and is financed by an insurance premium paid for by the recipient and federal government contributions. It covers physicians' costs, and it too has deductibles and co-payments.[6]

Social services have been provided in the health care system since 1909. (See Table 10.1.) Such services are mandatory for nursing home patients whose care is provided under Medicaid. The Veterans Administration facilities have been leaders in providing medical social services. Social services are also required in hospitals accredited by the Joint Council on the Accreditation of Hospitals. They are also a part of the services offered by some private medical practice groups, such as Health Maintenance Organizations (HMO) and maternal and child health services.

While the United States has not, to date, seen fit to develop a universal provision mechanism for the health care of its citizens, many other countries, including Canada and Great Britain, do have universal provision arrangements that cover the vast majority of the health care provided to their citizens. In Canada, national health care insurance is federally mandated but provincially administered. Funding is from

Table 10.1   Important Dates: Social Work in Health Care

| | |
|---|---|
| 1893 | Hull House medical dispensary opened. |
| 1905 | First medical social worker. Outpatient Department Massachusetts General Hospital |
| 1918 | American Association of Hospital Social Workers formed. |
| 1921 | Sheppard-Towner Act established child and maternal health centers. |
| 1926 | Social Services established in Veterans Administration hospital system. |
| 1935 | Social Security Act authorizes maternal and child health programs (Title V). |
| 1965 | Amendments to Social Security Act provide Medicaid (Title XIX) and Medicare (Title XVIII). |
| 1973 | Health Maintenance Organization Act requires social services as one component of care. |
| 1976 | Publication begun of two social work journals: *Health and Social Work* and *Social Work in Health Care*. |
| 1983 | Prospective payment — Diagnostic Related Groups (DRGS) introduced by U.S. Department of Health and Human Service for Medicare Services. |

federal general tax funds, provincial general tax base, and insurance mechanisms. All medical care, including doctor's fees, hospitalization costs, and some prescriptions drugs, are provided at no cost, though there has been some concern about overuse and the need for minimum fees to prevent this. Patients have free choice of doctors, who receive set fees for services rendered. Most hospitals are also provincially administered. In countries with universal provision for health care, all people have access to such care. Health care is seen as a right. There are two arguments used against such a provision, excessive cost and inferior quality of services. Counter arguments can be put forth against both. In relation to the cost, is there not a greater long term cost resulting from poor social functioning due to untreated health problems? Relative to inferior service, there are examples of inferior and superior service in the current system. Discussion of plans for universal provision of health care will probably continue until some solution is found for the problems that abound in the current system.

Thus, all arrangements used to provide social welfare services in the United States are also used to provide health care services. There are at least two levels of health care in the United States. One tier is for those who can pay for their care or who carry insurance that will pay for care. This tier's services are organized around a private practice system of medical care. Mutual aid, social insurance, and social services also provide services to this tier. The other tier, which provides services for those who cannot pay, relies heavily on mutual aid, charity-philanthropy, public welfare, and social services for services. One overlap between the health care system and the social welfare system falls in the area of the arrangements used to provide health care services. In the following sections of this chapter, as social services in health care settings are discussed, further areas of overlap will also become apparent.

## Social Services and Social Policy in Health Care

The relationship between the health care system and the social welfare system extends at least as far back as the late 1800s. Both the Charity Organization Societies and the settlement houses were concerned with the health care of the people they served. Hull House had a medical dispensary that Jane Addams organized in 1893. The Charity Organization Societies were concerned with programs to combat infant mortality, tuberculosis, and rickets and scurvy. Maternal and child health clinics and free dispensaries for the poor were also set up by social workers in some communities.[7]

At the same time, the use of hospitals for health care was growing. In 1905, Dr. Richard Cabot introduced social work at Massachusetts

General Hospital. Cabot had identified social factors he believed blocked effective medical treatment, and he identified social workers as understanding the environmental circumstances and having the ability to find ways of overcoming these blocks. Ida Cannon, a trained nurse who also had training in sociology and psychology, worked Massachusetts General and is considered to be the first medical social worker. Other hospitals, particularly the public hospitals, began to follow suit and use nurses with special training to deliver social services. Cannon traveled widely, attended conferences, gave papers, and generally spread the word about the value of social services in hospitals. By 1918, there were enough hospital social workers to form the American Association of Hospital Social Workers. This group saw the need for professional training and several schools of social work began to offer a specialized curriculum for medical social workers.[8]

After World War I, the federal government enacted two important pieces of health care legislation. The first was the establishment of the Veterans Administration (VA) in 1921. Health care for the veteran has always been an essential ingredient of the services available from the VA. These services can be seen as a different type of public health service. In the past, public health services were provided by local government for those who could not obtain care elsewhere because of poverty. The VA is a federal health care program offered as a benefit for those who served in the armed forces, with fairly broad eligibility requirements. This organization has always been a pacesetter in the area of medical social services; theirs were established in 1926. There are 171 VA hospitals, all of which provide social services to their patients. In addition, the VA has an extensive outpatient service made up of not only medical services but mental health, supportive personal care services, and professional supervision in the veteran's own home or a wide range of substitute residential services. Over three thousand professional social workers are employed in the various VA facilities.[9]

The second important act of that period includes another area where health care and social welfare overlap—child welfare services. In 1921, Congress passed the *Sheppard-Towner Act*, which established child and maternal health centers, most of them in rural areas. Under regulations developed by the Children's Bureau, states were helped to provide more adequate services to women and their children and to significantly lower the infant and maternal mortality rate. This program focused on health care with a preventive and developmental focus. Education of mothers was an important ingredient. Though the Act was not funded after 1929, its purpose was carried out after 1935 by the Social Security Act.[10]

Although the maternal and child health program was incorporated in the 1935 Social Security Act, it was not until the amendments of 1965 that health care received major consideration with the establishment of the Medicare and Medicaid programs. But earlier, in 1946, Congress passed the *Hill–Burton Act,* which assisted states in planning for health facilities and communities in building health facilities in underserved areas. It was a forerunner of the federal health planning programs to follow in the 1960s and 1970s.

During the 1980s, with the general cutbacks in federal spending for social welfare, came other important social policy developments. There was a lessening emphasis on planning and a general concern with the escalating cost of health care, particularly those services supported by governmental funds. The Medicare program received particular attention. *Prospective payment* mechanisms were developed. In these a hospital receives a fixed sum for the treatment of a specific medical condition. If the patient can be serviced for less, the hospital makes money; if the service costs more, they lose money. These *Diagnostic Related Groups (DRGs)* have caused hospitals to need people with discharge planning skills, one of the roles often filled by social workers.[11] Discharge planning involves placement in long term care facilities and provision of needed services if the patient returns home. These changes contributed to the rise of home health care services. They point to a change in the health care system as a response to changes in social policy. They point to changes in the roles and functions of health care social workers. They suggest a change in the relationship between the social welfare system and the health care system.

# Social Work in Health Care

In discussing the role of the social worker in the health care setting, it is necessary to define some of the characteristics of the health care setting. While there is no typical health care setting, the health care system can be divided into three major parts: the hospital, the long-term care facility, and the community setting. Each of these major components has different subcomponents. The *hospital* may be a large teaching hospital or a hospital specializing in one or more medical conditions or a general hospital in a large or small community or a VA facility. For the purpose of discussing roles of social workers, the hospital is considered the component that treats acute and short-term conditions requiring inpatient care. The *long-term facility,* while it may also be called a hospital, in this discussion will include all health care facilities where the patient is in residence over long periods of time (a month or more), including nursing homes and rehabilitation centers. The *community setting* includes private and group practices of physicians, health maintenance organizations (HMOs), home health care units, and outpatient clinics.

## The Role of Social Work in the Health Care System

The use of social workers in hospitals has continued to grow. In 1935, the American Association of Hospital Social Workers became the American Association of Medical Social Workers. For a time, this organization published *The Medical Social Worker Journal*. Social workers became recognized as health care professionals. Their roles expanded to include participation on health care teams and in comprehensive health care projects, clinical treatment, teaching, and consultation. They also became more specialized, following the trend in medicine. In 1955, with the formation of the National Association of Social Workers, medical social workers became a part of the unified organization.

During the 1960s and 1970s, social work roles in health care continued to expand—in part due to the growing influence of federal legislation on health care. The Social Security amendments of 1965 that also established the Medicare and Medicaid programs led to the establishment of positions for many social workers in hospitals and nursing homes. The 1966 Comprehensive Health Planning Act[12] was aimed at coordinating health care facilities, services, and funding with the needs, goals, and priorities of health planning bodies.

Slowly, social services have become an accepted part of all units of the health care system. In 1970, The Joint Committee on the Accrediation of Hospitals adopted a requirement that "social services must be available to patients and families." The 1973 Health Maintenance Organization Act that oversees HMOs (to be discussed later in this chapter) also requires that they make social services available.[13], thus fueling the gradual growth of social services in group medical practices as well as in hospitals, nursing homes, and maternal and child health programs.

During this period social work in health care has also grown and developed. Graduate social work schools have established specialty areas in social work in health care. Two specialty journals have been established and books on social work in health care have begun to appear.[14] Some discussion developed about the role of the BSW and the MSW in the health care field of practice, though there is still no definitive statement as to the role of each level of practice in health care settings.

Throughout the history of the relationship of the health care system and the social welfare system, there has been an ongoing debate about the control that physicians have had in the planning and delivery of health care. Although there is no doubt that a doctor must be in charge of the physical care, the psychosocial components of health care (i.e., those that focus on social and psychological effects of illness and treatment) and the health care planning (including the development of mechanisms for providing the fiscal supports for care) are areas where social workers have considerable knowledge. Health care can be enhanced by the use of this knowledge. Social workers have been particularly affected by this debate since they are often seen as an ancillary profession in health care. They have had to fight an ongoing battle to obtain and retain recognition for their expertise and contribution to the health care field of practice.[15]

The health care system is a multidisciplined one; important professionals in the system include: doctors, nurses, physical therapists, occupational therapists, speech clinicians, nutritionists. In some settings, psychologists, chaplains, and health educators may also be involved. This means the social worker must find a place among often overlapping areas of concern and must work within a team. Second, the physician is the primary professional in patient care, and either specifically or through previously chosen mechanisms determines the social worker's involvement with any patient. Physician desires must be dealt with and doctors must be kept informed of the social worker's plans and intervention. Third, in contemporary health care, a great deal of stress is placed on *accountability* —the means for establishing appropriateness and effectiveness of services. Documentation of work performed and contacts made on behalf of the clients, audits and surveys, and care plans are essential parts of work in the health care setting. It is usually assumed that social workers will deal with psychosocial problems, that they will work with families of patients, and that they will have knowledge of community resources that can benefit the patient or the family. In many settings, particularly if the worker is an MSW, teaching, consultation, and administration are also functions of social workers.

In 1984, 20.4 percent of all social workers were employed in health care settings. This represents a total of about 62,000 social workers.[16] As said before, the differentiation of roles between the MSW and BSW in the health care setting is still uncertain, as it is in the profession generally. However, MSWs tend to predominate in large teaching hospitals and hospitals in larger communities. They may direct social services in some long-term care facilities and in community agencies. BSWs tend to work in small hospitals or under the supervision of an MSW in a large hospital. They tend to be the social worker in a nursing home and carry case management roles in other long-term facilities. Their role in community settings is still unclear. The BSW tends to provide a good deal of the health care social work in nonmetropolitan settings.

Social workers are found in a variety of health care settings. The roles and responsibilities of these workers vary from setting to setting. Four settings are of particular interest in discussing the roles of social workers in health care settings: hospitals, long term care facilities, community settings, and maternal and child health programs.

## Health Care Settings

HOSPITAL SOCIAL WORK    When working in a hospital, a social worker must always be aware of the dual authority system existing in such settings: not only is there the medical authority of the physician but there is also administrative authority coming from the hospital administrator. Hospital administration has become a discipline in its own right, with responsibility for the ongoing functioning of the hospital facility. Also affecting the social worker's functioning is how patients are assigned. Some social workers are assigned to specialty units—such as neonatal, obstetrics, pediatrics, medical and surgical, oncology, renal disease, to name a few. Each of these specialty units has its own way of functioning and of determining how the social worker will be involved.[17] Other social workers receive referrals from physicians and other health care professionals for social services. In still other settings, *protocols* (rules for treating particular medical problems) have been developed and determine which patients are at risk, psychosocially, and should be automatically referred for social services.

Recently, health care social workers have moved into the emergency room. In the past thirty years, the number of emergency room visits has risen 945 percent. The emergency room is used as a source of primary care by many people. Emergency rooms also serve rape victims, battered women, child abuse victims, and suicidal and psychiatric patients. All of these situations call for psychosocial care as well as medical care. The role and function of the social worker in these settings still is not well-defined, but clearly, they are the team members that care not only for the patient but for the accompanying family members.[18]

Bracht has identified twelve services usually provided by social workers in hospitals:

1. Assessing the need for social work service.
2. Casefinding (finding those who need services), outreach, and high-risk population identification, and services to such groups.
3. Counseling to patients and families on their reactions to illness and disability, and facilitating a treatment plan.
4. Discharge planning service.
5. Preadmission planning.
6. Providing continuity of care.
7. Providing information and referral service.
8. Consulting with staff and outside agencies.
9. Institutional services planning.
10. Community liaison services.
11. Community planning and coordination activity.
12. Collaborating with physicians and other staff.[19]

Social services in hospitals are affected by outside accrediting agencies. Of primary importance in this area are the "Standards for Hospital Social Service" of the Joint Commission on Accreditation of Hospitals.[20] Because of funding implications the Professional Standards Review Organizations (PSRO), which operate in relationship to medical services provided under the Social Security Act (Medicare, Medicaid, and maternal and child health services), are important.[21] If the PSRO decides that a service is unnecessary, that service is not funded.

## A Case Study

The social worker on a pediatric unit was made aware that five-year-old John R had been diagnosed as having leukemia. Because of new treatments and the early stage of the disease, the prognosis for John experiencing a remission and surviving the disease is good. However, nursing staff have noted that the parents are distraught and unable to cooperate with the care of the child. The social worker came to the unit at a time both parents were scheduled to visit. She drew them aside, introduced herself, and asked if she could talk with them in her office. When the parents and the social worker got to the office, it was apparent that the mother was very upset, the father on the other hand seemed distant and distrustful. The worker explained that she could understand their shock at John's diagnosis and wondered what questions they might have about it. The mother broke down and became almost hysterical: the father seemed unable to respond to her and remained deep in his own thoughts. The worker told the parents that such feelings were natural and encouraged the parents to talk about how they felt. She listened to an outpouring from the mother and when this lessened somewhat, encouraged the father to talk about how he felt. He tentatively began to talk about how he found it difficult to express feelings but did talk about his concern for his wife. The worker probed, to help him express his frustration at not being able to do anything for John.

When the feelings had been dealt with to some extent, the worker asked if they understood the diagnosis. It soon was apparent they did not. Both parents had only heard the diagnosis and not the prognosis. They assumed John would soon die. The worker talked a little with them about new treatments and about some children she had known who had survived with leukemia. She suggested they set up a joint conference with John's doctor to further explore prognosis and treatment issues. With this the father asked the social worker how they should treat John, what they could do for him. The worker then discussed the meaning of having a sick child and together the three discussed some immediate ways the parents could relate to their child. As a followup, the worker set up the conference with the doctor and checked with the nursing staff about how the parents were relating to their child. The nursing staff reported a marked improvement in their ability to

*continued*

*A Case Study . . . continued*

participate in John's care. The social worker also noted that this situation would require ongoing social services to give the family support, help them to express feelings and ask questions, and to help them in parenting their child during his illness.

LONG-TERM CARE   Three groups of people usually make up the patients in long-term care facilities, those with life-long disabilities that require ongoing skilled nursing care, those with sudden disabilities like multiple sclerosis, disabling stroke, or trauma (quadriplegia or other extensive injury) resulting from accidents, and the elderly too frail to be cared for in a community setting. The two types of institutions usually considered long-term care facilities are nursing homes and rehabilitation hospitals. Though there are differences in the delivery of social services, depending on the reason for the need for long-term care and the particular long-term care facility, there is a commonality about the role of the social worker in these settings. Their role is different from that of a social worker in the hospital setting. First, social work plays a more central role and the physician role is often diminished. Second, the psychosocial needs are related, in part, to the long-term nature of the setting. Patients live in the facility, their ongoing needs for relationships, privacy, and activity must receive attention. Third, the medical condition is chronic, and often is not going to get better. Thus, the emphasis is on living with illness rather than curing it.

With patients who have had a life-long disability, the movement to the rehabilitation facility may come in adolescence or early adulthood, when the family can no longer meet the special needs of the patient. These patients will need help in separating from their families, making plans for how to live life in the most productive way possible, connecting with a variety of resources that may enrich life, and sometimes with plans for moving back to supported community living or to a more appropriate living facility.

With patients who have an unanticipated disability, the first task is helping them recognize the nature of the disability and how it will affect their life-styles. Many feelings will need to be dealt with at this stage. Patients' will need a great deal of support for the arduous tasks of rehabilitation. Families need help with their feelings. Ongoing tasks of development, such as education or parenting also need attention. Patients must be given help with developing ongoing living arrangements after the rehabilitation is completed. Resources must be found to support the patient either in a long-term care facility or in the community.

With elderly patients, the nursing home social worker will facilitate their entry into the facility with preplacement services and services to help the families and patients with the decision to enter the home. Families need help learning how to relate to family members in a nursing home and in dealing with their feelings about the patient. On admission, a social history and indepth assessment of the patient's needs must be developed. The social worker participates in the development of care plans. Ongoing tasks with nursing home patients include updating and revising goals and care plans, ongoing counseling or group activity, collaborating and consulting with staff, family, and volunteers about the needs of the patient, financial planning, and working to maintain family support and ties. Some patients progress to the point that they can be discharged. Discharge planning then becomes a social work task.

In long-term care facilities, the social worker carries some responsibility to see that the milieu of the facility is one that supports patient functioning at the highest level possible, one in which all the needs (not just the health care needs) of the patient are taken into account. To do this, the social worker consults with other staff about psychosocial aspects of care and the impact of the milieu on social functioning, participates in staff meetings where decisions are made about the facility's program and way of operating, and provides educational sessions for other staff in areas where the social worker has expertise. The social worker also coordinates the use of community resources to meet the needs of individuals or groups of patients in the area of social functioning. They will maintain the necessary records and serve as an advocate for patients. The social worker in the long-term care facility works with individuals, families, groups, and the institution itself, as well as the community of which it is a part. The social work role in these facilities is indeed a generalist role.

---

### A Case Study

The social worker went to see Mrs. B, who had just been taken by ambulance to a nursing home from a local hospital. Unfortunately, the social worker had not had an opportunity to visit Mrs. B or talk with her family prior to admission. Mrs. B was recovering from a fractured pelvis. The hospital asked for admission since she had used up her Diagnostic Related Group days and no longer needed acute care. The worker found Mrs. B confused and angry. She was not sure where she was and said no one asked her if she wanted to come here. The worker explained to Mrs. B that she was in Shadydale Nursing Home, and that together they would explore whether this is the type of care she would need on a long-term basis. The worker repeated that while she still needed care, she did not have to remain in the hospital any longer. The worker briefly described

*continued*

*A Case Study . . . continued*

the advantages of being in a nursing home over a hospital and assured her that this is not necessarily the "end of the line." Mrs. B became quieter and the worker asked about her living circumstances prior to hospitalization. She found that Mrs. B lived alone in low-cost senior housing. She told Mrs. B that she would check on how long the apartment could be held for her. The social worker asked Mrs. B if there was anything she would like from the apartment for her room here at the nursing home. They discussed this, and Mrs. B asked for some family pictures. The worker told her that she would get them and check on the apartment for her. Then the worker asked about her family and found Mrs. B had one daughter, who lived some distance away with a large family of her own that she could not leave just then. The daughter was notified of and gave permission for the move. The worker told Mrs. B she would like to call the daughter and talk with her. Hesitantly, Mrs. B gave permission for this. The worker then told Mrs. B she would be talking to her quite a bit in the next few days and gave a definite time for the next day.

The worker, in thinking about the situation of Mrs. B, noted how this was the third time in a month that Shadydale received a patient from the hospital who had inadequate preparation for the move. She noted that plans must be developed to prevent this from happening in the future. She called Mrs. B's daughter and found a very guilt-ridden woman who just did not know what to do about her mother. The worker assured her that her mother was being well cared for but that long-term plans would need to be made and that the social worker would keep in touch with her. She shared her plans to look into the apartment situation and bring the requested pictures and some of Mrs. B's clothes to the nursing home. The worker called the apartment manager and arranged to see him the first thing in the morning. She also recorded her contact in Mrs. B's chart and discussed her findings with the head nurse. She talked to an able long-time resident, who had a similar experience on admission to the home and suggested that she visit with Mrs. B.

COMMUNITY SETTINGS    The role that social workers play in community settings is still very unclear. For the most part, social workers, usually MSWs, have negotiated their role with the individual physician or clinic. There is also little information about how many social workers are practicing in community health settings. The literature from time to time contains articles that relate to specific situations. Arnold M. Gross, Jacqueline Gross, and A. Rosa Esenstein-Naveh have developed a list of psychosocial problems that are suitable for social work intervention in primary health care, which is a major function of community care.[22] Included are family problems, problems of children, geriatrics, physical illness, adult mental retardation, environmental problems, resource problems, mental problems, behavioral problems, and noncompliance with medical directions. This list covers many of the problems that social workers in other setting are concerned about. Doctors and social workers must work together to identify types of problems that both doctors and social workers agree need psychosocial care. Over time, a general consensus of the role of the social worker in these primary health care settings can emerge.[23]

One type of primary health care setting that has emerged in recent years is the *Health Maintenance Organization (HMOs)*. This is a voluntary, prepaid health system built around a group medical practice. The federal government has set standards and provided financial assistance to these organizations over the last twelve years. Originally, medical social services were required of those organizations receiving federal assistance; however, since 1981, this has not been the case. Social workers do continue to be employed in some HMOs. Jane B. Mayer and Gail Rubin believe the role of social workers in HMOs can only increase in importance in the next decade.[24]

Some of the services that social workers perform in HMOs are helping patients adjust to illness and understand and follow medical recommendations, helping patients with personal and behavioral problems that adversely affect their health, providing referral and resource development, coordinating rehabilitation services. In addition, they provide the medical team with information about social and emotional rehabilitation. They treat crisis-based mental health problems and are involved in educational activities. They handle grievances and discharge planning.[25]

*Maternal and child health programs* are other community programs that employ social workers. There programs serve children with special needs, those who have some kind of handicap, or those who are at risk because they live in poor families. Because each state administers its programs within federal guidelines, they differ considerably in practice from program to program. The social worker is a member of the team that serves the child in a holistic manner. Most of these positions require an MSW worker but BSWs are also used in some programs.[26]

Another component of the community health care delivery system, currently growing at a very fast rate is *home health care*. This growth is partly due to the fact that people are spending less time in hospitals, and going home needing continued nursing and other professional care. DRGs are partly responsible for this trend, as is the rising cost of hospital care. Many hospitals are organizing home health care units. Nurses, physical therapists, and other health professionals go into the home to provide the necessary care. Social workers also participate in this care.

Some of the services they provide include developing a patient's comprehensive social history, considering a patient's psychosocial needs in the admission and referral process, making recommendations for the care plan, helping the patient understand and comply with health recommendations, helping the family understand the patient's needs, counseling individuals, families, or groups, and referring people to and developing needed community resources.[27] Hospice care, care for terminally ill people, is also being organized as home care programs. Social workers are important members of the hospice team.

The social worker's role in delivering health care services, whether in the hospital, the long-term care facility, or the community setting, is important if holistic health care is to be provided. Social services can prevent some of the long-term negative results of illness and disability. They can facilitate the use of community resources to prevent overuse of hospitals and long-term facilities. As the health care system in particular and the community in general come to appreciate the value of these services, they cannot help but be in demand. This points to a growing importance of social work in the health care setting.

## Issues in the Relationship of Health Care and Social Welfare

Tremendous change is the contemporary theme in the health care system. A new method of determining payment (prospective payment) seems to be the method of the future, not only for Medicare patients but for those covered by health insurance and governmental payment mechanisms. This is only one response to the concerns about the rising cost of health care. In the future, there may be more reliance on professionals other than physicians for care. (Nurse practitioners and physicians assistants provide an increasing primary care service.) There is a growing emphasis on delivery of health care in the community rather than in institutions. (The growth of home health care services is one indication.) Prevention (health care rather than medical care) and a holistic approach are common themes in the popular literature. All of these changes can be interpreted to say that the role of the social worker will increase and become more central in the health care system. Change brings with it many unresolved issues. The health care system has many such issues today. Many affect the field of social work in health care. In this section, some of these issues will be raised and briefly discussed.

A primary issue that has not been resolved, though it has been discussed for some time is whether health care is a right or a privilege. Philosophically, many support health care as a right. However, social policy does not grant this right to all persons. The employed poor, if they have no health insurance, cannot afford health care. The federal medical programs and most health insurance programs do not pay for preventive care: rather, they pay for treating illness.

Quality of life issues also must receive attention. In recent years, enormous progress has been made in maintaining life through medical advances. New treatments and life-support systems are examples of these advances. However, little attention has been given to whether the preservation of life at all costs is in the best interest of the individual or society. Kidney dialysis, artificial hearts, the severely handicapped newborn all require expensive medical treatment, yet the quality of life that the individual can live is greatly limited. Society hesitates to provide funds for the needed medical care or for the life-supports that sustain the lives of people receiving *heroic medical measures,* such as the use of life support systems. Questions of the right to live or the right to die must be answered, and whether public funds should be used for heroic medical measures must be decided. Social workers need to be involved in discussions about biomedical ethics.

Not only is the health care system responsible for resolving these issues, so is the social welfare system. Many of the people affected by these controversial medical procedures will become recipients of financial support and services from the social welfare system. Ultimately, the general public will be involved in the resolution, as they support or fail to support social welfare programs. The general public needs information from the social welfare system as it makes these difficult decisions.

Another related set of issues concern preventive health care. The system, as it now operates, is focused on treating and curing illness. Many of the present-day medical conditions are chronic, incurable, and need to be managed. Prevention exists on both a primary and secondary level. The primary level is preventing chronic illness by educating the public and motivating change. At the secondary level, screening for chronic disease and managing these chronic illnesses prevents more serious effects, including the psychosocial. The emphasis on a holistic approach and on improving life-style is the best way to approach prevention.

Related to life-style issues are cultural issues. Little attention has been paid to the cultural aspects of illness and health care. Some cultural groups have their own health care providers, (the *curandero* of the Chicano and the medicine man of the American Indian). These resources can provide care but few health care agencies understand how to integrate these resources into a health care system that depends on highly trained professionals. Also understanding different life-styles, attitudes about what constitutes health, how illness should be treated, and self-help remedies is needed if these issues are to be addressed.

The social work profession has understanding and expertise that could be very useful in addressing the issues of quality of life, life-style, and prevention. The social welfare system has a considerable interest in resolving these issues, for they are closely related to human need and the mechanisms for meeting that need. Both the social work profession and the social welfare system should address the questions involved in these health care issues.

The financial aspects of health care are another major area of concern. There are issues of funding, of cost containment, of health care as big business, and of third-party insurance payments. These issues can be looked at individually or as a related whole. There is no doubt that with increased technology, the cost of health care has skyrocketed in recent years. With this escalation has also come the escalation in health insurance costs. Currently the quality of insurance provided by employers to employees (a major source of protection) has deteriorated due to these rising costs. Many families who do not have insurance coverage through employers no longer can afford to carry health insurance. Both the Medicare and Medicaid programs have serious limitations in what services they provide. Our society assumes that most people will pay for their health care or be covered by insurance. As costs rise and insurance coverage shrinks, this is no longer possible for many people. The problems of cost of and payment for health care must be resolved. If health care is a right, then it should be available to those who need it. Yet if the individual is expected to pay for health care—and the cost of either the care or the insurance to cover the care is so great that they cannot pay—then either government must pick up the cost or the individual's right to health care is not recognized. Some means must be found to provide health care institutions and professionals with a fair return for services and yet allow all people to receive care when they need it.

One solution, which to date has been rejected in the United States, is some form of a national health care insurance. Under such a program, everyone would pay a premium for health insurance that would then cover any medical care. The government would pay the premium for those who are too poor. This program could be administered by federal or state governments or by private insurance companies. There are problems with this system, but these problems are not as great as the ones generated by the present U.S. health care system.

Medical practices and institutions are now managed as businesses. Some feel that this places the major emphasis not on quality of care but on how much money can be made. With the rise of new professions such as physician-assistants, nurse-practitioners, or mental health professionals in the health care field, and old professions providing a broader range of skilled services, come questions about whether these new professionals should be reimbursed by insurance for their services. There are indications that some health care can not only be provided by professionals other than physicians but that it can be provided more cheaply. But without a system for reimbursing the new professionals, it is impossible to use this to reduce costs. The issues of health care as a business and of insurance coverage also must be addressed.

Another development is the proliferation of professions that function in the health care field. There is no agreement as to which profession should carry out which tasks. For example: in the area of discharge planning, should this be the task of a social worker or a nurse? Interdisciplinary turf battles must be settled. Some means must be developed to determine which profession is best qualified to carry out which tasks. Social work, as a profession expanding its role in the health care field, will be affected by these decisions, and if social work is to take its rightful place among health care professionals, the profession must give attention to the issue. In addition, the profession should consider and clarify the role of the BSW and the role of the MSW in the health care field. This should not be done from assumptions about what tasks each level of worker can carry out, but from careful study of the roles and tasks that are being carried out by both levels of social workers in the health field.

In this section of the chapter, issues have been raised. Few solutions have been suggested. Both the social welfare system and the profession of social work have contributions to make in the forthcoming discussions. Individual social workers will need to keep abreast of the unavoidable changes that will come and be prepared to answer the challenges change will bring.

## Summary

This chapter has discussed the nature of the contemporary health care system and the intertwining of that system with the social welfare system. It has noted the role that social work has filled in the health care system and given some indication of the expanded roles for social workers that can be a part of the future health care system. One last question needs to be raised: Can the social welfare system and the health care systems really be separate if the needs of individuals in a complex society are to be met? Hokenstad has stated:

> Universal health care and social services are fundamental building blocks of the modern welfare state. They are invariably discrete organizational and programmatic systems within the structure of government. From an administrative standpoint, this is rational and efficient. But for the consumer of services this structural arrangement may have negative consequences—particularly where there is little provision for linkage and collaboration between the two systems. The interrelationship of health, mental health, and social well-being is well documented. Emotional problems are frequently converted into health problems and lack of social support is sometime manifested as a health problem.[28]

This may be the most crucial of all issues. Until it is resolved, the social welfare system and the health care system will continue to overlap and be competitive for scarce funds. Social workers will find themselves relating to both systems in the health care field of practice with conflicting demands from the two systems. Individuals will continue to have social functioning needs met both by systems, often in a confusing and a clumsy manner.

## Key Words

| | |
|---|---|
| accountability | holistic |
| charity hospital | home health care agency |
| charity patient | hospital |
| community setting | long-term care facility |
| Diagnostic Related Groups (DRGs) | maternal and child health programs |
| Health Maintenance Organization (HMO) | Medicaid |
| | Medicare |
| health care system | prospective payment |
| heroic medical measures | protocol |
| Hill-Burton Act | Sheppard-Towner Act |

## Questions for Discussion

1. If the social welfare system and the health care system overlap as is discussed in this chapter, should they not be one unified system? What do you see as the obstacles to a unification of the two systems?

2. What is the impact on an individual's social functioning of the presence of a two-tier health care system?

3. What do you think are the reasons that the United States has not adopted National Health Care Insurance? Give arguments for and against such a mechanism.

4. In tracing the history of health care as it relates to social welfare, how do you see poverty, prejudice and discrimination, resource distribution, and social change contributing to that history?

5. What do you think should be the role of the federal government in the health care system? The state governments?

6. What should be the role of the physician in psychosocial care? What should be the role of the social worker? What should be the role of each in health planning?

7. Do you think prospective payment is an appropriate way to contain health care costs? Why or why not?

8. Do you think the U.S. health care system is making appropriate usage of the hospital, the long-term care facility, and the community setting?

9. How does the dual authority system of the hospital affect social work practice in the health field?

10. Discuss the difficulties and strengths of each of the methods for social workers to receive referrals in the hospital setting.

11. What do you see in the future for the role of social work in primary health care?

12. What changes do you think should be encouraged in the health care system? Support your thinking.

13. How do you relate quality of life and health care? What heroic measures should be supported with government funds?

# Notes

[1] Carel B. Germain, *Social Work Practice in Health Care,* (New York: The Free Press, 1984), p. 34.

[2] See: Stanley J. Brody, "Common Ground: Social Work and Health Care," *Health and Social Work* 1 (February 1976): 16–31.

[3] Michael J. Austin, Michael Baizerman, and Charles Guzzetta, "Public Health and Social Welfare: An Historical View of the Revitalization of an Old Partnership," *Arete* 3 (Spring 1974): 7–20.

[4] Austin, *Public Health*.

[5] Donald Brieland, Lela B. Costin, and Charles R. Atherton, *Contemporary Social Work* (New York: McGraw-Hill Book Co., 1975), p. 115.

[6] Bruce S. Jansson, *Theory and Practice of Social Welfare Policy* (Belmont, CA.: Wadsworth Publishing Co., 1984), chapter 12.

[7] Neil F. Bracht, *Social Work in Health Care: A Guide to Professional Practice* (New York: The Haworth Press, 1978), chapter 1.

[8] Toba Schwaber Kerson, *Social Work in Health Settings* (New York: Longman, 1982), chapter 1.

[9] Gene Rothman and Rosina M. Becerra, "Veterans and Veteran's Services," *Encyclopedia of Social Work*, 18th edition. ed. Anne Minahan (Silver Springs, MD: National Association of Social Workers, 1987), pp. 808–817.

[10] For further discussion of Shephard-Towner see: Sheila M. Rothman, *Woman's Proper Place: A History of Changing Ideals and Practices, 1870 to the Present* (New York: Basic Books, 1978), chapter 4.

[11] For further discussion of DRGs see: Marie A. Caputi and William A. Heiss, "The DRG Revolution," *Health and Social Work* 9 (Winter 1984): 5–14.

[12] Darwin Palmiere, "Health Services: Health and Hospital Planning," *Encyclopedia of Social Work*, 18th edition, ed. John B. Turner (Washington D.C.: National Association of Social Workers, 1977), pp. 595–620.

13 Bracht, *Social Work in Health Care.*

14 The journals are: *Health and Social Work* and *Social Work in Health Care.* Recent books on social work in health care include: Bracht, *Social Work in Health Care;* Rosalind S. Miller and Helen Rehr, *Social Work Issues in Health Care* (Englewood Cliffs, NJ: Prentice-Hall, 1983); and Carel Bailey Germain, *Social Work Practice in Health Care* (New York: The Free Press, 1984).

15 For a discussion of this issue see: Stephen R. Wallace, Richard J. Goldberg, and Andrew E. Slaby, *Clinical Social Work in Health Care* (New York: Praeger, 1984), chapter 1.

16 Sumner M. Rosen, David, Fanshel, and Mary E. Lutz, ed. *Face of the Nation 1987*, Statistical Supplement, *Encyclopedia of Social Work*, 18th edition, ed. John B. Turner (Silver Springs, MD: National Association of Social Workers, 1987), pp. 123–124.

17 See "Specialization and Specialty Interests," *Health and Social Work* 6 (November 1981 Supplement,)

18 Joan Clement and Karil S. Klingbeil, "The Emergency Room," *Health and Social Work* 6 (November 1981 Supplement,): 83S–90S.

19 Bracht, *Social Work in Health Care*, p. 122.

20 "Standard for Hospital Social Services," *Health and Social Work* 3 (May 1978): 4–12.

21 See: *Development of Professional Standards Review for Hospital Social Work* (Chicago: American Hospital Association, 1977).

22 Arnold M. Gross, Jacqueline Gross, and A. Rosa Eisestein-Naveh, "Defining the Role of the Social Worker in Primary Health Care," *Health and Social Work* 8 (Summer 1983): 174–181. While this article discusses practice in Israel, it could easily be applied to the United States.

23 Primary health care refers to the first health care professional to which one goes for such care.

24 Jane B. Mayer and Gail Rubin, "Is There a Future for Social Work in HMOs?" *Health and Social Work* 8 (Fall 1983): 283–289.

25 Bracht, *Social Work in Health Care*, pp. 57–58.

26 Virginia Insley, "Health Services: Maternal and Child Health," *Encyclopedia of Social Work*, pp. 602–610.

27 Jara P. Bonner, Joan M. Saci, Evelyn Rowlands, and Katharine Snouffer, "Medical Social Services in Home Health Agency: Luxury or Necessity," *Home Health Review* 1 (Winter 1978): 28–44.

28 M.C. Hokenstad, R.A. Ritvo, and M. Rosenberg, "International Prespectives on Linking Health and Social Services," *International Social Work* 22 (4): 13–21.

## Suggested Readings

Austin, Michael J., and Kosberg, Jordan I. "Social Service Programming in Nursing Homes," *Health and Social Work* 1 (August 1976): 40–57.

Bartlett, Harriet M. *Social Work Practice in the Health Field.* Washington, D.C.: National Association of Social Workers, 1961.

Bonner, Jara P.; Saci, Joan M.; Rowlands, Evelyn; and Snouffer, Katharine. "Medical Social Services in Home Health Agency: Luxury or Necessity," *Home Health Review* 1 (Winter 1978); 28–34.

Bracht, Neil F. *Social Work in Health Care: A Guide to Professional Practice.* New York: The Haworth Press, 1978.

Brody, Stanley J. "Common Ground: Social Work and Health Care," *Health and Social Work* 1 (February 1976): 16–31.

Cabot, Richard C. *Social Service and the Art of Healing.* New York: Moffat, Yard and Co., 1915, (NASW Classic Series).

Caputi, Marie A., and Heiss, William A., "The DRG Revolution," *Health and Social Work,* 9 (Winter 1984): 5–14.

Germain, Carle Bailey. *Social Work Practice in Health Care: An Ecological Prespective.* New York: The Free Press, 1984.

*Health and Social Work* 10 (Fall 1985) Special issue: "The Past as Prologue: Ten Years of *Health and Social Work* Tenth Anniversary Issue.

Horejsi, Gloria A. "Social Work in the Small Hospital," *Health and Social Work* 4 (August 1979): 10–25.

Jansson, Bruce S. *Theory and Practice of Social Welfare Policy.* Belmont CA.: Wadsworth Publishing Co., 1984, chapter 12.

Mayer, Jane B., and Rubin, Gail. "Is there a Future for Social Work in HMOs?" *Health and Social Work* 8 (Fall 1983): 283–289.

Miller, Rosalind S., and Rehr, Helen. *Social Work Issues in Health Care.* Englewood Cliffs, NJ: Prentice-Hall, 1983.

Minahan, Anne, ed. in chief, *Encyclopedia of Social Work* 18th Edition, Silver Springs, MD: National Association of Social Workers, 1987. Articles on "Health Care Specialization." "Health Planning," "Health Service System," "Hospice," "Hospical Social Work" "Primary Health Care," and "Public Health Care."

Reamer, Frederic G. "Facing Up to the Challenge of DRGS," *Health and Social Work* 10 (Spring 1985): 85–94

*Social Work in Health Care* 10 (Summer 1985) Special Section: Family Adjustments to Illness, pp. 15–54.

Wallace, Stephen R.; Goldberg, Richard J.; and Slaby, Andrew E. *Clinical Social Work in Health Care.* New York: Praeger, 1984.

# Chapter 11

## Social Welfare and Mental Health

One of the factors that contributes to inability to meet basic needs is the state of a person's mental health. The social welfare system then has developed partly because of needs that go unmet due to mental health problems. Different individuals respond in different ways to both their external environment and their internal state of being. This diversity makes it difficult to define what is meant by mental health. One definition of *mental health* is: "a positive state of personal mental well-being in which individuals feel basically satisfied with themselves, their roles in life, and their relationships with others."[1]

The extent of mental health problems is difficult to document. Many people do not seek help for such problems. However, in 1979, there were 8.1 episodes of hospitalization per 1,000 persons in the United States. During that same year, 20.6 episodes per 1,000 persons required outpatient services.[2]

What then is the relationship of social welfare and mental health? Does the social welfare system provide for the needs of people in poor states of mental health or who are in danger of falling into such states because they lack social and economic resources? Or does attention to their mental health prevent the need for social welfare services? These questions are related to whether a preventive or residual approach to social welfare is most desirable. The reality is that some individuals need help from the social welfare system because of poor mental health and others can, through maintenance of their mental health, be prevented from developing a need for help with problems in social functioning.

Another way the social welfare system and mental health services are related is in the functioning of the social worker. Social work is the central profession of the social welfare system. It is also one of the major providers of mental health services. Whether the service falls within the social welfare system or mental health system is often unclear. If social work services in mental health care for social functioning needs, they are a part of the social welfare system as well as mental health services.

Steven P. Segal and Jim Baumohl have discussed this issue in relationship to community mental health. "The community mental health movement's focus on community-based treatment and its emphasis on the impact of social life on mental status places it squarely within the domain of social welfare. Indeed, despite the greater authority accorded the medical profession, social workers staff more full-time positions and provide more services than any other professional group in community mental health centers."[3] Definition of what a mental health service is and what it is not is addressed in the first section of this chapter. Next, the development of mental health services, with particular emphasis on the role of social work in their delivery is considered. Then, this chapter examines the functioning of social workers in the mental health system, along with current concerns and issues for mental health social workers.

## Definition of Mental Health Services

*Mental health services* can be defined as those services provided to individuals who are defined as mentally ill. Officially, the definition of mental illness, or who is mentally ill, generally makes use of a medical (psychiatric) diagnosis, using DSMIII.[4] DSMIII is the official reference for diagnostic classifications of the American Psychiatric Association. An informal way of defining mental illness is to describe it as the manifestation of some emotional difficulty. This kind of definition is often used by the general public. But, these definitions are not as clear-cut as they first seem. Some individuals who, under stressful or difficult circumstances, might manifest symptoms of mental illness never actually do so because their environment is supportive and lacks excessive stresses, while other individuals become ill even in a very supportive, safe, environment. Cultural factors also influence the definition of mental illness.[5] In the mainstream of U.S. society, troublesome people tend to be labeled in some way—often the label is mentally ill. In other cultures the same behavior would not be considered abnormal and might even be valued. For example, in Puerto Rican culture it is believed that spirits of the dead communicate with the living. If a social worker does not understand this and a Puerto Rican client says they are hearing voices, the worker may label the client as psychotic. Mental illness consists of a wide variety of disorders with varying degrees of severity. Some types are short-term, due to loss, stress, anxiety, but *chronic mental illness* can last a lifetime and sometimes may be incurable. The boundary line between mental illness and mental health is often unclear.

If the definition of *mental illness* is based on the absence of mental health, another difficulty occurs. Using the definition of mental health discussed earlier in this chapter, it should be noted that what results in a sense of well-being for one person does not necessarily result in a sense of well-being for another person. Two people who fill the same roles in society may not view those roles with the same sense of satisfaction. One person may be satisfied with a fairly small circle of friends and prefer solitary activity for a good part of their free time. Another person may want ongoing activity within a large group of individuals. In addition, culture may provide individuals with different sets of expectations about life satisfactions.

Because of these difficulties in defining mental illness and mental health, no attempt will be made to define mental health services using these concepts. Rather, a functional definition will be used. In this discussion, *mental health services* will refer to those services which are provided by *mental health agencies*. It is further assumed that generally those agencies use a multidisciplinary approach to provide services, that psychology, psychiatry, and nursing, as well as social work, are core disciplines. Such agencies include *psychiatric hospitals* or psychiatric units in general hospitals, community mental health centers, and child guidance clinics. Services for those who have been diagnosed as chronically mentally ill and treatment for alcohol and drug addiction are included because those services are a part of a community mental health service. Services for the mentally retarded or developmentally disabled are also included because, historically, they have been considered a part of the mental health field.

## Development of Mental Health Services

The recognition of mental illness has existed throughout history. However, before the development of an industrial society, scant attention was paid to this phenomenon. Deviant behavior was much more tolerable in an agricultural society. Families could allow the deviant to participate in the work of the household or to be hidden away. For those with no family, the monasteries often provided a haven. With the onset of industrialization, the mentally ill became a part of the wandering vagrant group viewed as a threat to society. Mentally ill people became known as *lunatics*. They were considered incurable and dangerous. They were often placed in work houses or almshouses.

### Mental Health Care from the 1700s to World War I

This pattern of caring for the mentally ill was generally followed in the early years of U.S. history. (See Table 11.1) With the rise of special

Table 11.1   Important Dates: Social Work in Mental Health

| | |
|---|---|
| 1773 | First mental hospital established, Williamsburg, Virginia. |
| 1833 | Worcester State Hospital (Massachusetts) established and uses "moral treatment." |
| 1840s/50s | Dorthea Dix works for adequate treatment of the mentally ill. |
| 1854 | Congress passes act to provide support for care of mentally ill. President Pierce vetos. |
| 1908 | Publication of Clifford Beer's *The Mind that Found Itself.* |
| 1909 | National Committee on Mental Hygiene formed. |
| 1909 | Child guidence clinic established in Cook County, Illinois. |
| 1946 | Passage of the National Mental Health Act. |
| 1961 | Commission on Mental Illness and Health report. |
| 1963 | Community Mental Health Centers Act passed. |
| 1977 | President Carter establishes the President's Commission on Mental Health. |
| 1980 | Mental Health Centers Act. |
| 1981 | Reagan administration repeals budgetary authorizations affecting Mental Health Centers Act and includes federal support for mental health services in the health services block grant. |

institutions, the charity-philanthropy arrangement began to be increasingly relied upon. In 1773, a mental hospital was established in Williamsburg, Virginia. This and other mental institutions that followed the *insane asylums* established during the nineteenth century in most states, were in part developed to separate the mentally ill from the general population of the workhouses, poor farms, and jails. Since the mentally ill were considered incurable, little treatment was offered. Often the "lunatic" was confined in chains or in barred cells. Care was extremely poor, at best.

Word of enlightened ways of caring for the mentally ill being used in Europe did reach across the Atlantic. Of particular interest was the work of Phillippe Pinel in Paris, who used kindness and firmness to "cure" some mentally ill people. Worcester State Hospital, established in 1833 in Massachusetts, used what was known as moral treatment. *Moral treatment* was based on the concept of providing a quiet, supportive environment in which the patient could develop new behaviors. For a time this seemed successful. It was probably useful for the newly admitted patient, but its downfall was the growth of the long-term chronic population who did not respond as well to moral treatment. State hospitals tended to house individuals from the poorer classes, many of whom were immigrants and were experiencing difficulty in coping in a new culture. This population, due to their different cultures, was little understood by their caretakers and also appeared not to respond to moral treatment.[6]

In the 1840s and 1850s, Dorothea Dix spent a great deal of time speaking to politicians and others about the needs of the mentally ill. She went from state to state, calling for humane care of the insane—instead of isolation, neglect, and cruelty—for a special state institution for their care. She also worked to obtain medical care and moral treatment for the mentally ill. She was responsible for founding or enlarging thirty-two mental hospitals in the United States and abroad.[7] She also persuaded the Congress, in 1854, to pass a bill that provided public lands for the support of therapeutic programs for the mentally ill. However, President Pierce vetoed the bill on the grounds that care of the mentally ill was the responsibility of the states, not the federal government.

Another important influence on the care of the mentally ill was Clifford Beers. Early in the twentieth century, he spent several years in mental institutions. His book, *The Mind that Found Itself*[8] was widely read. In 1908, he founded the Connecticut Society for Mental Hygiene, and in 1909, the National Committee for Mental Hygiene (now the *National Association for Mental Health*). Originally, the purpose of this organization was for advocating more humane treatment of the mentally ill. To this day, this citizens organization is very influential in working for public awareness and for the development of services in the mental health field. It is the largest voluntary organization in the field of mental health today, with over one million members.

The National Association for Mental Health became interested in the prevention of mental illnesses, and saw the treatment of children who were displaying emotional difficulty as a promising measure. The child guidance movement began with a clinic in Cook County, Illinois, in 1909. By 1930, there were five hundred such clinics. *Child guidance clinics* use the interdisciplinary triad (psychiatrist, psychologist, and social worker) in providing services. They have been heavily influenced by Freudian psychoanalysis and make heavy use of play therapy.

## Mental Health Care from World War II

Following World War II, the Veteran's Administration began to establish what is now the largest psychiatric program in the country. In part, this was an outgrowth of the military experience of both World Wars I and II. World War I saw the first identification of psychiatric casualties. In World War II's selective service, the screening process identified mental illness as a major factor in rejecting men for service. The psychiatric casualties of the Vietnam War have also been heavy. To meet the needs of veterans, then, the Veteran's Administration facilities place considerable emphasis on psychiatric care.

*Mental hospitals*, that is hospitals caring only for mental illness and other emotional or developmental problems, remained the major resource for the treatment of mental illness until very recently. In 1955, there were 550,000 patients in state psychiatric hospitals.[9] By 1981 there were 122,073 patients in state and county hospitals.[10] Often, these institutions became the dumping ground for the unwanted, the nonproductive. This was especially tragic when the unwanted were children. Placed with the general population of the hospital, they received little treatment, nor did the hospitals make any effort to meet their special needs, including education. Gradually this has changed. Now special units for children are provided in some mental hospitals. More often, mentally ill children are placed in residential treatment facilities that provide treatment, education, and a social environment for the children. Specialized group homes have also been developed as a resource for mentally ill children. Private and religious agencies, once dedicated to caring for dependent children in orphanages, have now changed their focus to caring for emotionally disturbed children.

In 1946, as a result of a growing awareness of the problems relating to mental health, the National Mental Health Act was passed. A major thrust of this legislation was research on prevention and treatment of mental illnesses and the training of mental health professionals. This led to the formation, in 1949, of the *National Institute for Mental Health*. This act also encouraged states to designate an agency as its mental health authority. It provided grants-in-aid and technical assistance to the states for programs treating mental disorders.

Beginning in the 1950s, three developments provided new advances in the care of the mentally ill. First, new drugs, *psychotropic drugs* like tranquilizers, and others, made management of the mentally ill much easier. They reduced bizarre behavior and relieved anxiety in many patients. Second, the concept of a "therapeutic community," as developed by the British psychiatrist Maxwell Jones, became popular. This called for changing the institutional setting, the ward, into a therapeutic setting, using principles of democratic living. Third, many large state hospitals began to be organized geographically. Patients were assigned to wards or units that served a specific geographic area rather than specific types of illness. This allowed closer ties with outpatient facilities in that geographical area. These three developments laid the ground work for a shift from an emphasis on inpatient treatment to treatment in the community.[11]

## The Development of Community Mental Health Centers

The growing concern about mental health in the United States influenced Congress to pass the Mental Health Study Act. This act resulted in the formation of the Joint Commission on Mental Illness and Health and a 1961 report, *Action for Mental Health*. [12] The report called for

1) care for acutely disturbed patients in outpatient clinics and inpatient psychiatric units located in general hospitals,

2) improved care of chronic patients in state hospitals, to be limited to no more than 1,000 beds,

3) aftercare and partial hospital and rehabilitation services, and

4) expanded mental health education for the public. In December 1962, President John F. Kennedy sent a special message to Congress that proposed a national mental health program. [13]

The Community Mental Health Centers Act of 1963 called for the formation of catchment areas with populations of from 75,000 to 200,000 people, proposing that no more than one hour of travel should be necessary to reach a community mental health center. The original act made federal funds available for the construction of centers. It also emphasized state planning and called for state plans for the delivery of mental health services. In 1965, amendments to the act allowed grants to cover staffing assistance. In 1966, the Comprehensive Health Planning and Public Health Service Amendments required that a minimum of 15 percent of the grant go for direct mental health services. From 1967 to 1975, the provisions of the act were extended for additional periods of time.

*Community mental health centers* were expected to offer five services: inpatient care, outpatient care, emergency services, partial hospitalization, and consultation and education. Later, diagnostic services, rehabilitation services, precare and aftercare services, training, and research and evaluation were also required. Continuity of care was stressed. In 1970, legislation also covered the construction and staffing of facilities for the prevention and treatment of alcoholism and drug abuse and for services for children.

In 1977, President Carter established the President's Commission on Mental Health to identify the mental health needs of the nation and to make recommendations to the President. In 1980, The Mental Health Systems Act was passed by Congress. This act made available funds to continue many of the activities provided for under the Community Mental Health Centers Act. Grants were made specifically for the treatment of the chronically mentally ill, severely disturbed children and adolescents, and other underserved populations. The role of the National Institute of Mental Health was expanded to include ongoing planning activities. This act never had a chance to become fully operational, for in

1981, under President Reagan, the budgetary authorizations of the act were repealed and federal support for mental health services was included under the health services block grant. Some requirements for funding mental health services were retained at least until federal funding commitments were fulfilled.[14]

Assessing the community mental health movement, reveals a tendency to focus on verbal, middle class, nonpsychotic patients who probably do not need hospitalization. Aftercare and services for the chronic patient have been neglected.[15] The philosophy of treatment in a community mental health center is that the center meets the needs of the population it serves with a wide variety of approaches. This is done by using several professional disciplines, often with a team approach. Centers emphasize continuity of care, prevention, avoidance of hospitalization, and linkage with the human service network. They focus on health rather than illness. Citizen participation in their governance is essential.

With the development of mental health centers has come the movement for *deinstitutionalization*. Mental care professionals developed a strong belief that institutions were not therapeutic, and thus to be avoided at all costs, and that when used, patients should be discharged as soon as they are stabilized. During the late 1960s and 1970s, a considerable push was made to discharge many long-term patients. Populations in state institutions dropped by one-half or two-thirds from earlier numbers of patients. This movement was in part due to changes in the Social Security Act. Supplementary Income Assistance became available to discharged mental patients. Medicare and Medicaid also could be used for some costs of care. Many of the expatients became residents of nursing homes. Problems developed because neither the nursing home or the community mental health center were prepared to provide these individuals with the needed care and services. But today, the nursing home is still the institution that cares for the elderly mentally ill patient rather than the state hospital.

As the economy worsened in the late 1970s and early 1980s, public attention was given to the growing number of homeless people, "the street people."[16] Many of these people are chronically mentally ill and are on the streets because of deinstitutionalization and recent court rulings about the rights of mentally ill persons that prevent them being held in institutions against their wishes.[17] Another group of chronically mentally ill individuals has also been identified—young adults.[18] One problem in treating these new noninstitutionalized people needing mental health services has been the disinterest of mental health professionals to give service to them.[19] The chronically mentally ill do not respond to traditional methods of psychotherapy. A cure usually is not a realistic goal. Rather these people need long-term (perhaps life-time) services that support them, give them protected community living and work, and coordinate for them the wide range of community services they need.

What have come to be known as *community support programs* offer an approach that supplies the services needed by chronically mentally ill people, who formerly would have been institutionalized for life and who are still at risk of repeated hospitalizations.[20] BSW social workers have displayed both interest and skill in working with this client group, using a case management approach.[21]

## The Developmentally Disabled

Until the late 1800s, most mentally retarded people who needed care outside the home were cared for in the mental hospitals. In fact, there was little recognition of the special characteristics or needs of the *mentally retarded*. The mentally retarded are those people who have lower than average intellectual functioning that in turn affects their adaptive behavior. During the latter half of the nineteenth century, large state institutions were founded to care for this population, though many mentally retarded individuals continued to be cared for within the family. These institutions were usually in isolated areas. It should also be noted that in the past many retarded people did not grow to adulthood, since they were particularly susceptible to death from respiratory disease. During this time, awareness of the need for educational and training programs for the mentally retarded grew. A few programs were established, but this development halted during the Great Depression and World War II.

After World War II, the so-called miracle drugs successfully treated respiratory infections and extended the life expectancy of this population. Other scientific studies expanded the understanding of the causes of mental retardation. Early detection became possible, and thus early intervention came to be emphasized. The National Association of Retarded Children (now the National Association of Retarded Citizens) was founded in 1950. This group of concerned parents and others was influential in gaining attention to the needs of the mentally retarded. Educational programs, community workshop and activity programs, residential alternatives, and legislative reforms resulted. Federal funds became available for training professionals for work with the mentally retarded. The Education for All Handicapped Children Act of 1978 (see Chapter 8) had an important impact on services for the mentally retarded child. Handicapped children are now often referred to as the *developmentally disabled*.

Deinstitutionalization became a theme in services to the mentally retarded. As with the mentally ill, communities often did not have the needed services in place to serve them. With a growing group of adult mentally retarded, establishing new services for this group became important, including sheltered workshops, activity centers, and community living facilities. Because mentally retarded people often have multiple handicaps, a range of other services are also necessary to support them. Mentally retarded people often have mental health problems, thus they often need mental health services.[22] Today, services to the mentally retarded probably should not be classified under mental health services but should be considered a distinct field of practice with ties to mental health as well as to child welfare services and school social work services.[23]

## Substance Abuse

Because the treatment of alcohol and drug abuse are component services of a community mental health center, the history of caring for this major national problem is important for understanding the range of mental health services. Abuse problems can be considered from two points of view. The first is the misuse of alcohol and drugs. Many people who use these substances do not find it difficult to moderate their use; it is overuse that is the chief concern. The second is *addiction.* Some individuals become both physically and emotionally dependent on these substances to such a degree that they are unable to control their consumption. Of course, some drugs are powerfully addictive, others only mildly so. One theory holds that some individuals are prone to addiction and cannot use these substances in moderation.

Alcohol and drug use have been a part of civilization for many years, and there have always been some individuals who had problems controlling their use. Society has, until very recently, generally seen misuse as punishable behavior. For a time, in the United States, the response to the problem was prohibition of the use of alcohol (use of certain drugs is still illegal). This did not solve the problem and caused a great many other problems. The first attempt to deal with alcoholism other than by prohibition was through the formation of a self-help group—Alcoholics Anonymous, in the early 1930s. Self-help is still the solution of choice for many people with addiction problems. Public Law 91-61, passed in 1970, established a National Institute on Alcohol Abuse and Alcoholism. This law called for state plans using federal funds to develop both education and treatment programs. A variety of programs, in a variety of settings, with a variety of treatment philosophies are now attempting to address the problems of substance abuse. Some are within the mental health field of practice; some are not.[24]

## History of Social Work in Mental Health

Social work involvement in the field of mental health began in 1906 with the work of Cabot and Cannon at Massachusetts General Hospital (see Chapter 10). Mary Jarret, in 1913, developed a program at Boston Psychiatric Hospital that was known as psychiatric social work. Other such programs soon followed. In these programs, the social worker was primarily responsible for obtaining data from the patient's family. Later, social workers served as a liaison between the patient, the family, and the institution. In 1918, Smith College developed the first formal training in psychiatric social work. In 1926, the Veteran's Administration established a Social Services Department. This department has provided considerable leadership in the mental health field of practice. Because of the limited number of psychiatrists, social workers increasingly become involved in prolonged, intensive psychotherapeutic work under the supervision of psychiatrists. Social workers in the mental health field tended to work with more verbal, middle class clients in outpatient settings, though some social workers continued to work in institutional settings.

The definition of a *psychiatric social worker* has never been firmly established. Some said that it was a social worker who used psychoanalytic concepts. Eventually, the vast majority of social workers used these concepts. Others said it meant that the social worker worked in conjunction with a psychiatrist. Regardless of the definition used, psychiatric social work became a very prestigious kind of social work, and many social workers called themselves psychiatric social workers. Some sought post-graduate training in psychoanalytic-oriented programs, others engaged in personal analysis for training purposes. One of the member organizations that joined together to form the National Association of Social Workers in 1955 was the American Association of Psychiatric Social Workers, founded in 1926. Today, one seldom hears the term psychiatric social worker. Rather, a new group, similar in character, has developed—the *clinical social worker*. Usually, it is accepted that a clinical social worker must have the MSW degree, with training and supervised experienced in providing direct services to clients. Clinical social workers are therapists in the mental health field of practice.[25]

## The Social Worker in the Mental Health Setting

In 1972, twenty-two thousand social workers practiced in mental health settings and that number is believed to have increased substantially since that time. About one-third of these workers practiced in state and county mental hospitals. Outpatient clinics accounted for another 25 percent of the workers. At that time, 70 percent of the social workers in mental health setting held a MSW and 30 percent a BSW.[26] In 1985, 28.1 percent of all NASW members identified their field of practice as mental health. This would be fourteen thousand workers, but it must be remembered that not all social workers belong to NASW.[26]

To work effectively in the mental health field, regardless of the particular setting, a social worker should have special knowledge. Because most settings emphasize the use of the interdisciplinary team approach, the social worker must understand how teams function and be skillful in working within teams. The social worker also must understand the roles and ways of functioning of the other professional disciplines that are part of the mental health team. Of course, knowing about mental illnesses and their treatment is also essential, including the terminology, etiology (causes), and symptoms of the various syndromes. The ability to use psychiatric classification such as DSM III is important.[27] Understanding psychotropic drug treatment and its side effects, along with other kinds of care and treatment, is essential. There are legal issues to be understood as well. Each specific mental health setting will also have knowledge specific to that setting (i.e., rural clinics, inner city clinics) and the clients it serves that social workers must master to be effective in that setting.

Workers in mental health settings not only perform clinical social work or in-depth therapeutic direct service. They also use short-term approaches for working with patients/clients, with small groups, and with families. They engage in preventive as well as treatment activity. They use indirect methods to obtain needed services for patient/clients or to strengthen the social support network of the individual or family. Social workers are also involved in community organization, supervision and teaching, planning, and evaluation. Educational and consultation services are a part of many mental health agencies' services. Many social workers also are found in the administration of mental health agencies. One role that has recently become important is the case manager role. The case manager after assessment and planning develops an array of resources needed by each patient/client and continually coordinates services. As you can see, social workers in the mental health setting have many opportunities, many important roles to fill.

## Social Work in the Mental Hospital

Robert L. Barker and Thomas L. Briggs, in a study of social workers in state mental hospitals, found they fill twenty roles. Some of the more important include the following:

1. enhancing the patient's psychological functioning,
2. providing concrete social services to the patient,
3. enhancing the psychological functioning of the patient's family members,
4. enhancing social relationships between patients and their families,

5. providing concrete social services for family members,
6. educating the patient's family about the nature of the treatment of the patient,
7. stimulating healthy patient interaction in a therapeutic community,
8. providing information regarding the patient's social background and situation,
9. contributing to the psychiatric team's diagnostic and treatment program,
10. aftercare treatment of former patients,
11. developing service resources to help provide for patient needs.[28]

There is a wide variation in social work practice in mental hospitals. Much depends on the treatment practiced in a particular hospital. Also important is the particular population being served since many hospitals place patients with similar diagnoses on the same ward. Admissions wards are very different from continuing care wards. Units for the treatment of alcohol and/or drug addiction use approaches specific to the problems of addiction. In mental hospitals, the psychiatrist is usually the person in charge. The social worker is usually responsible for developing social histories, working with families, and for contacting community agencies. The work is a team effort. Both MSWs and BSWs practice in mental hospitals.

### Social Work in Community Mental Health Settings

Again, there is a wide range of work in the community mental health setting. Many MSW workers provide counseling for problems of depression and anxiety, provide help with other individual, marital, and family problems, and are involved in crisis intervention. They may do this through a team effort, but often they work as independent therapists. Other MSW workers are involved in service administration. When working in a child guidance clinic, the MSW is usually a member of the team, often works with parents, and may use play therapy with children either individually or in groups. MSW social workers use individual, family, and group approaches when working with clients. They also may be involved in community activity, training, and research.[30]

Both BSWs and MSWs may work with the chronically mentally ill and their families in community support programs. BSWs often are case managers for these clients. In filling this role, the worker engages in an ongoing assessment of the client's needs, develops plans for meeting those needs, links the client with resources to meet those needs, and generally monitors the plan by coordinating activity and work with the client.[31] Case mangers may supervise work programs or socialization activities. They may also work to develop resources in the community to meet the needs of these clients. This can involve working with the local Social Security Administration offices to see that clients receive benefits for which they are eligible. It can mean working with Job Service to find suitable part-time employment for clients. It can mean helping a landlord understand the particular needs of a client.[32]

## Addiction Treatment Programs

Some social workers have always been involved in working with problem drinkers or alcoholics. A few have also been involved in drug treatment programs. Some social workers believe that misuse of alcohol is only a symptom of other problems, and that treatment should focus on the other problems. For some clients this seems to be the case. For others, the alcohol abuse seems to be the primary problem. When working with this client population, the social worker combines generalist social work knowledge with specific knowledge of alcohol treatment. Recently, two social work journals published entire issues on work in alcohol treatment.[33]

## Work with the Mentally Retarded

Charles R. Horejsi, in a study of the literature, has identified six kinds of services social workers provide for the mentally retarded person:

1. providing individual and group counseling to the retarded individuals, their parents, and siblings,
2. conducting social evaluations as a part of the interdisciplinary diagnostic process,
3. developing alternative living plans,
4. offering protective services, social brokerage, and case advocacy services,
5. performing intake, release, discharge planning, and case management activities, and
6. community organizing, social planning, and administrative activity.

With the movement of the mentally retarded from the institution to the community, many social workers, especially BSWs, are finding positions as case managers in community facilities. Also, with the increased emphasis on rights to education, training, and treatment for the mentally retarded, there is an important role for the social worker in advocacy. Since the educational system has become the prime system to service mentally retarded children and adolescents, social workers place less emphasis on this age group, and more on the growing number of adult mentally retarded people.[34]

Social workers in every setting in the mental health field carry many responsibilities and provide a wide variety of services to patients/clients and their families. They also play important roles in developing community awareness of, acceptance of, and responsibility for services to the population served by mental health agencies. The role of the social worker in mental health services continues to broaden as more emphasis is placed on services in the community and on the community's and family's role in treating the mentally ill. Also the growing importance of mental health in our society should bring about increased support for mental health programs.

---

### A Case Study

Mary B is a twenty-five-year-old woman who has had three hospitalizations since she was eighteen years old. She was discharged three months ago from the state hospital with a diagnosis of undifferentiated schizophrenia. Her most recent hospitalization resulted from Mary failing to take her prescribed medication. She had been living with her parents and said they were "on her case to get out and go to work." She also reported that they said they would kick her out if she didn't straighten up. Mary has a General Education Diploma and has never been able to hold a job for more than two weeks. Her parents seem to have little understanding of her illness. On discharge from the hospital, she was referred to the local community support program.

The community support program operates a transition living residence, and Mary had been living there since her discharge. While living in the transition residence, she developed skills she will need to live independently. She particularly likes to cook and explained her mother would never let her do this. She also has attended a day treatment program where she works on socialization skills. The case manager tried to involve Mary's parents in a parent's educational group but they have refused to participate. The case manager determined that returning home is not in Mary's best interest since she needs to see herself as an adult. Also, the parents seem to make excessive demands on her. The case worker found that Mary is eligible for SSI benefits and helped her make an application for these benefits.

*continued*

Since Mary had been in the community support program for three months, it was time to review her progress and develop a plan for the next steps. The worker met with Mary to discuss her thinking about what she wants to happen. Mary expressed a desire to move to an independent living situation; she was, however, afraid to try a work situation. A meeting was called of everyone who had contact with Mary in the community support program. Also included were the housing specialist and the vocational specialist. The staff decided that Mary should be allowed an opportunity to move into an apartment that she would share with another client. In this housing situation, she would receive some supervision. It was suggested she remain in the day treatment program until she adjusted to the new living situation but that she also should be introduced to an evening group that meets once a week for socialization. The vocational specialist suggested that Mary be involved in a protected work situation after she adjusted to the living independently. He suggested a project where clients go in a group, twice a week, to the local newspaper office and stuff advertising material into the daily paper. If she can adjust to this, she will be encouraged to move on to more demanding work experiences later. Mary seemed to be doing well with the medication she was taking. She achieved some independence in medicating herself in the transitional living situation, but the staff felt this should be carefully watched as she moves out of transitional living. The staff suggested that the case manager discuss with Mary her relationship with her family, and help her make some decision about what she would like to happen. The case manager would remain available to the family, hoping they would decide to become involved with the parent's group.

After the staff meeting, the worker discussed the outcome with Mary. Mary was somewhat hesitant about sharing a minimally supervised apartment but finally said she would try it. The case manager and Mary discussed these feelings and planned to spend time discussing how it goes in the first few weeks of the new situation. Mary wanted to know when she will get her SSI so she would have some money to spend. The worker explained the time needed for this to go through. Also she pointed out that Mary will need to budget her money since she will have to pay rent and buy groceries in her new living situation. The worker decided that Mary worked enough for one session, but made a mental note of the other issues that will need discussion next time: the work experience, her parents, and other changes.

# Current Issues and Concerns in the Mental Health Field

As has been shown in this chapter, enormous changes in the care of the mentally ill have taken place in the last two decades. The move from an emphasis on institutional care to care in the community has been responsible for much of these changes. In addition, there has been a change in emphasis from mental illness to mental health. These changes have brought about a much greater community concern for mental health services. The need for and use of such services has become much more acceptable to the general public. Given the nature of this change, it is a natural consequence that tensions and problems would develop within the system. Those that seem most important are discussed in this section. They include issues rising out of a series of court decisions about the rights of the mentally ill, issues related to health insurance coverage, issues related to staffing of mental health services, and issues related to services for the underserved.

## Court Decisions

Over the last fifteen years, a number of court decisions have placed new constraints on involuntary care of the mentally ill and have required better care and treatment for these individuals. Essentially, the courts have developed a principle of the right to treatment in the *least restrictive environment*. In this setting, which can be either in an institution or community, people have fewer limitations on their movements and rights and are given opportunities to make their own choices as long as they do not endanger themselves or others. Prior to these decisions, mentally ill individuals could be committed to institutions with little recourse and with considerable loss of rights, both civil and personal. There is no doubt that there was considerable abuse of the commitment proceedings and that some reform was necessary. However, some people wonder if things have not gone too far, whether it is still possible to protect both the mentally ill patient and the community in general. The attempted assassination of President Reagan in 1981 is an example often used to illustrate this problem.

Some question whether community care is always in the best interest of the client, especially when good community care does not exist. Questions are also raised about whether mental health treatment is a right or a privilege. If courts mandate community care for some clients/patients, should it not be available to all who need it? But then who should be responsible for financing such care? Will the historic experience of two systems of care—institutional or community—be followed with one system paid for by public funds for those who can not pay for their own care, and another system for those who can pay for their care? Will these two systems provide similar quality of care, or will quality go to those who pay? What will happen to the relationship of the mental health system and the social welfare system? Will institutional care remain the responsibility of the states, while community care continues to be jointly funded by state and federal governments? All these questions will need to be addressed as the new mental health system develops.

These court decisions have also given the legal system a much stronger role in the care and treatment of the mentally ill. They have given rise to much litigation around mental health treatment, making it essential that mental health agencies and professionals be aware of the legal ramifications of any treatment used. The decisions have also forced mental health professionals to carry liability insurance, which adds to costs of care.

These same court decisions have brought attention to the implications of considering mental illness a medical condition. The statement that "deviance is in the eye of the beholder," has cast doubts on current definitions of mental illness. What is the responsibility of the mental health system and what is the responsibility of the criminal justice system and what should their relationship be?[35]

## Health Insurance

Most health insurance provides some, though usually limited, coverage for hospitalization in psychiatric settings. Some health care plans cover certain outpatient services. Coverage has been a major issue. Not only are there questions about the amount of coverage (how many sessions or what dollar amount) but which services can be provided by which mental health professionals. Services delivered by psychiatrists and, usually, psychologists are more often covered than those given by social workers and other professionals. The services covered can usually be categorized as intensive therapy. Newer understandings about treatment of mental illness indicate that this is not always the treatment of choice. Little or no provision has been made to meet the needs of the chronically mentally ill. The emphasis on prevention, which is receiving at least some attention, is not addressed by health insurance, nor in health care generally.

Social work, mostly through the National Association of Social Workers, has made a considerable effort to obtain what is known as *third-party payment* (insurance payment for services) for some social workers who provide mental health services, but this is almost exclusively restricted to the MSW worker involved in clinical social work. To facilitate this change, NASW has issued a *Clinical Register* that lists the social workers NASW considers competent to deliver clinical services. Some insurance plans have accepted MSWs listed in this register as eligible to receive payment for services under their plan. Because many workers listed in the register are not employed in mental health settings, this raises questions about the definition of mental health services used in this chapter. Of particular interest is the MSW in private practice. These workers indeed meet many mental health needs, but their place in the social welfare system in unclear. Also, what about mental health services provided by social workers not included in the register? Should they too not be reimbursed? There are still many questions regarding the issues of insurance for mental health services that need answering.

## Staffing in Mental Health Services

The sometimes conflicting roles of psychiatrists, psychologists, and social workers have been troublesome for some time. Answers have been worked out differently in different settings. In the hospitals, psychiatrists have tended, at least officially, to be responsible for treatment, using other disciplines as they see fit. This has often placed the social worker in an ancillary position. In the outpatient setting, a more egalitarian relationship has evolved, but often with a blurring of roles of the various professions. In this situation, the particular strengths of each profession are often overlooked. Another development has been the addition of professions to the group delivering mental health services, (e.g., nurses, occupational therapists, and rehabilitation counselors.) More study needs to be undertaken on the relative effectiveness and proper roles of the mental health care professionals in different mental health settings.

The third-party reimbursement also affect the staffing patterns of some mental health settings, for it is in the best interest of the agency to receive as much reimbursement as possible. This, however, hinders staffing decisions based on which professional can best deliver the service in the most economical and effective way. A related issue and familiar problem is the validity of the BSW as a professional degree. The role and function of the BSW in the mental health field is still very unclear. But since clinical services are not the treatment of choice for many clients/patients, and since many MSWs do not want to provide these services,[35] and since BSWs do indeed have the skills to provide these services (the case management function is an example), then the mental health system does have a place for the BSW, and insurance coverage should be provided for their services. If the mental health system is to meet the needs of people then all these issues of staffing must be addressed.[37]

## The Underserved

With the deinstitutionalization of the mentally ill and the mentally retarded has come a demand for vastly increased community services to meet the needs of this population. While many programs and projects have demonstrated that these needs can be met in the community,[38] a large group of deinstitutionalized people have not received such services. Some are being serviced by social welfare programs not equipped to meet their special needs. Others are in nursing homes.[39] The chronically mentally ill and mentally retarded remain both an underserved clientele and a serious community problem. Some of the needs of the mentally retarded have already been discussed in this chapter, particularly those related to deinstitutionalization and the growth in the number of adult mentally retarded persons. Also, as more is understood about mental retardation, new and more effective ways of responding become available. The mentally retarded person who is also mentally ill is a client/patient who has long puzzled the professional. Much more needs to be understood about this segment of the population.[40]

Other underserved groups include the poor and the aged. Each group has its special needs. With the drying up of federal funds to support mental health services, such services for those unable to pay either on their own or through third-party payments have been considerably reduced. And the best treatment and services for these groups have not been agreed upon. Attitudes in our society about aging and the aged have caused indifference toward their many unmet mental health needs, which must be addressed.

Some geographic areas of the country are also underserved. The rural sections of the United States have always lacked sufficient formal social welfare services, including sufficient mental health services. Individuals are forced to use institutions far from their homes or services developed on an urban model. But recently, some attention has been paid to providing mental health services to this population.[41] Much remains to be done.

There is a growing realization that services to various ethnic groups should be tailored to meet their particular needs. Some of these needs arise from the discrimination they have experienced. Cultural factors must be taken into account when serving people from minority groups.[42] The current interest in their needs must continue and be expanded.

## Summary

In this chapter, the mental health field of practice has been defined as those agencies and institutions that provide mental health services. The complex relationship of the social welfare system and the mental health system was described and discussed. The range of services in the mental health field was considered from both a historical and contemporary perspective. Social work's development as a mental health profession was examined. Also, a number of contemporary issues relating to the delivery of mental health services were raised.

This field of practice is one undergoing considerable growth and change. There is a change in focus from services within institutions to services in communities. There is also a change from emphasis on mental illness to one of mental health, which calls for more attention to preventive services. These changes require new kinds of service delivery and new roles for the social worker. They offer a challenge for creative and innovative work.

## Key Words

addiction
child guidance clinics
chronic mental illness
clinical social worker
community mental health center
community support programs
deinstitutionalization
developmentally disabled
insane asylums
least restrictive environment
lunatics
mental health

mental health agency
mental health services
mental hospital
mental illness
mentally retarded
moral treatment
National Association for
    Mental Health
psychiatric hospital
psychiatric social worker
psychotropic drugs
third-party payment

## Questions for Discussion

1. What do you see as the similarities and differences between social welfare and mental health?

2. Do you think that calling all social welfare services mental health services would reduce or abolish the stigma attached to receiving some social welfare services?

3. What is your definition of mental illness? How do you think mental illness should be diagnosed?

4. Do you think social workers can provide mental health services without working with psychiatrists and psychologists?

5. In what ways do you see earlier patterns of caring for the mentally ill still present in our response to the needs of this population?

6. Do you think services for the mentally retarded should be included in the field of mental health? If not, where should they be placed? Why do you think as you do about their placement?

7. Discuss the problems of deinstitutionalization. What do you see as means for overcoming those problems? Are there some individuals who should remain in institutions?

8. What do you see as major differences in the work done by MSWs and BSWs in the mental health field of practice?

9. Should social workers be more knowledgeable about treatment approaches for individuals involved in alcohol and drug abuse? Why do you think as you do? If you think more involvement is desirable, how can this take place?

10. Discuss the ramifications of the courts' involvement in the prescription of treatment of mental illness. Do you think this has led to better service or has it negatively affected the services? Support your thinking.

11. How can the rights of the individual and the protection of society be provided for when working with the mentally ill?

12. Do you think health insurance should cover mental health services? If yes, why and to what extent? If no, why not?

# Notes

[1] Milton G. Thackeray, Rex A. Skidmore, and O. William Farley, *Introduction to Mental Health: Field and Practice* (Englewood Cliffs, NJ: Prentice-Hall, 1978), p. 8.

[2] Scott Brier, et. al., 1983–84 Supplement to the *Encyclopedia of Social Work*, 17th ed. (Washington, D.C.: National Association of Social Workers, 1983), p. 241.

[3] Steven P. Segal and Jim Baumohl, "Social Work Practice in Community Mental Health," *Social Work* 26 (January 1981), pp. 19–20.

[4] American Psychiatric Association, *Diagnostic and Statistical Manual of Mental Disorders, III* (Washington, D.C.: American Psychiatric Association, 1980).

[5] For further discussion of this idea see: John S. McNeil and Roosevelt Wright, "Special Populations: Black, Hispanic, and Native American," in *Social Work and Mental Health*, eds. James W. Callicutt and Pedro J. Lecca (New York: The Free Press, 1983).

[6] For an indepth discussion of these ideas see: David J. Rothman, *The Discovery of the Asylum* (Boston: Little, Brown and Co., 1971).

[7] James Leiby, *A History of Social Welfare and Social Work in the United States* (New York: Columbia University Press, 1978), pp. 66–68.

[8] Clifford W. Beers, *A Mind That Found Itself* (New York: Longmans, Green, 1908).

[9] John A. Talbott, "Toward a Public Policy on the Chronic Mentally Ill Patient," *American Journal of Orthopsychiatry* 50 (January 1980): 43–53.

[10] Sumner M. Rosen, David Fanshel, and Mary E. Lutz, eds. *Face of the Nation 1978*, Statistical Supplement, of the *Encyclopedia of Social Work*, 18th Ed. (Silver Springs, MD: National Association of Social Workers, 1987), p. 91.

[11] Bernard L. Bloom, *Community Mental Health*, 2nd ed. (Monterey, CA: Brooks/Cole Publishing Co., 1984), pp. 13–14.

[12] Joint Commission on Mental Illness and Health, *Action for Mental Health* (New York: Basic Books, 1961).

[13] Bloom, *Community Mental Health,* pp. 16–22.

[14] For a helpful discussion of the history of community mental health see: Bloom, *Community Mental Health,* chapter 1, "Development of the Community Mental Health Movement."

[15] Walter E. Barton and Charlotte J. Sanborn, *An Assessment of the Community Mental Health Movement* (Lexington, MA: Lexington Books, 1977), chapter 4.

[16] For discussion of this issue see: Mark J. Stern, "The Emergence of the Homeless as a Public Problem," *Social Service Review,* 58 (June 1984): 291–301, and Madeleine R. Stoner, "The Plight of the Homeless Women," *Social Service Review* 57 (December 1983): 565–581.

[17] Bloom, *Community Mental Health,* pp. 34–36.

[18] See: James McCreath, "The New Generation of Chronic Psychiatric Patients," *Social Work* 29 (September–October 1984): 436–441.

[19] Nancy Atwood, "Professional Prejudice and the Psychotic Patient," *Social Work* (March 1982): 172–177.

[20] An excellent example of these programs is described in Mary Ann Test and Leonard I. Stein, "A Community Approach to the Chronically Mentally Ill," *Social Policy* 8 (May-June 1977): 8–16.

[21] Discussion at Council on Social Work Education sponsored workshop on education to work with the chronically mentally ill, Lawrence, Kansas, November 1984.

[22] See: Frank J. Menolascino and Brian M. McCann, eds., *Mental Health and Mental Retardation: Bridging the Gap* (Baltimore: University Park Press, 1983).

[23] For an indepth discussion of services to the mentally retarded see: Martha Ufford Dickerson, *Social Work Practice with the Mentally Retarded* (New York: The Free Press, 1981).

[24] H. Leonard Boche, "Alcohol and Drug Abuse Services" in *Handbook of the Social Services* eds. Neil Gilbert and Harry Specht, (Englewood Cliffs, NJ: Prentice-Hall, 1981), chapter 10.

[25] Also see: Martin Nacman, "Mental Health Services: Social Workers in," in Encyclopedia of Social Work, 17th ed., ed. John B. Turner (Washington, D.C.: National Association of Social Workers, 1977), pp. 897–904.

[26] Nacman, "Mental Health Services," 898.

[27] "Practice of Four Training Levels Examined," *NASW News* 30 (May 1985): 10.

[28] American Psychiatric Association, *Diagnostic and Statistical Manual.*

[29] Robert L. Barker and Thomas L. Briggs, *Differential Use of Social Work Manpower* (New York: National Association of Social Workers, 1968).

[30] For further discussion of the role of social work in community mental health see: Segal, "Social Work Practice in Community Mental Health," pp. 16–25, and Arthur J. Katz, ed., *Community Mental Health: Issues for Social Work Practice and Education* (New York: Council on Social Work Education, 1979).

[31] For further development of this role see: Peter J. Johnson and Allen Rubin, "Case Management in Mental Health: A Social Work Domain?" *Social Work* 28 (January–February 1983): 49–55, and Charlotte J. Sanborn, ed., *Case Management in Mental Health Services* (New York: The Haworth Press, 1983).

[32] Margaret W. Linn and Shayna Stein, "Chronic Adult Mental Illness," *Health and Social Work* 6 (November 1981, supplement): 54S–59S.

[33] Please see the special issues of *Social Casework* 59 (January 1978) and *Health and Social Work* 4 (November 1979).

[34] Charles R. Horejsi, "Developmental Disabilities: Opportunities for Social Workers," *Social Work* 24 (January 1979): 40–43.

[35] For details about the court decisions and their ramifications see: Levine, *History and Politics of Community Mental Health,* chapter 5.

[36] Allen Rubin and Peter J. Johnson, "Direct Practice Interest of Entering MSW Students," *Journal of Education for Social Work* 20 (Spring 1985): 5–16.

[37] Ruth I. Knee and Warren C. Lamson, "Mental Health Services," in Turner, *Encyclopedia of Social Work,* pp. 879–889.

[38] Allen Rubin, "Community-Based Care of the Mentally Ill: A Research Review," *Health and Social Work* 9 (Summer 1984): 165–177.

[39] Steven P. Segal, "Community Care and Deinstitutionalization: A Review," *Social Work* 24 (November 1979): 521–527.

[40] See Menolascino, *Mental Health,* for a discussion of the treatment of the mentally retarded, mentally ill individual.

[41] John S. Wodarski, *Rural Community Mental Health Practice* (Baltimore: University Press, 1983).

[42] McNeil, "Special Populations."

# Suggested Readings

Bloom, Bernard L. *Community Mental Health: A General Introduction,* 2nd ed. Monterey, CA: Brooks/Cole Publishing Co., 1984.

Callicutt, James W., and Lecca, Pedro J. *Social Work and Mental Health.* New York: The Free Press, 1981.

Dickerson, Martha Ufford. *Social Work Practice with the Mentally Retarded.* New York: The Free Press, 1983.

Horejsi, Charles R. "Developmental Disabilities: Opportunities for Social Workers," *Social Work* 24 (January 1979): 40–43.

Johnson, Peter J., and Rubin, Allen. "Case Management in Mental Health: A Social Work Domain?" *Social Work* 28 (January-February 1983): 49–55.

Levine, Murry. *The History and Politics of Community Mental Health.* New York: Oxford University Press, 1981.

Paradis, Bruce A. "An Integrated Team Approach to Community Mental Health," *Social Work* 32, (May–April 1987): 101–104.

Schulberg, Herbert C., and Killilea, Marie, eds. *The Modern Practice of Community Mental Health.* San Francisco: Jossey-Bass Publishers, 1982.

Segal, Steven P., and Baumohl, Jim. "Social Work Practice in Community Mental Health," *Social Work* 26 (January 1981): 16–25.

"Special Issue: Alcohol Problems," *Health and Social Work* 4 (November 1979)

Thackeray, Milton G.; Skidmore, Rex A.; and Farley, O. William; eds. *Introduction to Mental Health: Field and Practice.* Englewood Cliffs, NJ: Prentice-Hall, 1978.

Minahan, Anne, ed. *Encyclopedia of Social Work* 17th Ed. Sliver Springs, MD: National Association of Social Workers, 1978. Articles on: "Disabilities: Developmental," "Mental Health and Illness," and "Mental Health Services."

Wodarski, John S. *Rural Community Mental Health Practice.* Baltimore: University Park Press, 1983.

# Chapter 12

## Social Work and Corrections

The profession of social work and the field of adult and juvenile corrections have historically been partners in society's protection of its members from criminal behavior (acts that violate the law) and in providing rehabilitation and treatment. Hence, this chapter assumes that social work and the field of corrections are not two clearly separate and distinct responses. Rather, they should be viewed as a blending together of professional services that reflect concern for the treatment and rehabilitation of offenders. Social work has provided a wide range of services focusing on human needs, and its involvement in correctional services is a part of that response.

Special societal concern has focused on juvenile delinquency and juvenile corrections. Social workers in the child welfare system and in the juvenile court have responded to this concern. In recent years, improving the adult correctional system has been emphasized. The criminal justice system and the profession of social work have been at the forefront of these efforts.

This chapter examines the following: (1) the structure of the criminal justice system, including a brief overview of the fields of juvenile and adult corrections, (2) correctional services for youth, including the historical development of the juvenile court, types of juvenile offenders, legal perspectives, the provisions of services and treatment approaches to juvenile offenders, and the role of social work in the response, (3) correctional services to adults (including a brief overview of the theories about the causes of crime), an examination of the adult correctional system (including prisons and jails, the probation-parole system), alternative treatment and rehabilitation approaches in adult corrections, and the roles of correctional personnel (including social workers). Throughout

Table 12.1   Important Dates: Social Work and Corrections

| | |
|---|---|
| 1787 | Philadelphia Prison Society was founded to bring about reform in U.S. prisons |
| 1899 | Act to regulate the treatment and control of independent, neglected, and delinquent children, created the first juvenile court in the United States |
| 1964 | Cooper versus Pate Supreme Court decision established prisoners rights |
| 1965 | Prison Rehabilitation Act-Correctional Rehabilitation Study Act |
| 1967 | Gault v. Arizona Supreme Court decision gave due process of law rights to juveniles |
| 1970 | Presidents Task Force on Prisoner Rehabilitation encourages development of community based corrections for adults |
| 1974 | Juvenile Justice and Delinquency Prevention Act provided incentives for the deinstitutionalization of status offenders |

the chapter there are discussions of pertinent social issues and social changes that have influenced society's response to the problem of criminal behavior. (See Table 12.1.)

## Structure of the Criminal Justice System

The *criminal justice system,* both currently and historically has three component parts. They are law enforcement, the judicial system, and the correctional system.[1] The correctional system is the main focus in this chapter, although all three are discussed at various points.

To understand both the juvenile and adult correctional systems, it is important to define the term *corrections.* In a broad sense, corrections is the part of the criminal justice system that tries to prevent the reoccurrence of criminal behavior, to deal with its causes, to implement measures of social control that treat and rehabilitate both the adult and juvenile offender. Corrections is also thought of in a more narrow sense as a professional service that applies a criminology knowledge base to the control and rehabilitation of the criminal offender.[2]

There long has been a great deal of argument over what should constitute corrections. Differing values, philosophies, and ideologies have influenced the structure at different times. These arguments are expressed by such questions as, Should punishment be considered the primary method of corrections? If not, should treatment and rehabilitation be? What is rehabilitation? These issues are discussed throughout this chapter.

## The Structure of the Juvenile Corrections System

As previously mentioned, corrections implies that prevention, treatment, and rehabilitation processes are provided within the criminal justice system. Juvenile corrections, a subsystem, works with young offenders whose age is less than the legal age of majority (eighteen years old in most states). The structure of the juvenile corrections system consists of both institutional and *community-based services.* Institutional services are those in which the juvenile is placed in a closed setting, separated from the community and his or her family. Community-based correctional services are those in an open community setting, those that serve the juvenile offender without separation from his or her family or community. These two areas of services can be further broken down into formal and informal services. These are formal and informal institutional services, as well as formal and informal community-based services. Formal services are those services mandated and sanctioned by law. Informal services are those services that exist and are sanctioned by means other than the law.

Formal institutional services consist of reform schools, training schools, detention centers, youth authorities, or other correctional institutions provided for by law, and are usually directly operated by local, county, or state government. Informal institutional services consist of group homes, residential treatment centers, or other child-care institutions under the auspices of private nongovernment social service providers. Examples of formal community-based services are juvenile probation, court services, family court services, juvenile diversion programs, and youth service bureaus, which are mandated by law and administered by local, county, or state government. Most community-based services are informal. Examples include, family counseling agencies, child welfare agencies, mental health centers, Boys Clubs, Girls Clubs, YMCA and YWCA programs, Scouting programs, and church-sponsored agencies.

## The Adult Corrections System

The adult corrections system is similar to the juvenile system with both institutional and community-based services. Most of the services are institutional and formal. Examples include jails, prisons and other adult correctional institutions. Adult community-based services also tend to be formal, and include probation and parole services. The services provided by community mental health centers, drug and alcohol treatment programs, public social service agencies, employment assistance and vocational assistance programs, and family service agencies are part of the informal structure of community-based services for adult offenders.

# The Juvenile Corrections System

Both serious and minor crimes are committed by children and youth. In 1983, 1,725,746 juveniles were arrested for offenses varying from murder to status offenses.[3] Offenses committed by juveniles are also on the increase. This means that the juvenile corrections system has a difficult job in fulfilling its mission to further its understanding of juvenile delinquency and to treat and rehabilitate young offenders. To understand the functioning of the current system, it is necessary to understand the history of the juvenile corrections system. In the United States the system began in the late 1800s, with the emergence of the separate juvenile court. However, society's special concern for children and the creation of a separate judicial system for them began long ago.

In Roman common law the systems of law in most European countries, descended from the laws of the Roman Empire, the Latin term *parens patriae*, means the power of the state to act in behalf of a child as a wise parent would do. This legal precept has prevailed in most European countries since the 1700s[4] Later, English courts began the practice of implementing separate and special procedures for dealing with juvenile offenders. Rather than holding formal trials for children, as they did with adults, children were often dealt with in hearings in a judge's chamber. Prior to this, they were treated no differently than adult criminals. They were incarcerated in common lockups with adults, and subjected to the same harsh, often brutal, punishments. The "eye for an eye" philosophy, or society's extracting its "pound of flesh," seemed very inhumane and impractical when applied to the child offender.[5] Furthermore, by the early 1800s many came to believe that punishment was not an effective deterent to juvenile crime.

In the United States, these enlightened practices were not implemented immediately. There were few special institutions for young offenders. Children convicted of crimes were sent either to the almshouses, or to adult jails or prisons. These correctional institutions were deplorable places, with unsanitary conditions and staffed by violent officials who were ignorant and careless about the needs of children.[6] Gradually, after the American Revolution, states assumed jurisdiction over children and created juvenile correctional institutions, which in the beginning were nothing more than children's jails patterned after the adult correctional institutions. These practices continued until the late 1800s, when the response to juvenile delinquency began to change. The period of change has been referred to as the *juvenile reformation* and was signaled by several events.

First, society began to recognize that the system of juvenile institutions was not adequately dealing with the problems of juvenile delinquency. Children released from such institutions had not improved in behavior, and many committed further crimes, only to be institutionalized again. Punishing juveniles by incarcerating them in institutions had failed to rehabilitate them. Studies, particularly those conducted by the Juvenile Psychopathic Institute, which was located in Hull House in Chicago, indicated that the best way to treat the delinquent was not by incarceration, but by special home care.[7] As a result, several states began to create special "juvenile homes," or houses of correction. These special facilities marked the beginning of new, innovative practices in response to juvenile offenders. Such practices as the use of indeterminent sentences, and probation and parole were implemented by these new facilities.

With the growing emphasis on these new ways of treating young offenders came the realization that the laws needed to change to keep pace with these new developments. As a result, state courts began the use of special court procedures with children accused of crimes, which called for them to be dealt with separately and differently from adult offenders. Massachusetts was the first state to adopt such procedures. In Illinois, a battle had been underway for some time, spearheaded by the Chicago Bar Association and the settlement house workers, particularly Jane Addams, to create separate and special courts for juveniles. This lead to the passage by the Illinois state legislature of "an act to regulate the treatment and control of independent, neglected, and delinquent children.[8] This legislation created the nation's first separate juvenile court, which was established in 1899 in Chicago. Several other states followed suit by creating their own juvenile courts.

The *juvenile court* was not a criminal court. Instead of criminal procedure, a nonadversarial proceeding was used that took the best interests of the child fully into consideration. The aim of the court was to educate children, act as a parental guide in assisting the child and developing a plan of individualized treatment.

Though juvenile courts were philosophically dedicated to the aim of individualized treatment and the best interests of the child, this was not realized. Many juvenile courts became quite paternalistic and punitive in their approach to children. A system was created that in many ways was patterned after the adult court system. Children coming under the jurisdiction of the juvenile court were often removed from the custody of their parents without notification and placed in institutions. Parents had no rights to voice objections or have a part in decisions made by the court concerning the child's treatment or future. Children from minority groups especially suffered from these shortcomings. There were no attorneys to represent the child to insure their "best interests."

Naturally, serious questions arose about the constitutional rights of parents and children relative to due process of law. But punitive practices continued until 1967. In 1967, the United States Supreme Court, in the case of *Gault* v. *Arizona*, ruled that previous juvenile court procedures were in violation of due process of law, and that children and youths under the jurisdiction of the juvenile court must be afforded their due process rights such as

1. adequate notice to parents and child,
2. the right to legal counsel,
3. the right to confront and cross-examine witnesses, and
4. guarantees against self-incrimination.

This decision was responsible for overhauling the juvenile court system, by forcing the courts to establish new legal procedures that respected the child's due process rights. As a result states began to revise their statutes and laws pertaining to children to include provisions for insuring these rights.[9] The impetus provided by the Gault decision for reforming the juvenile court's legal procedures and the creation of the modern day juvenile court has been both a blessing and a curse.

## The Current Juvenile Court System

One of the basic goals of a corrections system is to understand the causes of crime and delinquency, and then to try to provide treatment and rehabilitative measures that will prevent crime from reoccurring. Therefore it is necessary to understand how children come to be under the jurisdiction of the juvenile corrections system. Historically, children brought before the juvenile court were considered *delinquent*. This catchall label was used for many years. However, as time passed, distinctions began to be made among certain types of offenses that children commit. The Gault decision again helped clarify this. Children commit offenses that if they were adults would also result in criminal charges. These include a range of offenses all the way from burglary to murder, misdemeanors to felonies. Children convicted of these types of offenses are labeled delinquent. However, the juvenile court also has jurisdiction over children who commit offenses associated with their status, such as minors running away from home, being out of parental control, or failing to attend school. These children are labeled as *status offenders*.

The causes of juvenile crime, as with all criminal behavior, is complex, and it is difficult to pinpoint exact causes. There are many theories concerning the causes of *juvenile delinquency*. These range from peer influence to the failure of the educational system to provide for educational needs of young people, lack of employment opportunities for youth, poverty, to alcohol and drug use. The list could go on indefinitely. One cause, however, agreed upon by most authorities, is that delinquency is usually associated with problems within the child's family system. The same causative factors emerge when speaking about the status offender. However, a clearer and more direct relationship exists between status offenders' behavior and family dysfunction.

## Treatment Approaches

Methods and approaches to the treatment of children who are adjudicated as being delinquent vary, depending on the child's individual situation. Juvenile court judges have some amount of discretion in deciding the treatment of such children. The following are examples of possible treatment approaches:

1. The child or youth may be placed on probation for a specific period of time.
2. The child or youth may be institutionalized in a correctional, child-care, chemical-dependency treatment, or psychiatric facility.
3. The child or youth may be ordered, along with his or her parents, into community-based treatment, such as family counseling or related mental health services.
4. The child or youth may be required to make *restitution* (repairing or paying for damages, returning stolen goods, etc.), particularly in the case of property offenses such as vandalism or burglary.
5. The child or youth may be required to participate in community service work.[10]

These treatment approaches may be used alone, or in combination with each other, as appropriate to meet the individual treatment needs of the child. Emphasis should be placed on the creation of a package of services that meet each child's particular needs, using any and all available resources in the process.

In the case of status offenders, the problem is not so much what treatment should be used, as who is responsible for providing services to them. Historically, the juvenile corrections system has been charged with this responsibility. Since the Gault decision in 1967, the juvenile justice system has begun the practice of *diverting* the status offender away from the system. There have been arguments both for and against this practice of *diversion*. Diversion involves the system not accepting legal jurisdiction over status offenders, or referral of the offender to other social service agencies for appropriate services. Some authorities contend that diversion of the status offender away from the system is a dangerous practice, since it creates a way for the formal system to "pass the buck." This leaves a considerable number of children and families without access to the appropriate correctional services. And some point out that diversion appears to have been no more successful than the use of the formal system when rates of recidivism (relapsing into unwanted behaviors) are compared.[11] Many people feel that status offenders should be removed altogether from the jurisdiction of the juvenile court,[12] believing that the needs of these children can better be met in community-based social service systems outside the formal juvenile justice system.[13] These arguments are not settled at the present time. In recent years, there has been considerable effort toward the deinstitutionalization of status offenders.

The Juvenile Justice and Delinquency Prevention Act of 1974 provided incentives to states, in the form of grant assistance, to remove status offenders from juvenile correctional institutions like detention centers and training schools, and to create community-based treatment programs for them.[14] This has been a successful approach in some states. A study done in 1982 reported that states that by law prohibited the institutionalization of status offenders were more likely to develop alternative services to treat the status offender than states that did not prohibit their institutionalization. Two states, Washington and Massachusetts, have developed specific community-based treatment services for status offenders.[15] Despite the reported efforts in developing community-based services or networks, the status offender is often poorly served. One obstacle has been the lack of coordination of the community resources that serve youth, in both metropolitan and rural area (and is a particularly serious problem in the rural areas). It has been pointed out that the lack of coordination of services to youth in rural areas results in duplication of services or a lack of services.[16] Although there are more resources for treating juvenile offenders, both delinquents and status offenders, in metropolitan areas than in rural areas, the problem with coordination results in some offenders "falling through the cracks in the system."

## Alternatives

Although significant numbers of children continue to be held in detention facilities and other correctional institutions, the trend in recent years has been away from their use. This has been seen as a movement toward a community-based corrections system for youth. However, a scarcity of community treatment resources can lead to the overutilization of institutions, which then appears to lead to higher rates of recidivism.[17] Several states have implemented the use of Youth Authorities, or *Youth Service Bureaus* that provide community-based services. The state of California, with its California Youth Authority, and the states of Minnesota and Wisconsin are examples of this approach. The services provided under these programs often include short-term placement of the child outside the family home, either in group homes or residential treatment facilities; family counseling and treatment; school and employment training programs; group counseling; and recreational services. Intervention should affect the offender's total world. These agencies also coordinate and link children and families to the community resources that serve youth.

The system also emphasizes prevention, by developing new prevention-oriented programs or by coordinating existing ones, such as the YWCA or YMCAs, Scouts, Boy's Clubs, Girl's Clubs, 4-H Clubs, and church youth programs, etc. Even though a rather elaborate set of treatment machinery has been set in motion within the juvenile corrections system, the total system is not perfect. Rates of recidivism continue to be higher than expected. Therefore, all parts of the system must make a concerted effort to develop additions and alternatives to the present system.

## The Role of Social Work in Juvenile Corrections

Social work historically has been more involved in the field of juvenile corrections than in the adult system. Social workers have assumed a variety of roles within both the formal and informal juvenile corrections system. The juvenile correction system was originally based on the philosophy of rehabilitation and treatment, as opposed to punishment, which is congruent with social work values. That is, in general, social work's goal is to provide treatment, rather than to impose punishment.[18] As the juvenile justice system developed, social workers working within it began to experience conflict between their values about rehabilitating offenders and the punitive response of the system.[19] Social work's values have also conflicted with those of other professions that are a part of the same system. Many social workers have been able to successfully manage these conflicts and have maintained social work's contribution to the system.

Social workers within the formal system work as probation officers or with probation officers and other professionals. They perform administrative roles in youth service bureaus. Social workers also work in juvenile correctional institutions, providing individual, family or group treatment, as well as planning, organization, and administrative services. Many social workers provide services to juvenile offenders in the auxiliary informal corrections system. Since the 1970s, the system has emphasized community-based treatment for juvenile offenders. Social workers perform a variety of roles in group homes, residential treatment facilities, family agencies, mental health centers, and traditional youth agencies, (YMCA, YWCA, etc.). These roles are most important to the overall functioning of the system. In recent years, social workers have become members of police crisis intervention teams, and have intervened in family domestic violence situations and in child protection. Juvenile corrections systems vary from one state to another in their organization, thus the role of the social worker will also vary from state to state.[20] To illustrate the social work role in the juvenile corrections system, the following case example is provided.

---

### A Case Study

Fred M, a fifteen-year-old youth was jointly referred by his school counselor and his mother to the intake unit of a county juvenile court located in a large city. Fred's problems, based on information provided by his counselor and mother, were that he was experiencing poor school performance, was skipping several of his classes, was belligerent and disruptive in class, was beyond the reach of his mother's attempts to discipline him, was staying out late, and was verbally and physically abusing his mother. His mother, a single parent, also worried that he could be abusing alcohol or drugs, and feared that he may be involved in delinquent activity with several of his friends. Since no formal charges were being brought against Fred, the intake worker referred Fred and his mother to the family services unit of the juvenile court. The family services unit had been created within the last year to deal with situations where there seemed to be the need for family interventions. The case was assigned to one of the unit's four social workers.

The social worker contacted the school counselor and the mother by phone for additional information and also arranged to meet with Fred and his mother. The social worker met with them on two occasions to assess their situation and to make suggestions on what could be done to assist the family in their situation. The social worker concluded in his assessment that Fred's difficulties stemmed from unresolved trauma and feelings associated with his parents' divorce, which had occurred several years earlier. His mother had also begun a serious relationship with a man. Marriage was being planned in the near future. Fred, although expressing no particular dislike for this man, seemed fearful or perhaps jealous of his mother's relationship with this man. The social worker also concluded that the supervision and discipline the mother used to try to control Fred's behavior were inappropriate and inconsistent.

*continued*

*A Case Study . . . continued*

The social worker made the following suggestions to the family:

1. That the family become involved in individual and family counseling sessions, including sessions with the mother's fiance.

2. That the mother and her partner attend the parenting training class being offered through the family services unit.

3. That Fred attend the peer influence prevention group and the teenagers from divorced families group provided by his school and conducted by his school counselor.

Although it sounds at this point as though the case of Fred M was on the road to a successful outcome, the situation was not easily resolved. The social worker's empathetic persistence, plus the mother's newly-learned parenting skills began to pay off. As Fred was able to understand and deal with his feelings about his parents' divorce, and as he began to see that the firm disciplinary approach meant love, care, and concern on the part of his mother, Fred's behavior began to improve. The problems that precipitated the referral to the juvenile court began to subside. After eight months of fairly intensive work, Fred M's case was closed by the family services unit.

Although the role of the social worker in the field of juvenile corrections can be rewarding, it can also be equally frustrating and challenging. Needleman has suggested several steps for improving the practice of social work in the juvenile corrections system:

1. Social workers need appropriate training in both direct and indirect service methods.

2. Social workers need to be able to communicate, develop relationships with, and move effectively to utilize community social service resources.

3. Social workers need to develop understanding about the community in which they practice. This includes the community's norms and tolerance around juvenile behavior, and crime, as well as socio-economic, cultural, ethnic, and racial factors of the community.

4. Social workers need, in order to reduce friction, hostility, and tension between themselves and other juvenile justice professionals to demonstrate the value of their contributions to the overall functioning of the system.

5. More social workers need to be a part of the juvenile justice system. Recruitment methods need to be developed to attract social workers.[21]

Social workers can also be effective in this field of practice by advocating for change that allows them increased opportunities to use their knowledge and skills in developing innovative intervention for use with juvenile offenders.

## The Adult Corrections System

Twelve million crimes were committed in 1983. Eight million adults were arrested in the same year.[22] Adult crime, as is true of juvenile crime, appears to be neither stabilizing or decreasing. *Crime* and *criminal behavior* are extremely serious social problems in contemporary U.S. society. Societies develop mechanisms to protect themselves from crime and criminal behavior, and to maintain social order and control. The adult criminal justice system that has developed in the United States provides that protection. The corrections part of the total system, as discussed earlier, has as its goal to understand and to treat the problem. The focus here is on the adult corrections system as a specific response to crime and criminal behavior. This concerns not only the policy issues associated with the correctional treatment of the offender but also to the broader issues of treatment of the victim and to the prevention of crime. In dealing with these issues it is helpful to gain an understanding of what constitutes and causes people in society to commit crimes or engage in criminal behavior. This will assist in furthering understanding about the nature of responses to crime and criminal behavior that have emerged within the adult correctional system.

## Causes of Crime and Criminal Behavior

Historically, explanations of the causes of crime and criminal behavior have varied. The earliest were based on religious thought—the criminal was possessed by evil spirits. Later, it was thought that the tendency toward criminal behavior was passed on to the individual through genetic inheritance. Later theories pointed to racial background, mental defect, and the use of alcohol.[23] In the 1900s it was widely believed that certain biological characteristics predestined certain individuals to a life of criminal behavior. A number of scientists, both biologists and anthropologists, adhered to this concept of *constitutional criminality*.[24] These theories attempted to pinpoint a single cause of crime criminal behavior and tended to foster the misconception that criminals were all a part of a large homogeneous group.

Currently, crime and criminal behavior are not attributed to one single source, but to a multiplicity of factors. This has been referred to as the multiple causation theory, which combines biological, social, psychological, economic and environmental factors together in explaining why crime and criminal behavior exist. Biological conditions such as poor health and physical handicaps may predispose certain individuals toward a tendency to commit criminal behavior. Social, economic, and environmental factors including poverty, racism, child abuse and neglect, socialization in criminal attitudes by family or peers, lack of educational achievement, and family breakup may also be involved. Mental illness, retardation and family character development are some psychological factors that can influence the individual toward committing crimes.[25] It must be emphasized here that any one or a combination of these factors will not necessarily cause an individual to become a criminal. These are solely predictive factors and may or may not be associated with the cause of crime and criminal behavior.

## Responses to Criminal Behavior

One might assume that society is interested in developing services that are designed to prevent crime. Such is not the case. Rather, society has been far more concerned with the practical issues of what to do with offenders than in preventing crime or understanding its cause.[26] Punishment and retribution have been the dominant response.[27] There has been considerable debate on whether current correctional policy is oriented to punishment or rehabilitation; there appears to be a movement toward punishment orientation in correctional policy. The criminal justice system currently faces a dilemma in the conflict between the philosophies of societal protection from crime and the rehabilitation of offenders. On the one hand, correctional policy seems to be dominated by the notions of "just deserts" or the "justice model." The offender receives deserved or just punishment. This is demonstrated by the fact that more dollars are being spent on building prisons than ever before. The renewed practice of *capital punishment* also reflects this view. On the other hand, rehabilitation efforts in correctional services have achieved few positive results. Therefore, the movement toward changing the structure to a more rehabilitative model has been difficult.

As noted earlier, correctional services for adult offenders consists of both institutional and community-based services. The largest and most predominant of the two are the institutional services. Jails, operated on a local community or county-wide basis, are usually reserved for short-term *incarceration* (confinement), but *prisons*, (operated by the states and federal government) are the backbone of the U.S. corrections system.

The development of the U.S. prison system has a complex history. Prior to the emergence of prisons, those who committed what were considered to be deviant or antisocial acts were dealt with in ways that today would be considered cruel and bizarre punishment. Both severe corporal (physical) and capital punishment (the death sentence) were used. Public hangings, beatings, torture, and other forms of physical punishment were carried out, to make a public example out of the offender. Beginning in the late 1700s, reform took place in the methods used to deal with adult offenders. A humanitarian protest by a group of Quakers led by Dr. Benjamin Rush has been credited with the beginning impetus toward the development of the modern penitentiary system in the United States. Rush and his followers founded the Philadelphia Prison Society in 1787, which in the years that followed brought about vast reform in the prison system in Pennsylvania. Their work became a model to other states, which adopted similar reforms. Reforms such as open exercise yards, larger cells, and discussion with prisoners about their lives and future were some of these reforms. The developing penitentiary prison system provided a more humane way of punishing the offender. Theoretically, penitentiaries offered opportunities to the offenders to think about their misdeed and to make amends for them.[28]

Although reform had taken place in the corrections system by the development of penitentiaries, the changes were not long-lasting. As the system grew with the establishment of state prisons, some of the earlier enlightened features were forgotten. State prisons became overcrowded and used severe disciplinary measures to control prisoners. This characterized a return to a punishment-oriented philosophy. The State Penitentiary at Auburn, New York, became a model for these new penal institutions. In the 1930s, a wave of reform began in the prison system. Impetus for this reform came from a better understanding of crime, criminal behavior, and rehabilitation, stemming from the new social science disciplines. Better designed prisons with more facilities, trained staff, and individual and group therapy began to be offered. The reorganization of the federal system of prisons in 1929 was at the forefront of these efforts. Although it served as a model, few states have adopted many of the innovative features of the federal system.

It was hoped that the Prisoner Rehabilitation Act of 1965, which provided community services for prisoners, and the Correctional Rehabilitation Study Act of 1965, which addressed personnel problems in the system, would move the system in the direction of prisoner rehabilitation. This did not prove to be the case. Efforts to rehabilitate offenders in prisons are thwarted by overcrowding; poorly trained, poorly paid, unqualified, staff; personnel shortages; poor sanitation and food; inadequate education, recreation, and treatment programs.[29]

Violence in prisons is a serious problem. The 1980 riot in the New Mexico State Prison in Sante Fe, where several inmates were killed and injured before order was restored, is a vivid example. Other problems such as suicide and homosexual rape also point out the inadequacies of the rehabilitative effort in the U.S. prison system. Correctional services in institutions fall far short of meeting the human needs of inmates.

Despite the problems, some positive changes have occurred in recent years. Numerous state, federal, and Supreme Court decisions have emphasized the protection of prisoner rights. Prior to the 1960s, the courts had maintained a hands-off policy toward prison administration. In 1964, the United States Supreme Court, in the case of *Cooper* v. *Pate*, ruled that prisoners in state prisons are entitled to the protection of the civil rights guaranteed by the Civil Rights Act of 1971. In this case, the court also ruled that prisoners could bring legal action against prison officials, under a law that imposed civil liability on people who deprive others of their constitutional rights. Since 1964, there has been a great deal of prisoner rights litigation. In 1966, 218 suits were filed in federal courts by prisoners; in 1984, 18,034 suits were filed. Several court decisions have protected other rights, such as freedom of religious practice, freedom of speech, freedom from cruel and unusual punishment, due process in prison discipline situations, and the right to adequate medical care and rehabilitative services.[30]

## Community-Based Correctional Services for Adults

In the 1960s, a new form of adult correctional services emerged, *community-based correctional services*, designed to provide treatment and rehabilitation in the community, as an alternative to institutionalization. The major goal of community-based correctional services is to make available a wide range of resources that justice system officials may choose from in dealing with offenders.

The impetus behind their development came from a variety of sources. The President's Commission on Law Enforcement and the Administration of Justice in 1967 dealt with the issue of incarceration versus community-based treatment, by making the point that the goals of offender rehabilitation were more likely to be achieved by community-based treatment.[31] Later in 1970, the President's Task Force on Prisoner Rehabilitation strongly urged that incarceration should be avoided in favor of community-based treatment.[32] In the 1970s, the National Council on Crime and Delinquency, and the Law Enforcement Assistance Administration also expressed favor of the development of community-based correctional services.

Probation and parole services had been in existence for some years prior to the more recent community-based programs. They are the most frequently used forms of community-based services. *Probation* is usually offered to first-time offenders as an alternative to incarceration. The offender is allowed to remain in his or her community, to maintain family ties, and to continue to study or work, yet remains under the supervision of the corrections system. Probation usually allows the offender to avoid the embitterment of institutional life, and allows the offender a second chance at a crime-free life. *Parole* is designed as a safeguard for both the offender and the community. It allows the offender, after a specified period of time, to be released from the institution into the community, with a plan for ongoing rehabilitation assistance. Parole offers the offender assistance in reintegrating into community life, while also protecting the community, within certain limits, from further criminal acts by the offender. Certain conditions must be met by the offender to keep the privilege of parole. Parolees must be under the supervision of local parole officers, who may restrict the work or travel of parolees. Needless to say, parolees cannot carry guns. The offender must avoid further criminal activity, and parole can be revoked at any time with just cause and the offender returned to prison. Other community-based alternatives include *work release* and *educational release* from institutional care back into the community (prisoners allowed short-term release to go to school or work but under close supervision), restitution, halfway houses, drug treatment programs, mental health services, and other social, health, and recreational services.

The advantages of community-based correctional services are numerous. To begin with, they avoid isolating the offender away from the community. Treatment resources are more available in the community than in correctional institutions. The offender is protected from the ills of the institutional system. Lastly, and perhaps most importantly, community-based services are more cost-effective than institutional care. Although it is estimated that the trend toward community-based services will continue, little evidence suggests they will ever totally replace the institutional system.

## Correctional Services and Human Diversity

No discussion of adult correctional services would be complete without mention of the influence and impact of human diversity issues. Criminal offenders are diverse, and not the homogeneous group they were once thought to be. Each individual has unique needs. There are differences in the way that society, through the corrections system, deals with individuals. For example, the prepondence of evidence points out that people from minorities are more likely to be arrested, convicted, sentenced, and incarcerated for crimes than white people. The forces of societal discrimination are operating here. One need only look at the populations of penal institutions to see first-hand that this is true. For example, blacks make up 12 percent of the United States population, yet they represent 45 percent of all persons who are incarcerated.

Socioeconomic status is a factor that can influence the kind of treatment an offender receives from the corrections system. White-collar offenders are more likely to receive more lenient treatment than blue-collar and unemployed offenders, who have a much greater chance of being incarcerated. In contrast, women are less often arrested, convicted, and incarcerated than their male counterparts. Correctional institutions for women also tend to be more humane and progressive than men's institutions. This is not to say that women's facilities are not without problems. Many of the same problems associated with men's facilities—social isolation and lack of rehabilitation and vocational programs for example—also exist in women's facilities. Some argue that the way women are treated within the system merely perpetuates sexism. But whatever the case may be, the correctional institutions for men could well take lessons from some of the innovations that have taken place in women's facilities.

The issue of the relationship between mental illness and criminal behavior has come into focus in recent years. The "not guilty by reason of insanity" plea has come into serious question, due to public sentiment and cases receiving national attention, causing several states to make changes in laws that provide treatment of the offender and protection of society by specified confinement in psychiatric institutions. But whether this practice offers any advantages, or whether mental illness should require differential correctional treatment of the offender have not been decided and will have to be faced.

Social work has assumed a somewhat limited role in adult correctional services, compared to juvenile corrections. During their early years, the Charity Organization Societies and the settlement workers worked with criminal offenders. In the 1900s, as the profession emerged, its concerns about human welfare broadened into other fields of practice seemingly more compatible with social work values. Social work and the field of adult corrections have traditionally experienced difficulties working together, in part because professional correctionists and social workers have different and conflicting sets of values.[33]

Correctionalists, although adhering to a philosophy of rehabilitation, conceptualize this as the offender having to make retribution for the criminal actions. This position is congruent with dominant societal values. Social workers, on the other hand, conceptualize rehabilitation as social adjustment, education, and preparation for living a normal citizen's life.[34] In a more practical sense, the correctionalists view social workers as idealistic and too soft-hearted. Social workers argue that correctionalists are hard-nosed and insensitive to offenders' needs. There has always been disagreement among social workers on the place of the profession in the correctional field. In 1945, Kenneth Pray, then Dean of the School of Social Work at the University of Pennsylvania, at the annual meeting of the American Association of Social Work, argued that social work should involve itself in the field of corrections. His address was not well received by many social workers.[35] Some social workers argue that since offenders are nonvoluntary clients, social workers who work with them violate the social work value of self-determination. That the offender client must involuntarily consent to treatment places the social worker in the position of imposing their services upon them, which social workers find unethical, impractical, and ineffectual. However, these same social workers fail to recognize that clients in other fields of practice are also nonvoluntary clients (e.g., child protective services).[36] Other social workers believe that social work should be involved in the field of adult corrections so they can contribute to needed changes in the field. H. Wayne Johnson states, "If social work refuses to have a role in corrections, then it surrenders this important human services field to other, often more repressive groups."[37]

## Social Work Roles in Adult Correctional Services

Social workers have performed a variety of roles, both within community-based correctional services and within some correctional institutions. Most social workers in correctional services have filled positions as probation and parole officers. In these positions, the main method of intervention has been what is termed direct intervention or social casework, which involves the use of the social work problem-solving process, including:

data collection (regarding the offender's life situation),

assessment (identifying problems, needs, and concerns),

developing an intervention plan (individual plus family counseling, and use of community resources),

intervention (carrying out the plan),

evaluation (examining the plan to ascertain its effectiveness), and

termination (preparing the offender for release from probation or parole).

The social worker, through the use of this process, helps the offender develop better self-understanding, strengthen relationships with family and friends, and change patterns of behavior so they are socially acceptable.[38] In addition, some social workers acting as a probation or parole officers use group intervention methods, working with groups of offenders for a variety of interventive purposes. Social workers in these positions may also be involved in community organization or advocacy roles. Offenders are often shunned by the community, making access to community resources difficult. Advocacy with the community on behalf of offenders is often necessary.

In recent years, social workers have also become involved in police work. Police departments in a number of instances have begin to employ social workers in crisis intervention and in domestic violence intervention programs.[39] Concern surfaced in recent years about the lack of qualified, trained professionals in this field; social work indeed can provide educated professionals to fill these roles. As early as 1959, social work began to address the needs of corrections through the development of curriculum in schools of social work. More recently, both undergraduate and graduate social work programs have begun to offer specific course work, including field placements, for students interested in correctional social work[40]

Many state prisons and most federal penal institutions employ social workers in their correctional treatment programs. Most often, social workers provide direct counseling or therapeutic services to the inmates, helping inmates explore their past and clarify their thinking about the future.[41] Social workers can also engage in group work treatment within the prison, working with inmates who have similar concerns, needs, or problems. The social worker can also be a part of a treatment team that might include other helping professionals. Social workers can also perform advocacy and resource development roles. Social workers have an important role in preparing inmates for release from the institution. This involves forging links between the inmate and community resources to assist them in reintegration into the community. The need for these services within correctional institutions is a crucial one. Social workers demonstrating competence in working within the corrections system will provide legitimacy for the profession's involvement in the adult correction field.

### A Case Study

Bonnie B, a twenty-three-year-old woman, was released on parole from the women's correctional facility. When released, Bonnie returned to live with her parents in a nearby city. As required, she made contact with her parole officer, a trained social worker. The parole officer knew from the parole board's report that in the past

*continued*

Bonnie had experienced a great deal of difficulty with alcoholism. Although she had become involved in Alcoholics Anonymous (AA) groups within the correctional facility, she had not received intensive treatment for this problem. Upon meeting with her, the parole officer also learned that Bonnie's two children had been temporarily removed from her custody at the time of her incarceration and had been placed in a foster home in another area of the state. Bonnie expressed her desire to regain custody of her children, once she was settled and able to provide for their care. She requested assistance from the parole officer in this effort. The parole officer knew from the parole report that Bonnie had received two years of secretarial training and had held various secretarial positions before her arrest and conviction. Bonnie also told the parole officer that living with her parents should only be a temporary arrangement. She worried that her parents would have trouble coping with her living independently since "they are over-protective of me."

In the following months, the parole officer helped Bonnie complete alcoholism treatment, along with continuing involvement in AA, find employment as a secretary with a local business, and secure her own living arrangements. The parole officer spent a great deal of time in intervention with Bonnie's family, helping to resolve the parents' feelings about Bonnie living on her own. The parole officer, working through the public social services department, was able to assist Bonnie with regaining the custody of her children. Eighteen months after Bonnie's release from the women's correctional facility, the parole officer recommended to the parole board that she be released from parole. The request was granted.

# Summary

This chapter has examined the responses made on behalf on society to crime, criminal behavior, and delinquency. Both the juvenile and adult corrections systems were explored, pointing out the responses made, the philosophies and values that have influenced the structure of the responses, and the strengths and weakness of the systems. The overall role of social work as a profession was discussed, and illustrated and supported the contention that involvement in the correctional system is a legitimate field of social work practice.

## Key Terms

capital punishment
community-based
  correctional services
constitutional criminality
corrections
crime
criminal behavior
criminal justice system
delinquent
diversion
incarceration

juvenile court
juvenile delinquency
juvenile reformation
*parens patriae*
parole
prisons
probation
restitution
status offender
work-educational release
Youth Service Bureaus

## Questions for Discussion

1. Discuss the term *corrections*. Should corrections be viewed as only services that are provided within the system or more broadly to include the entire social welfare system?

2. Discuss how the structure of adult correctional services differs from the structure of juvenile corrections.

3. What accounts for the fact that juvenile crime is on the rise? Why is there a high rate of recidivism among juvenile offenders, despite the efforts of the corrections system to treat these offenders?

4. Should the juvenile courts be tougher on the offender than is evident in the current system?

5. Should status offenders be removed from the jurisdiction of the juvenile court system? Who should be responsible for providing services to them?

6. Should society become more concerned with the causes of adult crime and criminal behavior, as opposed to developing service systems to punish the offender?

7. Does the penal system work? What do you think suggests that it does not? What alternatives to the current penal system do you think might be feasible and realistic?

8. How can violent behavior within the penal institution be dealt with? Would placing more emphasis on the treatment and rehabilitation of the offender be helpful?

9. Should there be more emphasis on community-based correctional services for adults? Do you think society should put more of its resources into this than in prison construction of prisons?

10. What do you think social workers can do to assist in bringing about of change within the adult corrections system?

# Notes

[1] Two sources agree on these three parts of the criminal justice system. They are Donald Brieland, Lela B. Costin, and Charles Atherton, *Contemporary Social Work: An Introduction to Social Work and Social Welfare* (New York: McGraw-Hill Book Co., 1985), and H. Wayne Johnson, *The Social Services: An Introduction* (Itaska, IL: F.E. Peacock Publishers, 1984).

[2] For further discussion of the definition of "corrections," see: Louis P. Carney, *Introduction to Correctional Science* (New York: McGraw-Hill Book Co., 1979), and Vernon Fox, *Introduction to Corrections* (Englewood Cliffs, NJ: Prentice-Hall, 1972).

[3] Statistics from the U.S. Federal Bureau of Investigation, *Uniform Crime Report* (Washington, DC: U.S. Government Printing Office, (Sept. 1984)), p. 1979.

[4] Maurice J. Boisevert and Robert Wells, "Toward a Rational Policy on Status Offenders," *Social Work* 25 (May 1980): pp. 230–234.

[5] Elizabeth Ferguson, *Social Work: An Introduction* (New York: J.B. Lippincott Co., 1975), pp. 359–360.

[6] Walter I. Trattner, *From Poor Law to Welfare State* (New York: The Free Press, 1979), p. 105.

[7] Trattner, *Poor Law*, p. 104.

[8] Trattner, *Poor Law*, p. 105.

[9] Ferguson, *Social Work*, p. 360.

[10] James Whittaker, "Family Involvement in Residential Treatment: A Support System for Parents," in *The Challenge of Partnership; Working with Parents of Children in Foster Care*; eds. Anthony N. Malviccoi and P. A. Sinanoglu (New York: Child Welfare League of America, 1980).

[11] Paul Nejelsk, "Diversion in the Juvenile Justice System: The Promise and the Danger," *Crime and Delinquency* 22 (October 1976): 393–480.

[12] C. Aaron McNeece, "Juvenile Justice Policy," in *Social Work in Juvenile and Criminal Justice Settings*, ed. Albert R. Roberts (Springfield, IL: Charles C. Thomas Publisher, 1983), pp. 19–44.

[13] James Ward, "Promises, Failures, and New Promises in Juvenile Justices: Implications For Social Work Education in the 1980s," *Journal of Education for Social Work* 15 (Fall 1979): 88–95.

[14] Arthur D. Little Inc., *Cost and Services Impacts of Deinstitutionalization of Status Offenders in Ten States: Responses of Angry Youth* (Washington, DC: Department of Health, Education and Welfare, 1977).

[15] Gary M. Nelson, "Services to Status Offenders and Delinquents under Title XX," *Social Work* 27 (July 1982): 348–353.

[16] "Report from the Colloquium of Rural Child Welfare Services," *Human Services in the Rural Environment* 3 (October 1978): 32–37.

[17] National Council on Crime and Delinquency, *Jurisdiction Over Status Offenses Should Be Removed from the Juvenile Court* (Hackensack, NJ: National Council on Crime and Delinquency, 1974).

[18] Rex A. Skidmore and Milton G. Thackeray, *Introduction to Social Work* (Englewood Cliffs, NJ: Prentice-Hall, 1982), p. 250.

[19] Carolyn Needleman, "Conflicting Philosophies of Juvenile Justice," in Albert R. Roberts, ed., *Social Work in Juvenile and Criminal Justice Settings*, (Springfield, IL: Charles C. Thomas Publishers, 1983), pp. 155–164.

[20] Needleman, "Conflicting Philosophies."

[21] Carolyn Needleman, "Social Work and Probation in Juvenile Court," in Roberts, *Social Work*, pp. 165–179.

[22] U.S. Federal Bureau of Investigation, *Uniform Crime Reports*, p. 1980.

[23] Carney, *Correctional Science*, p. 14.

[24] Walter A Friedlander and Robert Z. Apte, *Introduction to Social Welfare* (Englewood Cliffs, NJ: Prentice-Hall, 1980).

[25] Friedlander, *Introduction to Social Welfare.*

[26] Fergerson, *Social Work*, p. 378.

[27] Sheldon R. Gelman, "Correctional Policies: Evolving Trends," in Roberts, *Social Work*, pp. 45–65.

[28] Friedlander, *Introduction to Social Welfare*, p. 477.

[29] Johnson, *Social Services.*

[30] Todd R. Clear and George F. Cole, *American Corrections* (Monterey, CA: Brooks/Cole Publishing Co., 1986), pp. 442–467.

[31] President's Task Force on Prisoner Rehabilitation, *The Criminal Offender—What Should Be Done* (Washington, DC: U.S. Government Printing office, 1970).

[32] Clear, *American Corrections*, pp. 157–189.

[33] Johnson, *Social Services*, p. 220.

[34] Skidmore, *Introduction to Social Work.*

[35] Vernon Fox, "Foreword," in Roberts, *Social Work*, p. xii.

[36] Johnson, *Social Services.*

[37] Johnson, p. 221.

[38] Friedlander, *Introduction to Social Welfare*, p. 477.

[39] Harvey Treger, "Wheaton, Niles and Maywood Police Social Service Projects," *Federal Probation* 40 (September, 1976): 33–39.

[40] See: Elliot Studt, *Education for Social Workers in the Correctional Field* (New York: Council on Social Work Education, 1959) and Roberts, *Social Work.*

[41] Friedlander, *Introduction to Social Welfare*, p. 478.

## Suggested Readings

Brieland, Donald; Costin, Lela B.; and Atherton, Charles. *Contemporary Social Work.* New York: McGraw-Hill Book Co., 1985, chapter 13.

Friedlander, Walter A, and Apte, Robert Z. *Introduction To Social Welfare.* Englewood Cliffs, NJ: Prentice-Hall, 1980, chapter 19.

Johnson, H. Wayne. *The Social Services: An Introduction.* Itaska, IL: F.E. Peacock Publishers, 1982, chapter 11.

Roberts, Albert R., ed. *Social Work in Juvenile and Criminal Justice Settings.* Springfield, IL: Charles C. Thomas Publishers, 1983.

Skidmore, Rex A., and Thackeray, Milton G. *Introduction to Social Work.* Englewood Cliffs, NJ: Prentice-Hall, 1982, chapter 13.

# Chapter 13

## Gerontological Social Work

Working with the elderly is a fairly recent addition to social work. This is not to say that historically this group of people have been ignored, only that they have been traditionally considered as a part of the family. But with many elderly living alone and with a growing elderly population, the needs of older people have been recognized as an area of concern that must be given separate attention.

The elderly have many health problems, so social workers are now entering health settings. For example, mental health social workers help older people contend with loneliness and isolation, as well as more serious illness like Alzheimer's disease. Insufficient income and even poverty are major problems for this population. And while the elderly have always been recipients of income maintenance services, as life spans lengthen, the number of older people who will need special attention will also grow. To meet these and other needs, a special field of practice has developed that focuses specifically on the problems of older people. This field of practice, which has been referred to as social work with the aged or *gerontological social work*, includes people sixty years old or older.

Interest in gerontological social work dates from the mid-1940s. The Gerontological Society was formed in 1945 as a forum for professionals working with the elderly. The promotion of research on aging issues was one of its goals. Group work with the aged was the predominant mode of service. The National Council on Aging was established in 1960. This organization became a leader in stimulating interest in social work with older people and in developing practice methods and techniques for the particular needs of that population. In 1961, the first White House Conference on Aging was held. This conference identified the needs and concerns of older people that formed the base for several important pieces of legislation passed in the sixties. Included in this legislation was the *Older American Act* and the Medicare/Medicaid amendments to the Social Security Act. In the 1960s and 1970s, many conferences and projects took place that dealt with social work's need to recognize the aged as a special group and with enabling social workers to develop the special expertise needed for working in this new field of practice.[1]

# Who Are the Aged?

All human beings start aging from the day of their birth, but the word "aged" generally refers to individuals in the last stage of their life span. It is difficult to determine a definite age for this stage. Some say everyone over fifty-five is old; some, everyone over sixty; and others, everyone over sixty-five. And still others say that there are really two groups of aged people, those under seventy-five and those over seventy-five years of age. Usually the aged are defined as individuals older than either sixty or sixty-five years of age. This does not mean that younger people will not be the concern of this field; gerontological social work also helps younger people to avoid some of the problems the aged have.

## *Demographic Factors*

In 1985, 28.5 million Americans were over age 65, 12 percent of the total population of the United States and an 11 percent increase since 1980. Since 1900, the percentage of older people in the population has increased eight times from 3.1 million in 1900 to 28.5 million in 1985. In 1985 there were 17 million people in the 65 to 74 age group, eight times the number in that group in 1900. There were 8.8 million in the seventy-five to eighty-four age group. Eleven times the number in 1900, and 2.7 million in the 85 and over group; twenty-two times the number in 1900. Life expectancy in 1984 for a person 65 years old was 16.8 years (18.6 for women and 14.6 for men.)[2]

The aged are not a homogeneous group of people but contains individuals with a broad variety of characteristics: 18.8 million are women; 11.0 million are men. There are 149 women to every 100 men in this population. Of the men, 75 percent are married; of the women, 40 percent. Only 5 percent of the group are in nursing homes or other institutions. Of those not in institutions, 67 percent live in a family setting and 31 percent live alone. Women are more apt to live alone (43 percent of the women to 18 percent of the men). Whites make up 89 percent of the population over sixty-five; blacks 8 percent; Hispanics 2 percent; and other groups (Asians and native American) 1 percent. Thirty percent of this population assess their health as poor. Twelve percent are in the labor force.[3]

Geographically, certain parts of the country have a higher percentage of the older population. It is commonly thought that older people tended to live in the south and the west. But according to the 1980 census, while 17.3 percent of Florida's population is over sixty-five, states with more than 13 percent of their population over sixty-five include: Arkansas (13.7 percent), Rhode Island (13.4 percent), Iowa (13.3 percent), Missouri (13.2 percent), South Dakota (13.2 percent), and Nebraska (13.1 percent). Further examination of census data shows a considerable concentration of older people in the midwest.[4] More older people live outside metropolitan areas than do younger groups. If the elderly do live in cities, they tend to live in the central city, though this is changing as suburbia ages.

## Other Factors

When considering this age group, it is important to identify some of the biological, psychological, and social changes that take place at this time of life, since these are important in understanding the special needs of this population. Gradual physical changes that have been developing for some time now become apparent. The timing and extent of these changes varies widely from older person to older person. The skin is less pliable, wrinkles develop, the hair greys, the person begins to look old. The skeletomuscular system is more susceptible to stress, bones break more easily, arthritis can develop, joints are stiffer. Digestive problems become more common. Sensory functions are reduced; eyesight may dim; there may be a hearing loss; some sensitivity to touch may be lost. The cardiopulmonary system is subject to stress; high blood pressure, heart attacks, strokes, and chronic respiratory difficulty may develop. These physical changes can require a change of life-style and diminish an older person's capability to adapt.[5]

Many psychological and sociological theories have been developed about the later years in life.[6] These theories often conflict and offer little conclusive evidence of their validity. A useful means for considering the psychological factors involved in aging can be from a human developmental point of view. Erik Erikson, a noted psychologist, has identified this as the stage of integrity versus despair.[7] Robert Peck, Director of the Research Development Center for Teacher Education in Austin, Texas, has expanded on this to state that the tasks of this stage include: developing a sense of worth apart from the work role, developing a capacity to cope with the declining physical capabilities, and developing a capacity to deal with the prospect and meaning of death.[8] Maintenance of a positive self-concept is a most important task for the older person. Linda George, a psychiatry professor at Duke University, has identified four dimensions of the adult self-concept that are particularly important. These are

1. interpersonal aspects focused on social relationships,

2. altruistic aspects focused on ethical, religious, and philosophic concerns,

3. mastery aspects focused on competence, a sense of effectiveness, creativity, and autonomy,

4. the self-protective aspects focused on maintaining a sense of well-being.[9]

The sociological considerations important for older people are those characteristics of the society of which they are a part. Contemporary U.S. society displays considerable prejudice against the elderly. Attitudes toward older people and the aging process are generally negative. This has been referred to as *ageism*. There are few meaningful or important places for older people in our society. Our culture values youth, physical fitness, and productivity. Because of this, stress is inevitable for both the older individual and for society.

While not all people over sixty-five are in need of attention from the social welfare system, a considerable number find it a constant struggle to supply their own needs either from their own resources or from their immediate personal network. Factors that put older people at risk are insufficient financial resources, living alone with no family nearby, poor health, negative attitudes about aging, and being over seventy-five years of age. Some individuals with these risk factors manage quite well. But when these risk factors begin to affect the individual's capacity to function and when the individual's stress increases, social welfare resources become important. With a growing number of people not only in this population group but also with multiple risk factors, gerontological social work has become a field of practice, and the social welfare system has developed specialized means for meeting the needs of this population.

## Arrangements Used to Meet Need

Any consideration of the history of working with the aged must take into account that until the present century very few people lived to be as old as people are today. The number of older people was very small, and they were generally cared for by family mutual aid. Except for the institutional care provided by some private groups, it is only since the enactment of Social Security legislation in the 1930s that any recognition has been given to the special needs of the elderly. And our present care of the elderly has within it vestiges of attitudes and arrangements used in the past. It is important to consider how each of the six arrangements identified earlier in this book has been used to provide for the need of the elderly in our society.

## Mutual Aid

This has been the primary arrangement used throughout history to care for the older person. Families have been the major resource and, until very recently, their responsibility for relatives was enforced morally, culturally, and through law. *Relative responsibility laws* held adult children responsible for the support of their parents. If children could not take an older parent needing care into their homes, then they were responsible for paying at least some of the costs for caring for that parent in either an institution or some other place. Today, the relative responsibility laws no longer exist. And although the moral and cultural influence continue to pressure children to care for their parents, social change has made it increasingly difficult. Thus there is a gap between our expectations and the reality.

Another way that mutual aid has provided care for the elderly is through the personal resource networks that exist in communities and cultural groups. On a short-term basis, if older people are ill or unable to perform some of the tasks of daily living, neighbors and friends bring in meals or otherwise care for the needs that exist. Transportation for shopping, medical appointments, or church activities are often provided. Studies of community helping show that this mechanism is alive and well and still a very important mechanism for providing for the needs of the older person.[10]

## Charity-Philanthropy

The two historical examples of this arrangement (Charity Organization Societies and settlement houses) did not emphasize providing for the needs of the elderly, though both did provide some services. Settlement houses were one of the early agencies to develop group activities (Senior Citizens Clubs) for older people. Present-day family agencies (a contemporary example of this arrangement) provide counseling services for older people and their families, which can be particularly helpful when decisions about care must be made or when support in difficult situations is needed. Another agency very active in providing for the needs of older people has been the system of Jewish community centers. The Senior Citizens Centers developed in the last twenty-five years are yet another manifestation of this arrangement.[11]

Another use of this mechanism has been institutions for the care of the elderly. Most of these institutions charged either an entry fee or a monthly maintenance fee or both. In 1929, there were 1,268 such institutions. Of these, 43 percent were sponsored by religious groups, 35 percent by private philanthropic organizations, 10 percent by fraternal orders. The rest were sponsored by ethnic groups and trade unions. In addition, some were federal and state homes for veterans. Catholic orders, especially the Little Sisters of the Poor, operated homes for those without resources. In many cases, individuals served by these institutions had to be members of the church or other organization that sponsored the institutions.[12] The use of the charity-philanthropy institutions for the elderly has declined since the development of social welfare and social insurance programs that provide income maintenance for the elderly. Today most institutions for the aged care for the frail elderly who cannot live alone or whose health problems prevent their care by families. Nursing home care for those with medical problems is the primary use of institutional care today. It is generally accepted that 5 percent of those over sixty-five years of age live in institutional settings.

Retirement villages or apartment complexes where individuals maintain their own private space is also a popular housing arrangement with some older people. Many of these are developed and maintained by private and religious philanthropic organizations. These, like many of the private homes for the aged, require an entrance fee and/or a monthly maintenance fee. Charity-philanthropy is still a mechanism used to provide for some needs of some elderly people in today's social welfare system.

## Public Welfare

Elderly people were one of the groups that was provided for under the poor laws. If a family could not provide care for an elderly member, and if the elderly person had no resources, then that person became the responsibility of the town or county, and later, of the state. In the early days of the United States, these poor elderly individuals were cared for in families reimbursed by the governmental unit responsible for caring for the elderly. Later, with the development of almshouses, they were cared for in these all-encompassing institutions, along with children, the mentally ill, and others who could not care for themselves. As children and the mentally ill were removed from the almshouses, these institutions became largely populated by old people who had no other place to go. These institutions often came to be referred to as poor farms, the county home, or the old folks home. Life in an alsmhouse was dreary at best. There were many abuses in these institutions—funds were very limited, staff often cared little about the people in their care, little attention was given to providing proper food and shelter—unsanitary conditions, neglect, and even brutality abounded.[13]

Many older people were also cared for in institutions for the mentally ill. The diagnosis of senile dementia was popular: in 1936, 7.9

percent of all first-admissions to mental institutions were for people with this diagnosis.[14] The back wards also contained many individuals who, having been confined to mental hospitals, particularly the state hospitals, at earlier stages in life, had grown old in these institutions.

Some communities and some states came to believe that older people with no resources of their own could best be cared for by providing assistance payments, so they could remain independent within the community. A few states passed old age pension laws,[15] but it took the Depression and the Social Security Act to make financial aid to the elderly a part of the U.S. social welfare system. One part of the Social Security Act of 1935 was the *Old Age Assistance* program. Under this program, the federal government provided grants-in-aid to the states if the states set up programs to provide income assistance to those over sixty-five whose income fell under specified amounts. The grant-in-aid provided a percentage of the older person's income maintenance; states provided the rest. States had to meet certain other requirements to receive this grant. Each state had a different program with different payments. In 1973, at the time this program was discontinued, average monthly payments ranged from $56 to $121 a month. (See Table 13.1.)

In 1974, there was a major change in federal financial assistance to older people. The Supplemental Security Income (SSI) program was established. This program removed responsibility for income maintenance of the elderly from the states and placed it under the Social Security Administration. Eligibility, as for old age assistance, depends on income and resources. From July 1982 to June 1983, the maximum monthly payment was $285.50 for an individual and $426.40 for a couple. Automatic cost-of-living increases are incorporated in the payment system.[16]

Table 13.1   Important Dates: Gerontological Social Work

| | |
|---|---|
| 1935 | Social Security Act provides income maintenance for older people through both insurance and public welfare arrangements. |
| 1945 | Formation of the Gerontological Society |
| 1961 | First White House Conference on Aging |
| 1965 | Passage of the Older American Act |
| 1965 | Passage of the Medicare and Medicaid amendments to the Social Security Act. |
| 1974 | Supplementary Security Income provisions of the social security act replace Aid to the Aged. |

The SSI program remains the primary means for providing for the financial needs of those over sixty-five who have little or no other means or support. It is the present day use of the social welfare arrangement for meeting the needs of older people. Another program that falls under this arrangement is Medicaid, which was discussed in Chapter 10, an important means of providing for the health care needs of this group. The cost of nursing home care for many older people is provided from the Medicaid program.

## Social Insurance

The best example of this arrangement is the *Old Age, Survivors and Disability Health Insurance program (OASDHI),* commonly referred to as Social Security. The Social Security Act of 1935 established the program. Changes in the program have been mainly to broaden the number of people covered and to increase the amount of the benefits paid. At present, most people in the labor force are covered, and compulsory contributions from employees, employers, and the self-employed are required. Medicare, discussed in Chapter 10, which provides health care for individuals over sixty-five years of age is also a form of social insurance.

Over 90 percent of the people over age sixty-five receive benefits from OASDHI. It is the major source of income for people over sixty-five. The benefits depend in part upon an individual's earnings over the period worked in covered employment. Spouses can receive half the benefits of the worker. A surviving spouse receives benefits equal to those of the deceased worker. Benefits are payable at age sixty-five, with the option of payment at age sixty-two at a permanently reduced amount.[17]

With the growing numbers of older people in our society, our present OASDHI program is at risk. Many proposals have been made to give the program a degree of solvency. In future years, the age for receiving full benefits will be raised. Questions about benefits paid to women have been raised. Women are in the labor force for shorter periods of time, and at lower pay. Widow's benefits are lower than those of couples: thus, women tend to receive lower benefits than men. They are at greater risk of being below the poverty level. There is concern about how to provide a more equitable benefit for women. In the coming years, social security can be expected to change but will continue to be an important arrangement for meeting the economic needs of older people.

## Social Services

The needs of older people include not only a place to live or income maintenance, but also intangible services. In recent years, with the emphasis on maintaining older people in the community, it has been found that a variety of supportive services are needed. These include information and referral services, homemaker and home health services, home-delivered meals, socialization services, transportation services, and legal assistance. Some of these have been provided by the private social agencies for some time. The Social Security Amendments of 1962 provided the first federal support for these social services. In 1975, Title XX of the Social Security Act's major purpose was to provide services to reduce dependency and promote self-support. Eligibility was limited to those receiving income assistance or to those with incomes below the poverty line. Social services for older people under provisions of the Older American Act of 1965 further broadened the services for the elderly. Because this provision falls under the universal provision arrangement, it will be discussed in that section of this chapter.[18]

When considering the social service arrangement, it is important to note that this is a rather recent development. Only since about 1960 have such services been developed specifically for this population. Many demonstration projects have come and gone. Established private agencies, newly developed community-supported agencies, government agencies, and volunteers have all been active in developing services. Now it seems well established that an array of such services is desirable both to maintain older people in the community for longer periods of time and to enhance their quality of life. There are still questions about how such services should be structured, supported, staffed, and administered. They are, nevertheless, important in the overall service network for aging persons.

## Universal Provision

Growing concern about the plight of the increasing number of older people in the United States resulted in the White House Conference on Aging in January, 1961. This conference made a number of recommendations, some of which are encompassed in the *Older American Act of 1965 (OAA)*. White House Conferences on Aging held in 1971 and 1981 also made more recommendations and to some extent influenced additional legislation. There have been amendments to the original Older American Act. The result of this activity is a plan for meeting the needs of all older people, a plan that uses the arrangement of universal provision. There are no means tests; it is assumed that older Americans, regardless of income or other characteristics, all have needs that should be provided for within the social welfare system.

It must be noted, however, that funding has never been available to fully put into action the objectives of either the OAA or those set forth by the White House Conferences. But what has resulted is the identification of needs of the elderly and a framework for working toward provision of those needs. The framework consists of federal, state, and area (territory within a state) administrative units. The *Area Agency on Aging* is mandated to develop a comprehensive and coordinated service system. At present, because of the lack of funding, it makes considerable effort to get others—private agencies, local community groups, and various governmental agencies—to provide the needed services.

Services identified as universally needed by the elderly are: information and referral, informing older people of available services including developing and maintaining a data bank; outreach, services that break through the isolation of the elderly; transportation; in-home services; homemaker and home chore services and home-delivered meals; legal services; protective services; counseling services; socialization and recreation services; and educational services. A nutrition program that provides congregate meals in a central location in the community is a major thrust of the services available. In 1981 there were approximately twelve hundred such projects in the country.[19]

Although the provision of elder services is far from universal at this time, the philosophy for such services has been developed. Contemporary U.S. society recognizes that the elderly may need not only some kind of income maintenance but also a variety of other services. Since the family structure no longer supports the elderly, society recognizes the provision of these services as a right rather than as charity.

The material presented in this section of this chapter shows that a system for meeting the needs of older people has evolved by discarding earlier mechanisms that are no longer functional, by adapting some arrangements for use in a new time, and by developing new programs and services. Our social welfare system uses all six of the identified arrangements to care for older people's needs. While strongly rooted in the mutual aid philosophy of preindustrial societies, the current system emphasizes income maintenance through social insurance if possible, but uses social welfare where necessary. It also acknowledges the desirability of maintaining the older people in their communities rather than placing them in institutions. In addition, it recognizes that older people must have a wide variety of services if they are to live satisfying lives and be maintained in the community. There also seems to be a growing preference for these services to be provided by a universal provision arrangement. This system of care for elders is evolving, not static, and will continue to change as the social welfare system adapts to changing times and changing needs of older people.

## Current Problems and Issues

Current problems and issues in social work with the aged relate to each of the conditions that give rise to human need (social change, poverty, discrimination, and availability of resources). While discussing how each of these conditions affects aging individuals, service delivery issues will also be considered.

## Social Change

It should have been apparent from reading Chapter 3 that a tremendous demographic change has taken place in recent years in the United States. With the lengthening life span, the population of older people has grown at an extraordinary rate, not only in numbers but as a percentage of the general population, which means there are many more aging and dependent people in our society with fewer younger people to provide for their support. And the growth of the very oldest segment of the population (those over seventy-five) has been even faster. Because of their physical frailty and poor health conditions, this group's needs are considerable.

Two other significant factors closely related to demographics must be considered. First, there are more older women than older men. This is a fairly new phenomenon, since in the past many women died at a young age from childbirth complications or from the stress of raising large families under primitive conditions. And until very recently, most women depended on men to provide their financial support, so older women are not apt to have financial resources of their own; after their husband's death, they depend on their husband's social security or other insurance. Since most older women outlive their husbands, these widows often find themselves with limited resources. This change in the ratio of older men to older women contributes to the low average income of older people generally and of older women in particular.

The other significant factor is the increased quality of health care, which allows many people to live longer, lengthens the life span so that many individuals live into their eighties or even their nineties. But that also means that many more older people are living with chronic illnesses or are very frail, thus increasing their need for geriatric health care and their dependency on government programs.

But demography is not the only social change affecting social work with the aged. Changes in the family are also important to consider. Smaller families mean fewer children available to care for aging parents. And because of society's increased mobility, adult children often do not live as near to their parents as they once did. Another change that reduces the family capacity to care for its older members is the increase in the number of working women. Women have been the primary caretakers in our society, but as they have joined the labor force, their caretaking role has been reduced. While mutual aid, specifically family care, has been heavily used to meet the needs of many older individuals, it is easy to see that change in the family structure has affected the social welfare system.

*Retirement* is also a very new concept. Before the passage of the Social Security Law in 1935, only a very few older people were fortunate to have pensions and thus were able to leave the labor force through retirement. Most people were expected to work at some task until death. But mandatory retirement was instituted to make jobs available to younger workers during the Depression. Social Security provided income for retiring workers, so they could continue to provide for financial needs. However, work gives individuals a sense of self-esteem, a purpose for being, essential needs. Retirement forces older people to find new sources of their sense of belongingness and individual worth, not an easy task in our youth-oriented culture. Thus, retirement is another social change that affects the needs of aging people.

Social change has challenged older people in another way. The changes that have taken place in their lifetime have been tremendous and have called for constant adaptation. The life-style they observed in older people when they themselves were young no longer fits into today's society; adaptation without patterns or role models to follow is always difficult—and doubly hard for the elderly. Older individuals need to understand what is happening to them as they age and how they can best adapt to the new society.

## Poverty

Poverty, as discussed earlier, is indeed a condition that threatens the aging population: 12.6 percent of persons over 65 years old lived below the poverty line in 1985, contrasted with 14.1 percent in the general population. Another 8 percent were classified as "near poor" (had income between the poverty level and 125 percent of poverty). However, to truly understand the relationship between poverty and older people, it is important to look at which subgroups of elderly are most likely to live in poverty. Women, particularly those who live alone, are far more apt than men to be poor; 26 percent of women who live alone are poor while only 6 percent of those living in families are considered poor. Minority elders are poorer than white elders. While 14 percent of white elderly live in poverty, 32 percent of black elderly and 24 percent of Hispanic elderly live in poverty. Twenty-one percent of those living in nonmetropolitan areas are below the poverty line, compared with 13 percent in metropolitan areas.[20] Thus, if an older person is a woman who lives alone, is black or Hispanic, and lives in a nonmetropolitan area, the chances of her living in poverty are very great. It is not surprising that those groups of poor older people are the same groups with a history of working in low-paid jobs, which in turn affects the amount of social security benefits they receive—the economic "double-whammy" of employment discrimination.

Poverty for an older person means that health care may not be affordable, transportation may not be available, suitable housing difficult to find, good nutrition may be overlooked. While society tries to give special consideration in each of these areas for low-income elderly, resources and funds are simply inadequate. Older people in poverty risk living unsatisfying and difficult lives, risk unwanted institutionalization, and even premature death.

## Discrimination

*Ageism* is one kind of prejudice practiced by contemporary society, which rewards youth, physical fitness, and productivity. Aged individuals do not fit into the "valued person" criteria. Older people are "has beens," unable to offer much to society, who prevent younger people from "getting ahead" by continuing to occupy jobs when they are no longer productive. They are out of touch with contemporary society. Their wisdom has no value. In summary, they are incompetent. These are damaging misconceptions that take a toll on the older members of our society.

Ageism shows up in the contemporary scene in several ways. First, there is the work place. Discrimination against the older workers had become such a problem that by 1967, Congress passed the Age Discrimination Employment Act. This prohibits discrimination in hiring and other employment practices because of age. But laws do not change attitudes, and attitudes lead to finding ways to circumvent laws. It is very difficult for older people who want to work to find employment. When they do find jobs, it is often the minimum wage jobs where they must compete with young people. There are subtle pressures on older people still in the work place to retire.[21]

Discrimination is also manifest in the media. Because media images are so influential in our society, the negative depiction of older people reinforces the already negative thinking of the general public and contributes to the elderly's poor self-esteem. It leads to a sense of rolelessness, one of the major factors contributing to the attitudinal problems of the aged.[22]

It should also be noted that those groups discriminated against because of conditions other than aging are also discriminated against because of their age. These groups include ethnic and racial minorities, women, the mentally and physically disabled. Some older individuals are discriminated against in two, three, or even four ways. A woman, who is black, chronically physically disabled, and over sixty-five years of age thus can be said to have a fourfold jeopardy!

Several organizations have worked very hard to counteract discrimination in our society. These include the National Council on Aging, The

American Association of Retired Persons, The Gray Panthers, and the Gerontological Society. Older people, themselves, seem to be the best resource for counteracting the many myths and stereotypes that reinforce prejudicial attitudes and practices. But the social welfare system also must develop advocacy strategies to ensure that the rights of aged individuals are respected and that resources are developed to meet their needs.

## The Issue of Resource Availability

Because of decreasing personal capacity or decreasing income, the older individual must increasingly depend on other resources to meet needs. Traditionally the first line of defense has been the family, but in today's changing world, the family is not always able to meet these needs. So how does society cope with the needs of its older members?

Some of these needs are met informally in the community, through friends and natural helpers, which make up *personal networks*. However, these resources can meet only a part of the needs related to companionship, reassurance, and short-term emergency situations. Some older people have a limited circle of friends, others find their friends also less able to serve as resources due to their own declining health or strength, and, of course death takes its toll. Obviously, the informal network cannot be depended on to meet every need.

Many older people have been very self-sufficient, and up to now have not had to depend on resources outside their families and personal networks. They may think of use of public resources as "welfare," an affront to their pride, and thus not an acceptable means for meeting need. They may have no idea of the resources available to them. Thus, information and referral and educational services for elders become very important.

Community groups and public and private social service organizations have developed services that provide older people with meaningful opportunities to participate in community life. The *senior citizens centers* fall into this area and are important resources for the older person still able to be active outside the home. Food is often a part of the activity offered. Older individuals living alone may not maintain a nutritious diet since most people find it hard to cook for just one person. Nutrition programs, which offer a well-balanced meal several times a week, are funded under a section of the Older American Act.

Some older people have problems that would require institutionalization, where resources not provided to enable them to remain in their own home. These services include homemaker services, chore services, and home health services. Transportation services are important for those who can no longer drive or use public transportation. Housing adapted to the special needs of the elder is another resource that allows individuals to remain in their community for a longer period of time. Housing that places older people in close proximity to one other seems to encourage a natural helping network in which older people look out for and provide companionship for each other.[23] Some older people are abused by their family or other caretakers or are unable to manage their financial affairs. These people are in need of protective services.

Some older people can no longer live in their own homes and need institutional resources to provide for their special health care needs. Nursing homes are the most often-used resource for this purpose, but they must also consider how needs other than health care are met in these facilities so that the older person can live the least restrictive life possible with an opportunity for individualization and self-determination.

There are many issues about how the wide range of resources needed by aged people can be met. Which resources should be provided by community groups? Which resources can be provided by natural helpers or the older person's personal network? Which resources must receive governmental financial support? How can the resources be provided so that older people will not feel stigmatized? In a society that has a growing population of aged people, limited economic resources, and a changing social structure, answers to these questions are elusive. Only as communities and the professionals who work in these communities come to grips with these issues will answers be found. This is the time to develop new mechanisms within the U.S. social welfare system to meet the resource needs of aging.[24]

Fiscal support is crucial. Yet in a time of decreasing fiscal resources for the social welfare system, there is considerable question as to how adequate funding resources can be obtained. But how can we fail to meet the needs of the elderly in the community? If these needs are not met, then the aged are in danger of institutionalization, a much more expensive type of care. It is important at this time to identify what kinds of needs can be met by the natural helping system or community groups with little or no fiscal resources. The formal social welfare system then can work with them and help them. But needs not met by natural helping systems and community groups must be provided to maintain the aged in the community. These services should include supportive services to families caring for frail or disabled aged members. Respite care, stipends for family care, and support groups for caregivers can be useful in this supportive approach.

Aged people with an adequate income are less at risk of having unmet need. Therefore, attention needs to be paid to developing income maintenance programs and social insurance programs that support an adequate income for all aged. The funds that are available should be used to support those proven services and programs that meet critical needs that cannot be met in other ways. All of this requires a creative and critical approach to the use of all existing resources: personal, fiscal, and formal.

## Coordination

Another important issue is *coordination*. Coordination can be considered on two levels. First is the level of coordinating the services of all agencies and programs that provide resources to the elderly. The Area Offices on Aging are set up, in part, to do this. This effort must be strengthened. The coordination effort must identify and address unmet needs. The second coordination level is the personal resource network of the individual aged person. Social workers need to be given means for coordinating natural and formal systems, for including families in the planning process. For the family and other natural helpers to be used effectively, these must be balanced when making decisions about their use.

When thinking about this complex system of elderly services, a framework is needed. Such a framework is presented in Figure 13.2. This framework shows four levels of care. The first level, preventive care services, can be provided before an individual reaches the aged stage of life. If people prepare for this stage, they will be more likely to have resources for meeting their needs and a better understanding of those needs and how to meet them. The second level, socialization, are those services provided as an individual or spouse retires or changes life-style to help the individual cope with the adjustments involved and to develop a new, satisfying and adequate life-style. The third level, supportive and protective care, are those services provided to frail, ill or disabled older people, to support them and their caretakers in maintaining their capacity to live in the community. They focus on preventing premature institutionalization and supporting as active and satisfying a life-style as possible. The fourth level, institutional care, is for those who can no longer be maintained in a *community living* situation. It focuses on elders maintaining as much self-determination as possible and on maintaining contact with the important people in their lives, while developing a life-style with a positive and active stance.

The framework also divides service into four categories. These categories cover the most common problems of older people. These areas of service are economic; attitude, helping elders and society in general develop better attitudes toward aging; rolemaking, services that give the aged persons opportunities for meaningful roles in society; and health care.

This chart can help assess which services are available in a community and which need to be developed. Note that at levels one and two, preventive care and socialization, services can probably be provided through the natural and community systems and do not require a large amount of governmental funding. They can prevent or postpone the

Table 13.2   A Framework for Considering the Needs of Aging Persons

| | Economic Services | Attitudes | Rolemaking | Health Care |
|---|---|---|---|---|
| Preventive Care | Economic opportunity during adulthood that provides for one's older years. Education for self-responsibility in planning. | Development of positive attitudes toward aging. Development of a sense of self-responsibility. | Development of useful roles for older people in society. Development of a sense of social responsibility. | Good lifetime health care for everyone. Development of responsible attitudes toward health maintenance. |
| Socialization | Education and information about financial management for the elderly. Information and referral services. Opportunity for appropriate employment. Transportation services. | Peer group self-help experiences. Education about aging. Counseling services, Outreach services. | Meaningful and useful roles (volunteer, planning, political opportunities, etc.) for the elderly. | Geriatric health care for all. Self-responsibility for health care maintenance. Nutrition services. Health care counseling. |
| Supportive and Protective Care | Adequate income maintenance for people unable to provide for self. Services to maintain people in their own homes. Suitable and subsidized elderly housing. | Assessment of emotional and social needs. Maintenance of self-determination. | Day care centers. Volunteer visiting support. Supports to families maintaining elderly in the home. | Geriatric health care. Home help and health care aids. Meals-on-wheels. Support to families and others caring for ill and disabled aged persons. |
| Institutional Care | Funding for adequate institutional care when needed. | Services to provide social, entertainment, and counseling. Self-determination as possible. | Services to help maintain family- community contacts. Therapeutic activity. | Nursing and other needed health care. |

need for the more expensive supportive and protective care and institutional care. The chart does not indicate which services should be provided by private social service agencies, which by public social service agencies, which by other professionals or institutions within the social welfare network, which services should be provided by families, natural helpers, or community groups. This varies from individual to individual and from community to community, depending on resources available and on particular community functions. Frameworks like this should receive further study to learn how best to organize the social welfare system as it focuses on the aged person.

Another factor in coordination is the network of services developed to meet the needs of the elderly. Some individuals, particularly the frail and disabled, need many different services. Coordination is necessary for optimal use of resources. The case manager function, where one worker is responsible for seeing that the various services fit together in a coherent whole, seems most important. Social workers with a generalist frame of reference are a natural choice for filling this role.

## Social Work Practice with Older People

Social workers work with the elderly in both the community and in institutions. In the community settings, social workers are found in Area Agencies on Aging, Senior Citizens Centers, and in public social service agencies in the divisions providing services for older people. Social workers in a variety of other agencies servicing families, such as the family service agencies also may have older individuals in their case load.

Social workers use a wide variety of practice approaches with older people. Some of the more important roles a social worker can fill are

as a broker providing older people and their families with information about available services,

as a case manager coordinating a wide variety of services,

as a crisis intervener,

as a group worker providing a variety of group services,

as a community development and planning consultant working on services for older people,

as a coordinator with public and private agencies and with community groups,

as an administrator with responsibility for programs that benefit the elderly,

and as a social worker in a nursing home, hospital, or other residential or institutional setting.

## A Case Study

A hospital social worker was asked by Dr. C to find a nursing home placement for Mrs. F. Mrs. F was recovering from pneumonia and Dr. C felt she could no longer live alone since she came into the hospital malnourished. The social worker went to talk with Mrs. F and found that Mrs. F did not want to go to a nursing home. While she admitted it was difficult for her to get meals, she also found grocery shopping very hard. She did have a group of friends who kept track of her and came to see her, but her family lived in a distant city. The social worker contacted the local social service agency that provided both home-delivered meals and homemaker service to see if they could provide service to Mrs. F. The doctor was notified of the social worker's findings and, though reluctant, was willing to explore an in-home plan.

The social worker from the local social service agency visited Mrs. F and went to look at her home situation. This social worker, together with Mrs. F, developed a plan for Mrs. F to receive a home-delivered meal five days a week at noon until she regained her strength. A homemaker was provided for three days a week to do grocery shopping, some housework, and to assess just what Mrs. F was capable of doing for herself in daily living. A home health nurse was also involved in providing nursing care for a time.

After six weeks, the situation was reassessed. Mrs. F had made a good recovery and no longer needed home health care. Rather than the home-delivered meals, she would be provided transportation on the Senior Citizens Bus, so she could receive one meal a day at the nutrition site at the local Senior Citizens Center. Within a month, she was also attending other activities at the center. The homemaker hours were cut to two a week, as Mrs. F found she could do her own shopping on the Senior Citizens Bus. The social worker remains in contact with Mrs. F through the homemaker and through quarterly evaluations of her needs. At this time the situation seems stabilized.

# Summary

Given the growth in the aged population, not only will the social welfare system need to respond to the needs of this population, it will need to evolve new and different ways of responding. This evolution will be related to the characteristics of the aged population, to the current structure of the social welfare system and to the problems and issues that confront social work with the aged. In this evolving system the need for social workers will grow. They will support both the elderly and their families and the case managers for the frail and disabled elderly in the community. They will provide protective services and serve as advocates for those unable to stand up for their own rights and needs. They will provide services to the institutionalized aged person. They will help the mutual aid systems and communities to become more responsive to the needs of the elderly. They will work to blot out the discrimination caused by ageism. This relatively new field of practice will be very important in the social welfare system of the future.

## Key Terms

ageism
Area Agency on Aging
community living
coordination
gerontological social work
Older American Act of
     1965 (OAA)

Old Age Assistance
Old Age, Survivors and Disability
     Insurance (OASDI)
personal networks
relative responsibility laws
retirement
senior citizens center

## Questions for Discussion

1. At what age do you think people should retire?

2. Should gerontological social work be a separate field of practice? Why?

3. Why do you think so many people see old age as negative? How can this be changed?

4. What do you think should be the role of the family in meeting the needs of its aged members?

5. How should need be determined for an elderly person?

6. What changes would you suggest in Social Security benefits?

7. Discuss the changes that have taken place in the last sixty years and what changes those who are now aged have had to make in their way of life.

8. Describe the kind of personal network you believe is needed by an aged person to meet their needs.

9. What is a community's responsibilities in providing resources for aged people?

10. How do you think the coordination issues raised in the chapter should be addressed by social workers?

# Notes

1 For more detail about these developments see: Louis Lowy, *Social Work with the Aged*, 2nd ed. (New York: Longman, 1985), chapter 2.

2 These facts are taken from the pamphlet "A Profile of Older Americans: 1986." American Association of Retired Persons, 1909 K Street, N.W., Washington, D.C. 20049.

3 "A Profile of Older Americans: 1986."

4 Raymond T. Coward and Gary R. Lee, *The Elderly in Rural Society* (New York: Springer Pub. Co., 1985), pp. 39–41.

5 See Cary S. Kart, *The Realities of Aging: An Introduction to Gerontology*, 2nd ed. (Boston: Allyn and Bacon, 1985), chapters 4 and 5.

6 See Kart, *Realities of Aging*, chapters 6 and 7; and Lowy, *Social Work*, chapter 8.

7 Erik Erikson, "Identity and the Life Cycle," *Psychological Issues*, Monograph I (New York: International Press, 1959).

8 Robert Peck, "Psychological Developments in the Second Half of Life," in *Psychological Aspect of Aging*, ed., Joe Anderson (Washington, D.C.: American Psychological Association, 1956), pp. 42–53.

9 Linda K. George, "Models of Transitions in Middle and Later Life," *The Annals of the American Academy of Political and Social Sciences* 464 (November 1982): 22–37.

10 Eugene Litwak, *Helping the Elderly: The Complementary Roles of Informal Networks and Formal Systems* (New York: The Guilford Press, 1985), and Shirley Patterson and Eileen Brennan, "Matching Helping Roles with the Characteristics of Aging Natural Helpers," *Journal of Gerontological Social Work* 5 (Summer 1983): 55–66.

11 Lowy, *Social Work*, chapter 7.

12 Fred S. Hall, ed., *Social Work Year Book 1929* (New York: Russell Sage Foundation, 1930), pp. 31 and 55.

13 Amos Griswold Warner, Stuart Alfred Queen, and Ernest Bouldin Harper, *American Charities and Social Work*, 4th ed. (New York: Thomas Y. Crowell Co., 1930), chapter 16.

14 Russell H. Kurtz, ed., *Social Work Year Book 1939* (New York: Russell Sage Foundation, 1939), p. 253.

15 Russell H. Kurtz, ed., *Social Work Year Book 1960* (New York: National Association of Social Workers, 1960), p. 36.

16 Bennett M. Rich and Martha Baum, *The Aging: A Guide to Public Policy* (Pittsburgh: University of Pittsburgh Press, 1984), chapter 3.

17 Louis Lowy, *Social Policies and Programs on Aging* (Lexington, MA: Lexington Books, 1980), chapter 4.

18 Lowy, *Social Policies*, chapter 7.

19 Rich, *The Aging*, chapter 2.

20 See "A Profile of Older Americans," and Elizabeth D. Huttman, *Social Services and the Elderly* (New York: The Free Press, 1985), pp. 7–8.

21 For an excellent discussion of elderly housing options, see: Elizabeth D. Hutterman, *Social Services for the Elderly* (New York: The Free Press, 1985), chapters 8 and 9.

22 For an indepth discussion of the various programs and services that provide resources for aging people see: Donald E. Gelfand, *The Aging Network: Programs and Services*, 2nd ed. (New York: Springer Publishing Co., 1984).
23 Kart, *Realities of Aging*, chapter 13.
24 Kart, *Realities of Aging*, chapter 1.

## Suggested Readings

Atchley, Robert. *The Social Forces in Later Life*. 3rd ed. Belmont, CA: Wadsworth Publishing Co., 1980.

Beaver, Marion L., and Miller, Don. *Clinical Social Work Practice with the Elderly*. Homewood, IL: The Dorsey Press, 1985.

Biegel, David E.; Shore, Barbara K.; and Gordon, Elizabeth. *Building Support Networks for the Elderly*. Beverly Hills, CA: Sage Publications, 1984.

Brody, Elaine M. *Long-Term Care of Older People*. New York: Human Sciences Press, 1977.

Gelfand, Donald E. *The Aging Network: Programs and Services*. 2nd ed. New York: Springer Publishing Co., 1984.

Getzel, George S., and Mellor, M. Joanna, eds. *Social Work Practice in Long-Term Care*. New York: The Haworth Press, 1983.

Getzel, George S., and Mellor, M. Joanna, eds. *Gerontological Social Work Practice in the Community*. New York: The Haworth Press, 1985.

Hutterman, Elizabeth. *Social Services for the Elderly*. New York: The Free Press, 1985.

Kart, Cary S. *The Realities of Aging*. 2nd ed. Boston: Allyn and Bacon, 1985.

Litwak, Eugene. *Helping the Elderly: The Complementary Roles of Informal Networks and Formal Systems*. New York: The Guilford Press, 1985.

Lowy, Louis. *Social Policies and Programs on Aging*. New York: Lexington Books, 1980.

Lowy, Louis. *Social Work with the Aging*. 2nd ed. New York: Longman, 1985.

Matlaw, Jane R. and Mayer, Jane B. "Elder Abuse: Ethical and Practical Dilemmas," *Health and Social Work* 11 (Spring 1986): 85–84.

Minahan, Anne, ed. *Encyclopedia of Social Work*. 18th ed. Silver Springs, MD: National Association of Social Workers, 1987. Articles on: "Aged," "Aged, Services," and "Protective Services for the Aged."

Rich, Bennett M., and Baum, Martha. *The Aging: A Guide to Public Policy*. Pittsburgh: University of Pittsburgh Press, 1984.

# Chapter 14

## Old-New Fields of Practice: Industrial and Rural

Social work practice has developed within a field of practice framework. A field of practice is a system of policies, programs, services, and social work strategies that are based on knowledge, values, and skills. They focus on a specific area of the social welfare system. Each of the chapters in this section of the text has discussed what the authors consider to be well developed fields of practice. The fields focus either on a particular population (children, families, or the aged) or an institutional setting (health and mental health services or corrections or income maintenance services). Each field of practice has developed its services and ways of practice in response to the needs of people served by the setting and to societal concerns and demands about the problems encountered in the population or setting. The development of each field also reflects political and philosophical influences on that field of practice. Recently the idea of context (the environment of the practice) seems to be the focus around which fields of practice are developing. Two such fields are considered by the authors to be developing within a context. These fields of practice are rural social work and industrial social work. Both fields represent earlier interests of some social workers that at one point seemed to have waned in their importance, but are now re-emerging. Educational programs are developing that provide specific preparation for work in each field. Articles and books about each field are being written. A specific body of knowledge is developing for each area. In this chapter, each field is discussed separately.

# Industrial Social Work: An Historical Perspective

## Defining Industrial Social Work

Before discussing the new-old field of practice of *industrial social work*, a definition needs to be developed that will provide an understanding of the context of this field of practice. Paul A. Kurzman provides the following definition:

> Programs and services, under the auspices of labor or management, that utilize professional social workers to serve members or employees, and the legitimate social welfare needs of the labor or industrial organization. It also includes the use, by a voluntary or proprietary social agency, of trained social workers to provide social welfare services or consultation to a trade union or employing organization under a specific contractual agreement. The employing organizations are not only labor unions and corporations, but often government agencies and not-for-profit organizations.[1]

Kurzman notes that industrial social welfare is related to a third welfare system. The first two are the social and fiscal systems. The third system is the occupational welfare system. This system was conceptualized by Richard M. Titmuss, a British scholar of social welfare. Titmuss sees the occupational system as the benefits and services in which one may participate because of their employment status.[2]

Where other fields of practice have focused on social functioning within the family, on particular social problems, such as poverty, and on the social welfare system, this new field of practice focuses on the world of work. Work generates many tensions and problems for individuals. There are tensions between labor and management, tensions because of a troubled economy, tensions because of the rapid growth in the reliance on sophisticated technology, to name a few. These tensions affect the individual's functioning in the work setting as well as in the larger world of society. When social workers focus on the work world they enter the industrial field of practice. To get a better understanding of that field of practice it is important to first look at the history of industrial social work.

## Social Work and the World of Work: From the Middle Ages to 1930s

Kurzman traces the relationship of the social welfare system and the world of work back to the Middle Ages, when the medieval craft guilds set aside funds for members' economic security in case of misfortunes such as accidents, old age, or death. The guild was the major social welfare institution along with the church until the development of poor

Table 14.1   Important Dates: Industrial Social Work

| | |
|---|---|
| Late 19th Century | New England cotton mill owners concerned with moral life of female workers. |
| 1910 | Jane Addams involved in Hart, Schaffner, and Marx strike. |
| 1920s | Graduates of New York School of Social Work takes jobs as welfare secretaries in industry. |
| 1930s | Social workers support labor efforts. |
| 1940s | Bertha Reynolds worked with National Maritime Union. |
| Late 1960s | Industry begins to employ social workers. |
| 1970 | Industrial Social Welfare Center established at the Columbia University School of Social Work. |
| 1978 | First National Conference on Social Work Practice in Labor and Industrial Settings. |
| 1982 | Publication of *Work, Workers and Work Organizations* by Shelia Akabas and Paul Kurzman. |

laws in the 1600s. In the late nineteenth and early twentieth centuries in the United States, some employers started to pay more attention to the well-being of their employees.[3] For example, in the cotton mills of New England, they exercised control over the moral life of their female employees. In many cases, these single women were required to live in approved housing, keep proscribed hours, and allowed only approved social activities. Large industrial employers like mill and mine companies, set up entire towns, including houses, roads, stores, schools, and hospitals, for employees. There was a large element of social control mixed with this philanthropy. There was some concern over sanitary conditions and worker safety. Some companies hired individuals known as welfare secretaries to administer these programs and services.[4] In the 1920s many graduates of the New York School of Social Work took jobs as welfare secretaries. The 1930 edition of a social work textbook, *American Charities and Social Work*, contains a chapter on "Social Work in Industry."[5] But this system was openly paternalistic and was held in suspicion by the workers who saw that it did not have their best interests at heart. In the 1920s the position of welfare secretary began to die out and by 1935 had disappeared.

Another strand of early industrial social work was in the labor movement. Jane Addams, a founder of the settlement house movement, was involved in the clothing workers' strike against the Hart, Schaffner, and Marx store in Chicago in 1910. Other social work leaders supported labor's efforts in the 1930s.[6] The work of Bertha Reynolds with the National Maritime Union during World War II is documented in her book, *Social Work and Social Living*.[7] The *Social Work Year Book* of 1929 lists "Industry" as one of its groups of classified topical articles. Articles in that group included such labor-related topics as labor legislation for women, night work in industry, hours of work in industry, minimum wage, child labor, organized labor, unemployment, and vocational guidance.[8] The interest of social workers in the labor movement, with a few exceptions such as Jane Addams and Bertha Reynolds, did not lie in working with the labor union's organization but rather as a concern for poor working conditions that affected the people with whom they were working.

During the 1920s and 1930s social work moved away from concern for the environmental factors affecting individuals to focus on psychological concerns, focusing not so much on cause as on function. It paid scant attention to the environment, the context of an individual's social functioning. With these changes, the interest in social work with either industry or labor seemed to die. It was not until the late 1960s before any real interest in industrial social work resurfaced.

## The Reemergence of Industrial Social Work

While the involvement of social workers in industry was, at best, very limited from 1945 to 1965, two important developments in industry are important to note. First, although the position of welfare secretaries went out of vogue, concern for personnel issues by industry did not. Personnel management became a department in many companies, with responsibility not only for hiring, promotion, and firing but also for programs that provided health, education, and recreational benefits to employees. This development was important for the evolution of the contemporary industrial social work field of practice, for it is within personnel departments that the industrial social worker is now often found.

The other important development is the labor unions' concern for employee benefits. Martha Ozawa has noted that, in addition to concern about wages, labor unions have sought increases in health, security, and welfare benefits, including pensions, life insurance, and health care, including medical, hospital, and mental health care, which have encompassed programs ranging from treatment for alcoholism to marriage counseling. These fringe benefits may be termed an employee assistance program, a wage supplement program, an employee benefits program, or an industrial social welfare program. Ozawa believes the entrance of women and minorities into the labor force has been one factor in the development of these programs. She believes these groups of employees have special needs that can be met by such programs. She also sees a growing alienation from management in workers which has given rise to an increase in mental health problems related to the *workplace*.[9]

It should also be noted that during this period of time, the social welfare system saw the creation of several programs related directly to the workplace. These include Workman's Compensation for medical expenses and loss of time on the job due to accidents on the job, unemployment compensation, retirement benefits related to the Social Security Act, and special compensation for particular occupational diseases, such as the black lung disease affecting coal miners. There was a growing realization that social problems in the world of work were caused not only by factors within the individual but by the effects of a wide range of conditions within the workplace.

In the late 1960s and early 1970s, several large companies began to employ social workers in their personnel departments to deal with the mental health problems of their employees.[10] Early programs tended to focus on problems related to alcoholism. In 1974, it was estimated that five million workers were having some alcohol-related difficulty and that each problem-drinker cost his or her employer $3,000 a year.[11] The number and scope of mental health programs has continued to grow. As the employer-based programs developed, so did programs developed by labor organizations. An early example of this was the Sidney Hillman Health Center of the Amalgamated Clothing Workers of America, a labor-funded mental health and rehabilitation program.[12]

By the mid-1970s not only were employers dealing with a new work force (women and minorities), and the alienation of workers, they also were being affected by new legislation, such as the Occupational Safety and Health Act, the Age Discrimination in Employment Act, and Title VII of the Civil Rights Act. These, and an increased emphasis on the quality of life, caused employers to realize the need for expert help in work-related social services. Some industries employed social workers to provide this needed, expert help; other employers contracted with social service agencies.

The profession responded to this new demand for social workers. In 1970, the Industrial Social Welfare Center was established at the Columbia University School of Social Work. By 1974, Boston College, Hunter College, and the University of Utah also had industrial social work programs. From 1969 on, articles about social work in industrial settings began to appear in both *Social Work* and *Social Casework*. The National Association of Social Workers and The Council on Social Work Education underwrote a joint project on industrial social work that resulted in the First National Conference on Social Work Practice in Labor and Industrial Settings in 1978.[13] This conference yielded the first publication within this field, *Labor and Industrial Settings: Sites for Social Work Practice*.[14]

Industrial social work was well on its way to becoming an established field of practice.

However, another step was necessary if schools of social work were to prepare students for this field. The knowledge base that underlies the field had to be defined and developed. In 1982 a project to develop such material resulted in the publication of a book that provides at least a first specification of the necessary knowledge base for industrial social work students and practioners. This book, *Work, Workers and Work Organizations* covers such issues as the meaning of work from a historical perspective, work and social policy, the place of work in human development, work-related research, the nature of the workplace, and the special practice of the industrial social worker.[15] The industrial field of practice had emerged.

## Practice in the Industrial Setting

The new industrial field of practice came into being to serve a previously unmet need; the working-class population has been underserved by the social welfare system. It has not been eligible for many public services. Workers have found the traditional private services unusable because of value conflicts, agencies' lack of responsiveness to their special needs, or the fees involved seemed too high. But services delivered in the industrial setting have partially overcome these blocks. There, service is seen as an earned entitlement with no stigma attached to its use. There is no cost or little cost to the worker for using the service. Social workers in this field of practice have developed an understanding of the context of the work world. One very important aspect is the meaning of work to the individual. In our society, appropriately or inappropriately, individuals derive much of their identity from the work they do. If that work is not satisfying or does not provide a sense of accomplishment, people may feel a sense of alienation that then affects both their work functioning and social functioning.

How and what an industrial social worker does varies from setting to setting. There are three primary modes of service delivery: within the structure of a company, usually within employee assistance services; within the structure of a labor union; and on a contractual basis with a social service agency. In this latter mode, the social worker may actually go to the industrial setting, have a contract to provide services in the agency setting, or receive third-party payments (insurance reimbursement) for the service. Some social workers in industry also work with management as it carries out its civic responsibilities. They may consult on corporate giving, for example.

Ozawa notes that when social welfare service is provided in the industrial setting (company or union), there are four stages in the evolution of services. First, service is provided to deal with one or two specific problems, like alcoholism. At the second stage, the company or union recognizes that the specific problem is only a symptom of other underlying problems, and plans a more comprehensive program. Some of the services included in this comprehensive program can include counseling for personal or marital or financial problems; offering crises intervention; educating workers about preretirement planning or health awareness; giving information and referrals; instituting self-help programs such as Alcoholics Anonymous; creating recreational programs; or consulting with management on problems affecting workers and their productivity. At the third stage, the worker/recipient actually participates in identifying problems and proposing solutions. At the fourth stage, a blurring of the boundary between management and employees takes place, and worker/recipients share responsibility for implementing and managing programs.[16]

Social workers find that the industry's motivation for providing services rests in one of three areas.

1. The desire to increase employees' financial rewards. Thus, just as higher wages are seen as a reward, so are social services.
2. The service is a way of controlling employees, keeping them productive by reducing discontent and increasing well-being.
3. The desire to increase therapeutic services is similar to the first concern but also includes the assumption that disease is the cause of the problems and should be treated.[17]

It is important for the social worker working in industry to be aware of the concerns of the employer and to find means for responding to that concern while adhering to the ethical principles of social work.

In each field of practice, the social worker needs to be familiar with a special body of information about the history, tradition, functions, laws, and environments that affect the target population. When working in the industrial setting, the social worker must first understand the way industry and labor relate and function together and the structure and functioning of the particular setting. Each setting must be understood as its own social system. The social worker must know something of the history of industry in the United States, and the history of management-labor relations. Observing the channels of power, decision-making, and communications in the setting is also important. The social worker must learn how to work with new professional groups, such as laser-engineers or computer programmers, and understand the culture of the blue-collar wage earner, the pink-collar office support staffer, and the white-collar professional. The worker also has to become familiar with the local resource possibilities for client-referral on a wide range of problems.[18]

## *An Example*

This example will depict some of the activities that a social worker in an industrial setting may engage in.

### Daily Schedule

| | |
|---|---|
| 8:00 A.M. | Arrive at work and review the calendar for the day. Note two new referrals. Contact to make appointments. |
| 8:30 A.M. | Meet with vice-president to discuss company's participation in the upcoming United Way campaign. Discuss recent meeting for corporate givers. Answer vice-president's questions about the services of several agencies. Suggest content for a letter to be sent from management to employees urging their contributions to United Way campaign. |
| 9:00 A.M. | Session with a worker and his wife who are having marital problems. |
| 10:00 A.M. | First session with a worker who is in financial difficulty because of overuse of credit. Discuss possible solutions. Make an appointment to meet again in two days. |
| 11:00 A.M. | Set aside for recording. A foreman drops in to discuss a worker he believes may be having an alcohol problem. Worker is missing work more often than usual and seems irritable. Suggest means for making a referral. Stress confidential nature of the service. |
| 12:00 Noon | Lunch |
| 1:00 P.M. | New client. Problem is lack of resources for a retarded child. Social worker explores feelings. Discuss possible resources. Make an appointment for client and wife for later in the week. |
| 2:00 P.M. | Make phone calls to check out resources for the retarded child and the family. Return four phone calls that have come in. Finish recording interrupted this morning. |
| 3:00 P.M. | Conduct a session for employees who are approaching retirement. |
| 4:30 P.M. | Spend time with participants who have concerns about some aspect of retirement. |
| 5:30 P.M. | Review schedule for tomorrow. |

Industrial social work is new and growing very rapidly. It is an exciting challenge for the worker and the profession to provide this new type of service in the workplace.

# Issues in Industrial Social Work

Industrial social work is not only a practice in a setting not primarily a social work setting, it is practice in a nontraditional setting focused on production not service. In such a setting, inevitably there will be tensions and uncertainties between business goals and social work goals. Practitioners in industrial settings should be aware of these issues and work toward their resolution.

A primary issue is social work services' goal in the industrial setting. Is its goal to increase profits and production, industry's primary function? Or if the setting is a labor union, is social work's goal to encourage loyalty to the union? Or is its goal to promote the common good of the workers? This latter goal implies a commitment to improve the quality of life for the work force. If the goal of industrial social work is not the last one mentioned, ethical conflicts for social workers will arise. It is very important that social workers recognize this conflict and seek some resolution for themselves.

Related to the issue of conflicting purposes is the issue of placement of the industrial social work service. If it is located with either a company or union's offices, the social worker may feel pressure to serve the interests of the union or the industry, rather than the interests of the workers. A skilled social worker helps the sponsoring organization see that the best interest of the workers and those of the sponsoring body are indeed related, that they must recognize the unity of those interests. The best way to address the placement issues may be to locate the service in a neutral setting, such as a social service agency, or to use a third-party payment mechanism.[19]

Another important issue is confidentiality. Social agency records kept on individual workers must not become a part of the personnel file of that worker. Social workers need to skillfully explain the need for this protection. They also must be skillful in explaining the value of the service to individuals and to the sponsoring body without providing specific client-related information. Since this sometimes makes referrals difficult, referral sources sometimes need special help understanding this stance.[20]

A final issue that must be addressed is the role of the industrial social worker with individuals suffering from unemployment, outdated work skills, and poor preparation for entering the work force. These individuals have work-related problems. Is the workplace responsible for providing services to these individuals?

As this new field of practice, industrial social work, develops, it has great potential to become a needed resource in the social welfare system. Workers can be served in the workplace where their special needs can be considered. The workplace can become a more humane place, and thus, some problems can be prevented. The provision of universal services, so necessary in a complex society, can be nearer reality in the near future.

## Rural Social Work: An Historical Perspective

The second emerging field of practice is rural social work. Like industrial social work, this context received the attention of social workers in the past but seemed to die out before it became an established field of practice, only to reemerge in recent years.

It is hard to define *rural social work:* it is hard to define the word *rural.* The United States Census Bureau considers areas rural if they have under 2,500 people in any incorporated area. This would include very small towns and open country. Others define rural in terms of cultural characteristics.[21] Louise Johnson, one of this text's authors, has suggested that *nonmetropolitan* might be a better classification. That is, rural social work is practiced in any community with fewer than 50,000 people (the minimum U.S. Census designation for metropolitan communities). There are two reasons for this suggestion. One, services to small communities are not delivered from towns with a population of 2,500 or less, but rather from larger communities whose services reach out to the very small communities. Second, there is a distinct difference in both the service delivery system and some of the practice strategies, once a community falls into the nonmetropolitan category.[22] Finally, this classification takes into account the cultural definitions of rurality. The nonmetropolitan community does function within a rural culture. In this chapter then, rural social work will refer to social work practice in nonmetropolitan communities.

If the context of practice is the identifying characteristic, it is important to identify how rural social work practice differs from practice in metropolitan areas. First, the service delivery system is smaller and depends very heavily on the public social service agency. Second, that system functions more informally in its relationships with its component parts, agencies and service deliverers. Third, the people living in these areas are most comfortable with an informal rather than a formal style of functioning. This functioning might be characterized, to use Tonnies's formulation, in a *gemeinschaft* rather than *gesellschaft* relationship.[23] Fourth, the rural helping system places much more reliance on self-help, natural helpers, and grassroots groups, with fewer of the traditional services found in metropolitan communities. Fifth, the rural culture is more interested in individuals than in the degrees or positions they hold. And rural roles overlap, that is people carry several important roles at the same time. For example, local politicians are also full-time business people. Sixth, there is more attention paid to ecological concerns; weather is a very important concern.[24] The definition of rural social work, then, is a contextual definition that takes into account not only a census classification but the characteristics of that population.

## Before 1969

Since the modern social welfare system developed in response to the industrialization of society, it is no wonder that the system has not considered the particular needs of the rural society. The earlier heavy reliance on the self-help approach continued to be the major means for providing for human needs in rural areas. As institutions, poor houses, mental hospitals, orphanages, and so on developed, they were used to meet the needs of some rural people, particularly the "outsider." The COS and settlement movements had little effect on rural areas. Public welfare has never been an acceptable approach in rural areas. The Social Security Act's social insurance arrangements did not originally cover farmers and other self-employed people, thus offering little protection to rural populations. Overall, the system of social welfare that developed in the United States had limited impact on rural peoples.

However, the specific social functioning needs of rural people were not completely ignored. In 1908, Theodore Roosevelt appointed the Country Life Commission whose functions included developing awareness of the needs of rural communities. Emilia E. Martinez-Brawley, the historian of rural social work, considers this the "genesis of rural social work."[25] As a result of the Country Life Commission, the National Conference on Charities and Corrections and several schools of social work gave some attention to the need for services to rural people. *Survey*, the most important social work journal of the time, also published articles on rural problems and needs. During World War I, the Home Service of the Red Cross developed a regional approach to social service delivery and recognized the special characteristics of rural people and their social service needs. During the 1920s, some attention continued to be paid to the rural culture. 4-H Clubs were established in the U.S. Department of Agriculture Extention programs. These became the group work mechanism for rural youth, much as Scouting was the mechanism for urban youth. In fact, Extension Services provided many programs for farm families that can be seen as a part of the social welfare system. It is interesting to note that these services were universal and nonstigmatizing.

Many economic problems plagued the rural United States in the first two decades of the twentieth century, but the farmer and the surround-

## Table 14.2  Important Dates: Rural Social Work

| | |
|---|---|
| 1908 | Country Life Commission appointed by President Theodore Roosevelt. |
| 1920s | 4-H Clubs established. |
| 1927 | Grace Abbott, Chief of Children's Bureau discusses rural child welfare standards. |
| 1933 | Publication of *The Rural Community and Social Casework* by Josephine Brown. |
| 1969 | Leon Ginsberg presents paper, "Education for Social Work in Rural Settings" at Annual Program Meeting of Council on Social Work Education. |
| 1972 | Rural Task Force of the Southern Regional Education Board Manpower and Education and Training Project created. |
| 1973 | Council on Social Work Education workshops, "Education for Social Work in Rural and Small Communities," presented. |
| 1974 | Publication of *Social Work in Rural Communities: A Book of Readings*, edited by Leon Ginsberg. |
| 1976 | First Annual National Institute on Social Work in Rural Areas, Knoxville, Tennessee. |
| 1976 | Journal, *Human Service in the Rural Environment*, began publication. |

ing community still seemed to have the capacity to provide for their basic needs. Farming still had a subsistence aspect, which helped people provide for at least their own economic needs. With the onset of the Depression, the problems of rural American were especially great. Not only were farm prices down, but drought prevented the raising of subsistence crops. The emergency measures of the early 1930s benefited urban and rural people alike.[26] The Roosevelt administration's Agriculture Adjustment Act (AAA) addressed farm problems. It was aimed mostly at commercial farmers and provided means for controlling the market and providing farm subsidies. Farm subsidies can be considered a form of social welfare; they are a type of universal provision and thus are seldom seen as welfare, but they have helped meet the fiscal needs of the agricultural segment of U.S. society.

In 1927, Grace Abbott, then chief of the Children's Bureau, spoke to the National Conference on Social Work about standards for rural child welfare. The child welfare provisions of the Social Security Act of 1935 included services to these children. Because of these provisions, social workers began to provide social services in rural areas, and they quickly identified the differences between rural and metropolitan social work. Training for these workers was largely done under the Federal Emergency Relief Administration, often in the land-grant colleges. Two influential books that showed the differences in rural and urban practices appeared by the late 1930s, Josephine Brown's 1933 text, *The Rural Community and Social Casework* and Grace Browning's *Rural Public Welfare. Social Work Year Books* and professional journals contained articles on rural social work.[27] Schools of social work started paying attention to this budding field of practice.

But the growth did not continue. By the 1940s, the farm problem seemed to have ended. Social work was then moving toward a psychoanalytical base for practice, and it showed less and less concern for how the environment affected the individual. Probably the biggest detriment to the development of rural social work was the movement in social work education to demand graduate education for professional practice. The demise of the National Association of Schools of Social Administration (discussed in Chapter 2) meant that the undergraduate programs preparing the bulk of the workers for rural areas were no longer recognized. It should be remembered that practice in rural area, largely in public agencies that had limited numbers of masters-level practitioners, was the pattern in rural areas. Also rural people are suspicious of outsiders with "credentials," who often fail to understand their rural lifestyle and try to impose methods of work developed for metropolitan settings. Public social services in rural areas continued to develop and grow as federal funds became more available. Universities in rural states continued to prepare students for work in public welfare agencies, but these programs, usually found in sociology departments, lacked the sanction of the social work profession. Rural social work disappeared from the professional literature.

## Since 1969

During the late 1960s, several changes supported the re-emergence of rural social work. The National Association of Social Workers voted to recognize baccalaureate graduates of approved programs as professional social workers, and The Council on Social Work Education developed accreditation standards for such programs. The social welfare programs that had operated since the early 1950s were again acknowledged. This in turn allowed for the professionalization of services in many rural areas.

The unrest of the early 1960s had led social work to develop many new kinds of practice and to move into many new practice settings. The traditional psychoanalytic framework came into question. Social workers began to consider not only individuals but the environment aspects of human behavior. This was in part due to the "discovery" of social systems theory. Interest developed in what at that time was known as integrated practice, a practice that combined case work, group work, and community organization. In retrospect, these new practice approaches were much more acceptable to rural peoples.

The Appalachian Redevelopment Act of 1965 provided considerable funds for the provision of services to Appalachia. Health and social services were important recipients of the available funds. Most important, different approaches to practice, different service delivery patterns, were created for this rural area.

The contemporary rural social work movement dates its reawakening from 1969 and a paper, "Education for Social Work in Rural Settings," presented by Leon Ginsberg, then Director of the West Virginia University's division of Social Work. In the years that followed, a small group of practioners in various sections of the rural United States began to organize special knowledge bases for work in these settings and to present papers at national meetings.

In June 1970, a workshop sponsored by the Minnesota Resource Center for Undergraduate Social Work Education, "Effecting Rural Service Delivery through Education," was held. In 1972, a Rural Task Force of the Southern Regional Education Board Manpower and Education and Training Project created a statement of educational assumptions for educators preparing social workers for positions in rural areas. In 1973, the Council on Social Work Education sponsored a series of workshops around the country called, "Education for Social Work in the Rural and Small Community." Joanne Mermelstein and Paul Sundet of the University of Missouri were the resource people for these workshops. Papers continued to be presented at national conferences on rural social work. A few of these found their way into the literature. In 1974, the Council on Social Work Education published *Social Work in Rural Communities: A Book of Readings*, edited by Leon Ginsberg.[28]

The First Annual National Institute on Social Work in Rural Areas was held in Knoxville, Tennessee, in July of 1976. Since then, annual meetings have been sponsored each summer by social work schools and programs with an interest in rural social work. The proceedings of these meetings provide an important contribution to the literature about rural social work. A journal, *Human Services in the Rural Environment*, began publication. At the Knoxville Institute, the Rural Social Work Caucus was founded. This loosely-knit group of social workers with a concern for rural social work meets at most national social work conferences and has strongly advocated with both NASW and CSWE for recognition of rural social work as a field of practice. The caucus has been particularly successful in having rural content on the programs at most national social work conferences. Several books have been published on rural social work practice.[29] All in all, rural social work has emerged as a field of practice.

# Practice in Rural Settings

Two important considerations when working in nonmetropolitan settings must be kept in mind. First is the fact that the rural human services' delivery system is different from that of metropolitan communities. Second, there are greater differences among rural population groups than there are among groups in metropolitan areas. Each of these factors heavily influence the nature of practice in rural areas. Another generally agreed upon assumption about practice in rural settings is that practice should be in the *generalist* model.

Not only is the rural service delivery system smaller, its structure varies. Some communities have a variety of agencies, with emphasis on the public agencies located in the community. Other communities, especially the very small, have no formal agencies located in the community. All communities must rely on some metropolitan-based services for very special needs, for example, a child with a rare disease. The formal agencies located in nonmetropolitan communities often provide outreach services to the smaller communities in their region. There is also a tendency for more informal coordination among agencies than in larger communities. The other important difference in the service delivery system is the strength of the natural helping system. This system is akin to the mutual help network, but at times also takes on a more contemporary organization. This may be in the form of coalitions (e.g. against domestic violence, on aging); or organizations that provide resources (e.g. used clothing stores, food pantries). Community institutions, such as churches, and organizations, such as service clubs, are often heavily involved in the response to need. The social worker must be able to work with a wide variety of people and understand the differences between formal and informal functioning. Much time is spent linking people with needed resources of which they are unaware, and in helping community groups accomplish their goals. Rural social workers also help formal agencies with traditional, large city modes of functioning to respond to the needs of rural people in ways that are acceptable to and useable by them.[30]

When considering the differences among the various rural population groups, it is important to remember that some of the most discriminated-against minority groups are from rural areas (rural Southern blacks, native Americans, Chicanos). These groups often fall outside the mainstream, formal, community helping system. They do, however, have their own natural helping systems. The social worker often must play mediating and advocacy roles on behalf of these groups. There are many other nationality-based ethnic groups in rural areas. These groups have their own cultures and to work with them effectively, the social worker must understand the way the particular culture functions. Not all rural people are farmers, some are engaged in mining, logging, or the recreation industry, to name a few. Each has its own life-style, its own particular problems. There are boom towns; there are dying communities. The social worker in rural areas must adapt practice to people's needs within their cultural constraints and environmental conditions, and to use the resources available within that culture.

Observing rural practitioners leads to the conclusion that they must be skilled in the use of crisis intervention, mediation, support, problem-solving, resource brokering, work with multi-problem families, coordination, program development, and work for change in organizations. They also need at least some ability to work with various problems and age groups though there is some tendency to specialize in these areas due to the way service agencies split the work to be done. They need to be true generalists.[31]

### A Case Study

A social worker stationed in a community that provides services to five surrounding counties has discovered that in Small Town there are a number of older women who are living alone. As these women reach the age of about seventy-five, they find it a struggle simply to maintain themselves in their own homes. Some are no longer cooking adequate meals for themselves. They are all worried about falling and not being discovered for several days. It is also difficult for them to shop or get to the doctors, let alone go to church or community functions since they do not drive and are no longer able to walk downtown.

The social worker had previously identified the influential people in this community as the pastor of the major church, a county commissioner, and two women who belong to several organizations and have been helpful in the past in identifying natural helping resources in the community. The social worker talks to each of these individuals about her concern for the elderly. Each names several other people they are aware of who are isolated. They admit that they knew a problem existed but were really not aware of its extent and were not sure what to do. The social worker asks these four people to meet with her, so together they can decide what might be done. After some discussion, this group calls a community meeting to discuss the problem. In preparation for this meeting, they ask that the weekly paper run an article on the problem and publicize the meeting. Fifty people attend the meeting. A committee is formed to make suggestions on how the problem can be handled by using community resources.

*continued*

As the result of a long process, four different solutions were implemented: the community organized a nutrition site; the nursing home provided home-delivered meals; a telephone reassurance system was instituted; and a volunteer network offered essential transportation for these isolated older people. After two years, the worker noted that much more informal helping was going on with these elderly women. They are visited regularly by church visitors and friends, they are provided with transportation for church and other community events. The worker found it much easier to service these individuals since she had a well-developed resource system to rely on. Also, she found she had much more visibility and acceptance in the community, so that many situations were brought to her attention before they reached the crisis stage.

## Issues in Rural Social Work

One of the major problems faced by the rural social worker is recognition by those who work in metropolitan areas and those trained to work in metropolitan areas that the rural context indeed calls for a different kind of social work practice. The lack of recognition is particularly troublesome when the rural worker must depend on metropolitan services for specialized needs. It also causes difficulty when the worker is a part of the state social welfare agency. These agencies often are dominated by administrators with a bureaucratic orientation incongruent with the rural way of functioning.

A related concern is the education of rural social workers. Most graduate schools of social work are located in large cities. A few, such as the University of Missouri, do offer specialized curriculum in rural social work. Many of the baccalaureate programs are located in rural areas and prepare social workers for rural practice; the University of South Dakota program is one. Some believe that the baccalaureate worker has always been the major provider of service to the rural areas, and that the acceptance of the baccalaureate degree as professional has upgraded services in rural areas. Questions continue to be asked about the ideal educational program for rural social work practice. Much still remains to be done to develop the information base and practices needed for such work.

Another concern is how to adapt a profession developed in response to problems of industrialization and urbanization to meet the needs of the rural population. Attention should be paid to defining and differentiating between social work practice for all individuals, families, groups, and communities, and social work practice for only rural or only metropolitan service.

A final concern is how to develop means for coordinating the informal and formal systems of helping, both essential if individuals in rural communities are to have their needs met, yet because of the different ways the formal and informal systems function, the essential coordination of services is difficult. Social workers need to see that rural communities do not always have fewer resources for helping, but instead have *different* resources.

Each of these issues must be addressed if the rural field of practice is to continue to grow and develop. As social workers gain more experience and carry out the essential knowledge-building and research, certainly these issues will be addressed and resolved. The new rural field of practice will meet the needs of individuals often overlooked or inappropriately serviced by the U.S. social welfare system.

## Development of Fields of Practice

Before leaving the discussion of these two field of practice, thought needs to be given to the development of new fields of practice. Bartlett identifies three frames of reference that affect any field of practice. First are the essential elements of any social work practice. Second are the characteristics of the particular field. Third is social work practice as it develops for the particular field. Her analysis of the characteristics of the particular field are also useful in this discussion. These field characteristics include the problem or condition of central concern, the system of organized services, the body of knowledge, values, and methods, the sociocultural attitudes in society, and the characteristic responses and behavior of people served.[32]

For a field of practice, a practice with special characteristics for a particular population, to develop there must be a concern for that population. Both society in general and the professionals in particular must have responded to unmet needs or problems that exist within that population. In addition, both society and the social work profession must understand the system within which the needs and problems exist and the characteristics of the groups affected.

The question can then be asked, were these conditions not present at an earlier time, and why did a field of practice not develop in either rural or industrial social work? The answer is that though there was some concern, it was not sufficient for the development for a field of practice. This was probably due to social work's concern with individuals, rather than environment, to social workers' individual and professional values about work in either industry or the rural setting, and to the incongruence of traditional social work practice with the values and way of life of either the worker in industry or the rural person. The development of these two fields of practice reflects changes in the social work profession, and society in general. In the future, other fields of practice will develop as change takes place in society, in the profession, and in the populations to be served.

## Summary

A comparison of the two new fields of practice, industrial and rural, discussed in this chapter yields some commonalities even though the settings are different. As has been stated earlier, they are both contextual fields of practice, that is, they both take a person's environment into consideration. As such, they both call for the social worker to go where the needs are, to reach out to people in their natural settings. In addition, each has a very strong linking function; that is, they connect people with the resources available to them and facilitate their use of the resources. This also involves helping traditional resources (social service agencies) understand the particular needs and ways of functioning of workers and rural populations. Both fields of practice call for adapting traditional ways of meeting human need. Both also place social workers in a position where tensions exist; tension between labor and management, and tension between the informal way of rural functioning and the formal functioning of governmental agencies. Both call for workers who are flexible, who can listen to all parties involved in a situation, and who are creative in designing interventive strategies.

These two fields of practice reflect a perspective that calls for social services to be available within people's everyday environment. They are practices that are ecological in nature, practices that involve a wide range of individuals, influential and otherwise, in the development of the service delivery system. They are also practices that place emphasis on short-term service, and the development of strong personal support systems. And they are practices that are moving toward universal provision that works with and supports the self-help mechanisms of communities.

## Key Terms

generalist social work
industrial social work
nonmetropolitan

rural
rural social work
workplace

## Questions for Discussion

1. How does context affect social work practice?

2. Why do you think industrial social work took so long to emerge as a field of practice?

3. What are the advantages and disadvantages of each of the three modes for the delivery of social work services in the industrial setting?

4. Why do you think social workers were not more active in the labor movement?

5. Why do you think labor became interested in mental health services as a benefit?

6. How are the interests of worker and the interests of business or labor unions related?

7. Should business accept responsibility for services to the unemployed?

8. Why has the recognition of the rural field of practice taken so long?

9. Can a person really understand and work in rural communities who has not lived for a period of time in such communities?

10. What kinds of services are most appropriately delivered by informal helping systems and which by formal systems?

11. Is social work in rural areas truly generalist?

12. What are some of the special stresses that currently affect rural communities?

13. Why do you think there are more differences between rural populations than between metropolitan populations?

14. What do you think might be future fields of practice to be developed?

## Notes

1 Paul A. Kurzman, "Industrial (Occupational Social Work)," in *1983–84 Supplement to the Encyclopedia of Social Work, 17th Ed.* (Silver Springs, MD: National Association of Social Workers, 1983), pp. 57–68.

2 Kurzman, "Industrial," p. 57.

3 Kurzman, "Industrial," p. 59.

4 Phillip R. Popple, "Social Work Practice in Business and Industry, 1875–1930." *Social Service Review* 55 (June 1981): 257–269.

5 Amos Griswold Warner, Stuart Alfred Queen, and Ernest Bouldin Harper, *American Charities and Social Work*, 4th ed. (New York: Thomas Y. Crowell, Co., 1930).

6 Lou Ann B. Jorgensen, "Social Services in Business and Industry" in *Handbook of the Social Services* eds. Neil Gilbert and Harry Specht (Englewood Cliffs, NJ: Prentice-Hall, 1981), pp. 337–352.

7 Bertha Capen Reynolds, *Social Work and Social Living*, (New York: Citadel Press, 1951).

8 Fred S. Hall ed. *Social Work Year Book, 1929* (New York: Russell Sage Foundation, 1930).

9 Martha N. Ozawa, "Development of Social Services in Industry: Why and How?" *Social Work* 25 (November 1980): 464–470.

10 For a description of this see: David C. Blomquist, Daniel D. Gray, and Larry L. Smith, "Social Work in Business and Industry," *Social Casework* 60 (October 1979): 457–462. For description of specific programs see: Rosalie Bakalinsky, "People versus Profits." *Social Work* 25 (November 1980): 471–475; Elisabeth Mill, "Family Counseling in an Industrial Job-Supported Program," *Social Casework* 53 (December 1972): 587–592; and Andrew Weissman, "A Social Service Strategy in Industry," *Social Work* 20 (September 1975): 401–403.

11 Michael J. Austin and Erwin Jackson. "Occupational Mental Health and the Human Services: A Review," *Health and Social Work* 2 (February 1977): 93–118.

12 Kurzman, "Industrial," p. 61.

13 Kurzman, "Industrial," p. 62.

14 Sheila H. Akabas, Paul A. Kurzman, and Nancy S. Kolben, *Labor and Industrial Settings: Sites for Social Work Practice* (New York: Council on Social Work Education, 1979).

15 Sheila H. Akabas and Paul A. Kurzman, *Work, Workers, and Work Organizations: A View from Social Work* (Englewood Cliffs, NJ: Prentice-Hall, 1982).

16 Ozawa, "Development of Social Services."

17 Joseph R. Steiner and Ester C.C. Borst, "Industrial Settings: Undeveloped Opportunities for Social Work Services." *Arete* 6 (Fall 1980): 1–11.

18 Paul A. Kurzman and Sheila H. Akabas, "Industrial Social Work as an Arena for Practice," *Social Work* 26 (January 1981): 52–60.

19 Jorgenson, "Social Services in Business."

20 Paul A. Kurzman. "Ethical Issues in Industrial Social Work Practice," *Social Casework* 64 (February 1983): 105–111.

21 Robert C. Bealer, Fern K. Willits, and William P. Kuvlesky, "The Meaning of 'Ruality' in American Society: Some Implications of Alternative Definitions," *Rural Sociology* 30 (September 1965): 255–266.

22 For further development of this idea see: Louise C. Johnson, "Social Development in Nonmetropolitan Areas," in *Social Work in Rural Areas: Preparation and Practice* eds. Ronald K. Green and Stephen A. Webster (Knoxville, TN: University of Tennessee, School of Social Work, 1977).

23 Tonnes, in discussing relationships among people in an industrial society, saw as *gemeinschaft* as rural "we-ness" and *gesellschaft* as individuals related through structures in the community. Ferdinand Tonnes, *Fundamental Concepts of Sociology (Gemeinschaft und Gesellschaft* trans. Charles P. Loomis (New York: American Books, 1940).

24 This material has been developed by Louise C. Johnson through a fifteen-year project of observation and of participation in social work practice in nonmetropolitan areas.

25 This and subsequent material in this section draws heavily from Martinez-Brawley's work. See Emilia E. Martinez-Brawley, ed., *Pioneer Efforts in Rural Social Welfare: Firsthand View Since 1908* (University Park, PA: The Pennsylvania

State University Press, 1980 and Martinez-Brawley, *Seven Decades of Rural Social Work: From Country Life Commission to Rural Caucus* (New York: Praeger Publishers, 1981).

26 See Chapter 7 for a discussion of these measures.

27 Josephine C. Brown, *The Rural Community and Social Case Work*, (New York: Family Welfare Association of America, 1933); and Grace Browning, *Rural Public Welfare: Selected Records* (Chicago: The University of Chicago Press, 1941).

28 Louise C. Johnson, author of this text, participated in this development of rural social work. The information comes from unpublished material in her files.

29 H. Wayne Johnson, *Rural Human Services: A Book of Readings* (Itasca, IL: F.E. Peacock Publishers, 1980); O. William Farley, et al., *Rural Social Work Practice* (New York: The Free Press, 1982); and Julia M. Watkins and Dennis A. Watkins, *Social Policy and the Rural Setting* (New York: Springer Publishing Co., 1984).

30 For further discussion of the rural service delivery system see: Louis C. Johnson, "Human Service Delivery Patterns in Nonmetropolitan Communities." in Johnson, *Rural Human Services*, pp. 65–74.

31 The practice modalities used in nonmetropolitan communities are identified in Louise C. Johnson, "Nonmetropolitan Services Delivery Revisited: Insights from a Dozen Years of Participant Observation" *Human Services in the Rural Environment*. 9 (No. 2, 1984): 21–26.

32 Harriett M. Bartlett, *Analyzing Social Work Practice by Fields* (New York: National Association of Social Workers, 1961).

# Suggested Readings

### Industry

Akabas, Shelia; Kurzman, Paul A.; and Kolben, Nancy S., eds. *Labor and Industrial Settings: Sites for Social Work Practice.* New York: Council on Social Work Education, 1979.

Akabas, Shelia, and Kurzman, Paul A. *Work, Workers, and Work Organizations: A View From Social Work.* Englewood Cliffs, NJ: Prentice-Hall, 1982.

Austin, Michael J., and Jackson, Erwin. "Occupational Mental Health and the Human Services: A Review," *Health and Social Work* 2 (February 1977): 93–118.

Bakalinsky, Rosalie. "People versus Profits: Social Work in Industry," *Social Work* 25 (November 1980): 471–475.

Googins, Bradley, and Godfrey, Joline. "The Evolution of Occupational Social Work," *Social Work* 30 (September–October 1985): 396–402.

Jorgensen, Lou Ann B. "Social Services in Business and Industry," in *Handbook of the Social Services*, eds. Gilbert, Neil and Specht, Harry. Englewood Cliffs, NJ: Prentice-Hall, 1981), pp. 337–352.

Kurzman, Paul A. "Ethical Issues in Industrial Social Work Practice," *Social Casework* 64 (February 1983): 105–111.

Kurzman, Paul A. "Industrial Social Work (Occupational Social Work)" in Anne Minahan, ed. in chief, *Encyclopedia of Social Work*, 18th Ed., Vol. I, Silver Springs, MD: National Association of Social Workers, 1987, pp. 899–910.

Kurzman, Paul A., and Akabas, Shelia H. "Industrial Social Work as an Arena for Practice," *Social Work* 26 (January 1981): 52–60.

Ozawa, Martha N. "Development of Social Services in Industry: Why and How?" *Social Work* 25 (November 1980): 434–470.

Popple, Philip R. "Social Work Practice in Business and Industry, 1875–1930," *Social Service Review* 55 (June 1981): 257–269.

## Rural

Bealer, Robert C.; Willits, Fern K; and Kuvlesky, William P. "The Meaning of 'Rurality' in American Society: Some Implications of Alternative Definitions," *Rural Sociology* 30 (September 1965): 255–266.

Farley, O. William; Griffiths, Kenneth A.; Skidmore, Rex A.; and Thackeray, Milton G. *Rural Social Work Practice.* New York: The Free Press, 1982.

Ginsberg, Leon H. *Social Work in Rural Communities: A Book of Readings.* New York: Council on Social Work Education, 1976.

Green, Ronald K., and Webster, Stephen A., eds. *Social Work in Rural Areas.* Knoxville, TN: The University of Tennessee, School of Social Work, 1977.

Johnson, H. Wayne. *Rural Human Services: A Book of Readings.* Itasca, IL: F.E. Peacock Publishers, 1980.

Johnson, Louise C. "Nonmetropolitan Service Delivery Revisited: Insights from a Dozen Years of Participant Observations," *Human Services in the Rural Environment* 9 (No. 2, 1984): 21–26.

Martinez-Brawley, Emilia E., "Rural Social Work," in Anne Minahan, ed. in chief, *Encyclopedia of Social Work*, 18th Ed., Vol. II, Silver Springs, MD: National Association of Social Workers, 1987, pp. 521–537.

Watkins, Julia M., and Watkins, Dennis A. *Social Policy and the Rural Setting.* New York: Springer Publishing Co., 1984.

# Part Four

## The Contemporary Response to Human Need

Part Four serves as a summary for the book. Chapter 15 discusses contemporary social work practice, and Chapter 16 provides an overview of the social welfare system. Both of these chapters consider some of the ongoing change that may take place within our social welfare system. Both also provide the student with a preview of knowledge, values, and skills that will be developed in subsequent courses within a social work curriculum. An analytic framework within which to fit the various components of the social welfare system developed in the book is presented in Chapter 16, which will provide the student with a means of identifying the connection among the various components, and integrating the various parts into a meaningful whole.

# Chapter 15

## Social Work as a Profession

Social work is a profession dedicated to helping people meet their personal and social needs and to facilitating change in the environment to improve people's social functioning. Chapter 2 described the development of social work as a profession. In Part Three, various roles and functions that social workers perform within the social welfare system were addressed. This chapter expands the understanding of social work as a helping profession within contemporary society. Social work's purposes and mission are discussed, and its uniqueness as a helping profession is considered. Finally, this chapter makes some predictions about the future of social work.

## What Is Social Work?

Despite the fact that the profession has "done its work" for nearly a century, people still have trouble understanding exactly what social work is and what it is supposed to do.[1] Part of the difficulty lies in the fact that there is no single definition of social work. Social work can be defined in many different ways, reflecting the diversity that exists in the profession. In some ways, this can be viewed as a strength, but it also contributes to the confusion about the nature of the profession. The general public often confuses social work and social welfare. This confusion is easily understood, particularly given the close ties between social welfare, social work, and the system of social services identified in this book.

The National Association of Social Workers defines *social work* as "the professional activity of helping individuals, groups, or communities enhance or restore their capacity for social functioning and creating social conditions favorable to that goal."[2] Social workers help people singley, or collectively to solve life problems, so their lives can be more satisfying and rewarding. In attempting to enhance or restore people's social functioning, social workers also become "concerned with the interactions between people and their social environment, which affects the ability of people to accomplish their life tasks, alleviate distress, and realize their aspirations and values."[3] Social workers intervene to facilitate change, to enhance, restore, or promote a better relationship between people and their environments. This might include, but is not limited to

1. counseling at the individual, group, or family level;
2. linking people with resources, services, and opportunities to improve their functioning;
3. bringing about change in environmental systems, institutions, and organizations so they become more responsive to people's needs;
4. bringing about changes in existing policies or creating new social policies that provide for people's needs and well-being.[4]

These definitions help develop understanding about what social workers do; however, there is still a need to further discuss the nature of the profession.

Social work often has been described as a science. Its scientific nature can best be illustrated by pointing out that when social workers help people, they employ the problem-solving process, which is an application of scientific principles and methods. Social workers use a knowledge base in carrying out their tasks, which includes theories and knowledge extracted from several disciplines, among them sociology, anthropology, political science, and psychology.

Social work has also been described as an art. People's needs, concerns, and problems are complex. Environmental conditions that affect people are also complex. Thus, solutions to problems in people's social functioning can be difficult to find. The social worker's possession of knowledge alone is not sufficient for effective problem-solving. Being creative in blending knowledge with action is required. Just as a sculptor or artist uses creativity to produce a work of art, a social worker creatively blends knowledge, experience, values, and skills to help individuals, groups, or communities find solutions to life's problems. This is the *art of social work*.

In 1958, the National Association of Social Workers developed a working definition of social work practice, which continues to guide contemporary social work practice in all fields of practice. The working definition of social work practice has as a basic premise the proposition that professional practice is guided by a body of knowledge that assists the social worker to understand the nature of people's problems with their immediate environment and the causal relationship between the two. Another premise is that the profession possesses a set of values regarding human beings and the human condition that serves as a foundation for practice. The working definition also states that the knowledge base and values of the profession are put into action through a set of skills. Skills are the tools the social worker uses to effect change resulting in beneficial consequences for the people served. It is this constellation of knowledge, values, and skills that organizes the responses made to the concerns, needs, and problems of the people with whom the social worker is confronted.[5]

## Social Work's Knowledge Base

One of the basic criteria for any profession is a body of knowledge. The *knowledge base* of social work generally consists of

1) knowledge borrowed from the natural, social, and behavioral sciences,
2) knowledge developed from its own experiences in assisting and helping people, (referred to as "practice wisdom"), and
3) knowledge developed through research efforts.

This knowledge base is of little relevance unless it can be integrated into the helping endeavor. Siporin has suggested that the knowledge base can be divided into two practical component parts, assessment knowledge and intervention knowledge.[6] Assessment knowledge enables the social worker to assess and understand a person's concerns, needs, and problems as well as the situation in which they exist. It shows the social worker where and how to effectively intervene. Intervention knowledge is that knowledge utilized by the social worker to carry out the problem-solving process, thus helping individuals, groups, or communities effectively deal with the problems they face. Intervention knowledge is usually specific to the client problem, agency setting, and specific field of practice.

In today's world, a social worker must possess a broad knowledge base that includes but is not limited to the following:

1. Knowledge of human development and behavior, encompassing a holistic view of the person, and the reciprocal influences of the environment, including social, psychological, economic, political, and cultural influences. The main source of this part of the knowledge base comes from a strong and broad liberal arts education. It includes (a) knowledge extracted from the social and

behavioral sciences (sociology, psychology, anthropology, history, political science, and economics), (b) knowledge from the natural sciences for understanding the physical aspects of human functioning, and (c) knowledge gained through study in the humanities that helps explain the human condition by an examination of cultures, philosophies, and ways of thinking about and expressing the human condition.

2. Knowledge about human relationships and interactions. This includes knowledge of human communication, understanding person-to-person, family, small group, and group-to-group relationships and interactions, as well as the relationships and interactions between individuals, groups, and community organizations and institutions.

3. Knowledge of social work practice theories that embrace helping interactions. processes, and intervention methods and strategies appropriate for a variety of practice situations.

4. Knowledge about social policy and services, including knowledge of professional and institutional structures that deliver services to people in need of help, knowledge of the history of the movements that have influenced social policy, the impact of social policy on people's functioning, and the role of the social worker in the development of social policy.

5. Knowledge of self, which makes the social worker aware of and take responsibility for his or her own emotions, values, attitudes, and actions, when they would influence professional practice.

6. Specialized knowledge that enables the social worker to work with specific population groups or particular practice situations. This includes knowledge of specific clients, practice settings, and agencies. Social work's knowledge base has as its source a strong liberal arts base, professional practice, and research base.[7]

## Social Work, a Value-based Profession

Social work practice is guided by a set of values about human beings and the human condition. *Values* are strong beliefs that emerge from the way one feels. They guide human actions and behaviors. Social work's value base also serves as an ethical guide for the individual social worker in day-to-day work. Individuals hold values, learned through socialization at many levels within society. Individual values are diverse, differing from individual to individual. Some human values are held in common by most people and become societal values.

Social work's values are somewhat reflective of individual and societal values, but they are also unique to the profession. They fall into three areas: (1) values that reflect preferred conceptions of people, (2) values that reflect preferred outcomes for people, (3) values that reflect social workers' ethical responsibilities to the people they serve.[8] The following value statements are generally agreed upon as belonging to the profession:

*The Worth and Dignity of People.* Social workers believe in the inherent worth and dignity of all people, regardless of their individual or collective characteristics or status.

*The Self-Determination of People.* Social workers believe that people have the basic right to self-determination as long as their individual or collective actions do not endanger themselves or infringe upon the rights of others.

*The Purposefulness of Human Behavior.* Social workers believe that all human behavior has a purpose, however unusual it may appear, and however destructive it may be. Social workers strive to discover the meanings and purposes of behavior, rather than to label it, stereotype it, or otherwise react to it in a negative fashion.

*People Have the Capacity to Grow and Change.* No person should be viewed by the social worker as incapable of changing and growing in ways that will make their lives more rewarding. No person is beyond the capacity to accept constructive help.

*People Need Opportunities for Growth and Development.* Society and the profession must help people by providing the opportunities necessary for them to achieve their full potential in all aspects of their social functioning.

*People Have the Right to Participate Actively in Social Work Practice.* Social workers believe that people are capable of making decisions, and that social work is a mutual and cooperative endeavor between worker and client.

*Confidentiality.* In most instances, unless otherwise prohibited, social workers must respect people's right to privacy.[9]

The values of social work are further defined in the basic purposes and missions of the profession. In 1981, the National Association of Social Workers formulated a "Working Statement on the Purpose of Social Work."[10] This statement is presented in the working statement in the box on page 308. Social work values are further operationalized for use by social workers in their professional practice, through the social work *code of ethics* originally adopted by the National Association of Social Workers in 1960 and revised in 1980. All professional social workers are

# Working Statement on the Purpose of Social Work

The purpose of social work is to promote or restore a mutually beneficial interaction between individuals and society in order to improve the quality of life for everyone. Social workers hold the following beliefs:

The environment (social, physical organizational) should provide the opportunity and resources for the maximum realization of the potential and aspirations of all individuals, and should provide for their common human needs and for the alleviation of distress and suffering:

Individuals should contribute as effectively as they can to their own well-being and to the social welfare of others in their immediate environment as well as to the collective society.

Transactions between individuals and others in their environment should enhance the dignity, individuality, and self-determination of everyone. People should be treated humanely and with justice.

Clients of social workers may be an individual, a family, a group, a community, or an organization.

*Objectives*

Social workers focus on persons and environment in interaction. To carry out their purpose, they work with people to achieve the following objectives:

Help people enlarge their competence and increase their problem-solving and coping abilities.

Help people obtain resources.

Make organizations responsive to people.

Facilitate interaction between individuals and others in their environment.

Influence interactions between organizations and institutions.

Influence social and environmental policy.

To achieve these objectives, social workers work with other people. At different times, the target of change varies—it may be the client, others in the environment, or both.

Source: Ann N. Minahan, "Purpose and Objectives of Social Work Revisited," *Social Work* 26 (January 1981): 6.

expected to adhere to this code of ethics in their day-to-day work. The summary of its major principles is presented in the box below.[11]

Values, as can be seen, serve as the foundation upon which the profession of social work rests. They also form the basis of social work's self-regulatory function, which ultimately protects the people the profession serves.

---

# National Association of Social Workers Code of Ethics
## Summary of Major Principles

I.  The Social Worker's Conduct and Comportment as a Social Worker

    A.  *Propriety.* The social worker should maintain high standards of personal conduct in the capacity or identity as social worker.

    B.  *Competence and Professional Development.* The social worker should strive to become and remain proficient in professional practice and the performance of professional functions.

    C.  *Service.* The social worker should regard as primary the service obligation of the social work profession.

    D.  *Integrity.* The social worker should act in accordance with the highest standards of professional integrity.

    E.  *Scholarship and Research.* The social worker engaged in study and research should be guided by the conventions of scholarly inquiry.

II.  The Social Worker's Ethical Responsibility to Clients.

    F.  *Primacy of Clients' Interests.* The social worker's primary responsibility is to clients.

    G.  *Rights and Prerogatives of Clients.* The social worker should make every effort to foster maximum self-determination on the part of the clients.

    H.  *Confidentiality and Privacy.* The social worker should respect the privacy of clients and hold in confidence all information obtained in the course of professional service.

    I.  *Fees.* When setting fees, the social worker should ensure that they are fair, reasonable, considerate, and commensurate with the service performed and with due regard for the client's ability to pay.

III.  The Social Worker's Ethical Responsibility to Colleagues.

    J.  *Respect, Fairness, and Courtesy.* The social worker should treat colleagues with respect, courtesy, fairness, and good faith.

*continued*

*NASW Code of Ethics . . . continued*

    K. *Dealing with Colleagues' Clients*. The social worker has the responsibility to relate to the clients of colleagues with full professional consideration.

IV. The Social Worker's Ethical Responsibility to Employers and Employing Organizations.

    L. *Commitments to Employing Organizations*. The social worker should adhere to commitments made to the employing organizations.

V. The Social Worker's Ethical Responsibility to the Social Work Profession.

    M. *Maintaining the Integrity of the Profession*. The social worker should uphold and advance the values, ethics, knowledge, and mission of the profession.

    N. *Community Service*. The social worker should assist the profession in making social services available to the general public.

    O. *Development of Knowledge*. The social worker should take responsibility for identifying, developing, and fully utilizing knowledge for professional practice.

VI. The Social Worker's Ethical Responsibility to Society.

    P. *Promoting the General Welfare*. The social worker should promote the general welfare of society.

Source: National Association of Social Workers, *Code of Ethics of the National Association of Social Workers*. Washington, D.C.: National Association of Social Workers, July, 1980.

## The Skills of Social Work

Harriet M. Bartlett, has referred to the *skills* component as an "interventive repertoire," or a "bag of tricks" so to speak, that gives the social worker the means to facilitate change. The skills used by social workers are thought of in terms of the methods and techniques, as well as the ability to use knowledge effectively by transforming it into action in the helping process.[12] Social work skills from a more contemporary perspective are defined as "the social worker's capacity to set in motion with a client interventive processes of change based on social work values and knowledge in a situation relevant to the client.[13]

    The skills that social workers use can be organized into three general skill-areas; 1) interpersonal helping skills, 2) social work process skills, and 3) evaluation and accountability skills.

Interpersonal helping skills are basic to any professional people-helping endeavor. These skills include

1. Communication and listening skills include the social worker's ability to clearly communicate with a client, to understand and interpret the client's verbal and nonverbal communication; to help clients become clearer in their own communications; to be able to actively listen to the needs, concerns, and problems expressed by clients and so understand them in the reality of their situation, to be able to transform that which is understood through listening into action with the client, and so assist them in improving their social functioning.

2. Helping relationship skills include the social worker's ability to establish working relationships with clients, who either reach out for help, or to whom the profession reaches out to help. Involved here is the social worker's conscious use of self, including values and attitudes. Remaining honest, open, trustworthy, dependable, and nonjudgmental will promote the establishment of helping relationships.

3. Interviewing-counseling skills include the social worker's listening skills and such specific skills as confrontation, limit setting, support, ventilation, empathy, and self-disclosure to assess, question, and respond to the client's expressions of concern, need, or problems in their life situations.

Social work process skills are the "nuts and bolts" of social work practice activity. Here the knowledge base and values of social work come into play. Social work process skills involve creatively integrating interpersonal helping skills, with the problem-solving approaches contained in various methods of social work practice for work with individuals, groups, and communities. Use of these skills allows the social worker to be able to do the following:

1. To identify and assess problematic relationships between people and social institutions, where intervention is needed to promote, enhance, restore, protect, or terminate the relationships to improve social functioning.

2. To develop and implement appropriate intervention plans based on the assessment of problems involved in the client's situation, that address the client's concern and need.

3. To enhance or restore the client's capacity for problem-solving, coping, growth, and development.

4. To provide the link between people and community systems that will provide them with resources, services, and opportunities for improving social functioning.

5. To effectively intervene with and on behalf of vulnerable, disenfranchised, and discriminated-against people, to promote and restore their opportunities for social justice.

6. To promote the effective and humane functioning of community systems that provide people with resources, services, and opportunities.

7. To be involved with others (e.g. client-consumers and professionals) in the development of new service or the modification and improvement of existing community service and resource systems so that they become responsive to the needs of the client-consumers.[14]

Evaluation and accountability skills are the social worker's conscious use of self in evaluating the effectiveness of practice and being accountable to the people they serve, the delivery system they represent, and society in general. Again, value and ethical considerations in social work practice provide the guidelines against which social workers measures themselves.

## Methods and Approaches of Social Work Practice

Discussion of the elements of social work practice—its constellation of knowledge, values, and skills—has provided insight into the foundations upon which practice is based. Attention will be given now to discussing how knowledge, values, and skills are organized into methods and approaches for working with people. As social work has evolved as a profession, a number of practice methods and approaches have emerged. The development of these methods and approaches has been influenced by several factors: by contributions to the knowledge base of the profession; by the advances in technology; by advances in social work education; and the everchanging social, economic, and political climates over time. Chapter 2 briefly mentioned how social workers were educated in three practice methods: casework, groupwork, and community organization. These methods were developed from the early 1900s to the 1960s, and social workers before the 1970s were primarily educated in only one of these three methods. These methods are referred to as the *traditional methods* of social work practice.

*Casework*—Casework was the first method to be developed. It is the method of social work practice that assists individuals or families on a one-to-one or family group basis.

*Groupwork*—Groupwork is the process of working with individuals within groups and with the group itself. The focus of the groupwork process is placed on its individual members and the group as a whole. According to Knopha, the role of the groupworker is to enable the group to function so that group interaction and program activity help the individual members to grow, and so that the group as a whole reaches its mutual goals.[15]

*Community Organizing*—Community organizing is harder to define. One useful definition is: community organizing is the social work process of bringing about desired change in social welfare services, human relations, or social institutions by a variety of methods. It is the process of organizing a community to bring about desired change, focusing on specific areas and processes, such as changes in the law, improvement in existing service provisions, or improvement in community social conditions that are problematic for people.[16] Differing from casework and groupwork, the client of the community organizer becomes the whole community, or designated parts of it.

# Current Conceptualizations of Social Work Practice

In the late 1960s, social work practiced within these three traditional methods began to change, due to a rethinking using a broad perspective, about what constitutes social work practice. The new conceptualization incorporated new theory development in the social sciences, particularly social systems theory.[17] *Social systems theory* brought new understandings about the earlier social work view of people having a reciprocal relationship with their environment, and further developed the notion that social work processes should focus on what was called "the person in the situation," that is that people are involved in life situations that include interaction with various social systems in the environment that affect their social functioning. Assessing the person in the situation now involved understanding the relationship between individuals and environmental systems, and the problems of social functioning that arise out of that interaction.

New practice approaches surfaced in the early 1970s. In part, the new practice approaches solved long-standing arguments about which is the most desirable way for social workers to facilitate change. This argument can be stated as: Should intervention be focused on the individual or family—to improve their coping skills and thus improve their interaction with their environment (which the traditional caseworker would believe)? Or, should the change occur in the environmental systems that cause difficulties for people and families (as community organizers would think is the case)? It was argued that the traditional methods "encourage the dichotomous thinking of changing the individual or changing the environment, instead of maintaining the primary focus of social work intervention on the person-situation interaction."[18]

Integrating the knowledge and skill bases of the traditional methods with the broadened person-situation practice perspective was first termed *integrated social work practice*. Also, what were termed the *micro* and *macro* approaches became popular. *Microintervention* focuses on the social worker intervening with small client systems (e.g., individuals, families, and groups). Practice principles from the methods of casework and groupwork are integrated here. *Macrointervention* focuses on social workers intervening with large client systems (e.g., communities, societal organizations, and institutions at the local, state, and national levels). Education in macrointerventions also prepares social workers to assume administrative, social policy, and program evaluation roles. Macrointervention, then, incorporates the principles of community organizing practice with knowledge about administration and evaluation.

As discussed in Chapter 2, the bachelor's degree in social work was recognized as the first professional degree in 1974. With this recognition came concern over how undergraduate social work programs should educate beginning-level practitioners, and how to identify the knowledge and skills needed by the bachelor-level social worker, to prepare them practice. What eventually emerged was what began to be called the *generalist approach*. It was based on the integrated approach, particularly the focus on the person-situation interaction but did not lead to a "jack-of-all-trades" approach. Rather, the generalist social worker assesses the needs, problems, and concerns of people in situations, and then uses knowledge and skill to develop and implement change strategies with any size client system. The following case study illustrates the generalist approach to practice.

---

**A Case Study**

Bobby L, a eight-year-old boy, was referred to the family services unit of the State Department of Social Services by the guidance counselor at his elementary school, upon the request of his mother. A social worker in the family services unit was assigned to his case. The information provided in referral indicated that Bobby was experiencing difficulties in academic performance, was inattentive in class, was disruptive and sometimes belligerent toward his classmates and his teacher. He had been fighting on the playground and

*continued*

had been generally disruptive in the school lunchroom and in other special activities, such as music and physical education. His guidance counselor also reported that Bobby's mother was finding it hard to control his behavior at home and had confided that she was "at her wits end", in attempting to discipline him. She also mentioned that she was considering having him placed in a foster home or some sort of institution. The family services social worker began her assessment of the situation by interviewing the guidance counselor and Bobby's teachers for additional information. The worker contacted Mrs. L to discuss the situation with her. In the interview with Mrs. L, the social worker learned that she was a single parent, divorced for two years, and that Bobby and his mother had moved to the community at the beginning of the school year. Mrs. L explained that Bobby had similar problems in his previous school setting and had always been a somewhat difficult child to discipline, although not as difficult as in the current situation. His mother stated that her work schedule and other family obligations left her little time to deal with his problems. Based on the interviews with the school officials and Mrs. L, the social worker suggested that Bobby undergo a complete physical examination by a physician, and that he receive psychological testing and evaluation at the Child Guidance Clinic of the local community health center. Mrs. L was also referred to the Child Guidance Clinic for participation in its parenting skills and child management education group.

The results of the physical examination revealed that Bobby was displaying symptoms of organically-based hyperactivity. The psychological testing and evaluation also confirmed this, and also revealed that Bobby, although having above-average intelligence, may have been experiencing minimal brain dysfunction causing him to be learning-disabled. The clinic recommended that Bobby be taken out of his regular classroom and placed in a special classroom for learning-disabled children. The school officials initially resisted this recommendation since their special education classes were at full capacity at the time. The social worker intervened with the school officials and advocated in behalf of Bobby and Mrs. L for his placement in this classroom, reminding the school officials that Public Education Law 94-142 made them responsible for Bobby's special education needs. The social worker had for some time been aware of the school system's reluctance to provide for the special educational needs of children in the community. Based on this case and several others that had occurred in recent months, the social worker, along with several other professionals in the community, formed a Community Task Force to advocate in behalf of children and families in the community for a more responsive program of special education services.

The generalist social worker is sufficiently skilled to assume the following roles in social work practice:

*Outreach* —The social worker recognizes that some people who need services and are eligible to receive them are often unaware of them or are blocked in some way in their attempts to gain access to them. The worker identifies such individuals and assists them in finding the appropriate social services.

*Broker* —The social worker has knowledge of and the skills to link individuals with appropriate community resources that will meet their needs and assist them in solving their problems.

*Advocate* —The social worker has the ability to intervene on behalf of people seeking community resources, or people experiencing problems in gaining access to community resources. Advocacy may be on an individual case basis (case advocacy) or in behalf of a number of individuals whose needs are not being met, or are being disadvantaged in some way (cause advocacy).

*Teacher* —The social worker has the knowledge and skill to teach clients useful specific behaviors and skills in such areas as job seeking, parenting, or homemaking.

*Enabler-Mobilizer* —The social worker has the ability to form productive professional relationships with people, and through encouragement, support, and role-modeling, enables or mobilizes the client system to make changes, engage in problem-solving, or appropriately use social services.

*Behavior-Changer* —The social worker has the knowledge, experience, and skills to help clients change their problem-causing behaviors through the use of individual or group counseling or other interpersonal methods.

*Consultant* —The social worker has the skills to work along with community professionals to help the community resource system become more responsive to the needs and problems of community members.

*Community Planner* —Within limits, the social worker assists community groups in planning for the development of needed services or changes in existing services.[19]

Currently, undergraduate social work programs prepare beginning-level social workers to use the generalist approach. Graduate schools prepare social workers for advanced specialized practice. This level of training focuses on a particular field of practice, such as family therapy or mental health, or specific training in administration or social planning.

# Professional Concerns

As social work has evolved, several professional concerns have come to the forefront. People contemplating social work as a career choice should be aware of the following in responsibly deciding on a career in social work.

## Personal Characteristics of Social Workers

Social workers are first individuals with diverse characteristics. Many people have attempted to describe characteristics or qualities that professional helpers such as social workers need to have. Generally, social workers possess natural helping skills (e.g., empathy, sensitivity, warmth, and caring for others), which are then enhanced by and combined with professional knowledge, values, and skills. People who wish to pursue social work as a career must know that social work is a broad profession, focusing on working with many different types of people and situations, ranging from individual to group therapy to work with communities. However, given these broad practice parameters, explicit practice guidelines do not exist; thus the individual social worker must be able to take responsibility for exercising creativity and judgement in social work practice.[20] Beyond this, social workers must be self-aware, committed, and flexible individuals, capable of coping with the day-to-day stress, pressures, and criticism always present in the realities of their work.

## Employment Opportunities and Requirements

One of the most frequent questions asked by students considering a career in social work is, what may I expect to do with my degree? What jobs are available when I finish my education? Social workers are prepared for employment at many levels within the social welfare and human services delivery structures. Depending on their specific education and experience, professional social workers are experts in assisting many people in many different situations. Practice settings include, but are not limited to, public social welfare and social services, children and family social service agencies, health care areas (both in and outside of medical facilities), mental health agencies, correctional agencies, and business and industry. Employment opportunities currently exist and will continue to exist within this broad structure. Professional requirements for employment within these settings vary. As discussed earlier, there are two points of entry into the profession of social work, the first at the bachelor's level and second at the graduate level. There still is confusion as to what a baccalaureate social worker can do or not do compared with a master's level social worker. In 1979, NASW commissioned a task force charged with the responsibility for classifying levels of social work practice. The classification system proposed by the task force designated four practices.

BASIC PROFESSIONAL   The entry-level requires a *Bachelor of Social Work (BSW)* from an undergraduate program accredited by the Council on Social Work Education (CSWE). This level of practice requires the application of theoretical knowledge, professional practice skills, and values, in intervention with clients. Bachelor-level practitioners are distinguished from paraprofessionals (e.g., social workers with associate degrees), people working in the field who have degrees other than a social work degree and other nonprofessional helpers.

SPECIALIZED PROFESSIONAL   This level requires a *Master of Social Work (MSW)*, from a graduate social work program accredited by CSWE. Practice at this level requires that the social worker demonstrate mastery of specific therapeutic techniques in at least one knowledge and skill method (e.g. individual or group therapy, community organizing administration, social planning, social program or policy education, or research. The social worker should have a working knowledge of all areas listed above in addition to the area of specialization.

INDEPENDENT PROFESSIONAL   This requires the MSW degree and at least two years post-masters experience under appropriate professional supervision. This level contains experienced social workers who engage in private practice, or who practice in an agency where they assume primary responsibility for representing the profession, training staff, or administering the agency.

ADVANCED PROFESSIONAL   This requires a doctoral degree in social work or a closely-related social science discipline. Social work practice at this level may include responsibility for the education and training of social workers; specific and in-depth research; policy planning and analysis; or the administration of social welfare or social service programs, organizations, or agencies.[21]

SALARIES   Salaries within the profession are not very high. People who enter the profession do so to achieve other personal goals and to derive satisfaction from providing purposeful assistance to people. Salaries of social workers at all of the practice levels vary so much throughout the United States that it is impossible to state specifically what they are at any given time or place. In 1981, NASW developed a recommended minimum salary schedule for the four practice levels.

These are only recommendations and may or may not reflect actual salaries paid. They are as follows:

Basic Professional—$15,220
Specialized Professional—$18,990
Independent Professional—$21,980
Advanced Professional—$26,660[22]

OTHER PROFESSIONAL REQUIREMENTS   A basic professional requirement not addressed thus far, is *professional identification*. This may be accomplished informally through relationships with professional peers and the social work agency in which the social worker is employed. Professional identification may also be accomplished, in a formal sense, by membership in professional organizations, particularly NASW. Professional social workers at both the bachelor's and master's levels are eligible for membership in NASW. Through participation in the association, the social worker has the opportunity to become socialized and professionally immersed in the formal culture of the profession, including the NASW code of ethics.

In recent years, many states have passed legislation requiring social workers to be *licensed* to practice social work. This has added another dimension to the sanction and public regulation of the profession. Most state licensing laws provide for a number of levels of licensure, similar to the classification of levels of practice suggested by NASW in 1979. Some states have become members of the American Association of State Social Work Boards. Membership in this association requires the standardization of requirements for social work licensure and gives a national consistency to the whole matter of licensure. A forerunner to social work licensing was the creation in 1961 within NASW of the *Academy of Certified Social Workers (ACSW)*. The requirements for membership in the Academy are a MSW degree, two years of post-master's professional experience under the supervision of a person holding the ACSW, and the successful completion of a written examination. Members of the Academy are considered to represent the highest level of competence within the profession.

In addition, NASW publishes the *Register of Clinical Social Workers*. The *Register* contains an updated listing of qualified social work practitioners. To be listed, a social worker must meet strict educational and practice requirements and document that he or she has a broad knowledge of social work and demonstrated clinical experience. A basic purpose of the Register is as a consumer resource reference.

Professional requirements and sanctions provide opportunities for social workers to identify with their profession. They also regulate and sanction the profession, to promote quality social work services, and to protect client-consumers from incompetent or unethical practitioners.

## The Future of Social Work

Predicting the future of social work forces one to gaze into a crystal ball that is not at all clear. Perhaps the best way to accomplish this is to turn to the past as a basis for viewing the future. Social work as a profession made significant advances during the 1960s and 1970s, branching out to serve more people than ever before, in an expanded human services delivery system. The national political climate nurtured such advancement by placing a high priority on serving the concerns and needs of people, which were fostered by a humanitarian spirit. As we have moved through the decade of the 1980s, the political climate has changed, bringing about a shift to new economic, social, and political priorities, such as concern for economic stability and national security. These shifts in national priorities have cast doubt on the future of some social welfare and social service programs that traditionally have been staffed by social workers. Since 1980, federal support and funding for some social welfare and social service programs have decreased. Although this has had an impact on certain vulnerable groups within society, particularly the poor and the elderly, the profession has worked hard to insure the continuance of social welfare programs that meet the needs of these people.[23]

Despite current policies, there is little likelihood that the need for professional social workers will be eliminated. People's problems will continue, despite the cutback in services. The nature of social work practice may, however, need to change in response to the recent political and social changes. New strategies and methods of practice will likely need to be developed to accomplish the missions of the profession. This is already occurring to some extent, exemplified by social work's involvement with business and industry, and its commitment to advocacy—as demonstrated by its entrance into the political arena on an individual and collective basis.

In recent years, some social workers have run and been elected to political office. The NASW also has formed a political action coalition known as PACE, which lobbys and makes campaign contributions to candidates who support social policy that benefits the poor or underprivileged.

Social workers are reacting to funding cuts by using creative measures to develop and support mechanisms for self-help and by making maximum use of natural helping systems. As Anne Minahan has put it, "Social workers have a dual responsibility. In assisting other people to gain control over their lives, they help them establish goals and make plans to adjust to or shape their future. And, if social workers want to do for their profession what they help others to do, they can work to gain some control over the future of their own profession by making a conscious decision to shape the future instead of serving, ignoring, or adjusting to it."[24] Social work will survive the changes as it has in the past and continue to mature as an even stronger profession committed to the ideals of serving humanity.

## Key Terms

Academy of Certified Social Workers (ACSW)
advanced professional
advocate
art of social work
Bachelor of Social Work (BSW)
behavior change
basic professional
casework
code of ethics
community organizing
community planner
consultant
enabler-mobilizer
generalist approach
groupwork

independent professional
integrated practice
knowledge base
licensing
macrointervention
Master of Social Work (MSW)
microintervention
outreach
professional identification
skills
social systems theory
social work
specialist practice
teacher
traditional methods of practice
values

## Questions for Discussion

1. Discuss the differences between social work and social welfare? How are they similar?

2. Discuss social work's mission to improve people's social functioning. How, and at what levels within society, does social work seek to accomplish this?

3. Discuss social work practice as a creative blending of knowledge, values, and skills.

4. Identify the traditional methods of social work practice. Why are they considered to be the traditional methods? How do they differ from the social work practice conceptualizations of today?

5. Discuss the generalist approach to social work practice. What is a generalist social worker? How is the generalist approach different from specialist social work practice?

6. Discuss the levels of professional social work practice, as classified by the National Association of Social Workers, and their relevance to contemporary social work practice.

7. In what ways can a social worker develop identity with the profession? Do you think professional identity is necessary? Why?

8. Discuss what you believe might be the possible roles and missions for social work in the future.

# Notes

[1] Arthur Fink, Jane H. Pfouts, and Andrew W. Dobelstein, *The Field of Social Work* (Beverly Hills, CA: Sage Publications, 1985), p. 14

[2] National Association of Social Workers, *Standards for Social Service Manpower* (Washington, DC: National Association of Social Workers, 1973), pp. 4–5.

[3] Allen Pincus and Anne Minahan, *Social Work Practice: Model and Method* (Itaska, IL: F.E. Peacock Publishers, 1973), p.9

[4] Pincus, *Social Work Practice.*

[5] Louise C. Johnson, *Social Work Practice: A Generalist Approach* (Boston, MA: Allyn and Bacon, 1983), p.48.

[6] Max Siporin, *Introduction to Social Work Practice* (New York: MacMillan Publishing Co., 1975), chapter 4.

[7] Johnson, *Social Work Practice*, pp. 53–54; and Armando Morales and Bradford W. Sheafor, *Social Work: A Profession of Many Faces* (Boston, MA: Allyn and Bacon, 1986), p. 173 and 177; and Betty L. Baer and Ronald Federico, *Education of the Baccalaureate Social Worker: Report of the Undergraduate Curriculum Project* (Cambridge, MA: Ballinger Publishing, 1978), chapter 9.

[8] Morales, *Social Work*, p. 205.

[9] Charles S. Levy, *Social Work Ethics* (New York: Human Services Press, 1976); Charles S. Levy, "The Values Base of Social Work," *Journal of Education for social Work* 9 (Winter 1973): 37–38; Morales, *Social Work*; and Elizabeth Ferguson, *Social Work: An Introduction* (New York: J.B. Lippincott Co., 1975).

[10] Anne N. Minnehan, "Purpose and Objectives of Social Work Revisited," *Social Work* 26 (January 1981).

[11] National Association of Social Workers, *Code of Ethics of the National Association of Social Workers* (Washington, DC: National Association of Social Workers, July 1980), pp. 1–2.

[12] Harriet M. Bartlett, *The Common Base of Social Work Practice* (New York: National Association of Social Workers, 1970), pp. 80–83.

[13] Morales, *Social Work*, p. 228.

[14] Baer *Education.*

[15] Gisela Knopka, *Social Groupwork: A Helping Process* Englewood Cliffs, NJ: Prentice-Hall, 1972), p. 15.

[16] Murray G. Ross, *Community Organization: Theory and Principles* (New York: Harper & Row Publishers, 1955).

[17] Johnson, *Social Work*, p. 13.

[18] See Siporin, *Introduction to Social Work*, chapter 7.; Beulah Compton and Burt Galaway, *Social Work Processes* (Homewood, IL: Dorsey Press, 1984), chapter 1.; and Pincus, *Social Work Practice.*

[19] Ronald C. Federico, *The Social Welfare Institution* (Lexington, MA: D.C. Heath & Co., 1980), pp. 244–246.

[20] Morales, *Social Work*, p. 11.
[21] National Association of Social Workers, *Standards for the Classification of Social Work Practice* (Washington, DC: National Association of Social Workers, September, 1981).
[22] *NASW News* 26 (November 1981): 16.
[23] Robert P. Stewart, "Watershed Days: How Will Social Work Respond to the Conservative Revolution?" *Social Work* 26, (July 1981): p. 272.
[24] Anne Minahan, "Social Workers and the Future," *Social Work* 26 (September 1981): 363.

## Suggested Readings

Baer, Betty L., and Federico, Ronald. *Education of the Baccalaureate Social Worker: Report of the Undergraduate Curriculum Project*. Cambridge, MA: Ballinger Publishing, 1978.

Compton, Beulah, and Galaway, Burt. *Social Work Processes*. Homewood, IL: Dorsey Press, 1984.

Johnson, Louise C. *Social Work Practice: A Generalist Approach*. Boston, MA: Allyn and Bacon, 1983.

Morales, Armando, and Sheafor, Bradford W. *Social Work: A Profession of Many Faces*. Boston, MA: Allyn and Bacon, 1983.

National Association of Social Workers. *Code of Ethics of the National Association of Social Workers*. Washington, DC: National Association of Social Workers, July 1980.

# Chapter 16

## The Contemporary Social Welfare System

This book has considered the U.S. social welfare system as the chief means our society uses to meet human need. The text has done this by discussing factors that have contributed to the development of the contemporary system. First, general trends were considered, then specific fields of practice were discussed. In this chapter, discussion again returns to the whole system. This is done to help the reader form an integrated picture of our social welfare system and thus pull together the information provided in the earlier chapters of the book. First, the chapter presents a framework for analysis that shows the relationships among the major themes presented in the book. This framework is used to show how any response by the social welfare system to human needs can be analyzed and better understood. This then provides a basis for considering modifications that may be needed if the system is to more fully fulfill its purpose. Next, the chapter discusses several major issues facing the contemporary social welfare system. While solutions to these issues are complex and beyond the scope of this book, several changes that have been suggested will be noted. Finally, the chapter suggests some steps for the student to gain greater understanding of the system.

## A Framework for Analysis

One way to understand a complex system like the U.S. social welfare system is to identify several major concepts that explain the nature of that system, and then to develop an analytic framework that shows the relationships of the parts (the major concepts) to the whole (the social

## Figure 16.1   An Analytic Framework: U.S. Social Welfare System

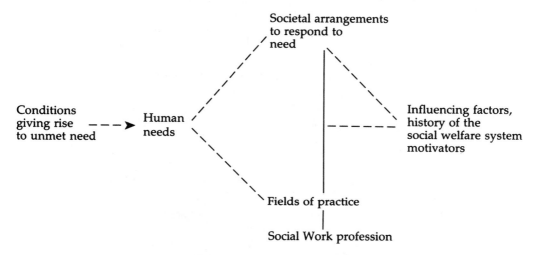

welfare system). Such a framework is presented in Figure 16.1, which shows the relationship of the major themes of this book to each other. The center of the framework is occupied by the *human need* concept. Human need was defined, at the beginning of this book, as those resources which people must have if they are to survive as individuals and to function appropriately in the social situation of which they are a part. (See Chapter 1.) It should be apparent from subsequent discussion that human need is both individual and collective. A major impetus for the development of the social welfare system was the necessity of society to have a means for helping individuals, families, groups of individuals, and communities meet needs they are unable to themselves. The book also developed other major themes that explain, at least in part, the causes of unmet need and describe how the social welfare system responds to need.

*Conditions giving rise to need* was the theme of Part Two of the book. Four major contributors to human need were identified: social change, poverty, lack of resources, and prejudice and discrimination. Other contributors also could be identified, such as chronic illness or disability, status as a dependent person (children or frail elderly), lack of opportunity in education or work, but these four contributors are the major sources of difficulty in meeting human need. Other contributors have their roots in them.

Another theme of the framework is *societal arrangements to respond to need*. This theme was also discussed in Chapter 1. Arrangements identified and discussed were: mutual aid, charity-philanthropy, public welfare, social insurance, social services, and universal provision. These arrangements refer to the different kinds of private and governmental structures and philosophies that have come into existence to help needy people. When analyzing how any need is met by the social welfare system, it is useful to first determine the arrangement traditionally used to meet the need, the strengths and limitations of that arrangement and whether the traditional arrangement is the most appropriate arrangement to use.

Contributing to the decision of which arrangement to use are two influencing factors: *the history of the social welfare system* and *motivators*. The historical development of our social welfare system was analyzed in two ways: Chapter 1 discussed the major milestones of its development, and Part Three presented the historical development in each field. The motivators, mutual aid, religion, politics, economics, and ideology, were presented in Chapter 1 and were referred to from time to time throughout the book. Usually more than one motivator has influenced the choice of an arrangement to meet a particular need. To understand the choice, one must first understand the influence of both the historical context of the arrangement and the societal motivations for providing for that need. Looking at the choice from that kind of analysis also provides clues to other choices that might have been made.

*Fields of practice* was the organizing framework for Part Three. The fields of practice discussed were: income maintenance services, services for children, family services, health care, mental health services, correctional services, gerontological services, industrial social services, and rural social services. These services could have been divided into other sets of fields of practice. Some would include health and mental health in one field of practice. Some would include children and family services into one field. Others would suggest that developmental disabilities is a separate field of practice. Some would not consider rural social work a field of practice. What is important to remember is that the social welfare system developed and is organized around a number of distinct fields of practice and that services do originate in those organized subsystems. Some fields, such as health care and services to children, are seen in a more positive light by the general public than are income maintenance or correctional services. Society's response to need is influenced not only by the traditional organization of services within a particular field of practice but also by how much that field is valued and supported by the general public. In analyzing how any need is met, it is important to consider which field of practice has traditionally met the need and the structure of its services. Furthermore, it is important to ask if the field being used is the most appropriate one and whether its services are structured to meet the need in the most effective and efficient manner.

It is within the fields of practice that the *social work profession* has evolved. This evolution is discussed in Chapters 2 and 15. The fields of practice not only have been a major influence on the development of the profession, social work practice has influenced the services provided in each field. Thus, the analysis also should ask questions about the social work profession within the field of practice. These questions should include: What social work practice modality(s) are traditionally used to meet the need? Has the response been effective? Why or why not? What changes need to be made in the professional response to the need?

The major themes presented in the book should now fit into a framework for analysis. The following example further clarifies its use. To use the analytic framework, a particular need is identified—whether it is one individual's need or many people's need. Then, that need is analyzed from three perspectives: conditions that give rise to the need, arrangements the social welfare system uses to respond to it, and the fields of practice that deal with it. Influencing factors, such as the historical development and motivators, are also considered, as are the practice methods used by social workers to respond to the need. With this understanding, the current problem(s) in meeting that need can then be examined in order to find solutions.

### Identification of Need

Loneliness and isolation have been identified in a number of needs assessments concerned with services to the elderly in small communities. The population affected are primarily single individuals, often widows, over seventy-five years of age, and living alone in small towns or on farms. These people find it increasingly difficult to get out to attend business or social functions, even to shop. Their children tend to live at some distance and thus not available for day-to-day help and companionship.

### Conditions Giving Rise to Need

Social change is the major contributor to this need. As pointed out in Chapter 3, older people are living longer and the U.S. population tends to be more mobile. This creates a longer period of life when people become frail and not able to get around, but at the same time, they are also without the daily support of an extended family, unlike earlier generations. Thus, another contributor to this problem is a lack of appropriate social supports as substitutes. The problems of loneliness and isolation are not simply the lack of vital social interaction with others, there is a risk that without people to care for them, these older women face premature institutionalization or a fall, other injury, or illness without anyone to help them.

### Traditional Arrangement Used to Meet the Need

As noted, the traditional arrangement has been mutual aid, depending on the family for assistance. But the rise in the number of older people with these needs and the mobility and subsequent removal of traditional family resources, has shifted this responsibility to other parts of the mutual aid arrangement, friends, neighbors, and others. In some cases, these resource persons are also reaching a point in life where they not only are unable to meet the need of someone else, they may have loneliness and isolation problems themselves.

More recently, the social service arrangement has been used to provide some monitoring and transportation services. But with the cutback in funds for social services, it has been impossible to fully meet these needs through the social service arrangement. The social services arrangement may have been a poor choice. The kind of help needed is one where the helper is available fairly often and with a quick response in case of an emergency. The social worker often can not respond this way because of large caseloads, and it is probably a poor use of the skilled professional.

The institutional arrangement also has been used, placing these individuals in nursing homes. This is very disruptive to the life-style of the older person and something they often resist. This institutional arrangement is also very expensive, often calling for the use of governmental funds to support the placement.

It would seem that the use of traditional mutual aid may indeed be the best response to this kind of need. However, different resources (other than family and age peers) must be developed. Research has shown that this is the most available and useable arrangement.[1] Mutual aid and religious motivators support the use of the arrangement. Current economic and political motivators also support its use since limited funds for services and a disinterested political climate points to the fact that resources that do not require governmental funding are very acceptable and a resource of choice where possible.

## Field of Practice

Two fields of practice traditionally respond to this need, gerontological and rural social work. These two fields are not mutually exclusive, as one responds to an age group and one to a specific context of practice. Both fields have made use of volunteers and natural helpers as a part of the service delivery system. Both fields have special understandings, that must be drawn on when designing a response to the needs of the rural elderly.

## Analysis of the Problem in Meeting the Need

The problem in meeting need, then, lies not in the arrangement or the field of practice but in the resource being expected to meet the need. Many social workers who work with elderly people living alone use a community approach within a generalist method and develop motivation for a younger population (largely the young elderly—those from sixty to seventy-five years of age) to provide the needed friendly visiting, telephone reassurance, and transportation services. This response has been effective in many communities. The strategy used by the social workers places major responsibility for planning and providing those resources in the community. This is congruent with rural culture and with what is acceptable to the frail elderly person. It requires a limited professional input, thus is economically and politically acceptable. The changes that need to be made are (1) social workers working with the elderly in rural communities should be directed to devote part of their time to motivating and supporting the community in meeting this need; and (2) continue to make use of the mutual aid arrangement, but with different segments of the informal system than has previously been used. A segment motivated by mutual aid and religion, and also with the time and physical capacity to provide the needed resource. Thus we see how the use of an analytic framework enhances the understanding of an identified need. This understanding then gives direction to the choice of responses to the need. Choices made after an indepth analysis of the need provide some assurance that the response will be one that cannot only provide the needed resources but can do so in a manner that will be supportable by the immediate situation in which the need exists and within the larger societal context. The analytic framework also gives recognition to the complexity of the U.S. social welfare system.

## Major Issues in the Contemporary Social Welfare System

Throughout the book, many issues and concerns about the contemporary social welfare system have been raised. Only limited attempts have been made to answer the questions involved in developing some solutions to the problems involved. Primarily, this is because the questions are too complex and must be worked out in the ongoing interchange between the political and economic processes of our society and the various parts of the social welfare system. The issues and concerns have been raised so the reader might become aware of them and might consider possible responses—both of society as a whole through its various mechanisms for decision-making and of individuals in their professional and personal endeavors.

Many of the issues and concerns raised were related to the specific fields of practice (Part Three), or the conditions that give rise to need (Part Two). They were concerned with specific sectors of the social welfare system. In this concluding chapter, the focus will be on five primary issues currently facing the contemporary social welfare system. In other words, the focus is on the system as a whole. No attempt will be made to address all the problems and issues facing the system. Rather, the focus is on drawing together major issues facing all parts of the system. Then, a few of the overarching proposals for change of the system will be presented.

## Structure of the System

The structure of the social welfare system very much reflects the influences of an earlier time. The use of a particular arrangement to meet a particular need may be more a choice based on tradition than on careful analysis. Also, the fields of practice structure has allowed the system to develop in piecemeal manner. An ongoing issue, then, is whether this structure is the most effective and efficient organization for meeting human need. The next question must be how to attain the best structure. In a society made up of many special-interest groups, it is most difficult to see the overall picture. Yet priorities must be set, decisions must be made. Somehow, society must provide a system that functions equitably across the entire country, yet allows for appropriate local control.

Other concerns related to the structure of the social welfare system are related to whether the present fields of practice should be the organizing mechanism for service delivery. Does this structure segment and compartmentalize problems, so that holistic views of individual, family, and community are overlooked? Does it prevent various parts of the system from working effectively together? Are the current fields of practice the most appropriate ones for the contemporary scene, or are they merely a relic of historical development? Should new fields be developed?

Further questions exist about the relationship of the social welfare system to the health, mental health, education, and corrections systems. Are these systems really a part of the overall social welfare system? It could be assumed that they are all part of the social welfare system, yet they function as separate but related systems. Social workers are found in all these systems. If they are not a part of the social welfare system, then what should its relationship be to each of these other systems? What should the role and function of the social worker be in these systems?

The social welfare system is complex. There is little basic agreement on its role and function in contemporary society. It is costly, it often stigmitizes individuals, it creates multilayered services and responses (those for the person who can pay and those for the person who must rely on governmental support). The system must change with the changing needs of people in a changing society. The answers to questions about what change is needed, and how that change can be facilitated, are also very complex. The system's change will be heavily affected by ideological, political, and economic motivators. If future change follows the pattern of earlier change, it will be incremental.

## Professional roles and responsibilities

As the social welfare system changes, the major profession within that system will change as well. One area of concern are the roles and functions of the BSW and the MSW within the current system. Which tasks can each best perform? Other professionals, such as nurses, psychologists, and the clergy work within the system. What should their roles and functions be? What should be the relationship of the social worker to these other professionals? Answers to these questions will come not only from the social work profession but from the demands of the social welfare system and its various motivators.

The need to expand resources as the government-funded resources shrink makes additional use of informal resources essential. The role of professional social workers in developing and working with those informal resources is still in question. There is a growing belief that broker and case management roles are best filled by the BSW. A closely related concern is the role of paraprofessional, volunteer, natural helper, and self-help group in the delivery of social services—about which tasks, which functions, these helping people and groups can carry out— and about the role of the social worker in working with these helping individuals.

Other questions relate to the role of the MSW. Social workers at this level generally have been found in two very different types of roles, the clinical or therapist role and the administrative role. While both of these roles will still be needed in the U.S. social welfare system in the foreseeable future, the numbers of workers needed for each role and which programs and agencies should provide the clinical services are not clear. Also, how interchangeable are these two roles? At the present time, many MSWs move from the clinical role into the administrative role without additional administrative education. Are social workers appropriate administrators in the social welfare system? Some insist that to administer a social service program, the administrator must have knowledge derived from social worker practice. Others believe this is not the case, that preparation in public administration is required. The supervisory role for the MSW is a related concern, as is the nature of supervison needed by the range of people employed in the social welfare system. The social work profession will wield considerable influence over the resolution of these concerns about professional roles and responsibilities—but political, economic, and societal ideology will also be influences.

## Poverty, Prejudice, and Discrimination

That poverty, racism, and discrimination continue to exist can not be disputed. (See Chapters 4, 6, and 7.) They are primary reasons why some people must receive income maintenance services. Where discrimination affects who will get jobs that provide basic income, poverty and discrimination become closely related. While racial discrimination is certainly basic to the issue, so are other kinds of discrimination, toward ethnic groups, women, the handicapped, and the aged. While one of the functions of the social welfare system is to provide for people affected by these conditions, it is also the function of that system to work for the elimination of these conditions. Thus, one of the pressing concerns when considering change in the U.S. social welfare system must be to eliminate poverty, prejudice, and discrimination in our society. This is a goal that must be approached incrementally, that is, for fewer individuals and families to be affected each year until, over time, poverty, racism, and discrimination are wiped out.

As noted earlier, solutions to the problem of poverty remain elusive and complex, with no consensus on how to solve the problem. Those who work must have a liveable wage and thus meet their own needs without relying on the social welfare system. In addition, those unemployed who can and want to work should have opportunities for employment at a liveable wage. Those who cannot work, because of age or handicaps or because they are needed to care for dependent family members, should be helped to live above the poverty level. In a society as affluent as ours, it is intolerable that people still live below the poverty level. A major task confronting our society is the development of feasible, acceptable, and workable solutions to the problems of poverty.

One way to reduce the amount of poverty in the United States is by reducing prejudice and discrimination. Discriminatory practices in the social welfare system contribute to the difficulties of those discriminated-against to find satisfying, secure, and well-paid jobs. Poverty, prejudice, and discrimination remain major social problems that strongly affect the capacity of the social welfare system. They must remain a target for change until they are eliminated.

## Resource Availability

It should also be apparent in the discussion of the various fields of practice, that a major impediment to meeting human need is the lack of resources. (Also see Chapter 5.) Questions around this issue are many. Some of the more important are what resources should federal, state, and local governments be responsible for providing? Which governmental unit should be responsible for providing which resources? Which resources should be the responsibility of the community's informal helping systems, neighborhood, friendship groups, and family? How should the governmental services support these natural helping systems?

When decisions about resource provision are made, attention needs to be paid to social change and its impact on the family, the changing structure and functioning of the family, and thus a changing need for new and different resources. For example, the entry of large numbers of women into the labor force has brought about new needs for child care resources. Attention also must be paid to the changing population patterns. For example, the growth of the aging population requires an emphasis on resources that provide for community care wherever possible. Changes in other parts of the social welfare system also affect the need for new, expanded, or different resources. For example, the policy of deinstitutionalization calls for a whole range of new community resources to meet the needs of the affected population.

Given the current political and economic situation, substantial increases in funding for social welfare programs cannot be expected. In fact, we may continue to see cuts. A critical question is—how can the availability of resources be expanded with little or no expansion in dollars? The use of the informal system must be explored further to determine what resources it can provide. Accountability, effectiveness, and efficiency become important; it is essential that decisions about service provision consider these factors.

## Social Provision

The U.S. social welfare system has no unified philosophy for the use of arrangements or for establishing policy that guides the delivery of services. The question of whether the primary purpose of the system is for social provison or social control continues to be unanswered. Depending on the prevailing political and ideological philosophy, the balance changes between care and control, yet the balance is never discussed or identified as such. Far greater understanding needs to be developed about this issue and its influence on both social policy and social work practice.[2] The decisions about which social arrangement to use has often been related to issues of social control and social provision. When social provision prevails, there is a tendency to use social insurance and universal provision arrangements. When social control prevails, public welfare arrangements are often the choice.

A closely related issue is whether social welfare should have a residual or universal approach. Generally, U.S. policy-making has used a residual approach. This has resulted in services reaching those in need too late to prevent major impacts on their social functioning capacity, thus contributing to the need for more intrusive and expensive interventions. For example, institutional care has often been needed for mentally ill clients because their problems were not identified soon enough or there were not enough resources to support them in the community. Services should be available near potential recipients and tailored to their life-styles. If hard facts comparing the relative costs of the current residual system to a universal system focused on prevention and support, informed decisions could be made about the relative merits of the two systems from both a financial and a humanitarian point of view.

The issues raised in this section are not all inclusive. Attached to each of the five major issues identified are many other issues. Some of these have been raised in earlier sections of this book. Others have yet to be raised. It is hoped that the reader has become aware of the complexity of the issues involved in the ongoing development of the U.S. social welfare system.

## Change in the System

From time to time, plans arise for changing the social welfare system so that it will become more responsive to human need. Because of the system's complexity the political and economic implications for any extensive change, such change has proven very difficult to bring about.

A plan introduced during the Carter administration may be characterized as the "continuity of care—developmental approach." According to Arabella Martinez, Assistant Secretary for Human Development Services, Department of Health, Education, and Welfare, under President Carter, "we have moved from looking at social services as an act of individual charity for the destitute to a nation-wide network of public and privately financed services for the poor, the handicapped, the elderly, and children, youth, and families."[3] She also notes the complexity and cost of the present system. She also sees difficulties in coordinating the various parts of the system as a deterrent to optimal operation of the system.

The plan highlights the need to remove barriers to coordination and suggests the concept of service focal points as one means for doing this. Service focal points locate services targeted for a particular population, such as services for the aging. By having these services in a common site, it is projected that not only will the services be more accessible to the clients, but coordination of the various services will be facilitated as workers communicate more readily and gain greater understanding about their services.

The Carter administration's plan had a developmental approach that assumed services are designed to meet predictable human need throughout the life cycle.[4] This approach recognized "the influence of social and physical environment on human functioning at all stages of life, and that the modifications of social factors in the family, neighborhood, and community generally can play a vital role in preventing social dysfunction in the individual."[5] It thus takes on a preventative stance. It implies that services based on age group needs are desirable and that such services may best be available at sites where other age group functions are placed, such as schools for children, maternity wards for new parents and infants, and so on. By recognizing age group needs and placing services so they are readily available and usable, the individual's development is facilitated, and need is met at the spot where obstacles to growth exist.

A final component of the plan is the recognition of five levels of care: professional, paraprofessional, caring network, self-help, and non-service. Non-service care is indirect assistance, such as tax credits for child care, or beneficial changes in the tax structure. This component requires some facilitation to meet need through alternative sources while maintaining coordination. It calls for the use of resources that involve no subsidy or fee when appropriate.

While parts of the Carter plan have been put into action, it has never had an opportunity for development as a whole. One barrier to adoption of the plan is that it has never been fully conceptualized. However, perhaps as it is incrementally accepted, it can become fully operational.

If it is accepted that incremental change is the realistic way to expect change in the social welfare system, then it is important to consider how that change might be influenced by those who have concern for and knowledge about meeting human need humanely and comprehensively. Withorn has suggested five political strategies that can be used to integrate social work goals and practices into our attempts to achieve a social welfare system that more adequately meets human need.[6]

The first of these suggestions is developing *public responsibility*. For change to take place, the general public needs to place a higher priority on human need, and understand that it is in the best interest of all citizens. The general public must understand why a social welfare system is necessary for the functioning of modern society, and also understand why individuals and families are sometimes not able to meet their own needs and the long range implications for not meeting those needs.

Second is the *debureaucratization* of helping. People must recognize that alternatives exist, that skill and competence can be organized so that consumer demand is an important influence in decisions about service delivery. People must find ways to minimize the influence of large organizational structures, and keep them from imposing rules, regulations, and ways of functioning that impede the meeting of human need.

Doing good work in a *deprofessionalized* setting is a third strategy. Working for the best interest of the client means acknowledging the importance of all helpers, regardless of their professional status.

Achieving *reciprocity* is the fourth strategy. This strategy acknowledges the need for collective effort both in providing aid to the needy and in political efforts to obtain needed change. It calls for recognition that clients have roles to play in both helping and in change efforts.

*Building an outside constituency* is the last strategy Withorn suggests. This strategy calls for alliances with other groups and movements that have similar goals. It calls for collective effort rather than singular effort and spreading the base for influencing change.

The U.S. social welfare system is not a static entity. It is evolving. The student of social welfare or social work must not only consider the past, but how the past influences the present. Then that student would be well advised to consider what the future may hold and how human need could more adequately be met as the evolution of the system takes place. If, as these authors believe, the U.S. social welfare system is on the brink of another milestone, a time of extensive change in the system, then the present opportunity for influencing for change is great.

## A Student's Next Step

A major purpose of this book has been to provide a solid knowledge base about the social welfare system for students preparing for work in one of the human service professions, particularly those preparing to become social workers. The survey of the fields of practice should be useful for students who are making a decision about whether social work is the profession for them and, if it is, which of the areas they may be especially interested in. The historical material should help students understand the nature of the contemporary social welfare system in which social work is practiced. The analytic frame of reference should give them one means for looking at human need and the usual responses to that need, so they can determine whether the most appropriate response is being used. This, then, can lead to identifying what changes need to take place in the social welfare system if human need is to be met. These understandings are needed by all who would work in the social welfare system.

For social work students, the development of these understandings is only a beginning. They will need to develop knowledge and skill in policy analysis, an understanding of legislative processes, of ways to influence those processes, and what is involved in the development of social welfare programs and policies. This knowledge is usually taught in a social welfare policy course in a social work curriculum.

Social work students will also need to learn the knowledge, values, and skills needed for social work practice. Anne Minahan and Allen Pincus have stated that "The objectives of social work emerge from the assignment given to the profession by society to deal with certain social problems and the professions's own sense of what promotes and prevents the achievement of its mission."[7] Alvin L. Schoor has stated that "professional practice is an expression of policy."[8] Without an understanding of the social welfare system as the context of practice, the knowledge, values, and skills used in practice lack an important ingredient for their mastery.

# Summary

It is hoped that this book has provided the reader with an in-depth understanding of the development and the contemporary nature of the U.S. social welfare system. This understanding should provide a basis for the kinds of decisions that all citizens need to make as they participate in the democratic process. The social welfare system is subject to much criticism. Many issues over values are involved. Much misinformation exists about the system and those who benefit from its provisions and services. Discussions in the political arena, as they affect the development of social policy, need to be influenced by knowledge from the past and understanding of the contemporary issues. Citizens need to have this understanding as they vote their political preferences and as they influence the development of public policy. An informed citizenry is essential if the social welfare system is to address the needs of individuals in a changing society.

This book, then, has attempted to present one conceptualization of the U.S. social welfare system, in hopes it will be of value to all who use it to develop their understanding of that system. Human need is a central concern of social living. The response any society makes to human need reflects that society's values, political structures, and philosophies, economic base, and its ecological and demographic makeup. What is functional in one society at any one time may not be functional in another society or at another time. Change in the structure and functioning of the social welfare system is inevitable. For the change to truly benefit the citizens of the United States, the change must be influenced by an informed citizenry and knowledgeable professionals who work within that system.

# Questions for Discussion

1. Choose a social problem of which you are aware and use the analytical framework presented in this chapter to decide what an appropriate response to that problem would be.

2. Identify other major issues facing the U.S. social welfare system (not those discussed in the chapter) and discuss why you see them as major issues.

3. Choose one of the major issues discussed in this chapter and develop the historical background of the issues and the current concern using material previously presented in the text.

4. Assess one of the proposals for reorganizing the social welfare system presented in the chapter. What do you consider its strengths, its limitations? What influences are there for the adoption of the proposal, what influences for rejection of the proposal?

5. What do you see as your next steps for gaining additional understanding of the U.S. social welfare system? This may take the form of additional reading, courses, or experiences.

## Notes

1 Eugene Litwak, *Helping the Elderly: The Complementary Roles of Informal Networks and Formal Systems* (New York: The Guilford Press, 1985).
2 Phyllis J. Day, "Social Welfare: Context for Social Control," *Journal of Sociology and Social Welfare* 8 (March 1981): 28–44, and Joan Higgins, "Social Control Theories of Social Policy," *Journal of Social Policy* 9 (1980): 1–23.
3 Arabella Martinez, "Relating Human Services to a Continuum of Need," in *The Social Welfare Forum, 1979*, National Conference on Social Welfare (New York: Columbia University Press, 1980).
4 Martinez, "Relating Human Services," p. 49.
5 Cecil G. Sheps, "A Developmental Approach to Meeting Human Needs," National Conference on Social Welfare, *The Social Welfare Forum*, pp. 45–61.
6 Ann Withorn, *Serving the People: Social Services and Social Change* (New York: Columbia University Press, 1984), chapter 7.
7 Anne Minahan and Allen Pincus, "Conceptual Framework for Social Work Practice," *Social Work* 22 (September 1977): 347–359
8 Alvin L. Schoor, "Professional Practice as Policy," *Social Service Review* 59 (June 1985): 178–196.

## Suggested Readings

Day, Phyllis J., "Social Welfare: Context for Social Control," *Journal of Sociology and Social Welfare* 8 (March 1981): 28–44.

Higgins, Joan. "Social Control Theories of Social Policy," *Journal of Social Policy* 9 (1980): 1–23

Minahan, Anne, ed. in chief, *Encyclopedia of Social Work,* 18th Ed. Silver Springs, MD: National Association of Social Workers, 1987. Articles: "Federal Social Legislation Since 1961," "Legislative Advocacy," "Policy Analysis: Methods and Techniques," "Political Action in Social Work," "Social Problems and Issues: Theories and Definitions," and "Social Welfare Policy: Trends and Issues."

Minahan, Anne, and Pincus, Allen. "Conceptual Framework for Social Work Practice," *Social Work* 22 (September 1977): 347–359.

Schoor, Alvin L. "Professional Practice as Policy." *Social Service Review* 59 (June 1985): 178–196.

# Index

## A

Abbott, Edith, 34
Abbott, Grace, 288
Absolute deprivation, 64
Abuse. *See specific listings*
Academy of Certified Social Workers
    (ACSW), 319
Accreditation standards, 40, 111, 289
Act for the Punishment of Sturdy
    Vagabonds and Beggars, 121
*Action for Mental Health*, 214
Addams, Jane, 109, 147, 189, 236, 279, 280
Addiction, 217
    treatment programs, 221
Administration, 331
Adolescence, 87–88
Adoption, 160–162
    agency, 162
    independent, 162
    legal aspects of, 160, 161, 162
    social work role in, 162
Adoptions Assistance and Child Welfare
    Reform Act, 149, 158
Adulthood, 88
Advanced professional, 318
Affluence, 71, 76
*Affluent Society, The* (Galbraith), 6
Aged. *See* Elderly
Age Discrimination in Employment Act,
    267, 281
Ageism, 107, 258

Agency adoption, 162
Agriculture Adjustment Act (AAA), 288
Aid to Dependent Children (ADC), 11, 12,
    14, 22, 126
Aid to Families with Dependent Children
    (AFDC), 11, 24, 126–128, 133, 136,
    147, 174
    case study, 136–137
    criticism of, 127–128
Aid to the Blind (AB), 11, 22, 24, 126
Aid to the Disabled (AD), 11, 22, 24
Aid to the Physically and Totally Disabled,
    126
Alcohol abuse, 159, 217, 221
Alcoholics Anonymous (AA), 7, 159, 217
Alms house, 8, 20
    life in, 144–145, 260
Altruism, 26, 30
Alzheimer's disease, 255
American Association of Group Workers
    (AAGW), 36
American Association of Hospital Social
    Workers, 190, 192
American Association of Medical Social
    Workers (AAMSW), 35, 192
American Association of Psychiatric Social
    Workers (AAPSW), 36, 218
American Association of Retired Persons,
    268
American Association of Social Workers
    (AASW), 35, 36, 37, 249
American Association of State Social Work
    Boards, 319

*American Charities and Social Work*, 279

American Home Economics Association, 168

American Psychiatric Association, 209

American Public Welfare Association, 79, 132, 137, 149

American Revolution, 123

Anderson, Ralph E., 49

Antipoverty movement, 74

Antipoverty programs, 77–78

Appalachian Redevelopment Act, 290

Apprenticeship, 32, 144, 145

Area Agency on Aging, 263–264, 272

Area Office on Aging, 270

Asian Americans, 105–107

Assimilation, 97

Association for the Study of Community Organization (ASCO), 36

Association of American Universities, 34

Association of Training Schools of Professional Social Work (ATS), 34

Atherton, Charles, 94

# B

Bachelor's in Social Work (BSW), 39, 40, 41, 289, 314
  fields of practice, 136, 192, 193, 203, 216, 218, 220, 221, 226, 293, 331

Barker, Robert L., 219

*Barrios*, 103

Bartlett, Harriet M., 294, 310

Basic professional, 318

Battered child syndrome, 152

Baumohl, Jim, 209

Beers, Clifford, 213

Beggars, 18, 121

Bellevue Hospital, 187

Bible, 29

Black Americans
  children, 149
  discrimination against, 66, 98–100, 149
  incarceration of, 247
  poverty of, 66
  segregation of, 98

Black Muslims, 100

Black Panthers, 100

Black Power Movement, 100

Blind, 129. *See also* Aid to the Blind

Block grants, 148

Boston, 33, 35

Boston Psychiatric Hospital, 218

Brace, Charles Loring, 25, 145

Bracht, Neil F., 194

Brennan, Earl C., 41

Brieland, Donald, 94

Briggs, Thomas L., 219

Brown, Esther Lucille, 37, 38

Brown, Josephine, 289

Browning, Grace, 289

*Brown* v. *Board of Education*, 99

BSWs. *See* Bachelor's in Social Work

Bubonic plague, 120

Bureaucratization, 50, 335

Bureau of Indian Affairs (BIA), 67, 101, 102
  child welfare programs, 147
  income maintenance programs, 129–130

# C

Cabot, Richard, 189–190, 217

California, 239–240

California Youth Authority, 239, 240

Cambodians, 106

Canada, 16, 188–189

Cannon, Ida, 190, 217

Capitalistic economy, 71

Capital punishment, 244, 245

Carmichael, Stokely, 94

Carter, Irl, 49

Carter, Jimmy, 131, 214, 334–335

Case manager role, 219, 220–221, 272, 331

Case work, 14, 32
  methods and processes, 32, 37, 135, 313
  teaching, 34

Categorical assistance, 11, 18

Charity hospitals, 186

Charity Organization Societies (COS), 8–9, 14, 145–146, 189, 246
  history of, 21, 31, 32, 48, 54, 75, 123, 177, 189

Charity patients, 186–187

Charity/philanthropy arrangement, 6,
    7–10, 17, 21
  in child welfare, 20, 144–146
  disadvantages to, 9–10
  and the elderly, 259–260
  in health care, 186
  historical perspective of, 31, 123,
    144–416
  religious motivation in, 25, 30
Chavez, Ceasar, 104
Chestang, Leon, 106
Chicago, 33–34
Chicago School of Civics and Philan-
    thropy, 34
Child abuse
  causes of, 152–153, 176
  defined, 151
  legislation on, 146, 151–152
  statistics, 151–152
Child care, 31, 185
Child guidance clinics, 9, 212
Child labor laws, 31
Childless family, 170
Child Protective Services (CPS), 150
Children. *See also* Child welfare
  adoption of, 160–162
  dependent (*see* Dependent children)
  handicapped (*see* Handicapped children)
  mentally ill, 213
  mentally retarded, 221
  poverty of, 68, 149
  resources needed for, 87
Children's Aid Societies, 9, 25, 145
Children's Bureau, 147, 190
Children's services. *See* Child welfare
    services
Child welfare, 9. *See also* Child welfare
    services
  defined, 141, 146
  focus of, 141, 146
  historical perspective on, 142–149, 190
  recent trends, issues, and concerns,
    148–149, 151–156
Child Welfare League of America (CWLA),
    148, 161
Child welfare services
  case study, 159

current programs, 150–156
  emphasis in, 150, 172
  in rural areas, 288–289
  protective programs, 150–153
  scope of, 141, 142, 147, 148
  social workers' role in, 153
  substitute care programs, 156–162
  in their own homes, 155–156
Chinese Americans, 105
Chinese Exclusion Act, 105
Christianity, 25, 29, 30
Chronic mental illness, 209, 215–216, 220
Churches. *See* Religious groups
Civil rights
  of blacks, 98, 110
  of Mexican Americans, 103, 104
  of Native Americans, 102
  of prisoners, 237, 246
Civil Rights Act, 100, 246, 281
Civil rights movement, 26, 65, 77, 99–100,
    110
Class structure, reinforcement of, 9
Clinical social worker, 218, 219
*Closing the Gap in Social Work Manpower*
    (HEW), 40
Cohabitation, 170
Colonial times, 30, 101, 122–123, 142–144
Communicable Disease Center, 15
Community Action Program, 77
Community-based correctional services,
    234–235, 240, 244, 246–247
  case study, 250–251
Community health settings, 191, 198–200
Community Mental Health Centers Act, 214
Community mental health services, 9, 156,
    210
  development of, 214–216
  social work in, 220–221
Community organizations and services,
    86, 156, 268, 291
Community organizing, 313
Community support programs, 216
  case study, 222–223
Comprehensive Employment and Training
    Act (CETA), 133
Comprehensive Health Planning Act, 192,
    214

Conference of Charities, 32
Congress of Racial Equality (CORE), 100
Connecticut, 128
Connecticut Society for Mental Hygiene, 212
Conservativism, 56, 74, 131
Constitution, U.S., 10, 98
Constitutional criminality, 243
Cook County General Hospital, 187
*Cooper* v. *Pate*, 246
Coordination of services, 270, 294, 334
*Core of Competence for Baccalaureate Social
    Welfare and Curriculum Implications*,
    A, 40
Correctional Rehabilitation Study Act, 245
Corrections system, 233
    adult, 234–235, 243, 248–250
    basic goals in, 237
    historical perspective, 233, 235
    institutions, 20, 235, 244
    juvenile, 232, 234
    punishment versus rehabilitation,
        244–246
    recidivism, 239, 240
    services in, 244, 247–248
    social work in, 248–250
Costin, Lela B., 94
Council of Economic Advisors, 63
Council on Social Work Education
    (CSWE), 34, 35, 36, 39, 40, 110, 111,
    281, 289, 290
Counseling
    for the elderly, 259
    by private agencies, 9
Country Life Commission, 287
Crime
    causes of, 237–238, 243–247
    juvenile, 237–238
    prevention of, 244
Criminal behavior
    causes of, 243–247
    mental illness and, 248
    responses to, 20, 244–246
Criminal justice system, 233–235
Crisis poverty, 73
Cuban Americans, 67, 104
Cultural change, adaptation to, 58. *See also*
    Social change

Cultural factors
    in health care, 201–202
    in mental health, 209, 227
    in rural social work, 287
    in usability of resources, 89–91
Cultural pluralism, 97, 98
Cultural pride, 97, 102
Culture, defined, 49

# D

Darwin, Charles, 124
Dawes, Anna L., 32–33
Day-care services, 153–154
Debureaucratization, 335
Deinstitutionalization
    of the mentally ill, 215, 226–227
    of the mentally retarded, 216–217, 221,
        226–227
Delaney, Anita J., 90
Delinquent, 237, 238
Department of Agriculture (USDA), 128,
    287
Department of Health and Human
    Services, 147
Department of Health, Education and
    Welfare (HEW), 40
Dependent children
    aid to, 126–128
    historical perspective on, 122, 143–144
Deprivation
    absolute, 64
    relative, 64, 65
Deprofessionalized setting, 335
Detroit riots, 100
Developmental approach, 119, 334
Developmentally disabled, 216. *See also*
        Handicapped; Mentally ill
Diagnostic Related Groups (DRGs), 191, 199
*Differential Use of Social Work Manpower*, 40
Disabled. *See specific disabilities*
Discharge planning, 191, 197, 203
Discrimination
    against Asian Americans, 105–107
    against blacks, 66, 98–100
    against the elderly, 107, 258, 276–268

against Hispanics, 102–104
against native Americans, 67, 101–102
against the poor, 73
causes of, 95–98
in child welfare programs, 149
defined, 94
in employment, 99, 267
in the media, 267
in public facilities, 26
racial, 66, 94–98
sexism, 68, 107–108
social change and, 59
social welfare response to, 109–112, 332
Discussion clubs, 35
Divorce, 169
causes of, 174–175
effects of, 175, 315
mediation, 175
Dix, Dorothea, 212
Drug abuse, 217
treatment programs, 221
Drugs
miracle, 216
psychotropic, 213, 219
DuBois, W.E.B., 109
Dust Bowl drought, 25

# E

Economic change, 47–48, 55–56, 215
Economic factors
in poverty, 65, 70–72
in social welfare system, 25
Economic Opportunity Act, 77
Economic philosophy, 123–124
Economic theory, 76
Education. *See also* Schools
compulsory, 146
discrimination in, 99
equal opportunity in, 99, 100, 103, 154
formal, 32, 39–41, 110
Education of All Handicapped Children
Act (PL–94–142), 154, 156, 216, 315
Educational services, 154, 155–156
Elderly
case study, 273

coordinating services of, 270–271
demographic factors, 51, 54–55,
256–257, 265
discrimination against, 107, 258, 267–268
health care for, 187, 255, 271
income maintenance, 255, 264
long-term care, 196–197
mental health care, 215, 227, 255
poverty of, 67–68, 266–267
problems of, 255, 257, 263
in rural areas, 292, 328–329
services needed for, 8
social work with, 272–273
stereotypes, 107
theories about, 257–258
women, 265, 293
Elitism, 10, 15, 39
Emergency Employment Act (EEA), 133
Emotionally disturbed children, 213
Employer-employee relationship, 50. *See
also* Industrial social work
Employment
discrimination in, 99, 103, 108
equal opportunity in, 100
Endowment, 8
England. *See* Great Britain
English Poor Law, 10, 18–19, 30, 47, 122,
278–279
Environmental factors, 31. *See also* Rural
social work
in poverty, 73–74
Episcopal Charity Society, 123
Equal Opportunity Act, 100
Equal protection of the law, 103–104
Equal Rights Amendment, 108
Erikson, Eric, 257
Esenstein-Naveh, A. Rosa, 198
*Essay on the Principle of Population*
(Malthus), 124
Ethics
biomedical, 201
in social work, 110, 307, 309–310, 319
Ethnic identity, 97, 102
Ethnic minorities. *See* Minorities; *specific
names of groups*
Ethnocentrism, 94, 95
Europe, 7–8, 13, 29–30, 119–122

Executive Order 8802, 99
Extended family, 57, 169–170

# F

Family. *See also* Family services
   as basic social unit, 142–143, 169, 172
   childless, 170
   defined, 168
   divorce in, 174–175
   dual-career, 172–173
   economic impacts on, 56–57, 172–174
   extended, 169–170
   functional changes in, 49, 84, 156,
      171–172
   illness in, 185, 186, 197
   integrity of, and child welfare, 146, 150
   mobility, 57, 84
   nuclear, 170
   relationships in, 174–176
   reconstituted, 170
   single-parent, 170, 172, 241–242
   social change and, 57, 168–169
   structural changes in, 56–58, 169–171,
      265
   violence in, 176–177, 179
Family Allowances (Canada), 16
Family Assistance Plan (FAP), 130, 133
Family foster care, 157
   case study, 159
   professionalizing, 157
   social work role in, 158
Family life education, 177–178
Family Service Association of America
      (FSAA), 8, 177–178
Family services, 9, 173
   for abuse, 176–177
   case study, 178–179
   development of, 177–180
   for divorce, 175
   homemaker services, 154
   social work and, 178–179
Farmers, 58, 69, 287–288
Farm subsidies, 288
Federal Emergency Relief Administration,
      289

Feudal system, 8, 120
Fields of practice, 327, 330 development
      of, 277, 294–295
Filipinos, 67
Financial services, 85
First National Conference on Social Work
      Practice in Labor and Industrial
      Settings, 281
Flexner, Abraham, 36–37
Food assistance programs, 128–129
Food Stamp Act, 128
Food stamps, 12, 128
Foster care, 145, 149, 157
   issue of duration, 150, 158
Foster parents, 145
   minority, 158
   selecting, 157–158
Fourteenth Amendment, 98
Frail elderly, 54, 260, 329
France, 211
Fraud, welfare, 128
Free enterprise, 26
French Benevolent Society, 123
Freud, Sigmund, 37, 212
Friendly visitors, 31
Funding, issue of, 320, 328

# G

Galbraith, John Kenneth, 73, 74, 76
*Gault* v. *Arizona*, 237, 238
*Gemeinschaft* and *gesellschaft* relationship, 6,
      286
General assistance programs, 125
Generalist approach, 291, 314, 316, 329
   case study, 314–315
George, Linda, 257
Germain, Carel, 184
German Americans, 105
German's Society of New York, 123
Germany, 13, 19
Gerontological social work, 255, 328. *See
      also* Elderly
   current problems and issues, 264–265
   historical perspective, 258–264
Gerontological Society, 255, 268

Ginsberg, Leon, 290
Good Samaritan, parable, 30
Graduate programs, 34–35, 39, 192, 316.
    *See also* Master of Social Work
Grants-in-aid programs, 126, 147, 261
Gray Panthers, 268
Great Britain, 8, 13, 119–122, 188–189
    history of social welfare in, 10, 18–19, 30
Great Depression, 10, 22, 25, 48, 75–76, 79
Greenwood, Ernest, 38
Gross, Arnold M., 198
Gross, Jacqueline, 198
Gross National Product, 70
Group homes, 160, 213
Group service agencies, 9
Groupwork, 313
Guaranteed income programs, 133–134
Guilds, 120, 278

# H

Hamilton, Charles V., 94
Handicapped, 11, 12, 86, 129
    children, 147, 153, 155, 216, 315
    discrimination against, 108
Harrington, Michael, 74, 77
Headstart, 78
Health, defined, 184
Health care system
    accountability in, 193
    business aspects, 202
    community settings, 198–200
    costs, 185, 191, 200, 202
    cultural issues in, 201–202
    defined, 184
    delivery in, 186–189, 192, 200
    development of, 189–191
    HMOs, 199
    holistic approach, 185–186, 199, 200, 201
    home care, 155–156, 191, 199–200
    hospitals, 193–196
    levels of services, 189
    long–term care, 196–198
    major components of, 191
    maternal and child care, 199
    multidisciplines in, 193, 203

physicians in, 192
preventive approach, 200, 201
primary care, 199, 200
quality of life issue, 201
right or privilege issue, 201
social services in, 188–191
social work in, 185–189, 191–200
unresolved issues in, 200–203
Health insurance, 202, 225–226
Health Maintenance Organization Act, 192
Health Maintenance Organizations
    (HMOs), 188, 191, 199
Helfer, Roy E., 152
Heroic medical measures, 201
Hill-Burton Act, 191
Hispanics, 67, 102–104
Hodson, William, 37
Hokenstad, M. C., 203
Holistic approach, 185, 199, 200, 201
Hollis-Taylor Report, 39
Home health care, 191, 199–200
Homeless people, 215
Homemaker services, 154
Home Service of the Red Cross, 287
Homestead Act, 101
Homosexual family, 170
Hoover, Herbert, 76
Horejsi, Charles R., 221
Hospice care, 200
Hospitalization
    costs of, 225
    psychosocial effects of, 185
Hospitals
    accreditation, 188, 194
    administration, 194
    aid to the poor, 8, 120, 186
    charity, 186
    emergency rooms, 194
    functions of, 191
    history of, 189–190
    mental, 211, 212, 213, 219–220
    psychiatric, 210
Hospital social work, 193–196, 273
    case study, 195–196, 273
    protocols in, 194
    services provided, 8, 186, 194
Houston, 33

Hull House, 189, 236
Human diversity perspective, 111
Humanitarianism, 26
Human needs
    arrangements used to meet, 325, 327,
        328–329
    conditions giving rise to, 327
    identifying, 327
    life-span, 87–89
    middle-class perceptions of, 90
    range of, and available resources, 83–87
    societal response to, 5–16, 325–326
    variations in, 3–5

# I

Ideology, 97
Illegal aliens, 103
Illinois, 236
Immigrant Protection League, 109
Immigrants
    Asian, 106
    Chinese, 105
    Cuban, 104
    Japanese, 105
    Mexican, 103
    mutual aid of, 6
Immigration
    effect on social welfare, 19–21, 25, 48,
        52–53, 109, 212
    restrictions, 104–105
Immigration Act, 105
Inadequate income support, 71
Incarceration, 244, 246
Incest, 151, 152
Income
    defined, 117
    distribution of, 70–71
    fixed, 67
    levels of, necessary, 118
    sources of, 173
Income maintenance
    concept and definitions of, 12, 117–118
    developmental approach to, 119
    earliest forms of, 120, 122
    institutional approach to, 119

    residual approach to, 118–119
    work ethic and, 124, 127, 130, 132–133
Income maintenance services
    alternative programs, 130–135
    case study, 136–317
    current programs, 125–130, 331–332
    current proposals, 131–132
    eligibility for, 122, 125, 127, 133, 187
    government involvements, 125
    historical development of, 119–124, 147
    local programs, 125–126
    rejected proposals, 130–131
    role of social work in, 135–137
    state programs, 126–130
    structure of, 118–119
Income tax, negative, 134–135
Income transfers, 125
Indenture, 122, 145
Independent adoption, 162
Independent professional, 318
Indian Child Welfare Act, 149, 161
Indians. *See* Native Americans
Individualism, 26
Indoor relief, 10, 20, 122, 123
Industrialization, 21, 146, 170, 210
Industrial Social Welfare Center, 281
Industrial social work
    daily schedule, sample, 284
    defining, 278
    delivery systems, 282
    evolution of services, 283
    historical perspective, 278–282
    issues in, 285–286
    personnel management and, 280–281
    practice in, 282–285
*Industrial Society and Social Welfare* (Wilen-
    sky and LeBeaux), 118
Inflation, 72
Inherited poverty, 74
In-kind provision, 174
Insane asylums, 211
Insanity plea, 248
Institutional approach, 119
Institutional care
    for children, 144–145, 149, 160
    for the elderly, 259–260, 268–269, 270,
        328

history of, 19–20, 47, 123, 144–145
for the mentally ill, 260, 333
Institutional corrections services, 20, 234, 235, 244
Insurance
   health, 202, 225–226
   national health care, 187–189, 202
   social, 6, 12–14, 17, 262, 264
Integrated practice, 290, 314
Internal Revenue Service (IRS), 135
Interpersonal relationships, 86, 311
Ireland, 19

# J

Jackson, Jesse, 65
Jails, 244
Japanese Americans, 105
Jarret, Mary, 217
Jewish community centers, 259
Jim Crow laws, 98, 99
Job Corps, 77, 78
Jobs and Income Security Program (JISP), 131, 133
Job Service, 221
Jobs programs, 131
Johnson, H. Wayne, 249
Johnson, Louise, 286
Johnson, Lyndon, 77–78, 100
Joint Commission on Mental Illness and Health, 214
Joint Commission on the Accreditation of Hospitals, 188, 192, 194
Jones, Maxwell, 213
Judaism, 25, 29
Judicial system, 233
   and child welfare, 157
   and family violence, 177
Juvenile corrections system, 232
   case study, 241–242
   diversion system, 238–239
   history of, 235
   social work in, 240–243
   structure of, 234
   treatment approaches, 238–240
Juvenile court system, 31, 236–238

Juvenile delinquency, 232, 236
   causes of, 237–238
Juvenile Justice and Delinquency Prevention Act, 239
Juvenile Psychopathic Institute, 236
Juvenile reformation, 236

# K

Kellog, Charles, 32
Kempe, Henry C., 151, 152
Kennedy, John F., 76–77, 100, 214
Kerner Commission, 100
King, Martin Luther, Jr., 77, 100
Koreans, 106
Ku Klux Klan, 99
Kurzman, Paul A., 278

# L

Labor unions, 280, 283, 285. *See also* Industrial social work
Ladies of Charity, 30
Laissez-faire economics, 76, 124, 134
Language barrier, 90–91, 106
Laotians, 106
Lathrop, Julia, 147
Law Enforcement Assistance Administration, 246
Least restrictive environment, 224
LeBeaux, Charles, 118
Lee, Porter R., 34
Legal aspects. *See also* Judicial system
   in adoption, 160, 161, 162
   in mental health, 219, 224–225
Less eligibility, principle of, 11
Lewis, Oscar, 65, 75
Liberalism, 56
Licensing, 319
Life-cycle poverty, 73
Life span, 54
   and resources needed, 87–89
   stages in, 87–88
Life-styles, changes in, 55, 58
Life-support systems, 201

Little, Alan, 73, 74
Little Rock, 99
Little Sisters of the Poor, 260
Local control, 18, 19
Local government, 18
Locke, John, 124
Locke, Thomas, 124
Long-term care, 196–198, 215–216
    case study, 197–198
Long-term facilities, 191, 196
Lunatics, 210, 211

# M

Macarov, David, 24
Macrointervention, 314
Maintenance, defined, 117. *See also* Income
    maintenance
Malthus, Thomas, 123–124
Manpower, 39–40
Manpower and Development Training
    program, 133
Marital relationships, 85
Martinez, Arabella, 334
Martinez-Brawley, Emilia E., 287
Massachusetts
    correctional system, 236, 239
    foster parents program, 145
    health care, 189–190
    mental health care, 211–212, 217–218
Massachusetts General Hospital, 189–190,
    217
Master of Social Work (MSW), 34–35, 39,
    40, 41
    fields of practice, 136, 192, 193, 198, 203,
        218, 220, 225–226, 331
Maternal and child health programs, 199
Mayer, Jane B., 199
Meals on Wheels, 128
Means test, 127, 129
Media, discrimination in, 267
Medicaid program, 11, 24, 190, 192, 202,
    155–156, 158, 187, 215, 262
*Medical Social Worker Journal, The*, 192
Medical treatment, effects of, 185
Medicare (Canada), 16

Medicare program, 13, 24, 187, 190, 191,
    192, 202, 215
Melting pot theory, 97
Mental health, 184, 215, 224–227, 281. *See
    also* Mentally ill
    definition of, 208
Mental health agencies, 210
Mental health services, 9
    case study, 222–223
    church-affiliated, 178
    community, 156, 210
    costs of, 224–226
    definition of, 209–210
    delivery of, 210–216, 224
    for the developmentally disabled,
        216–217
    development of, 210–216, 217–218
    role of social work in, 208–218
    staffing in, 226
    for substance abuse, 217
    underserved, 226–227
Mental Health Study Act, 214
Mental Health Systems Act, 214
Mental hospitals, 211, 212, 213
    social work in, 219–220
Mental illness
    chronic, 209, 215–216, 220
    criminal behavior and, 248
    defined, 209–210, 225
    diagnostic classification, 209
    interdisciplinary approach to, 219
    prevention of, 212, 225
Mentally ill
    defined, 209
    deinstitutionalization of, 215, 226–227
    discrimination against, 108
    rights of, 215, 224–225
    services for, 86
Mentally retarded
    adults, 222, 227
    children, 155, 156, 221
    defined, 216
    deinstitutionalization of, 216–217
    discrimination against, 108
    services for, 86, 221–223
Mermelstein, Joanne, 290
Mexican Americans, 65, 67, 102–104

Mexican-American War, 103
Microintervention, 314
Middle class
    growth of, 22
    perspective, 118
Military disability, 129. *See also* Veterans
Milwaukee, 35
Minahan, Anne, 320, 336
*Mind That Found Itself, The* (Beers), 212
Minnesota, 240
Minority children
    adoption of, 161
    in court system, 237
Minority foster homes, 158
Minority groups. *See also specific names of*
        *groups*
    assimilation of, 97
    and assistance programs, 125–126
    and corrections system, 247–248
    and discontinuity of services, 90–91
    discrimination against, 96, 98–107,
        125–126, 247–248, 291
    poverty of, 66–67
    in rural areas, 291
Minority social workers, 110–111
Mississippi, 127
Mizio, Emelicia, 90
Monasteries, 30, 120
Monetary economy, 47, 48, 55–56, 120,
    170
Monetary provision, 48, 55, 56
Moynihan, Daniel, 80
MSWs. *See* Master of Social Work
Mutual aid, 7, 14, 17, 25
    and the elderly, 259, 264
    in health care, 186
    historical perspective, 5–7, 29, 30
    in rural areas, 7, 291
Mutual assimilation, 97

# N

National Association for Mental Health,
    212
National Association for the Advancement
    of Colored People (NAACP), 100, 109

National Association of Black Social Work-
    ers (NABSW), 110, 161
National Association of Retarded Children,
    216
National Association of Retarded Citizens,
    216
National Association of School Social
    Workers (NASSW), 36
National Association of Schools for Social
    Administration, 289
National Association of Social Workers
    (NASW), 36, 39, 41, 79, 132, 137, 192,
    218, 225, 281, 289, 303, 304, 319
    Code of Ethics, 110, 307, 309–310, 319
    Purpose of social work, 307, 308
National Center on Child Abuse and
    Neglect, 152
National Committee for Mental Hygiene,
    212
National Conference on Charities and
    Corrections, 32, 34, 35, 36, 287
National Conference on Social Welfare
    (NCSW), 79, 137
National Conference on Social Work, 37, 288
National Council on Aging, 255, 267
National Council on Crime and Delin-
    quency, 246
National health care, 187–189, 202
National Humane Society, 151
National Institute of Mental Health, 213,
    214
National Institute on Alcohol abuse and
    Alcoholism, 217
National Maritime Union, 280
National Mental Health Act, 213
National Social Workers Exchange, 35
Native Americans
    child welfare programs, 147, 149
    culture of, 89
    discrimination against, 67, 101–102
    income maintenance programs, 129–130
    poverty of, 66–67
    reservations, 67, 101, 102
Natural disasters, 120
Natural selection, law of, 124
"Need for a Training School in Applied
    Philanthropy, The," 33

"Need for Training Schools for a New Profession, The," 32
Needleman, Carolyn, 242
Needs. *See* Human needs
Negative income tax, 134–135
Neglect, child, 151–153. *See also* Child abuse
New deal, 10–11, 22, 76
New Federalism, 79, 131, 132
New Mexico State Prison, 245–246
New Orleans, 144
New York Association for Improving the Condition of the Poor, 31, 123
New York Childrens Aid Society, 145
New York Society for the Prevention of Cruelty to Children, 146
New York Society for the Prevention of Pauperism, 31, 123
New York state, 31, 32, 33, 35, 127
Nixon, Richard, 78, 132
Nuclear family, 170
Nursing homes, 188, 191, 196, 197–198, 215, 260, 269, 273
Nutrition services, 155, 264, 268

# O

Occupational Safety and Health Act, 281
Office of Economic Opportunity (OEO), 77, 78, 133
Old Age, Survivors, Disability, and Health Insurance (OASDHI), 13, 173, 262, 266
Old Age and Survivors Insurance, 13
Old Age Assistance (OAA), 11, 22, 24, 126, 261
Old Age Security (Canada), 16
Older American Act, 15, 24, 256, 263, 268
Old Testament, 29
Omnibus Reconciliation Act, 148
Orphanages, 144
*Other America, The* (Harrington), 74, 77
Outside relief, 20, 123
Ozawa, Martha, 280, 283

# P

PACE, 320
*Parens patriae*, 234
Parental neglect. *See* Neglect, child
Parents
    abusive, 152
    foster, 145, 157–158
    needs of, 85
    role of, 171
    surrogate, 172
    unmarried, 155
Parents Without Partners, 7
Parole, 246, 247, 249
Pauperism, 413
Peck, Robert, 257
Pensions, veterans', 129
*People* v. *Hall*, 105
Permanency planning, for children, 149, 150, 158, 161
Personal networks, 268
Philadelphia, 33, 35
Philadelphia Prison Society, 245
Physically disabled. *See* Handicapped
Pierce, Franklin, 10, 212
Pincus, Allen, 336
Pinel, Phillippe, 211
Plague, 120
*Plessy* v. *Ferguson*, 99
PL-91-61. *See* National Institute on Alcohol Abuse and Alcoholism
PL-94-142. *See* Education of All Handicapped Children
Poison Control Centers, 15
Police work, 250
Political factors
    in poverty, 65, 74–75, 77
    in social welfare system, 25, 335–336
Politicians
    black, 100
    Mexican American, 104
    and the poor, 74
Poor. *See also* Poverty
    able-bodied, 18, 19
    charity to, 8

discrimination against, 73
identifying, 66–69
and mental illness, 212
stereotypes, 63, 66
working, 68–69
"worthy" or "deserving," 12
Poor house. *See* Alms house
Poor laws. *See* English Poor Law
Poor Peoples' March on Washington, 100
Poor relief system, 30–31, 125, 142–144
Population patterns
immigration and, 19
shifts in U.S., 51–58
and social insurance, 13
Poverty. *See also* Poor
causes of, 69–75, 332
children and, 68, 149
crisis, 73
culture of, 65–66
cycle of, 68, 73
defining, 63–66
discovery and rediscovery of, 75–78
in economic terms, 64, 70–72
elderly and, 67–68, 266–267
families and, 172
geography of, 69
inherited, 74
life-cycle of, 73
as political problem, 65, 74–75, 77
problem of, 62
relative, 63
social change and, 59
societal response to, 75–79
sociological perspective on, 64, 72–74
Poverty line, 64, 332
Pray, Kenneth, 249
Prejudice, defined, 94, 95. *See also*
Discrimination; Racism
President's Commission on Civil
Disorders, 100
President's Commission on Law Enforcement and the Administration of
Justice, 246
President's Commission on Mental Health,
214
President's Task Force on Prisoner Rehabilitation, 246

Prisoner Rehabilitation Act, 245
Prisoners, rights of, 246
Prisons, 244–245
reform efforts, 245
social work in, 250
violence in, 245–246
Private family service agencies, 177
Probation, 246–247, 249
Progress, victims of, 59
Professional identification, 319
Professional organizations
establishment of, 35–36
and poverty, 79
response to racism, 110
Professional Standards Review Organiza-
tions (PSRO), 194, 195
Profession, attributes of a, 38. *See also*
Social work
Prospective payment, 191, 200
Protective services
for children, 150–153
for the elderly, 270
social workers in, 153
Protestants, 18, 25, 30, 72
Protocols, in hospital social work, 194
Psychiatric diagnosis classifications, 209,
219
Psychiatric hospitals, 210
Psychiatric social worker, 218
Psychiatrists, 226
Psychological theory, 37, 289
Psychotropic drugs , 213, 219
Public health services, 15
Public responsibility, 335
Public schools, 99, 128
Public Service Employment (PSE), 133
Public welfare, 6, 10–12, 17, 20, 22,
260–262, 287
Puerto Ricans, 65, 67, 104, 209
Punishment
in corrections system, 244–246
as deterrent to poverty, 122, 213
Purchasing power, 71
Puritan-Calvinism, 19

# Q

Quakers, 123, 245
Quality of life issues, 201

# R

Racial discrimination. *See* Discrimination;
    Racism
Racial minorities. *See* Minority groups;
    *specific names of groups*
Racism, 66
    causes of, 95–98
    defined, 94, 95
    individual, 94, 96
    institutional, 94, 96, 101, 103
    and poverty, 77
    problems and solutions, 96–98
    social welfare response to, 109–112, 332
Radicalism, 37
Rape, 151
Reagan, Ronald, 24, 79, 215, 224
Reciprocity, strategy of, 335–336
Reconstituted family, 170
Reform. *See* Social reform; Welfare reform
Refugee act, 106
Register of Clinical Social Workers, 225, 319
Rehabilitation, in corrections, 244, 245,
    246, 248
Rehabilitation centers, 191, 196
Relationships
    identifying and defining, 50
    interpersonal, 86, 311
    marital, 85
Relative deprivation, 64, 65
Relative responsibility, principle of, 18, 259
Religious groups. *See also names of religions*
    and the elderly, 260
    family services, 178   primary care by,
        19, 29–30, 120, 123
    support of private agencies, 9
Residency laws, 18, 19, 122
Residential care services, 160, 213
Residual approach, 118–119, 333

Resources
    accessibility to, 89, 93
    availability of, 89–90, 268–270, 331, 332–333
    coordination of, 90
    defined, 84
    delivery of, 90
    distribution of, 65, 89
    inadequate, 56
    range of needs for, 83–87
    usability of, 89
Restrictive opportunity theory, 72
Retirement, 266
Retirement villages, 260
Reynolds, Bertha, 280
Ricardo, David, 124
Richmond, Mary, 33, 34, 37
Right to die, 201
Role-overload, 172
Roman Catholic church, 8, 18, 25, 30, 260
Roosevelt, Franklin D., 10, 76, 99, 288
Roosevelt, Theodore, 187, 287
Rubin, Gail, 199
Rugged individualism, 4
Rural areas. *See also* Farmers
    immigrants from, 52
    mutual aid in, 7, 291
    poverty in, 69
*Rural Community and Social Casework, The*
    (Brown), 289
*Rural Public Welfare* (Browning), 289
Rural social work, 328
    case study, 292–293
    defining, 286
    delivery systems, 227, 286, 287, 328–329
    generalist model in, 291
    historical perspective, 287–290
    issues in, 293–294
    literature on, 290
    practice in, 291–292
Rural Social Work Caucus, 290
Rush, Benjamin, 245

# S

St. Louis, 33, 35
Salaries, 318

Schiller, Bradley, 72
Schools, public, 99, 128
    breakfast programs, 128
    social services, 154–155
Schools, social work training, 8, 32–35, 39,
    111, 281–282
Schoor, Alvin L., 336
Scientific charity, 9
Scot's Charity Society, 123
Segal, Steven P., 209
Self-help groups, 7
Senile dementia, 260–261
Senior citizens centers, 259, 268, 272
Serfs, 120
Services, defined, 84. *See also* Resources;
    Social services
Service society, 55–56
Settlement, concept of, 122
Settlement houses, 8, 9, 14, 33
    history of, 21, 48, 54, 75, 145–146, 259
    work style in, 31
Sexism, 68, 107–108
Sexual abuse
    causes of, 153
    of children, 151–152, 153
Sexual exploitation, 151
Sheppard-Towner Act, 147, 190
Sidney Hillman Health center, 281
Single-parent family, 170, 172, 241–242
Siporin, Max, 305
Skill obsolescence, 58
Skills, in social work, 310–312
Slums, 21
Smith, Adam, 124
Smith College, 218
*Social Casework*, 281
Social change
    and child welfare, 144, 146, 156
    effect on individuals, 48, 58–59
    effect on social welfare, 47–59
    effect on societal system, 48, 51–58, 84
    and the elderly, 265–266, 327
    and family services, 168–169
Social control
    defined, 47
    social welfare as, 8, 18, 19, 20, 122, 333
Social Darwinism, 124

*Social Diagnosis* (Richmond), 34, 37
Social insurance, 6, 12–14, 17, 262, 264
Social philosophy, 123–124
Social reform, 21, 37, 109
    in child welfare, 145, 146
Social Security. *See* Old Age, Survivors,
    Disability, and Health Insurance
Social Security Act of 1935
    Amendments, 12–13, 23, 129
    as basis of social welfare system, 11, 18,
        22
    child welfare assistance, 54, 147, 158,
        136, 288–289
    development of, 11, 14, 22–24, 48, 76
    elderly assistance, 54, 261, 262, 263
    health benefits, 187, 190, 192
    income maintenance assistance, 118,
        124, 126, 136, 147
    social insurance program, 14–15, 147,
        148, 287
Social Security Administration, 64, 65, 129,
    261
Social services, 6, 14–15, 17
    delivery of, 331, 334–335
    for the elderly, 262–263, 328
    in health care systems, 187–191
Social system, components of, 49–50
Social systems theory, 287–288, 313, 321
Social welfare, defined, 4
*Social Welfare and Professional Education*
    (Abbott), 34
Social welfare system
    analytic framework of, 324–329
    change in, 334–335
    components of, 4–16, 17, 24
    function of, 88
    history of, 8, 16–24, 25, 325, 326
    issues in, 90, 329–334
    motivators of decisions in, 22, 24–26
    resource availability, 332–333
    roles of professionals in, 331
    social change and, 47–59
    social provision, 333–334
    structure of, 330
*Social Work*, 110, 281
Social work
    art of, 304

careers in, 317–319, 336
educational requirements, 39–41,
    317–319
employment opportunities in, 317–319
fields of practice, 277, 294, 327 (*see also*
    *names of services*)
future of, 320–321
history of, 29–42, 109
knowledge base of, 305–306, 311
methods of practice, 312–316
profession of, 9, 21, 30–41, 79, 109–110,
    135, 281, 326
purpose and mission, 303–305, 308
science of, 304
skills of, 310–312, 316
value-base of, 307–310, 311
*Social Work and Social Living* (Reynolds), 280
*Social Work Education in the United States*, 39
Social Work Research Group (SWRG), 36
Society
    boundary, 49
    early civilizations, 29
    as a social system, 48–51
    stratification in, 7, 21
Society of Saint Vincent de Paul, 30
Sociological factors
    in corrections system, 248
    in poverty, 64, 72–74
Sociology, 35
South Dakota, 66, 102, 293
Southern Regional Education Board, 40
Specialized professional, 318
Spenser, Herbert, 124
Spouse abuse, 176
*Stanley* v. *Illinois*, 161
State governments, 10
State Penitentiary at Auburn, New York,
    245
Status offenders, 237, 238–239
Statute of Laborers, 121
Steady state, 49
Step-family, 170
Stigma. *See* Welfare stigma
Student Nonviolent Coordinating Commit-
    tee (SNCC), 100
Subsistence economy, 47, 48, 55
Substance abuse, 217

Sundet, Paul, 290
Sundquist, James L., 78
Supplemental Security Income (SSI), 12,
    24, 126, 129, 147, 174, 215, 261–262
Supreme Court, U.S., decisions
    on discrimination, 99
    on parental rights of biological fathers,
        161
    on prisoner rights, 237, 246
*Survey*, 287

**T**

Talmud, 29–30
Tax
    compulsory, 122, 123
    negative income, 134–135
    payroll, 13
Tax monies, 10, 16, 56
Thais, 106
Therapeutic community, concept of, 213
Third-party payment, insurance, 225
Thirteenth Amendment, 98
Tithes, 8, 19
Titmuss, Richard M., 278
Tonnies, Ferdinand, 6, 286
Traditional methods of practice, 312
Training. *See* Schools, social work training
Trattnor, Walter, 120

**U**

Underemployment, 71–72, 173
Undergraduate programs, 35, 39, 40, 281,
    289, 293, 316. *See also* Bachelor's in
    Social Work
Unemployment, 48, 173
    causes of, 72
    and poverty, 71–72
    of racial minorities, 67
Unemployment Insurance, 13
United Farm Workers, 104
United States Commission on Civil Rights,
    103
United Way, 178

Universal provision, 6, 15–16, 17, 26, 263–264
University of Chicago, 33, 34
Unmarried parents, 155
Urban areas, 69. *See also* Industrial social work
Urbanization, 21
Ursuline Convent, 144

# V

Vagabonds, 212
Vagrancy, 18, 122
Vermont, 128
Veterans
  assistance to, 129
  health care for, 190
  mental health care for, 213
Veterans Administration (VA), 129, 188, 190, 212, 218
Vietnamese, 106
Vietnam War, 78, 213
Vincent de Paul, Saint, 30
Violence
  family, 176–177, 179
  in prisons, 245–246
  racial, 100, 102, 105
VISTA (Volunteers in Service to America), 77
Voting rights, of blacks, 65, 98
Voting Rights Act, 100

# W

Wald, Lillian, 147
War on Poverty, 77–78, 79, 80
Warren, Roland L., 50
Washington state, 239
Watts riots, 100
Wealth
  redistribution of, 8, 70
  responsibility and, 8
Welfare fraud, 128
Welfare reform, 130–135

Welfare secretaries, 279, 280
Welfare stigma, 9, 11–12, 13, 15, 69, 174
Western Reserve University, 34
White House Conferences on Aging, 255–256, 263
White House Conferences on Children, 146
White House Conferences on Families, 173
Widows, 7, 265, 292, 327
Widow to Widow, 7
Wife abuse, 176
Wilensky, Harold, 118
Wisconsin, 240
Withorn, Ann, 335, 336
Women
  in correctional institutions, 248
  discrimination against, 68, 107–108
  elderly, 265, 293
  in labor market, 49–50, 51
  poverty of, 68
  traditional roles, 51
  widows, 265
Women's labor laws, 31
Worcester State Hospital, 211
Work–educational release, 247
Work ethic
  in colonial times, 122
  influence on social welfare, 72, 122, 124, 127, 130, 132–133
Work experience programs, 132–133
Workfare, 127, 133
Work Incentive Program (WIN), 127, 133
Working poor, 68–69
Workman's Compensation, 13, 281
Workplace, 278, 281. *See also* Industrial social work
*Work, Workers and Work Organizations*, 282
World War I, 213
World War II, 76, 105, 213
Wounded Knee, 102

# Y

Youth Service Bureaus, 239, 240